The Newspapers Handbook

This new edition of *The Newspapers Handbook* presents an enlightening examination of an ever-evolving industry, engaging with key contemporary issues, including reporting in the digital age, and ethical and legislative issues following the hacking scandal, to display a comprehensive anatomy of the modern newsroom.

Ian Reeves and Richard Lance Keeble offer readers expert practical advice, drawing on a wide range of examples from print and digital news sources to illustrate best practice and the political, technological and financial realities of newspaper journalism today.

Other key areas explored include:

- the language of news
- basic reporting
- the art of interviewing
- feature writing
- the role of social media in reporting
- investigative reporting
- court reporting
- reporting on national and local government
- guidance on training and careers for those entering the industry.

Ian Reeves is Deputy Director at the University of Kent's Centre for Journalism. An award-winning former editor of *Press Gazette*, he continues to write about business and media issues for a variety of newspapers and to provide digital consultancy for online news content. He is co-editor of *What Do We Mean By Local? Grass-Roots Journalism – Its Death and Rebirth* (with Neil Fowler and John Mair, 2012). He designed and built the Centre for Journalism's website and its iPad app – the first app for a university department to appear on the Apple App Store.

Richard Lance Keeble is Professor of Journalism at the University of Lincoln. He is author of *Ethics for Journalists* (second edition, 2008), editor of *Print Journalism: A Critical Introduction* (2005) and co-editor of *The Journalistic Imagination: Literary Journalists from Defoe to Capote and Carter* (with Sharon Wheeler, 2007), and is co-editor and author of 25 other titles.

Media Practice

Edited by James Curran, Goldsmiths College, University of London

The *Media Practice* handbooks are comprehensive resource books for students of media and journalism, and for anyone planning a career as a media professional. Each handbook combines a clear introduction to understanding how the media work with practical information about the structure, processes and skills involved in working in today's media industries, providing not only a guide on 'how to do it' but also a critical reflection on contemporary media practice.

The Advertising Handbook
3rd edition
Helen Powell, Jonathan Hardy,
Sarah Hawkin and Iain MacRury

The Alternative Media Handbook
Kate Coyer, Tony Dowmunt and
Alan Fountain

The Cyberspace Handbook
Jason Whittaker

The Digital Media Handbook
2nd edition
Andrew Dewdney and Peter Ride

The Documentary Handbook
Peter Lee-Wright

The Fashion Handbook
Tim Jackson and David Shaw

The Film Handbook
Mark de Valk with Sarah Arnold

The Graphic Communication Handbook
Simon Downs

The Magazines Handbook
3rd edition
Jenny McKay

The Music Industry Handbook
Paul Rutter

The Newspapers Handbook
5th edition
Ian Reeves with Richard Lance Keeble

The Photography Handbook
2nd edition
Terence Wright

The Public Relations Handbook
4th edition
Alison Theaker

The Radio Handbook
3rd edition
Carole Fleming

The Sound Handbook
Tim Crook

The Television Handbook
4th edition
Jeremy Orlebar

The Newspapers Handbook

Fifth edition

Ian Reeves with
Richard Lance Keeble

 Routledge
Taylor & Francis Group

LONDON AND NEW YORK

First published 1994
Second edition published 1998
Third edition published 2001
Fourth edition published 2006

Fifth edition published 2015
by Routledge
2 Park Square, Milton Park, Abingdon, Oxon OX14 4RN

and by Routledge
711 Third Avenue, New York, NY 10017

Routledge is an imprint of the Taylor & Francis Group, an informa business

British Library Cataloguing in Publication Data
A catalogue record for this book is available from the British Library

Library of Congress Cataloging in Publication Data
Keeble, Richard, 1948–.
 The newspapers handbook/Richard Lance Keeble and Iain
 Reeves. – Fifth edition.
 pages cm – (Media skills)
 Includes bibliographical references and index.
 1. Newspaper publishing – Handbooks, manuals, etc.
 2. Journalism – Handbooks, manuals, etc. I. Reeves, Iain.
 II. Title.
 PN4783.K44 2014
 070.5'722 – dc23
 2014006841

ISBN: 978–0-415–66651–0 (hbk)
ISBN: 978–0-415–66652–7 (pbk)
ISBN: 978–0-203-14361–2 (ebk)

Typeset in Helvetica Neue and Avant Garde
by Florence Production Ltd, Stoodleigh, Devon, UK

Printed and bound in Great Britain by
TJ International Ltd, Padstow, Cornwall

Contents

Notes on contributors

Mark Hanna is Senior Lecturer in the Department of Journalism Studies, Sheffield University. He worked on newspapers for 18 years for various titles including *The Western Daily Press*, *Sheffield Morning Telegraph* and *Sheffield Star*, specialising in crime reporting and investigations, and also for *The Observer* as northern reporter. He won awards at national and regional level, including Provincial Journalist of the Year in the British Press Awards. Since 2009, he has been co-author of *McNae's Essential Law for Journalists*.

Nick Nuttall is the former Programme Leader for the MA courses at the University of Lincoln School of Journalism. His latest book, with co-author Jane Chapman, is *Journalism Today: A Themed History*. He has also contributed chapters to *The Journalistic Imagination: Literary Journalists from Defoe to Capote and Carter* and *Global Literary Journalism: Exploring the Journalistic Imagination*.

Dr John Turner runs a political research agency and has worked with *The Guardian*, *Channel 4 News*, the Conservative Party, Reform, the Countryside Alliance and the BBC. He has been a member of the Central Regional Consultative Committee of the ITC and has contributed to training programmes at the BBC. Previously he was a Principal Lecturer in Politics at Oxford Brookes University and has written on the Conservative Party, Europe, the media, news management and the London mayor and dirty tricks, and has contributed to a number of politics and media textbooks. He has also run courses for Oxford County and City councils, and for Harrow Borough Council.

Preface

Just as the previous edition of this book was being published in 2006, *The Economist* ran one of its more provocative cover stories, asking readers a bold question: Who killed newspapers? Its story condensed the arguments that had been depressing industry executives and journalists for a while, examining the perfect storm of events that were conspiring to devastate the economic model that had supported newspaper publishing for more than a century.

The initially steady leakage of lucrative classified advertising from print to online became a flood, and was now a torrent; regular buyers of printed journalism had continued to dwindle as lifestyles changed; publishing organisations tied themselves in knots as they tried to work out whether to cut costs to protect the bottom line, or invest in new digital technology in the hope of improving it.

But it wasn't just the economics of news that was showing signs of significant change. There were big social changes afoot too, largely driven by technology. Eighteen months or so earlier I had run my own cover story for *Press Gazette*'s audience of professional journalists, headlined: 'I Have Seen the Future. And We're Not In It.'

Armies of amateur bloggers had begun to rise, challenging the hegemony of the professional journalists; mobile technology had already became sophisticated enough that anybody could break a story, in full colour video if necessary, that could be seen by millions of people within minutes; social media, primarily in the guise of Facebook and Twitter, had just swaggered on to the digital landscape like a garrulous guest at a party that nobody could resist paying attention to.

Seven years later, these trends have accelerated. Surveying the newspaper industry at the end of 2013, it's clear how seismic those changes have been in a time span short enough to have witnessed just one World Cup tournament.

In 2006, Facebook was not yet two years old, and just starting to extend its influence beyond students at universities in the US. Twitter had only just launched, to rather mixed reviews, as a 140-character embodiment of what at the time was becoming known as the 'real-time' web. Today Facebook has more than 1 billion global active users, and audience engagement figures that 'traditional media' would die for. Twitter has more than 200 million active users. Even the Pope has an account.

Over the same period, almost 3 million people in the UK have stopped buying a national daily newspaper (11,024,094 in July 2006, down to 8,176,555 in August 2013). The biggest circulating Sunday newspaper, the *News of the World*, has closed. Regional newspapers in the UK have lost more than 30 per cent of their sales.

Press Gazette, the weekly newspaper I edited as it celebrated its 40th anniversary in 2005, fell victim to the very economic changes it had so diligently reported. It closed as a print publication before its 47th birthday, having tried to make a living as a monthly, then a quarterly. It now exists online with a fraction of the reporting staff.

But another story was beginning to unfold in 2006 that would have arguably even more drastic an effect on newspapers than this economic meltdown. Senior *News of the World* journalist Clive Goodman spent the end of that year awaiting trial on charges of having intercepted mobile phone messages involving Royal family members. Although there was some concern, particularly amongst those who understood how national newsdesks worked, that this would not prove to have been an isolated incident, nobody foresaw how toxic this story would become.

As the story unravelled, so did News International's initial claim that Goodman was a lone rogue reporter. The evidence of the industrial scale at which mobile phone accounts of celebrities and others had been illegally accessed by journalists led right to the heart of government; David Cameron had hired Goodman's former boss Andy Coulson as his communications director.

The Leveson Inquiry that Cameron set up to extract himself from this political difficulty continues to exert a fallout on the entire industry. Dozens of journalists were arrested in the renewed police investigations into phone hacking and the corruption of public officials. At the start of 2014 there were more British journalists facing trial over the way they went about their work than at any time in history – including some of the best known names in the business. Senior police officers had begun prison terms for passing information to journalists.

The industry is under intense pressure to overhaul its system of self-regulation. For the first time in the country's history, we face the prospect of a statutory involve-ment in the way journalists do their work. Editors, academics, politicians, celebrity-led pressure groups and members of the public remain at loggerheads over the fundamental principles of what should happen next. Trust in journalists – never a currency with a particularly high value – drops and drops again. From most angles, it looks like a tale of unrelenting despair. And yet.

The British newspaper industry is a resilient beast. Two of its newspapers regularly appear in the top 10 lists of the world's most popular websites, their journalism reaching audiences vastly greater than at any time in history. Online advertising is beginning to show signs that it could pick up more of the tab than at one time had been feared. Publishers' continued experiments with paywalls appear to give the lie to a belief that online news is a valueless commodity.

Meanwhile, its journalists are benefiting from a dazzling array of new storytelling techniques, giving them more options than they have ever had to engage and engross their audiences. And they show no sign of losing their appetite for holding power to account, or for entertaining, educating and informing their readers. Newspapers may not be enjoying their most ebullient time. But they're certainly Not Dead Yet.

To reflect these fundamental changes to the newspaper industry, I've made some significant changes to the format of this new edition of its handbook. While much of Richard Keeble's excellent work on the previous four editions continues to underpin it, I've changed the structure of the chapters somewhat.

I hope, though, that I have continued to make the important link between theory and practice that Richard set out to encourage back in 1994 when he wrote the first edition.

Ian Reeves
October 2013

Acknowledgements

The authors and publishers gratefully acknowledge permission to reproduce copyright material from the following:

The National Council for the Training of Journalists for permission to reprint the Journalists at Work Survey 2012.

Press Gazette for permission to reprint the following articles:

Ian Reeves, 'I have been, I hope, an agent of change ...', *Press Gazette*, 25 November 2005 (www.pressgazette.co.uk/node/32634).

Gavriel Hollander, 'Local World's David Montgomery: "We will harvest content and publish it without human interface"', *Press Gazette*, 21 May 2013 (www.pressgazette.co.uk/david-montgomery-we-will-harvest-content-and-publish-it-without-human-interface).

Paul Dacre, 'Society of Editors: Paul Dacre's speech in full', *Press Gazette*, 9 November 2008 (www.pressgazette.co.uk/node/42394).

Jonathan Stray for permission to reprint Jonathan Stray, 'Designing journalism to be used', 26 September 2010 (http://jonathanstray.com/designing-journalism-to-be-used).

Subscraft blog for permission to reprint Gameoldgirl, 'Another sad week at *The Times*', Thursday, 13 June 2013 (http://subscraft.blogspot.co.uk/2013/06/another-sad-week-at-times.html).

David Weinberger for permission to reprint Joho the Blog, 'Transparency is the New Objectivity', 19 July 2009 (www.hyperorg.com/blogger/2009/07/19/transparency-is-the-new-objectivity/).

The Croydon Advertiser for permission to reprint excerpt of piece (8 August 2012) by Gareth Davies.

Solo Syndication/*Daily Mail* for permission to reprint the following material:

> The front page of the *Daily Mail*, Tuesday, 1 October 2013.
>
> Kieran Corcoran, 'Female referee called off cup match after being told to "get her handbag and go home"', *Daily Mail*, 22 September 2013 (www.dailymail.co.uk/news/article-2429044/Female-referee-called-cup-match-told-handbag-home.html).
>
> David Jones, 'The Designer Baby Factory', *Daily Mail*, 5 May 2012.

David Yelland for permission to reprint 'Former Sun editor David Yelland: "I was drunk every night for nearly 24 years but I was saved by the love of my son"', *Daily Mail*, 27 March 2010 (www.dailymail.co.uk/femail/article-1261200/Former-Sun-editor-David-Yelland-I-drunk-night-nearly-24-years-I-saved-love-son.html).

Daily Mirror for permission to reprint the following material:

> Ryan Parry, 'Our Man In The Palace: My Life As A Footman', *Daily Mirror*, 19 November 2003.
>
> Tom Parry, 'I come here all the time to pray for my friend who was washed away . . .', *Daily Mirror*, 10 March 2012, pp. 26–7.

Derby Telegraph for permission to reprint the front page of *Derby Telegraph* from Wednesday, 14 November 2012.

Evening Standard for permission to reprint the following material:

> '"David Cameron runs his Government with an Eton-Oxford old boy clique", blasts top woman civil servant', *Evening Standard*, 1 November 2012.
>
> Joshi Herrmann, 'The Sussex School Whose Pupils Vanish At 16 To Join Scientology's Secret Elite – And Return Married', *Evening Standard*, 11 July 2012.

KM Group for permission to reprint page 6 of *Medway Messenger*, Friday, 3 May 2013.

Liverpool Echo for permission to reprint the following material:

> *Liverpool Echo*, Tuesday, 11 September 2012, pp. 4–5.
>
> Paddy Shennan, 'Warts and all? It just cannot begin to describe an abhorrent scandal', *Liverpool Echo*, 12 September 2012.

Socialist Worker for permission to reprint quotations from *Socialist Worker* articles published 10 July 2004 and 3 June 2000.

Guardian News and Media Limited for permission to reprint the following material:

> the *Guardian* website home page, 7 October 2013.
>
> 'David Montgomery's "robot" journalism will terminate both jobs and local news', the *Guardian* (Comment Is Free section), 23 May 2013 (www.theguardian.com/media/media-blog/2013/may/23/david-montgomery-robot-journalism).
>
> Sam Jones, 'Emergency services: Thirty rescued after fire on tourist "duck bus"', the *Guardian*, 30 September 2013.

Mark Townsend, Martin Bright and Tony Thompson, 'News Investigation: Police and Racism: Inside the Ranks of Police Racists', the *Observer*, 26 October 2004, p. 7.

Ghaith Abdul-Ahad, 'Syrian rebels who paid ultimate price as ammunition ran out', the *Guardian*, 26 August 2012, p. 1.

Alfred Hickling, '"How's things?" "Oh, you know – drugs, violence"', the *Guardian*, 31 March 2003, p. 10.

Jonathan Glancey, 'Just three quid, and lots of change', the *Guardian*, 10 January 2000, p. 12.

Miranda Sawyer, 'Something Of The Nighy', the *Observer Magazine*, 31 October 2004, p. 14.

Charles Arthur, 'They've got your number', the *Guardian* (online), 13 April 2009 (www.guardian.co.uk/media/2009/apr/13/investigative-journalism-protecting-sources).

Owen Bowcott, 'Press Intrusion: Don't name suspects in the media until charged, urges MP', the *Guardian* (online), 21 April 2013 (www.theguardian.com/media/2013/apr/21/press-intrusion-name-suspects).

Independent Print Limited for permission to reprint the following material:

the *Independent*, Monday, 14 January 2014, p. 17.

Tony Paterson, 'Invasion of rowdy English-speaking tourists leaves Oktoberfest bitter', the *Independent*, 1 October 2013, p. 30.

Peter Popham, 'Assignment of a lifetime', the *Independent*, 21 April 2004.

Cole Morton, 'A Man Can Take Away My Freedom . . .', *Independent on Sunday*, 7 November 2004.

Tiffany Rose, 'Jennifer Tilly: Little voice, big talent', the *Independent*, 19 November 2004.

Morning Star for permission to reprint 'A lesbian couple . . .', *Morning Star*, 10 November 2004.

News UK Syndication for permission to reprint the following material:

The front page of the *Sun*, Tuesday, 23 July 2013.

Gary O'Shea, 'Leaking Duck', the *Sun*, 30 September 2013.

Vikki Orvice, 'Villa Are Pants: Deadly Defoe Makes Certain It's Over As Quick As A Flash', the *Sun* (Super Goals section), 25 September 2013, front page.

Page 34 of *The Times*, Monday, 14 January 2014.

'On this day', *The Times*, 1 January 1855.

'On this day', *The Times*, 18 January 1940.

Catherine Philp, 'US paratroopers send Saddam a dramatic message', *The Times*, 28 March 2003.

Tanya Gold, 'Can we have the keys to your Lamborghini, madam?', *The Sunday Times Magazine*, 25 March 2012.

Janice Turner, 'What do you want to know? Do I worm the cat?', *The Sunday Times*, 2 June 2013.

The *Voice* for permission to reprint Elsa O'Toole, 'Profile of Nia Long', the *Voice*, 1 November 2004.

Politics and the English Language by George Orwell (© George Orwell, 1946). Reprinted by permission of Bill Hamilton as the Literary Executor of the Estate of the Late Sonia Brownell Orwell.

Every attempt has been made to obtain permission to reproduce copyright material. If any proper acknowledgement has not been made we would invite copyright holders to inform us of the oversight.

CHAPTER 1

From Grub Street to pub tweet

Anatomy of an industry

WHAT IS A NEWSPAPER?

When the first edition of this book was published in 1994, that wasn't a difficult question. It was a bundle of stories, pictures, adverts and puzzles collected together as a stylish printed package made of lightweight paper. Its production was a daily or weekly miracle brought to life by a devilishly complex chain involving journalists, photographers, editors, advertising executives, publishing managers, compositors, print engineers, delivery drivers, newsagents and paper boys and girls.

In its daily format it was the most perishable item on the high street, whose contents were largely past their sell-by date by the day's end, and in the main never to be seen again by anyone other than archivists and historians. It was a product with a secure, if not rosy, commercially viable future ahead of it. Today the question is less easily answered.

The printed product remains, but the output of the people who produce it is far more likely to be read on some sort of screen. A modern newspaper typically encompasses a website, a tablet app, a Facebook page, multiple Twitter accounts, a YouTube channel, collections of bloggers, a series of podcasts and more besides. Its contents are interactive, multimedia extravaganzas. It can be accessed just as easily in Bogota as it can in Basingstoke. And it often remains available long after the day it was published, a potentially permanent record that can be augmented, corrected and republicised should the situation demand it. Commercially, its future is troubled. Rocked by the massive disruption of the internet, the commercial foundations upon which it has rested for more than a century are crumbling.

The question of what constitutes a newspaper is more than simply a matter for academic musing. The way in which a publication is categorised may well have a significant impact on the rules that govern its content in future – and could make a dramatic difference over its liability for libel costs, for example. As I write this, the debate continues to rage – and I use the term advisedly – over the way the press will be regulated in the UK. And it stands to reason that, before we can decide how to regulate it, we need to define exactly what it is we are regulating.

Brian Leveson, Lord Justice of Appeal – about whose report into press standards there will be much more to come in this book – was given as his terms of reference multiple mentions of the term 'the press' without defining what it actually encompasses. Most of his inquiry focused on newspapers. Subsequently, the government's draft Royal Charter, one of the possible implementations of Leveson's recommendations on how the press should be regulated, was designed to cover any business whose purpose is publishing news-related content – even those that operate only online – according to Maria Miller, the Culture Secretary at the time of writing.

That would mean it includes professional blog sites, such as Guido Fawkes, which makes money and publishes political news, gossip and scandal online, and certainly sees itself as in direct competition to traditional newspapers, editorially speaking. But throw in the fact that the computer servers that host the Guido Fawkes site are deliberately sited overseas to avoid potential libel suits in this country, and you see how muddied the waters can very quickly become.

Yet, however you define it, the newspaper industry in the UK remains a spectacularly vibrant place. As you read this its journalists are vox-popping high street shoppers, grilling chief executives, analysing hospital spending plans, lampooning prime ministers, watching tomorrow's television programmes, poring over crime statistics, hanging around grubby music venues, challenging court orders, road-testing cars, risking their lives to cover foreign wars, photographing sporting triumphs, raising money dressed as cartoon characters, compiling Freedom of Information requests, composing four-deck headlines, death-knocking, setting up fashion shoots, rewriting blog posts, tweeting road traffic accident updates, forecasting economic outlooks, cold-calling criminals, buying drinks for diplomats and countless other things detailed in John Dale's book *24 Hours in Journalism* (Dale 2011).

Its advertising staff are helping its readers to sell their cars, their houses, their unused toys; to commemorate the deaths of their loved ones, mark the births of their children, find their soulmates and celebrate their weddings. They are helping local carpet-dealers and multinational conglomerates shift their stock, and reinforcing the brand values of handbag manufacturers, car makers, restaurant chains and high street butchers. They are finding work for carpenters, plumbers and nannies.

UK newspapers influence policy makers in national and international governments, the armed forces, courts, town halls, corporate boardrooms, sports dressing rooms and beyond. Their output is read by tens of millions of people across the globe.

They reflect and feed the views, prejudices and principles of a diverse society. Without them, this country would cease to be the thriving democracy that it prides itself on being.

A VERY SHORT HISTORY OF NEWSPAPERS: INNOVATION, INNOVATION, INNOVATION

News has been circulating in print in this country since the early part of the sixteenth century, when pamphlets known as 'relations' gave accounts of specific events. The earliest surviving example, recounting the battle of Flodden in 1513, is entitled *Hereafter Ensue the Trewe Encountre of Batalye lately Don between Englande and Scotlande*. There's a copy at the British Library.

Although such publications increased in number as the century progressed, it wasn't until the beginning of the seventeenth century that the idea of printing news at a regular frequency began to take hold in Europe, although a 1586 decree by the Star Chamber forbade this happening in England. In 1621, printer Nathaniel Butter acquired a licence to publish a series of 'corantos' containing news translated from German. The opening of Parliament in 1640 heralded regularly published 'newsbooks' containing domestic news, such as the snappily titled *The Heads of Severall Proceedings in This Present Parliament*. These newsbooks, as the Civil War raged, increasingly became vehicles of propaganda for each side. So the battle between the *Mercurius Auricus*, on behalf of the Royalists, and the *Mercurius Britannicus*, on behalf of the Parliamentarians, was the first newsprint rivalry on political lines.

The Printing Act of 1685, following the Restoration, reasserted licensing of news publications. The launch of the *Oxford Gazette*, later the twice-weekly *London Gazette*, during this period is often described as the first newspaper (although the *Oxford English Dictionary* records the first coining of the term as being in 1667) – since it was printed at regular frequency and on both sides of a single sheet.

The first English daily newspaper was *The Daily Courant*, launched in 1702 in London. Its unique position in this new 24-hour news cycle did not last long, though. Within seven years, the evening newspaper was born, and papers including the *Whitehall Evening Post* (1718–1801) began to report on-the-day events.

The Stamp Acts of 1694 and 1712 subjected newspapers to taxes on the paper they used and the advertising they sold. Ostensibly a revenue-raising policy, the taxes were also perceived as means by which the more radical leanings of news publishing could be curtailed. As James Curran notes:

> The intention of these press taxes was twofold: to restrict the readership of newspapers to the well-to-do by raising cover prices; and to limit the ownership of newspapers to the propertied class by increasing publishing costs. The belief was that substantial stakeholders in society would conduct newspapers 'in a

more responsible manner than was likely to be the result of pauper management', and that it was potentially dangerous to the social order to allow the
lower ranks to read newspapers at all.

(Curran and Seaton 2003)

Among those to conform to this system was the *Belfast News-Letter*, first printed
in 1737 by the Joy family. Although it did not become a daily for more than a
century, it retains the record as the oldest continuously published English daily
newspaper in the world. It additionally has claim to one of the greatest newspaper
scoops, publishing news of the American Declaration of Independence in 1776
before King George III or Parliament had seen it, thanks to the fact that the ship
carrying the document had docked in the city, seeking shelter from a storm.

This period also saw other launches that would stand the test of time. The *Daily
Universal Register*, launched in 1785 using a new form of printing, was later
rechristened as *The Times*, and the world's oldest Sunday newspaper, the *Observer*,
debuted in 1791. The abolition of the Stamp Duty in 1855 was a significant milestone
in the development of a mass-market free press. It heralded the 'Blitz of Paper',
a dramatic expansion of newspaper publishing that was also driven by other
developments neatly summarised by Andrew Marr in *My Trade* (2004).

> ... the Victorians did four things which made Britain the newspaper-mad
> nation it remains even today. They cut the taxes and lifted the legal restraints
> which had stopped newspapers being profitable; they introduced machinery
> to produce them in large numbers; they educated a population to read them;
> and they developed the mass democracy that made them relevant.

The *Daily Telegraph* emerged in 1855 from this flurry of publishing entrepreneurialism,
as did a London paper called the *Evening Standard* in 1859, and dozens of
newspapers printed for the growing provincial centres such as Birmingham,
Liverpool, Leeds and Bristol. By the beginning of the twentieth century, more than
a million people every weekday were handing over their penny for a copy of the
Daily Mail, launched just four years earlier. The era of true mass-market publishing
had begun.

Thereafter, the launches of enduring mastheads came thick and fast, and with that
febrile atmosphere of rivalry came advances in technology and improvements in
the packages on offer. The *Daily Express* (launched 1900) would introduce the daily
crossword; the *Daily Mirror* (launched 1903) was the first to be illustrated entirely
with photographs; the short-lived *Illustrated Weekly Budget* (launched 1908) was
some way ahead of its time as the first mass-market newspaper with colour printing.
Readers were treated to the first cartoon strip (*Mail*, 1915), and the first half-tone
photograph reproduction (*Times*, 1914). By 1933, the *Daily Herald* (launched in
1911 as a strike sheet for the printing unions) had become the world's largest-
circulating newspaper, reaching a daily sale of 2 million.

The first colour advertisement would appear in the *Glasgow Herald* (1936); the first photograph to be transmitted by radio waves from Australia in the *Mail* (1938). After the Second World War, when newsprint rationing had curtailed the circulation ambitions of the newspaper industry, sales once again began to surge. Daily and Sunday circulations reached dizzying heights. In 1947, the *News of the World* came within a whisker of selling 8 million copies per issue.

The regional press was booming too. Several big city dailies were shifting upwards of 200,000 copies a day (including the *Manchester Evening News*, the *Liverpool Echo*, Glasgow's *Evening Times*, the *Yorkshire Post* and the *Birmingham Mail*). Often owned by local businessmen, these were powerful cultural touchstones that helped to define the communities they served. By 1966, the *Daily Mirror* had broken through the 5 million circulation barrier – the only UK daily ever to reach that mark.

Other innovations continued. *The Sunday Times* launched the first colour supplement magazine in 1962; in 1976 the *Nottingham Evening Post* became the first title to use direct input computer systems for its journalists; in 1982 the *Mail on Sunday* was the first newspaper produced using photocomposition.

In 1984, Chris Bullivant launched the *Birmingham Daily News*, Britain's first free daily newspaper, and Eddie Shah, owner of the *Warrington Messenger*, fought a significant battle against the print unions. His victory paved the way for Rupert Murdoch to move production of his national newspapers from Fleet Street to Wapping – which resulted in bitterly fought confrontations between union supporters and workers at the new plant. Shah would go on to launch the first national daily newspaper printed in full colour, *Today*, in 1987.

By the mid 1990s, though, the focus of the technological innovation that had characterised the industry's development was showing the first signs of shifting away from the physical printed product. In 1994, the *Telegraph* became the first national newspaper to launch a website, allowing computer users with a dial-up internet connection to read short versions of selected stories from the day's newspaper on their screens.

The idea of web-based news was at once intensely exciting and profoundly disturbing for many in the industry. The enthusiasts could see the opportunities, both commercial and editorial, that this new era allowed: the chance to update stories in real time; the possibilities of delivering tailored content, including highly targeted advertising, to individual readers; the value that could be added to a text story with sound, and even video. To others, such as veteran journalist Robert Fisk, it portended an era where the checks and balances of professional journalists would be overrun by stampeding hordes sharing gossip and trivia. 'To hell with the web', he told a public lecture in New Zealand. 'It has no responsibility.' (Lyon 2008)

By the turn of the century, the first dotcom bubble was already fit to burst. The first set of 'paywalls' had come and gone – having generally, with one or two notable exceptions (such as the *Financial Times*), failed to deliver anywhere near enough paying customers. As the tech stocks crashed and burned, there was even, for a while, a sense of calm within the newspaper world. An investment in new colour presses meant that ink-on-paper advertising revenues were actually higher than they had ever been for national newspapers (Reid 2000). The *Independent*'s bold move to change from a broadsheet to a 'compact' format – like many regional evening newspapers before it – paid brief dividends in circulation terms. *The Times* followed suit, while the *Guardian* opted for the mid-sized Berliner format.

But if the view that the upstart web had somehow been seen off ever did gain any real traction, it wasn't long before it started slipping again. By the middle of the twenty-first century's first decade, digital media came roaring back in the shape of Facebook and then Twitter. 'Social' was the buzzword as publishers realised the appetite amongst some web users for getting involved in the content-creating process – for joining the conversation.

In his seminal book *We the Media*, Dan Gilmor (2004) describes his realisation of how significantly the ground had changed immediately after the 2001 attacks on New York's twin towers:

> But something else, something profound, was happening this time around: news was being produced by regular people who had something to say and show, and not solely by the 'official' news organizations that had traditionally decided how the first draft of history would look. This time, the first draft of history was being written, in part, by the former audience. It was possible – it was inevitable – because of new publishing tools available on the internet.

Today, technology continues to feed the innovation of news content. The development of new generations of smartphones and tablet devices means that news is more than ever accessed 'on the go' by readers and viewers. More than a quarter of *Financial Times* readers use a mobile device to consume its content. And while the iPad – and tablet revolution that it inspired – has not proved the saviour of the newspaper industry, as Rupert Murdoch once hoped, they have nonetheless found new ways of reaching audiences with immersive multimedia features.

So what next? As I write this, BBC Radio 4 is running an item on *The Media Show* about Google Glass – which not only feeds text information directly in front of its wearers' eyes, but will no doubt in time also allow them to stream real-time video of what they are seeing to an online audience. Clearly, innovation in news will continue at a terrific pace. But what of those original printed products? In his book, *The Vanishing Newspaper*, Philip Meyer (2004) published a graph showing what would happen if American newspaper readership continued its long-term decline at the existing rate. An extrapolation of the graph would show a zero point at April 2043 – although Meyer later pointed out that the economics of printing for such tiny audiences would force publishers to have thrown the towel in considerably before then (Meyer 2008).

Thirty years out from Meyer's zero point, it's hard to make a strong case that the printed newspaper market in the UK will be anything like as vibrant and competitive as it is now. More regional daily newspapers will go weekly. National titles will close. What remains will, by definition, be products aimed at more elite, niche readerships. Newspapers as we know them probably are in the early stages of their endgame. But newspaper journalism? I have a strong feeling that will survive much, much longer – as I hope we'll see in later chapters of this book.

NEWSPAPER OWNERSHIP: PROFIT OR PROPAGANDA

The agents of change

Despite Lord Beaverbrook's claim to the First Royal Commission on the Press in 1947 that he ran the *Daily Express* 'purely for the purpose of making propaganda and with no other motive', newspaper proprietors generally have a more forceful motivation underlying their ownership: the generation of profit. Even in the eighteenth century, when newspaper owners often had political ambitions of their own, their titles were still primarily businesses. As Bob Clarke points out in his meticulous history *From Grub Street to Fleet Street*: 'Most provincial newspapers in the 18th century were politically neutral. They were intended for profit, not propaganda.' (Clarke 2010)

The era of the press barons, led by Lords Beaverbrook and Rothermere, was characterised by Prime Minister Stanley Baldwin's depiction of them. Their products were, he said ' . . . the engines of propaganda for the constantly changing policies, desires, personal wishes, personal likes and personal dislikes of two men . . . What the proprietorship of these papers is aiming at is power, but power without responsibility – the prerogative of the harlot throughout the ages.' (Curran and Seaton 2003)

With their contemporaries the Berry brothers – Lords Kemsley and Camrose – these powerful men controlled vast swathes of the newspaper landscape and exerted immense power on national politics. Characterised not inaccurately as ruthless, capricious egomaniacs, they boasted of their ability to oust prime ministers and make or break governments. But they overestimated the extent to which a newspaper's influence could be turned into the harder currency of votes.

Backed by Rothermere, Beaverbrook announced the formation of a new political party, the United Empire Party, which would take on Stanley Baldwin's Conservatives. In a key by-election, however, the UEP man was defeated, and, as legendary *Mirror* editor Hugh Cudlipp would note: 'The baleful influence of proprietorial journalism was diminished. The personal prestige of Beaverbrook and Rothermere as Press Barons, which rarely extended beyond mutual genuflection, plummeted: so did their power, though not their pride or arrogance.' (Cudlipp 2009)

Cudlipp would come to see with his own eyes the damage that a monstrous ego could do to a newspaper proprietor. As editor of the *Mirror* through its most successful period, during which its circulation reached a heady, never-to-be-beaten 5 million in 1964, Cudlipp's chairman was Cecil King. By 1968, King had become convinced that disaster was about to befall the country because of Prime Minister Harold Wilson's economic policies, and involved himself in a bizarre plot to overthrow the government. Riding roughshod over the editorial independence of the newspaper, he wrote a front page editorial headlined 'Enough Is Enough'. But once again, a proprietor had wildly mistaken the real political power of the title at his disposal, and within three weeks King had himself been cast into oblivion by his own fellow board directors.

The following year saw a young Australian entrepreneur named Rupert Murdoch take the newspaper industry by the scruff of the neck. After buying the *News of the World*, and then the *Sun* from IPC, his influence and success grew as rapidly as its circulation. By the early 1980s, by which time he had bought *The Times* and *The Sunday Times* too, Murdoch controlled around one-third of the UK's newspaper market by circulation. The *Sun* had outstripped the *Mirror* and was selling more than 4 million copies a day. And while he never attempted anything quite so overt as launching his own political party, or bringing down a government, his political influence has undoubtedly been vast. In his authorised *History of* The Times, Graham Stewart (2005) puts it this way:

> Murdoch was not interested in owning *The Times* as a ticket into the British Establishment, and nor was it deployed effectively as his prime weapon in exerting political power. Rather, Murdoch's motivating interests seemed to relate more clearly to its central place in the history and development of his first and greatest hobby – newspapers.

Be that as it may, Murdoch has had the ear of prime ministers and senior cabinet ministers throughout much of the past 40 years. Lance Price (2006) likened him to the 24th member of the cabinet in a post on the *Guardian*'s Comment Is Free blog.

> Rupert Murdoch doesn't leave a paper trail that could ever prove his influence over policy, but the trail of politicians beating their way to him and his papers tells a different story . . . his presence is always felt.

Murdoch himself claims that too much is made of his influence along the corridors of power. In an interview he did for the 40th anniversary issue of *Press Gazette*, Murdoch told me:

> I've been, I hope, fairly radical, and an agent of change. I've brought in competition in the popular press. My insight, my feeling was that there was room for that.

Then there was the turning of the industry upside down at Wapping to its total benefit and then dragging *The Times* into the modern age, and *The Sunday Times*. It is perfectly natural that people would be a bit paranoid about me.

(Reeves 2005a)

Among the modern press barons, Richard Desmond appears the most transparent. With no apparent aspiration for political influence, his motivations for buying the *Express* titles in 2001 seem clear enough: to allow him a degree of respectability – his early fortune having been made in the porn publishing business – and the realisation that he could make the newspapers extremely profitable by cutting costs without worrying unduly about falling circulation.

Likewise with the Barclay brothers Sir Frederick and Sir David. As owners of the Telegraph Media Group (having bought the newspaper titles from disgraced mogul Conrad Black in 2004), they were named at the top of 2013's *Sunday Times* Rich List of people in publishing, PR and advertising.

The newest press barons on the block are Russian father and son Alexander and Evgeny Lebedev, whose companies own the *Independent* titles and a majority stake in the *Evening Standard*. Lebedev senior, a former KGB spy, has pledged not to interfere with his newspapers' editorial stance and has a track record of allowing independent journalism to flourish – he owns *Novaya Gazeta*, a Russian newspaper which focuses on issues that the state-owned press dare not touch. The Lebedevs also appear to have another vital quality that the modern newspaper owner cannot do without: a shrewd business sense. Having controversially turned the *Evening Standard* into a free newspaper in 2009, they have turned a dramatically loss-making enterprise into a modestly profitable one. (Greenslade 2012)

They have also launched *i*, the cut-price 'lite' version of the *Independent*, which in circulation terms has been one of the few success stories of the past few years.

In his speech at the 2013 Orwell Prize, *Times* columnist Matthew Parris responded thus to criticisms of newspaper proprietors made by Labour MP Chris Mullin:

Does he realise how precarious now is the whole future of daily newspapers in Britain? Apart from historic buildings and football clubs I know no other sector where owners and investors appear so willing to pay for the privilege of losing money in the public interest.

But as Colin Sparks (1999) stressed,

Newspapers in Britain are first and foremost businesses. They do not exist to report the news, to act as watchdogs for the public, to be a check on the doings of government, to defend the ordinary citizen against abuses of power, to unearth scandals or to do any of the other fine and noble things that are sometimes claimed for the press. They exist to make money just as any other business does. To the extent that they discharge any of their public functions, they do so in order to succeed as businesses.

The nationals: monopolies rule

One of the most striking features of the British national press is its diversity. The London-based mainstream newspaper industry comprises 10 Sundays and 11 dailies. Three out of every four national newspapers are bought unordered from newspapers each morning: hence the hyper-competition between the titles. Yet behind the façade of extraordinary diversity lies an industry dominated by monopolies and conformism. There is a lively 'alternative' press including leftist, religious, municipal, trade union and ethnic minority publications. But their circulations are relatively small and their impact on the national debate only marginal. Power, influence and financial resources lie with the mainstream local and national press.

Here competition has not promoted variety. By 1974 only London, Edinburgh and Belfast had directly competing paid-for local morning or evening papers. Since then, the concentration of media ownership has intensified, reducing many newspapers to tiny outposts of vast, highly profitable multinationals (Williams 1994; Sarikakis 2004). As John Pilger stressed in an interview in *Socialist Worker* (20 November 2004): 'In 1983 there were 50 multinational companies effectively controlling the world's leading media. Today there are six. The "new global media" is less diverse than ever before.'

Monopoly ownership has similarly intensified at the national level. In 1947, the three leading corporations accounted for 62 per cent of the national daily circulation and 60 per cent of national Sunday circulation. By 1988 these figures had increased to 73 and 81 per cent. Kevin Williams (1998: 228) commented:

> In the post-war period the press has become integrated into British finance and industry. So much so that today there is no national newspaper or major regional newspaper group that does not have a tie through cross-ownership to interests outside publishing and the media.

Overall, the trend in ownership of the British press since 1945 has been towards concentration, conglomeration and internationalisation. By 2000, Fleet Street was dominated by just four companies. This trend was best typified by Rupert Murdoch, head of News Corporation (in which his family own a controlling 30 per cent share), whose London-based newspapers (*The Times*, *The Sunday Times*, the *Sun* and the *News of the World*) constituted a small subsidiary of a vast empire, yet amounted to more than 30 per cent of the national market.

Today, News UK (as Murdoch's newspaper division is now known – and with the *News of the World* now deceased) shares the national market with Associated

Newspapers (owner of the *Daily Mail* and the *Mail on Sunday*); Telegraph Media Group (the *Daily Telegraph* and the *Sunday Telegraph*); Express Newspapers (the *Daily* and *Sunday Express*); Mirror Group (the *Daily* and *Sunday Mirror*, the *People*); Pearson (publisher of the *Financial Times*); and Independent Print Ltd (publisher of the *Independent*, the *Independent on Sunday*, *i* and the *Evening Standard*). Accompanying this monopoly ownership has been a serious decline in sales. Fleet Street's figures show circulations dropped by one-fifth between 1990 and 2002 and by a further one-third over the following decade.

Similar crises are afflicting newspapers in America and across Europe, although in China, India and Asia circulations are racing ahead and global newspaper sales have continued to rise (Preston 2004a). But as we shall see later in this chapter, print circulation is now just one measurement by which the newspaper industry can be judged. Alongside those vertigo-inducing print drops, we must also take into account the dramatic surges in web traffic seen by all newspapers.

Robert Andrews (2012) of Paid Content analysed data from the Audit Bureau of Circulation between 2003 and 2012, comparing net print circulation figures for six national newspapers with their average daily unique browsers. Using these data – while acknowledging that they are not entirely equivalent measurements (but print readership figures are notoriously unreliable) – Andrews concludes that the 'tipping point' came in November 2010. That's the point at which web overtook print. By the end of 2012, the web figure was more than double print circulation.

The regionals: monopolies falter

The history of ownership of the regional press reads like a succession of family sagas. Typical among them are the Storeys. Samuel Storey, a Liberal MP, co-founded the *Sunderland Echo* in 1873 as an evening newspaper that would reflect his radical views. His business later acquired other newspapers in the Midlands and Portsmouth – including what would become the *News* in Portsmouth. Storey's son Frederick soon took the reins of the newspaper group, and when he died the mantle passed to his son – another Samuel, who later became Lord Buckton. When he died in 1978, his son Richard became chairman of the group – by then known as Portsmouth and Sunderland Newspapers. But Sir Richard Storey's son Kenelm was not destined to become the fifth generation of his family to take charge. A family disagreement destabilised the group just as a takeover frenzy was taking hold of the industry in the 1990s.

At this stage, the Storey family's saga becomes intertwined with that of the Johnston family, which had also passed its newspapers down the family line since 1846 – having been in the printing business since 1767. After listing on the London Stock Exchange in the late 1980s, it was on the acquisition trail – buying newspapers from Emap, among others. Taking advantage of the Storey clan's bickering,

Johnston Press acquired the Portsmouth and Sunderland business for £266 million in 1999.

By this stage, Johnston was one of the top five newspaper publishers in the country. No doubt Samuel Storey would have been flabbergasted to know that the company that owned the newspapers he founded was worth a staggering £1.5 billion in 2004. But the family ties continued to loosen. When Freddie Johnston stepped down as chairman in 2010, it was the first time in almost 250 years that there had been no family member on the board of Johnston Newspapers. His son Michael left the company in 2012 – severing the final link.

There are plenty of other family sagas like those of the Storeys and the Johnstons: among many others, there are the Iliffes and the Grahams in the West Midlands; the Forman-Hardys in Nottingham; the Colmans (of mustard fame) and the Copelands in East Anglia; the Burgesses in Cumbria; the Boormans in Kent. Some from that list – notably the latter two – have held out as entirely family-owned concerns, but for most the corporate takeover of the regional press reached its peak in the 1990s and 2000s. During a period of unprecedented consolidation, 77 per cent of the entire industry changed ownership between 1996 and 1999.

The new corporate structure involved giant players backed by banks and venture capitalists, including Trinity International and Newsquest. In the late 1990s, the financial successes of the local press began to attract the attention of US companies, and in June 1999 the US media giant Gannett (owner of 74 papers including *USA Today* and 22 television stations, all with their interlocking websites) purchased Newsquest, UK's largest local group with 63 paid-for titles and 120 frees, for £904 million. The same year, Trinity became the UK's largest newspaper group with its £1.5 billion merger with the Mirror Group.

At this point just four companies – Northcliffe (part of Associated Newspapers), Trinity Mirror, Johnston Press and Newsquest – between them controlled 73 per cent of the regional market (Greenslade 2004). Johnston's chief executive Tim Bowdler, reflecting the corporate culture in a way no member of the Storey or Johnston family would ever have countenanced, would describe the newspapers he managed as 'cash generating units'.

One key player in this explosion of corporate involvement in newspapers was Chris Oakley. A former editor of the *Liverpool Echo*, he twice led management buyout teams to take control of newspaper groups with money from private equity investors in the early 1990s. His fascinating account of the period, 'The men who killed the regional newspaper industry' (Oakley 2012), reflects on the corporate frenzy. City investors, he says, failed to understand how significantly the publishing world was about to be devastated by internet technologies, and remained convinced for far too long that the cyclical advertising core could be ramped up year after year to produce margins of 30 per cent or more. 'The willingness of banks to provide loans on ever more arcane assumptions – cashflow forecasts for five or more years ahead – helped to ensure the valuation of newspaper groups did not reflect the new reality.'

The new reality would set in quickly enough. From the high point of the mid 2000s, the collapse has proved spectacular. Johnston's share price, for example, had collapsed by 97 per cent in just five years, giving it a market capitalisation of £47 million in 2009 – around a fifth of what it had paid for just the Storey family's titles 10 years earlier. By 2013 the company was saddled with more than £300 million debt (Cookson 2013), which it struggled to service, and became the subject of continual speculation of takeover or even collapse. Northcliffe Newspapers, which had put its newspaper portfolio up for sale in 2005, hoping to find a £1.2 billion buyer, eventually sold out to Local World, a new company led by an old name – former *Mirror* boss David Montgomery – in 2013 for just £53 million plus a stake in the new business.

In 2013 the overall monopoly structure of the regional press remains as concentrated as ever. The top 20 publishers now account for 87 per cent of all audited press titles, and a whopping 97 per cent of all audited circulation. The top four alone account for nearly 60 per cent of circulation. The turmoil of the past two decades has seen a net loss of almost 300 local newspapers, down from 1,333 in 1990 (Franklin 2005) to 1,054 at the beginning of 2013, according to the Newspaper Society. In that time, 10 daily newspapers have shifted to a weekly frequency, and a number of titles – notably the *Manchester Evening News* – have experimented with a part-paid, part-free circulation. Oakley, for one, is pessimistic about the future of some parts of the industry, and says the big city daily papers are the most vulnerable:

> They are almost exclusively owned by publicly quoted companies which have huge debt burdens to service while attempting to maintain or improve year-on-year profits and margins at a time of falling revenues. As a result costs continue to be cut in ways which have rendered regional dailies less readable and less relevant. Editorial workloads have been increased to service online media while staff has been reduced to a level where the generation of original, well-researched material or the undertaking of local investigations is almost impossible.
>
> (Oakley 2012)

But, for all its troubles, the sector remains a giant part of British cultural life. Some 44 million local newspapers are sold every week, while 30 million are distributed free. In all, 84 per cent of adults in the country read a regional newspaper, according to the Newspaper Society. The sector's time as the darling of the City may be over, but that's not to say that its time is up altogether.

If we look across the Atlantic, Warren Buffet – one of the country's shrewdest corporate investors – bought a business that publishes 63 regional daily newspapers for $142 million in 2012. As analyst Jack Shafer (2012) wrote for Reuters: 'Buffet isn't romantic about newspapers. He buys when he sees value that others don't.' Alongside the acquisition in 2013 of the *Washington Post* by Jeff Bezos, the founder of Amazon (Kelion 2013), comes the sense that forward-thinking business brains can see a future for this ailing industry.

Meanwhile, in the UK there are still family businesses determined to survive as the generations before them did – the Kent Messenger Group, Cumbria Newspapers, Midland Independent Newspapers, to pick out just three. Then there's Sir Ray Tindle, who has suggested that his ideal model would be a newspaper for every street (Tindle 2012), and has successfully, painstakingly, built a small empire of weeklies serving highly localised communities. They all believe that there's life in the old dog yet. Which might even give old Samuel Storey a reason to spin slightly less quickly in his grave.

DIGITAL STRATEGIES: A HOT AND COLD ROMANCE

The newspaper industry's relationship with the online world has been a bit like that of Richard Burton and Elizabeth Taylor. One moment it's a very public romance burning with white-hot passion. The next the two sides have fallen out, citing irreconcilable differences. Ever since the *Telegraph* launched Britain's first newspaper-based web service, the Electronic Telegraph, in 1994, there has lurked an inherent suspicion that these digital interlopers were out to steal the newspaper industry's lunch. From the word go, there was uncertainty over whether any investment would pay dividends. Derek Bishton, co-founder of the Electronic Telegraph, recalls:

> We didn't have a clue how we could make money out of it. But we knew it was an exciting new development and if we were on the cusp of it, then whatever possibilities might exist we would be the first to be able to try to exploit them.

Many in the industry took the ostrich approach and eschewed the internet altogether until it was too big to ignore. Others, like Rupert Murdoch's News Corporation, tried on various occasions to buy their way into the game. His list of purchases is long and not especially auspicious: he bought Delphi, one of the first companies to allow ordinary people access to the internet, in 1994. He ploughed millions into iGuide the following year, the first attempt at a standalone web news service, but closed it down soon after. Then there was the entertainment service pagesix.com, which had two equally doomed short lives: the first during the initial dotcom bubble, the second in 2008. But most infamous was his $580 million purchase of social media site MySpace in 2005. After an early burst of growth and the prediction that it would be worth $1 billion a year in advertising, users began to quit the site in their droves. Six years later he offloaded it for just $35 million (Garrahan 2011).

Others chose to invest in their own teams to develop new services. The *Guardian*, for example, established a new media lab in 1995 to oversee the development of the newspaper's internet presence. It launched standalone sites for its technology section, and for its coverage of the European football championships in 1996, but it wasn't until 1999 that its first broad-based news service, Guardian Unlimited – which published content from the daily newspaper and from the *Observer* – was born. Since then, it has embraced the web as a delivery mechanism for its journalism more enthusiastically than most.

Certainly more enthusiastically than Richard Desmond, owner of the *Express*, who has also had a capricious relationship with the web. He famously sold the newspaper's websites to a friend of his for £1 when he bought the group in 2001, saying there was no money to be made from them. He later re-registered the domain names and returned to the web fray two years later.

Meanwhile, in the regional press, the experimentation was just as patchy and the confusion just as great. In the initial burst of web enthusiasm in the 1990s, many regional groups allowed some of their more tech-savvy staff to experiment with putting rudimentary content from their newspapers online. By 1999, though, bosses of several of the large regional publishing groups had decided that a unified approach to the threat of the internet was their best bet. Four of the big players – Trinity Mirror, Northcliffe, Newsquest and Guardian Regional Media – backed a 'gateway' approach called ThisIsBritain, which was intended to become a central hub that users would access in order to be directed to news content from their local editorial teams. Alongside this was a separate gateway for classified advertising called Fish4it.co.uk, which was intended to link up the cars, property and jobs advertising being sold by newspaper sales staff throughout the country in one giant searchable database.

Confused? So were the readers. The familiar mastheads of the newspapers they loved and trusted did not appear on these new gateway sites, so they didn't establish the connection. ThisIsBritain was dropped in 2000. Fish4 still exists, but only as Trinity Mirror's recruitment advertising platform.

It wasn't until the advent of widely available broadband access to the internet that the potential of many of these new information services really began to take off. Until then, the dial-up connection using a standard telephone line was slow and costly. For all the potential promise of the medium, the basic technology simply hadn't been able to deliver. But with service providers now able to deliver good resolution images, near broadcast-quality audio and higher definition video into people's homes at a relatively inexpensive cost, a second wave of web development began as newspaper groups realised what a fundamental part of their future digital journalism was likely to become.

By the mid 2000s, national newspapers were beginning to put the web at the heart of the operation – a strategy central to the design of the *Telegraph*'s new newsroom. The *Guardian* had already implemented its groundbreaking 'web first' strategy, in which the journalism of its major correspondents was published online before appearing in the newspaper. This was followed five years later by the announcement of a 'digital first' strategy in 2011 (Sabbagh 2011), signalling the *Guardian*'s intention to put digital investment at the heart of its strategic thinking. Editor Alan Rusbridger said: 'Every newspaper is on a journey into some kind of digital future. That doesn't mean getting out of print, but it does require a greater focus of attention, imagination and resource on the various forms that digital future is likely to take.' One result has been a plethora of stories – all of them rubbished by the *Guardian* – that it has been seriously considering closing the print edition entirely and focusing all its efforts on a global digital future (see for example Rushton 2012).

In 2012, the *Financial Times* followed suit with a dramatic restructuring and a fundamental shift of focus for its journalists. In an email to staff, editor Lionel Barber said: 'We need to ensure that we are serving a digital platform first, and a newspaper second. This is a big cultural shift for the *FT* that is only likely to be achieved with further structural change.'

The astonishing rise of the *Daily Mail*'s website is a further case in point. In the mid to late 1990s, when other news organisations were establishing their brands online, the *Mail* chose not to. Its parent company did launch a series of sites – thisisLondon.co.uk, charlottestreet.com and thisisMoney.co.uk, among others – but they were staffed and branded entirely separately from the main newspapers. It wasn't until 2003 that the strategy changed and dailymail.co.uk was born, with some content from its print editions cautiously being published online for the first time. Within nine years it was the biggest newspaper website on the planet. Comscore's web usage figures for January 2013 showed the Mail Online had 54.2 million unique users in the month, putting it ahead of the websites of the *People's Daily* (China), the *New York Post* (USA) and the *Guardian*.

Its relentless focus on celebrity gossip, grisly crime and offbeat weirdness from around the globe has been described by its editor Martin Clarke as 'journalism crack' (Steel and Edgecliffe-Johnson 2013). Much of the *Mail*'s growth in web traffic has come from the US, a territory recognised by many British newspapers as the most obvious place to expand their digital offerings. The *Guardian* too has grown its US staff rapidly as it seeks to compete for online readers with the *Washington Post* and the *New York Times*, among others.

But it's one thing to attract a lot of new overseas readers; it's quite another to turn those eyeballs into profit. For a short while, hopes flared that the answer to that would lie in new devices launched by computer giant Apple. When the company announced the arrival of its iPad in 2004, Rupert Murdoch famously heralded it as a device that 'may well be the saving of the newspaper industry' (Kalb 2010).

Would that it were so simple. The explosion of the tablet market that followed the iPad did, indeed, lead to the feverish development of tablet apps that could deliver paid-for content directly to these new devices. Murdoch put his money where his mouth was by launching The Daily, an iPad-only tablet newspaper for the US market staffed by a dedicated team of reporters, editors, designers and programmers, in February 2011. Less than two years and around $60 million later, the experiment was closed. The Daily is understood to have attracted around 100,000 subscribers paying less than $1 per week for the newspaper – nowhere enough to sustain its $500,000 per week running costs (Bates 2012). Tablet editions do continue to play a part in newspaper groups' digital strategies – the *Sun* and the *Daily Mail* both launched theirs in 2013 – but they're not seen as the silver bullet that they once were.

Paywalls: knocking them down, building them up

The year 2010, an *Economist* headline announced with its usual admirable certainty, was going to be the year of the paywall (*Economist* 2010). Driven by a sharp drop in online advertising spending after several years of impressive growth, the piece said, big newspapers including the *New York Times*, and the *Sun* and *The Times* in London, were becoming convinced the time was right for them to start charging readers to access their news online. *The Times* of London duly did erect its paywall that year, although it would be 2011 before the *New York Times* closed part of its site, and another couple of years after that until the *Sun* did the same. By 2013, the *Daily Telegraph* has also announced plans for its own digital payment system.

Not that this newfound enthusiasm was entirely universal. In 2010, Johnston Press, one of the largest of the UK's regional newspaper publishers, abandoned a trial in which it had experimented with six different methods of online payment for several of its daily and weekly titles. And in 2012 the UK's biggest circulating evening regional newspaper, the *Express & Star* in Wolverhampton, stopped its paywall experiment after a nine-month trial (Pugh 2012a).

The Economist might also have noted that this would be the second time around for a strategy that had already been tried on a fairly hefty scale a decade earlier, and abandoned by most of its early proponents. Only the *Financial Times* and the *Wall Street Journal*, of the significant European and American newspapers, had managed to make a paywall operation add up in any sustained sense. The *New York Times*, for example, abandoned its first paywall operation after two years in 2007. In that experiment, it calculated that the $10 million a year it was making in digital subscription revenue was less than the amount it was losing from online advertising revenue as web traffic fell because of the paywall block (Perez-Pena 2007).

So what's changed to make these companies think things can work this time? Partly it's down to perceived changes in the public's attitude to paying for low-value items online, and partly it's down to important tweaks to the paywall model. The first wave of paywalls tended to be 'all or nothing', meaning that if you didn't pay, you couldn't access any content. This generally resulted in spectacular drops in online readership because the newspapers' content stopped appearing in search engines – which is where a significant proportion of their traffic comes from. This time, though, many are adopting a 'porous paywall' approach, which allows readers to access the site initially, but requires them to pay usually after viewing a certain number of articles – the 'metered paywall' – or after a certain length of time. (With *The Times*, readers get short previews of articles before being asked to pay.) This has a far less negative effect on traffic as the search engines still list their stories.

But are they working? It's still too early to judge definitively. In the case of the *New York Times*, its first published figures indicated that it had around 700,000 digital subscribers paying for various packages under its metered paywall system. The company valued these at $150 million (£98 million) per year in revenue – that's around $200 (£130) per customer per year (Chittum 2013). The *New York Times* brings a further $210 million (£140 million) per year in digital advertising revenue.

It's worth comparing those digital revenue figures with those of the *Guardian*, a newspaper with similar global reach, and similar numbers of online readers, but with an avowedly anti-paywall strategy. Its figures show it has total digital revenues of £85 million, but that its digital advertising revenue is growing at an annual rate of 29 per cent – as opposed that of the *New York Times*, which is falling. The *Daily Mail*, another paywall-free title, expects its websites to bring in more than £100 million in annual revenue in the next three to five years (Sweney 2013).

The Times is far more reticent about sharing revenue figures, but has published figures showing that 140,000 digital subscribers had signed up in the first three years of its paywall – mainly accessing its content through tablets. Sceptics, though, suggest the 'giveaway' of a Google Nexus tablet computer to early subscribers will have skewed the figures. Its stablemate, the *Sun*, launched its paywall in the summer of 2013, with the added enticement that subscribers would be able to watch Premier League football goals exclusively on the site – likely to be a significant carrot to fans.

The *Telegraph* introduced its metered paywall in March 2013, with a 20-article limit before readers were asked to take out a subscription. Commenting on the newspaper's strategy to *Press Gazette*, Douglas McCabe of Enders Analysis said: 'There's almost no downside that we can see to this approach. The *Telegraph* demonstrates the point and this could be what everyone's been waiting for.' (Ponsford 2013c) Early figures indicated that the paywall had not led to a drop in traffic to the site.

Another major American publisher, Gannett, has also built paywalls across its 82 newspapers – with the notable exception of its national flagship *USA Today*. It claimed to be on target to reach 250,000 digital subscribers by the end of 2013.

If those are a sustained success, then we can expect the company's titles in the UK – where it owns Newsquest – to follow suit.

The paywall debate will continue to ebb and flow, as newspaper publishers remain in search of that elusive goal: the digital structure that can sustain large-scale journalism newsrooms. Some will go for greater reach that they hope will sustain improved advertising rates; others will opt to sacrifice that reach in the hope of achieving recurring revenue from a more loyal core of readers.

CHAPTER 2

From print to multi-platform

Anatomy of a newspaper

The *Daily Universal Register* of 1 January 1785, for all its quaintness, would still be recognised as a newspaper if you put it on a newsstand today. For a start, there's that distinctive title-piece coat of arms, which still appears every day on its modern counterpart (the newspaper changed its name to *The Times* in 1788). Then there's the grid format of its layout, the use of large type for headlines and sub-headings, and the basic typography of its presentation of text – none of these has changed dramatically in more than 200 years.

True, there are plenty of things that have been introduced in that time – pictures and colour being the most obvious – but newspaper buyers, from every point on the political compass, are essentially conservative in their outlook. They have become accustomed to the conventions and traditions that journalists and newspaper designers have conspired to develop over many, many decades. Ask any editor who has risked a significant redesign of a title, and they will show you their battle scars from readers outraged that 'their' newspaper has been ruined.

In this chapter we'll take a brief look at some of the elements that help make up the modern newspaper package – including its newer web, mobile phone and tablet formats.

THE NEWSPAPER FORMAT: SHAPES AND SIZES

In some circles there's still a distinction made between 'broadsheets', 'mid-market' newspapers and 'tabloids'. In truth, the first and last of these terms – which are based on the historical physical size of the newspapers serving a particular part of the market – are no longer that useful. In 2003, the *Independent*, which had launched in 1986 as a broadsheet – roughly the same size as existing dailies *The Times*, the *Daily Telegraph*, the *Financial Times* and the *Guardian* – made what seemed a radical gamble. It changed its physical size to a package that was roughly the same size as tabloids the *Sun*, *Daily Mirror* and *Daily Star*, and mid-markets *Daily Mail* and *Daily Express*. Eschewing the word 'tabloid', which could have damaging downmarket connotations for a serious newspaper, it chose to call the new size 'compact'. Readers loved it, and pretty soon *The Times* had followed suit. Not long after that, the *Guardian* reformatted too – although it chose a 'Berliner' format, somewhat taller and wider than a compact, but smaller than its original broadsheet size.

Actually the radical gamble followed a pretty well-trodden path. The *Mail* had gone from broadsheet to tabloid size in the 1970s. Many regional evening and morning newspapers had made similar transformations, partly because of the economics of the print process – there were more suppliers who could print at a tabloid size, and not having to make that final fold took something off the cost too – and partly because commuting readers found them easier to handle.

THE GRID SYSTEM: KEEPING ORDER ON THE PAGE

Every newspaper page starts life as a basic grid – a simple set of ruled lines that govern the placement of items such as pictures and text boxes. The grid has both editorial and commercial functions. Editorially, it ensures that there is a consistency of design between editorial pages; commercially, it is used as a measurement to sell advertising space. Tabloid and compact-sized newspapers – which account for the vast majority of titles in the UK these days – largely use a five-column editorial grid. So papers as diverse as the *Sun*, *The Times*, the *Daily Mail*, the regional daily *Ipswich Evening Star* and the weekly *Epsom Guardian* in Surrey all share an underlying design structure. In 2013, the *Independent* bucked that trend with a new six-column design.

But although it sounds like a terrible constraint, skilled newspaper designers and layout subs are able to use the grid in creative ways to design pages that are uniquely identifiable as belonging to their own newspaper. We'll see more about their work in Chapter 3.

The *Guardian*'s Berliner format uses a six-column grid, as do some weekly regional newspapers such as the *Kent Messenger* series. Of the broadsheets, some use a six-column grid (the *Daily Telegraph* for example) while others, including the *Financial Times* and *The Sunday Times*, use an eight-column format.

FIGURE 2.1

The Times's five-column grid; the *Independent*'s new six-column design; and the *Kent Messenger*'s six columns

THE TITLEPIECE: ESTABLISHING IDENTITY

Sometimes known as the masthead, the titlepiece is the most fiercely protected element of any newspaper. This is its brand, the most obvious point of differentiation from its competitors in the frantic melée of the newsagent's shelf. Cover up the titlepiece of *The Times* and the *Independent* and you will be surprised how many casual newspaper readers are unable to tell you which is which. That's one of the reasons why titlepieces are very rarely redesigned. To all but the most pernickety of typographers, today's *Daily Mail* masthead is virtually unchanged from the one it was using at the turn of the nineteenth century.

Only on the rarest of occasions do titlepieces change. Of today's national newspapers, the *Guardian* has tinkered with its masthead more than most, making notable changes in 1959 (when the word Manchester was dropped), 1969, 1988 and 2005. The *Sun* playfully changed its titlepiece to '*The Son*' on the birth of the Duke and Duchess of Cambridge's son Prince George in the summer of 2013 (see Figure 2.2).

SECTIONS OF THE NEWSPAPER: PACKAGING THE BUNDLE

The sectionalisation of British newspapers is best exemplified by the juggernaut that is *The Sunday Times*. Its 2013 manifestation comes in no fewer than eight regular separately printed newsprint sections (the main newspaper, News Review, Business, Sport, Money, Travel, Homes and Motors), and three magazines (Culture, Style and *The Sunday Times Magazine*). This is partly driven by a commercial imperative. Separate sections mean separately targeted advertising to specific subsets of readers with high purchasing power and very clearly expressed interests – the Holy Grail of the ad world. They also allow the paper to market itself with a 'something for everyone' message.

But daily newspapers, particularly at the quality end of the market, are split into well signposted sections too – a development that has grown over the past 30 years or so.

So, for example, the *Daily Telegraph* runs sections of Home News, International News, Comment and Opinion, Business, Obituaries and Sport. The *Guardian* was the first daily to have a separately printed features section – G2, launched under the editorship of Peter Preston in 1992. *The Times* followed suit (as briefly did the *Independent*). But other sections of the *Guardian* that were printed separately – including Media, Society and Education – have since been taken back into the main newspaper as the classified advertising that once funded them has moved into the far-less-lucrative online space.

FIGURE 2.2
The Sun becomes *The Son*

Daily Mail

TUESDAY, OCTOBER 1, 2013   www.dailymail.co.uk   60p

GOOD HEALTH
STARTS PAGE 36

FREE CD

TCHAIKOVSKY SWAN LAKE
CLASSICAL COLLECTION

Ultimate soothing classics
SEE PAGE 42 FOR DETAILS
PICK UP TODAY FROM TESCO, WHSMITH & EASON

Tories' answer to out-of-hours care crisis

GPs TOLD TO OPEN SURGERIES UNTIL 8PM EVERY DAY

FAMILY doctors should open surgeries seven days a week and outside office hours, David Cameron will say today.

The Prime Minister will set out plans for the first wave of surgeries which will be open from 8am to 8pm every day, making it easier for patients who struggle to

By James Chapman
Political Editor

fit in visits with their family and work commitments.

The move is a response to growing concern over the quality of out-of-hours care.

Labour allowed GPs to opt out of responsibility for patients outside office hours and at weekends as part of a botched deal which came into

force in 2004. Since then, private companies have taken over and in many cases have been forced to employ foreign doctors, many of whom have a poor grasp of English.

The Daily Mail has repeatedly highlighted the deterioration in the service since the contract was changed.

A poll for this newspaper showed that 60 per cent of Britons believe that out-of-hours care has got

Turn to Page 2

Stunning: Catherine Zeta-Jones, who was wearing her wedding ring at a charity event in New York

Troubled Zeta's dazzling again

SEE PAGE 27

FIGURE 2.3
A typical *Daily Mail* splash

THE SPLASH: THE STORY THAT SAYS 'BUY ME'

The splash is the most important story in the newspaper. It's the story that is given the greatest prominence on the most crucial page – the front. The splash headline is usually the only one the reader will see before making the decision whether or not to purchase the newspaper. Its style and tone speak volumes about the newspaper's place in the market and help to position it in the minds of readers.

On most days, the *Sun* and the *Mirror* will use block headlines, all caps, in headline font of up to 200 point. They will often reverse out the headline – setting it as white text on a black or coloured background – to give a greater emphasis and an almost poster-like quality. And they will make heavy use of puns and streetwise cultural references to appeal to their target readership. The *Daily Mail* will be more sparing in its use of all capital letters (caps, in the jargon) for the splash – reserving them for its more bombastic declarations – and will rarely use humour in a splash headline either. Compare both of these with the relative sobriety of splashes in *The Times*, for example.

The choice of splash also helps to position the title. For example, the *Daily Express* went through periods when it regularly splashed on stories about Princess Diana. When Piers Morgan edited the *Daily Mirror* (1995–2004) he underwent a brief Damascene conversion when he decided he would no longer splash on nonentity 'celebrities' such as those made famous by the TV show *Big Brother*. It was a laudable idea, but sales dived and the policy was quietly dropped (Morgan 2005).

On rare occasions, when they had a particularly stunning exclusive that they wanted to protect, tabloid newspaper executives would print what's known as a 'spoof' front page for their first edition – which rolls off the presses in time to be delivered to far-flung corners of the country, early enough to give rivals a chance to catch up on the story for their own main editions. The spoof – usually a less interesting story – was designed to throw rivals off the scent, so that the main edition would have the scorching exclusive entirely to itself.

THE BYLINE: THE REPORTER'S BRAND

To the journalist, the byline is vital. Most will have a very clear memory of the first time their name appeared above a piece of reporting. The byline is a reinforcement of their personal value to the newspaper they work for and its readers, a validation of the individual reporter's place at the heart of the news machine. Readers generally couldn't care less (Culbertson and Somerick 1976).

Newspaper articles were, until relatively recently in the scheme of the industry's history, written anonymously. Victorian editors believed that by publishing everything without attribution to an individual author, the authoritative voice of the newspaper would be maintained (Reich 2010), a convention that remained largely intact for more than a century. *The Economist*, uniquely among mainstream news publications, maintains that principle to this day.

But by the middle of the twentieth century bylines began to be awarded, sparingly, to star journalists or to well-known guest writers. Slowly, the convention began to spread into the news sections. In some publications, by the 1990s it was common practice for the page lead – a news page's most prominent story – to be bylined, but not the 'downpage' stories. Today, bylines are prevalent throughout most newspaper pages.

In their analysis of news sources in UK newspapers, Lewis *et al.* (2008) found that 72 per cent of the 2,207 newspaper stories they studied were attributed to a bylined reporter. The 24.5 per cent that carried no byline were typically News in Briefs.

Partly that's down to a seepage of online culture back into newspapers. In the internet era, the byline is arguably more important than it ever has been. Journalists are now able to build and maintain their own personal brand online, almost independently of the organisation they work for. In the US, data journalist Nate Silver, having made his name with his shrewd analysis of baseball statistics, became a celebrity when his fivethirtyeight blog accurately predicted the state-by-state results of the 2012 US presidential elections. The *New York Times* quickly signed him up – with his blog – and saw a huge increase in its online readership. At one point his content accounted for 20 per cent of all traffic to the newspaper's website. When he left the newspaper to join ESPN eight months later, and again took his blog brand with him, it was perceived as a major blow to the publication.

The online byline is more than just a matter of vanity. In this interactive age, readers expect to be able to respond directly to the individual reporters whose journalism they are reading. Online bylines are just as likely to be linked to Twitter accounts and professional Facebook pages of the reporter in question. Being visible and accountable are key qualities for the modern journalist, and the byline – both in paper and on the web – is an essential aspect of that.

THE LEADER COLUMN AND THE OP-ED PAGES: FINDING A VOICE

The leader column is the voice of the newspaper. Its conscience. Its heart and its soul.

It sets out the newspaper's views of what its editors consider to be the most important stories of the day and interprets them for its readers, usually in a trenchant and robust style. Its tone and content say more about the political, cultural and social positioning of a newspaper than any other piece of journalism within it.

The leading article, as it is sometimes also known, has its roots in the Victorian newspaper age. Historian Dallas Liddle suggests the term was already in use as newspaper jargon before 1800, and by 1820 had passed into relatively common usage (Liddle 1999). What's more, he explains, it had acquired a powerful force all of its own:

> The Victorian leading article was a discursive creation of remarkable cultural and political authority. To many nineteenth-century readers it was a voice of almost superhuman wisdom.

For many readers of that era, when news reporting as we know it now was still in its infancy, a newspaper was pretty much defined by its leading articles. In modern newspapers, the leader may not quite have the same kudos or power, but it is still a vital part of the title's DNA. It generally takes its place in a section of the publication often called the Op-Ed (derived from Opinion and Editorial). This is the place where objective journalism is notionally put to one side (although see the section on objective journalism in Chapter 7), and where journalists and guest writers are given free rein to voice their opinions, allowing them to 'take the lead in establishing the dominant interpretive frameworks within which ongoing political events are made sense of' (McNair 2000).

Increasingly, though, as Wahl-Jorgensen (2008) points out, opinion journalism is no longer confined to the Op-Ed pages but 'pervades every section of the newspaper'. Most of the 'quality' British newspapers devote between three and five pages to their Op-Ed sections, which tend to be characterised by a more sober layout style with fewer illustrations and a heavier emphasis on text – although most will also include a regular satirical cartoon among these pages too. (The slight exception here is that the *Independent* put its leaders on page 2, well away from the rest of its Op-Ed coverage, as part of its compact redesign in 2013, a move that *The Times* had previously experimented with between 2004 and 2013).

For the mid-market and tabloid sectors, the Op-Ed sections are less clearly delineated – they don't have their own separate section headers as the quality titles tend to do – but, nonetheless, there is a formula to which they stick. The *Daily Mail*, for example, always puts one of its more strident regular writers next to its leader column. These are the pages in which the newspaper's political stance should come across loud and clear, where parties are endorsed or ditched at election time, and where 'opposition' strategies are dissected and lampooned.

In the regional press, leading articles are rarely overtly political in nature. Regional newspaper editors have a more difficult balancing act to maintain as they generally can't afford to alienate swathes of readers within the relatively small geographical footprint in which they have to sell copies. Notably, though, the newer 'lite' newspapers with a national reach such as *Metro* do not have leader columns at all.

Writing a leader column is a speciality skill, and many of its practitioners tend to be drawn from the political arena. For example *The Times*'s chief leader writers include Philip Collins, who was the chief speechwriter for former prime minister Tony Blair, and Daniel Finkelstein, who was an advisor to former PM John Major. Meanwhile, the rise of the blogosphere, described elsewhere in this book, is also having an impact on opinion journalism. For Wahl-Jorgensen (2008) it:

> . . . highlights a greater diversity of discursive strategies in a context divorced from the conventions of editorial and op-ed pages. As such it appears to further challenge the separation of news and opinion, and along with it any remnants of the ideal of objectivity.

THE WEBSITE: A COMPLEX FEAT OF ORGANISATION

Web design has come a long way since the *Daily Telegraph* first put a list of stories up on a web page on 15 November 1994, and promptly crashed its server. The design of the Electronic Telegraph, as it was called, was understandably rudimentary. In the days when internet access was via a dial-up modem connection, and most people used a browser called Netscape, pictures simply took up too much precious bandwidth, and so the front page illustrations consisted of tiny thumbnail images – mainly logos. There were no navigational aids to get the user to other parts of the website – because there were no other parts of the website. The individual news stories allowed the user to click back to the front page – or home page, as it would eventually be called – but otherwise that was it.

Since that trailblazing experiment, newspaper websites have adapted and changed to exploit developing technologies – most significantly the arrival of broadband connections to the domestic market – that have improved the browser experience beyond measure.

Today's newspaper websites are immeasurably more complex feats of organisation and design than that first site, containing thousands of pages of individual stories, tens of thousands of pictures, hundreds of thousands of links, detailed navigational structures and hundreds of interactive multimedia storytelling features. They are powered by content management systems, which allow journalists to create and upload individual pieces of content, adding text, headlines, pictures and, where appropriate, audio and video files – all without having to know any of the underlying computer code. Each piece of content is also 'tagged' with words and phrases that dictate which part of the site that they appear in.

From a design perspective, newspaper sites have gone through a number of iterations, from those early single-list home pages, through framesets – in which areas of the page had their own independent scroll bars – to the navigational tabs and social media-friendly design elements commonly in use today.

7 October 2013 Last updated less than one minute ago

Google™ Custom Search

theguardian

Weather | London 🌤 20°C 12°C

News | Sport | Comment | Culture | Business | Money | Life & style | Travel | Environment | Tech | TV | Video | Dating | Offers | Jobs

News ▶ UK | World | Development | US | Politics | Media | Education | Society | Science | Women | Law | Data | Football | Observer

Breaking news: Most female doctors suffer sexual harassment, say researchers in Australia ◀▪▶

Browne and Moore sacked as reshuffle gets under way

Last updated one minute ago

 LIVE Michael Moore biggest casualty so far, but Esther McVey and Norman Baker promoted

💬 709 comments

LATEST
"Iain Dales has taken Grant Shapps to task over the reshuffle for hardworking people. (See 3.39pm.)"
Politics live blog: government reshuffle

- Osborne allies promoted in Tory reshuffle
- Tory and Labour reshuffles follow Lib Dem rejig
- Coalition government reshuffle – the full list
- Alistair Carmichael to be new Scottish secretary

Fears for Greenpeace activists' health

 Some activists and two journalists held in solitary confinement in Russia while others are being kept in very cold cells after rig protest

💬 223 comments
📷 Greenpeace speaks out over activists' detention

Cabinet 'in dark' over GCHQ

 Ex-minister Chris Huhne says he was in 'utter ignorance' of Prism and Tempora and calls for more oversight

💬 678 comments
- Chris Huhne: cabinet were kept in dark
- Peter Sommer: how to improve GCHQ oversight

Libya tackles US on suspect 'kidnap'

 Questions over raid, but John Kerry insists Libyan held was a 'legal and appropriate target'

💬 410 comments
- US silent over aspects of Libya and Somalia raids
- US capture Libyan al-Qaida leader
- Al-Liby in US custody following 15-year manhunt
- Adam Wishart: the truth about the 'white widow'

World Cup: Rio claims favela

This is what fear looks like
Terrified faces at Canadian 'haunted house'

GTA Online
Hands-on review

David Byrne
If the 1% stifles New York's creative talent, I'm out of here

The top 10 ...
Romantic movies

Nobel peace prize
Pick your winner

Sport

Redknapp: 'FA haven't got a clue'

 Football: Harry Redknapp says he would not trust the FA to show him a good manager 'if their lives depended on it'

- Cole faces scan on rib injury
- Hodgson feels the heat before qualifiers

Premier League: 10 talking points

 Guardian writers: Brendan Rodgers's grumblings were justified, Manuel Pellegrini finds his release button and all hail Sam Allardici!

💬 590 comments
- Tottenham fan bailed over chant
- Poyet 'set to be named Sunderland manager'
- United to offer Januzaj long-term contract
- Wilshere admits smoking wasn't a prank

'It was lonely for me, really tough'

Charlotte Edwards tells Donald McRae how she rose from leading a team of schoolboys to become an Ashes-winning captain

Franchitti hospitalised after crash

IndyCar: Scottish driver Dario Franchitti suffers fractures and concussion after a huge accident in Houston

FIGURE 2.4

The *Guardian*'s grid-based website home page

Most current newspaper home pages are based on a grid system, which allows a variety of stories to be showcased in different areas of the page (see Figure 2.4). We have also recently seen a division between two schools of thought regarding the most effective navigational structure – horizontal versus vertical navigation (Lazaris 2010).

In a vertical navigation structure, the most significant elements in a column appear on the left-hand side of the home page – on the basis that most western readers will focus on this side of the screen first. Some newspapers – the *New York Times* is one – still use this system. But the case for horizontally structured navigation is that a vertical structure takes up too much of the most valuable space on the screen – getting in the way of real content. Most contemporary designs (see Figure 2.4) instead place their main navigational menus across the top of the screen, underneath the masthead.

The growth of smartphones and tablets as devices used increasingly for web browsing has brought further complication to the equation. Some news organisations – including the BBC – are looking at what's called 'responsive' design (sometimes called 'reactive' design) for their websites, which means that on a small iPhone screen the user sees a different version of a page from the one they would see on a laptop.

THE MOBILE EDITIONS: NEWS WHERE THE AUDIENCE IS

According to some estimates, sometime between now and 2016 there will be more people accessing the internet using a mobile device than doing so using a personal computer. In the US, the number of people accessing the internet through PCs will shrink from 240 million consumers in 2012 to 225 million in 2016. At the same time, the number accessing the internet through a mobile device will increase from 174 million to 265 million (IDC 2012). Journalism organisations are already seeing those changes take root.

The Poynter Institute has published statistics showing that 25 per cent of Americans already consume news on a mobile device. And for regular consumers of news, the figures show an even more striking take-up rate; the Pew Internet and American Life Project found that more than half of Americans who regularly read news do so on handheld digital devices. Another report, *Other Trends*, conducted by the Pew Research Center's Project for Excellence in Journalism in conjunction with the Economist Group, suggests that the tablet is a medium that encourages a different relationship between reader and device. For example, industry figures show that users of tablet devices are likely to watch long-form videos for 28 per cent longer than they do on a desktop PC (Ooyala 2013).

Parker (2007) noted the '360 degree strategy' being adopted by many larger publishing organisations, whereby content is made available to consumers on a multitude of platforms so they can consume it on whichever device is most suitable for them at that time. Jonathan Stray, in his online essay 'Designing journalism to be used', writes:

> Since journalists don't make tangible objects, the product is defined by the user's experience. It's whatever the user interaction with the news is. It's picking up the paper at breakfast, or watching CNN in bed, or waiting for your mobile app to update the headlines on the bus. And yes, the product includes the stories delivered by the medium, but those stories alone are not the product; they never were. The stories were packaged into a newspaper or a television show, and that was the product. Or more precisely, the newspaper and the television show as the user chose to use it was the product.
>
> (Stray 2010a)

This importance of news as a carefully crafted package has been understood by journalism innovators for centuries. W. T. Stead transformed British newspapers as editor of the *Pall Mall Gazette* in the late nineteenth century, by introducing bold banner headlines and using pictures, diagrammes and illustrations to create a product that was far more visually compelling than anything that had gone before.

Digital news design has, like other new platforms before it, tended to follow the conventions of its predecessors. So early radio bulletins involved newscasters simply reading out newspaper or wire copy. Early television news bulletins featured a disembodied voice with no visible sign of the newsreader. Early websites mimicked newspaper layouts. And early experiments with journalism on tablets has borrowed heavily from the conventions of the magazine industry: a recognisable 'cover', tables of contents and lavish use of high-resolution colour pictures.

In her study of the presentation of journalism in newspapers, television and print over 40 years, Lynn Cooke notes that a visual convergence of media has become more pronounced (Cooke 2005). These similarities are not random, she says, but emerge from a 'dynamic media environment that is shaped by technological, social and cultural forces'. So, for the mobile tablet user, we are in the foothills of the journey towards providing them with a news experience that they feel comfortable with and that maximises the capabilities of the device they are using.

The tablet is neither a 'lean-forward' device like a desktop PC, nor does it quite offer the 'lean-back' experience of television news consumption. The tactility of the user's relationship adds an entirely new dimension to Stray's idea of 'whatever the user interaction with the news is'.

The Poynter Institute's 2012 study included analysis of how news is consumed on tablet devices (Dickinson-Quinn 2012). For the tablet Eyetrack study, 36 subjects were monitored as they read, watched and interacted with real news stories using an iPad. These 20 news stories were arranged in three different prototype app formats: a traditional browser-style format; a carousel format; and a clipboard-style format. And each story contained narrative text, with at least one additional media element from a range including still photographs, photo galleries, video clips and pop-ups.

The most significant of the early findings of the study seems to be the importance that is placed upon touch by the users. The study breaks the subjects down into two broad groups – 'intimate' readers and 'detached' readers – depending upon how they used touch to engage with the content on the screen. The intimate group were more or less in constant contact with the device, using finger movements to continually keep text elements within a very narrow field of vision on the screen. This group made up the majority of the sample, at 61 per cent. The smaller detached group tended to carefully arrange elements on the screen first, then leant back to read or watch. The early findings also indicate that users tend to prefer either portrait or landscape orientation for their reading, which they tend to stick to throughout a session.

Mario Garcia, the design guru who played a key role in the establishment of the Eyetrack experiments, has published an e-book about design of content for tablets, based on his work with journalism organisations around the world (Garcia 2012). He suggests that the tablet is being used by news consumers more in the evening and at weekends, when they have more time to catch up on longer-form pieces of journalism, both in text and in video.

> Based on a variety of surveys, the majority of users engage with their tablets in the evening, while 'snacking' on mobile phone and online information during the day . . . We do this news 'snacking' for two-to four-minute periods. Chances are that this time is not the most opportune for us to see a gallery of photos, spend time with a video or digest a length article. These activities are better suited to the tablet, that more relaxing lean-back platform that we engage with when we are kicking off our shoes and enjoying much-needed downtime at the end of the day.

TYPES OF NEWSPAPER STORY: HARD NEWS TO SOFT FEATURES

For the purpose of simplicity, let us say that hard news is the reporting of issues or events in the past, or about to happen. It is largely based on selected details and quotations in direct or indirect speech. Hard news begins with the most striking details and thereafter information progressively declines in importance. Some background details may be needed to make the news intelligible, but description, analysis, comment and the subjective 'I' of the reporter are either excluded, or included only briefly. Hard news has the highest status in newspapers and tends to fill front pages. But Anne Sebba (Allan 1999: 130) is critical of the emphasis on hard news. 'Writing about numbers of planes shot down and military hardware is the "soft" option male journalists often go for because it is easier and less taxing to one's emotional being.' Hard news differs from a range of newspaper genres that have emerged over the past couple of centuries (see Pöttker 2003) which include the following – some of which are discussed at greater length in subsequent chapters.

- *Soft news*: the news element is still strong and prominent at or near the opening, but is treated in a lighter way. Largely based on factual detail and quotations, the writing is more flexible and there is likely to be more description and comment. The tone, established in the intro section, might be witty or ironic. The separation of hard and soft news emerged in the second half of the nineteenth century: the first, linked to notions of accuracy, objectivity and neutrality, was for conveying information; the second was more an entertainment genre.

- *News feature*: usually longer than a straight news story. The news angle is prominent though not necessarily in the opening paragraph(s) and quotations are again important. It can contain description, comment, analysis, background historical detail, eye-witness reporting, and wider or deeper coverage of the issues and range of sources.

- *Timeless feature*: no specific news angle, the special interest is provided by the subject or sources. For example, a feature could explore youths' experiences of coming out gay.

- *Backgrounder/preview/curtain-raiser news story or feature*: emphasis is not so much on the news, but on explaining the news or setting the scene for an event about to happen. It might focus on historical background and/or seek to explain a range of issues and personalities involved. A *retrospective* is a similar feature looking back at an event.

- *Colour feature*: an article of feature length concentrating on description, eye-witness reporting, quotations and the build-up of factual details. It can also contain historical background material, and need not have a strong news angle.

- *Eye-witness news feature*: based on the reporter's observations of a newsy event, it can incorporate descriptions, conversations, interviews, analysis, comment, jokes. The 'I' of the reporter might also be present.

- *Participatory feature*: in which the reporter engages in an activity (such as joining a circus for a month) and describes the experience.

- *Sketch*: opinionated, colourful, light piece usually associated with Parliament, for example, the late Simon Hoggart in the *Guardian*, Matthew Parris in *The Times*, Quentin Letts in the *Daily Mail*.

- *Opinion piece/personal/think piece*: emphasis on the journalist conveying their views and experiences, usually in an idiosyncratic, colourful, controversial fashion. Journalists with regular slots are known as columnists.

- *Diary items*: short, light-hearted, opinionated, gossipy news items, generally grouped together under a single byline.

- *Profile* (sometimes labelled *interview*): description of a person, usually based on interviews with them and sometimes with their friends/critics/relations/work colleagues. A news dimension is often prominent.

- *Obituaries*: profiles appearing after the death of the subject, though often prepared beforehand.

- *Vox pop*: collection of quotes on topical issues, usually accompanied by mug shots of sources (and it is important to be race/gender/age-sensitive over the selection).

- *Reviews*: descriptions and assessments of works of art, television programmes, exhibitions, books, theatre shows, CDs, rock gigs and so on.

- *Lifestyle features*: including advice columns (such as on health or education matters, slimming, gardening, do-it-yourself, computer problems), shopping features, fashion, travel.

- *Editorials*: commentary reflecting the institutional voice of the newspaper. Usually carried in a larger font than that of the basic body text and without a byline. They can be written by the editor, but most newspapers have editorial-writing specialists.

- *Graphics-driven feature*: here the emphasis is on the graphics, with the text playing a supportive role.

- *News and feature packages*: stories in a range of genres are increasingly being 'packaged' together. Thus a main investigative piece, say, will be accompanied by short profiles of the leading players, a 'fact box' outlining the chronology of events, an opinionated, bylined piece on a particular issue and a graphic (produced by the artist with input from the sub-editor and reporter).

- *Audio slideshow*: an emerging online package that combines compelling audio with still pictures.

- *Interactive feature*: software packages such as Adobe Flash can be used to create standalone interactive presentations that combine text, pictures, audio and video in a way that allows the user to navigate through the story following a route, and at a pace, of their choosing.

- *Data visualisation*: the growth of data journalism has seen an explosion in online and print stories that use statistical information as the key driver. Online versions tend to be interactive – allowing users to interrogate parts of the data that will be most interesting to them – and might use mapping tools, for example, to plot points on a local map (Mair and Keeble 2014).

- *Podcast*: a downloadable format, often in the style of a radio show, in which newspaper staff and guests discuss topical stories relatively informally.

CHAPTER 3

Press gangs and endangered species

Anatomy of the modern newsroom

I wonder what W. T. Stead (1849–1912), or Arthur Christiansen (1904–63), or Sir David English (1931–98) would make of the modern *Telegraph* newsroom. Those legendary editors, all ground-breaking innovators in their own eras, would surely marvel at the lines of sleek computers radiating out from a central hub at the company's premises in London's Victoria, unveiled amid great excitement in 2006.

They would certainly gawp at the huge open-plan workspace, which in a previous life had been the trading floor of Salomon Brothers bank, and at the gigantic screens surrounding them displaying continuously updated web pages and 24-hour TV news channels from around the world. And they would doubtless be baffled by the jargon-filled job titles of some of the people at the desks: head of search engine optimisation; digital content strategist; convergence manager.

But what would they make of the lines of command in this new multimedia nirvana? All three men were notoriously scrupulous in maintaining a very strict control over the titles they edited. Christiansen issued a daily bulletin giving a critique of the day's newspaper in minute detail; Stead even corrected page proofs from his prison cell (having been locked up for three months for the abduction of a girl, which he had arranged as part of a *Pall Mall Gazette* investigation into child abduction and prostitution); English was a notorious perfectionist who could humiliate his executives if they failed to live up to his demands for the style and content of his *Daily Mail*. Yet such is the vast extent of the modern newspaper's output, it would be physically impossible for one person to read, watch and listen to it in its entirety.

The *Daily Telegraph* is by no means alone in reimagining its newsroom for the 'converged' era. Its hub set-up is only one solution to the demands of supplying journalism content to multiple platforms. The *Guardian*, having moved from

Farringdon Road, London to new premises at King's Cross in 2008, describes its newsroom structure as a 'pods in a matrix' approach, in which small clusters of subject-specific reporters work to line managers from different media platforms.

But what impact are these new organisational structures having on the people who work within them? Is the editor still the most powerful beast in the newsroom jungle? Do sub-editors still have a part to play? Does a fancy desk layout really make any difference to the way in which a reporter covers a story? We'll cover the work of the reporter – the most important role in any newsroom – in depth in Chapter 5. In this chapter we'll take a look at some of the other key roles in newspaper journalism, and how they are continuing to change and develop in this time of radical restructuring. And we'll take a look at some of the new roles that have emerged in recent years as the digital side of the business becomes, in some cases, pre-eminent.

THE WORKFORCE: A HARD-PRESSED GROUP

Who are these people providing and packaging the words, pictures, sound, video and interactive data that fuel the 24-hour furnaces of the modern newspaper industry? In the next section we'll look more closely at the individual personnel who make up the typical (if there is such a thing) newsroom. But for now let's examine the overall working population of the sector. The Journalists at Work survey of 2012, funded by the National Council for the Training of Journalists (NCTJ), puts the number of journalists working in the UK at around 60,000 (NCTJ 2012a). Some 56 per cent of these, according to the survey, work at least partly for newspapers. It also found that 28 per cent of journalists are self-employed, as opposed to 14 per cent of all in employment. As a result of this, the proportion of journalists who are permanent employees is much lower than for the economy as a whole – 68 per cent as opposed to 81 per cent.

Journalists at Work survey data also show that 34 per cent of respondents have another job outside journalism. These additional jobs vary widely. There are some clusters of related occupations, such as education, PR and general administration. Examples of such work are:

- education: college lecturer (in journalism), online journalism tutor, tutor, trainer in blogging, writing workshop leader, university lecturing
- public relations: corporate publications, press officer, media relations
- journalism-related: copywriter, publisher, chief sub-editor, editorial librarian, writer/author
- media-related: photographer, documentary film maker, screenwriter, wedding photographer
- general administration roles: public sector official, administration assistant, building services administrator

- miscellaneous job roles: bar manager, barman, part-time waiter, working in a supermarket, wood-yard assistant.

In 2013, Alan Geere (2013) conducted a small survey of young journalists who had joined a division of Northcliffe Newspapers as trainees between 2008 and 2011. Of the 60 respondents, he found that fewer than half (26) were still working in newspapers – some still at Northcliffe, the rest with other employers. A further 14 were still in journalism, but had moved into other sectors such as magazines, television, online publications and agencies. Ten of the group were working in PR. As one of Geere's respondents put it:

> This can be the best job in the world but also the worst . . . it's not just a job but a way of life. You must be prepared to work for a pittance and be the poorest you have ever been in your life and live hundreds of miles from home, but there is no other job like it. As a warning, when your heart's not in it any more it's time to get out and there is limited progression on local papers.

The editor: who's in charge of the clattering train?

Legend has it that Lord Beaverbrook (1879–1964) would ring the newsroom at his *Daily Express* late at night, and bellow a question to whichever hapless hack happened to pick it up: 'Who's in charge of the clattering train?' Newspaper production has an unstoppable momentum all of its own, and the individual with ultimate responsibility if it all goes wrong – who could go to prison if the wrong sentence appeared in a particular court report – is the editor. It is the most demanding of roles, and it's taken its toll on many men and women. In a candid piece for the *Daily Mail* several years after he had left newspapers, former *Sun* editor David Yelland described how the pressures of his five-year stint in the top job had affected him.

> My typical working day would start late the previous evening when I would read the first editions of the following day's newspapers. Sometimes I would go to bed at 3am and get up at 7am, already knowing what would be setting the day's news agenda. In the office, Les [Hinton, chief executive], and sometimes Rupert [Murdoch], would wander down the corridor at Wapping and we'd go through the *Daily Mirror* – our big rival – and *The Sun*, page by page.
>
> At an 11 am conference, senior executives would tell me the stories their departments were working on. It is one of the editor's jobs to make decisions very quickly on which stories should appear in the paper and how to approach them.
>
> There's a new government initiative on crime – is it a good thing? A Cabinet Minister has been caught in a compromising position – is he guilty of all-too-

human frailty or a disgrace who should be drummed out of office? By the early afternoon I'd have a good idea of what would be in the next day's paper and I'd know pretty much what the 'splash' – or main front page story – was. Then I'd start writing the leader column, an opinion piece that represents the soul of the paper. As the rest of *The Sun* took shape, page proofs would be delivered to me for approval. In the evening, the presses would start rolling and then the cycle would start again.

(Yelland 2010)

Yelland's spell at the *Sun*'s helm finished in 2003, but you'll see from his brief job description how the print edition newspaper was clearly his primary focus. The *Sun*'s website in those days was not much more than a rerun of some of the paper's top stories. Compare that with *Independent* editor-in-chief Chris Blackhurst, explaining his promotion to the elevated title of Group Content Director in his final letter to readers in June 2013:

My new, elevated title ... , I accept, has an Orwellian *1984* or John Birt's BBC ring to it. But we could not find a better name that summarises our changed, multi-platform organisation and our ability to cope with the insatiable demands of the internet, print titles and television.

(Blackhurst 2013)

Note the pecking order. Internet first. Print titles second.

The modern editor is expected to be much more than an arbiter of what makes it into the final print edition. He or she is, perhaps first and foremost now, a business strategist whose remit involves finding the optimum way to reach audiences on different platforms and often with very different ideas as to the value of the product. The *Financial Times*'s 'digital first' strategy, announced in 2012, came partly as a result of editor Lionel Barber's trip to Silicon Valley in the US. Here's what Barber said in a 2013 memo to staff about the changes he was making:

'The 1970s-style newspaper publishing process – making incremental changes to multiple editions through the night – is dead,' he continued in the memo.
    'In future, our print product will derive from the web offering – not vice versa'.

(Bartlett 2013)

From that point on, he said, the newspaper would be pre-planned and produced, with production journalists publishing stories to meet peak viewing times on the web rather than old print deadlines. The new process would be planned more like a broadcasting schedule rather than with page lay-outs at the centre of it.

Similarly, Alan Rusbridger's tenure as *Guardian* editor has been characterised in recent years by his vision for a digitally driven organisation. But if these national newspaper editors are spending much of their time wrestling with fundamental issues about their future, in the regional press, meanwhile, there is a school of thought developing that makes the editor's job entirely redundant. Johnston Press is one of a number of companies that no longer has a role of 'editor' at several of its weekly newspapers (Lambourne 2012).

Similar reorganisations have taken place at Archant (Lambourne 2012; Linford 2013). At York's the *Press*, one of the country's longest-established evening newspapers, Newsquest forced its editor, Kevin Booth, to compete for his own job against the managing director in 2009 (Dyson 2010). And here's editor-turned-media mogul David Montgomery, chief executive of business consortium Local World, describing his view of the editorial process after his new organisation acquired a group of historic newspapers in 2013:

> The editor title will survive but the job has to be much broader and compre-hensive. The modern editor will be the content director, managing content, organising content and disseminating it on the appropriate platform; print, online or mobile. It's about getting people to organise themselves sufficiently to manage the amount of content a local publisher exploits. Not a two-fold increase but a 20-fold increase in the amount of content a local publisher exploits.
>
> (Ponsford 2013a)

The job has always been something of a merry-go-round. But like football managers in the Premiership era, there's a sense that the modern editor gets less and less time to prove him or herself. When James Harding was removed from the editorship of *The Times* in 2012, *Press Gazette* noted he was the sixth national editor to lose his job in 16 months (Pugh 2012b).

Harding would go on to become the head of BBC News – the first newspaperman to hold that job. For others, though, the question of 'what next' after they lose tenure in the editor's chair is trickier. Former *Lancaster Guardian* editor Sue Riley (2012) wrote in *InPublishing* about the increasing frequency of her former peers in the regional industry losing their jobs. She quoted Society of Editors executive director Bob Satchwell, who said there were special reasons for more upheaval because of the big pressures that the industry found itself under:

> I always thought that editors, particularly on dailies, needed to have a bit of a shelf life ... you are in your prime in your 30s and 40s; not to say you are on the scrap heap after that but you are at the height of your energy and creativity then.

In his interview with the *Daily Mail*, David Yelland acknowledged how the stress of the job had fed his alcoholism and may have contributed to the end of his time at the helm (Yelland 2010). Christiansen, too, became exhausted from the job, and retired from newspapers after becoming ill. Perhaps he knew the rest of the Milliken poem, 'Death and His Brother Sleep', that his boss was quoting in those late-night telephone calls.

> *Who is in charge of the clattering train?*
> *The axles creak and the couplings strain,*
> *and the pace is hot and the points are near,*
> *and sleep hath deadened the driver's ear,*
> *and the signals flash through the night in vain.*
> *For death is in charge of the clattering train.*
> Edwin J. Milliken (1839–97)

The content editor: a new breed

In simpler times, editors edited. News editors enforced. Features editors commissioned. Reporters reported. And sub-editors kept everybody honest.

Today, newsrooms are more complicated places, and the pecking order much harder to fathom. One of the newest breed now goes under the title 'content editor' (which somewhat begs the question, what other type of editor is there?). The word itself is troubling for some. As Peter Cole and Tony Harcup note in *Newspaper Journalism* (2010): 'Content is simply what occupies the space, and to use it to describe the products of journalism is to devalue the spirit and practice of intellectual inquiry and analysis that is the hallmark of good journalism.' Yet it has become pretty pervasive.

In May 2013, the boss of the regional newspaper industry's newest company, Local World (see Chapter 1) appeared before a parliamentary select committee. David Montgomery told MPs:

> We have to be truly digital, so that in three or four years from now, much of our human interface will have disappeared. We will have to harvest content and publish it without human interface, which will change the role of journalists. Journalists collecting stories one by one is hugely unproductive. They will have to have new skills, greater responsibility for self-publishing on different platforms.
> (Hollander 2013)

For many in the industry, this notion of the 'robot' journalists harvesting content – as though good journalism was something that could so simply be plucked like a ripe apple from a tree – completely undermines almost everything that the industry stands for. Michelle Stanistreet (2013), general secretary of the National Union of Journalists (NUJ), responded:

> Amid the management-speak, Montgomery's vision is a chilling one. Does he really have so little inkling that it is high-quality journalism and top-quality writing that is the key to successful newspapers and websites? His thinking is sadly

not unique; it is a pattern we are already seeing. Journalists are being reduced to pouring words – sorry content – into pre-determined grids, with the danger of turning newspapers into open sewers.

Whether or not their role actually conforms to Montgomery's nightmarish vision, there are scores of people in different organisations with the title 'content editor'. Their roles vary widely. In some cases they are essentially 'repurposing' existing material to suit the format of new devices such as tablets and smartphones. In others their job is not dissimilar to that of the traditional sub-editor, which we'll look at next, with extra responsibility thrown in for new requirements such as search engine optimisation (see Chapter 6).

The sub-editor: endangered species

In his book *Essential English for Journalists, Editors and Writers*, Harold Evans (2000) runs through the roles of several job titles that are now essentially defunct. Revise editor, projection editor, copy taster: very few journalists still rejoice in these job titles that hark back to simpler days of the print production process. But today a more fundamental role, that of the sub-editor, appears to be under threat.

In the traditional newspaper newsroom, the subs were an essential bulwark between reporter and reader. Described in the NCTJ's production journalism syllabus as the 'reader's champion', the sub's role was to turn the raw copy from the newsdesk into the final, polished product that the reader would enjoy. The job involved checking facts; spotting legal difficulties; correcting grammatical errors and esoteric spellings; cutting copy to fit the page; writing compelling headlines and captions; and proofing final copies of every page before they went 'off stone' to be printed.

But is this job title finally disappearing? It has been on the endangered species list before. At the launch of the *Independent* in 1986, its executive team initially thought its new direct input system meant that it could do away with the traditional 'back bench' – the section of the newsroom dedicated to page production and copy-subbing. And in the 1990s, some management teams began experimenting with input systems that allowed reporters to key copy and headlines directly to page templates. Others tried production teams located in centralised 'hubs', designing and copy-fitting pages for multiple newspapers in the group, far from the newsdesks that supplied them with a constant stream of copy and pictures.

But, often as not, these experiments tended to return to the traditional role. The *Indy* (as it is affectionately known) certainly did, shortly after its launch. The subs, meticulous in their knowledge of grammar, media law and typography, encyclopaedic in their recollection of local personalities, geographical peculiarities and historical feuds, and wondrous with their flair for great headlines, standfirsts and captions, generally came bouncing back. Yet, in the current swirl of newsdesk reorganisations, there are signs that the sub may finally be disappearing for good. *The Times*'s most recent restructure saw a revamp of the backbench so that news desks would have greater responsibility for the structure and positioning of stories and the quality of the copy. As an anonymous sub put it in *Press Gazette*:

> So designers will draw pages, news editors will fill the holes – and subs will be allowed 'to concentrate' on headline writing. Which probably translates as 'shovel it through as fast as possible' for print, web, tablet, smartphone, android and whatever new invention Apple comes up with next week. They are no longer thinking, talented journalists, masters of language, mistresses of design, but 'producers', conveyor-belt handlers of copy, fit only to write a Google-friendly heading.
>
> (Subscraft blog 2013)

But one sub's catastrophic step into the abyss is another executive's logical streamlining of an archaic, cumbersome process. Trinity Mirror editorial director Neil Benson explained to *InPublishing* (Sands 2009) the rationale behind setting up production centres that take care of the creation of pages for multiple newspapers. He said the five-step editorial process had been shortened to three in most cases, and even to two steps in some centres. In Birmingham, for example, the old workflow of 'reporter to newsdesk to designer to sub to revise' had become 'reporter to multimedia hub to page finishing'.

> Key pages such as the front, back and spreads are still designed from scratch. But how many ways are there to design a page 27 with a quarter-page ad on it?

The production process, Benson said, now also incorporates new online skills, such as tagging, search engine optimisation and headlining for the web, so the work of the sub has both moved 'upstream' in the editorial process and is no longer just about print. David Montgomery, chairman of Local World, gave an even clearer indication in his depiction of the sub to the select committee in May 2013.

> I see a situation where experienced journalists that can be trusted have no barrier to communication with their audience. Sub-editing is a twilight world, checking things you don't really need to check. Senior people will always monitor the content, a core group will create the product.
>
> (Hollander 2013)

Susan M. Keith's paper 'Sinking subs and collapsing copy desks?' (2009) interviewed practitioners of the sub-editing and copy-editing art from newspapers in the UK, Canada, the US, Australia and South Africa. She dates the sub-editor's role in UK newspapers back to the 1840s, and examines the transformation in the work from the technological changes of the 1980s, when direct input systems began to appear in editorial newsrooms, to the present day. One of her interviewees, a former sub on a British newspaper, puts the case succinctly:

I think subs are now processors. They just check out copy – conveyor belt style. They turn out templated pages – that look good enough. But maybe that's where we are at now. Maybe there isn't time to craft a newspaper – nor does the reader have time to appreciate it. Maybe there will be subs who do a good job at turning round copy for online and what's left of the print industry. . . . But I don't think we have seen the end of changes. So perhaps the reader will be writing the content soon. Perhaps we won't have subs at all.

The picture editor: power of the still image

In his unsurpassed book on photojournalism, graphics and picture editing, *Pictures on a Page*, former *Sunday Times* editor Harold Evans makes an unequivocal case for the importance of the still image in news journalism. In his introduction to the 1997 edition, Evans reprints the searingly shocking image taken by Kenneth Jarecke during the first Gulf War of 1991 of an Iraqi soldier charred and mutilated having been burned alive during an allied Scud missile attack. When the *Observer* printed that picture in 1991, readers were outraged and even fellow professionals were shocked at the decision to publish taken by picture editor Tony McGrath. Why, asks Evans, when we had become so used to seeing moving colour pictures of great violence being visited in various war zones through our television sets, was this grainy black-and-white picture so shocking?

> It was a solitary individual in the transfixation of a hideous death. In the absence of a photograph of this power, it had been possible to enjoy the lethal felicity of designer bombs as some kind of video game. It had been possible to be caught up in the excitement of people rushing to escape the Scuds. There was no escape from the still silence of the corpse in Jarecke's photograph. Once seen, it has a permanent place in one's imagination. Anyone who can replay moving images in his mind has a very rare faculty. The moving image may make an emotional impact, but its detail and shape cannot be easily recalled. Anyone who saw that still photograph will never forget it.
>
> (Evans 1997)

For all the newspaper industry's investment and experimentation in videojournalism, the primacy of the still image remains untouched, and rightly so. But as with all other parts of the industry, digital technology continues to have an invasive impact. The development of image manipulation software in the 1980s and 1990s made the alchemy of the darkroom available on every newsroom desktop – with all the temptations that brings – and since around the turn of the century virtually all press photographs have been shot with digital cameras, which, coupled with digital transmission of files, allows an immediacy that press photographers even 20 years ago could only dream of. In the cut-throat world of newspaper rivalry, however, photographers and picture editors do succumb to those temptations.

- In 1998, the *Sun* airbrushed Shelley Ann Emery, who uses a wheelchair, out of a photograph taken at an England cricket match. The newspaper initially said the manipulation was for page balance, not because of Emery's disability.

- The *Evening Standard* manipulated a photograph in 1996 to show John Prescott, then the deputy prime minister, drinking champagne rather than beer.

- Reuters freelance Adnan Hajj was dropped by the agency in 2006 when it emerged that he had digitally doctored his own photographs showing the aftermath of Israeli airstrikes on Beirut to make the damage look more widespread.

Significantly, a redrafting of the Press Complaints Commission's Code of Practice in 1998 did extend the 'accuracy' clause to include photographs: 'Newspapers and periodicals should take care not to publish inaccurate, misleading or distorted material, including pictures.' Around the time of that redrafting, there was debate within the industry as to whether some kind of kitemark should be introduced to indicate that an image had been manipulated. But the practicalities of news production – and, in truth, the emergence of far more pressing issues – have largely ended that discussion.

One of those additional pressing issues has been the ubiquity of the high resolution digital camera carried in pockets and handbags throughout the country. We'll look more closely at user-generated content in Chapter 7, but here it's worth noting that the modern picture editor's skill set now has to include an ability to verify the multitude of images – such as those generated by the *Guardian*'s Witness project, which encourages readers to send in their photographs and videos for use on its website – that routinely arrive from amateurs all around the globe.

The videojournalist: moving pictures

Anybody doubting the importance of web video in the new media landscape only has to look at the extraordinary success of YouTube. From its beginnings in a makeshift office in a garage in 2005, it has grown to be one of the internet's hottest properties – and was bought by Google for a staggering $1.65 billion less than two years after its launch. By 2012 its users were uploading more than 60 hours of video to the site every *minute* (Oreskovic 2012).

Newspapers were not slow to realise the public's appetite for video was an opportunity, and many invested in training their reporters in the use of the newly available, relatively cheap, lightweight camcording equipment. By 2010, newspaper websites were collectively uploading more minutes of streaming video content than their broadcast news counterparts (Ingram 2010). The NCTJ introduced a video-journalism exam for its National Certificate Examination and diploma qualifications in 2008.

But, as many newsrooms also quickly discovered, putting together even rudimentary video packages and publishing them on a website can be a frustrating and time-consuming task. Editing software can still be fiddly and prone to crashing; integrating video with existing content management systems remains a major headache. And so, although many newspapers experimented with video and spent money on equipping their reporters with new multimedia production skills, much of their early enthusiasm has been tempered by reality.

In Phil McGregor's longitudinal study of the *Northern Echo*'s web strategy between 2006 and 2011, he notes what he describes as a prevailing view in his final interviews that 'mentalities of print persisted as the primary shaping force' (McGregor 2013). One example of this is that no video is allowed online without an accompanying text story, and he quotes a staff member as saying:

> Video is just to enhance the story . . . it is never a replacement for the story. It is a secondary thing; we know it is important but we are going to these jobs ultimately to put them in the newspaper and the video follows that.

In some cases, the idea of equipping reporters with lightweight video cameras has been overtaken by the development of smartphone technology – many of these devices have high definition video built in. In 2013, for example, Johnston Press boss Ashley Highfield announced plans for a series of 'mini ultra local TV stations', for which the company would issue its journalists with smartphones in order to increase significantly the video content on their newspaper websites (Lambourne 2013a).

A number of newspaper groups, at both national and regional level, are involved in new franchises for local television services whose licences are being rolled out by Ofcom. In London, the service went to London Live, owned by Evgeny Lebedev, who also runs the *Evening Standard* and *Independent* titles (see Chapter 1). The channel, due to launch in 2014, will include five-and-a-half hours of daily news and current affairs programming, produced by journalists from the newspaper newsrooms.

The data journalist: stories from tables

> Journalists need to be data-savvy. It used to be that you would get stories by chatting to people in bars . . . But now it's also going to be about poring over data and equipping yourself with the tools to analyse it and picking out what's interesting. And keeping it in perspective.

The author of this quote is someone who ought to know a thing or two about the digital world. After all, he created the best known chunk of it. It's Tim Berners-Lee, in his widely reported speech to launch an initiative to make government data more widely available (Arthur 2010). And it's certainly true that the avalanche of information that is now available in digital formats for journalists to investigate shows no sign of slowing down any time soon. Take one of the biggest newspaper scoops of recent years – the *Daily Telegraph*'s exposé of parliamentary expenses in May and June 2009. That came about through the sale to the newspaper of a disk (turned down in the first instance by a couple of other national titles, but that's another story) containing details of claims made by MPs over a number of years. And the disk itself was only made available because of a long series of Freedom of Information requests made by Heather Brooke.

The story led the news agenda for days, but before that could happen, a team of journalists had to pore painstakingly over the information contained on the disk. The public release of data that followed then enabled the *Guardian* to set its own readers loose on a crowdsourcing exercise, to which individuals could contribute by checking individual receipt scans against the tables showing the claims that were made. All of this required data processing skills of varying degrees of sophistication.

We'll cover more about what journalists can do to use data as part of their reporting, including some useful places to look for public data sets, in Chapter 7. But if you are still not convinced as to how useful the interpretation of data can be, take a look at David McAndless's *Information Is Beautiful* (2009), which takes sets of data and finds fascinating ways to interpret them visually – often revealing hidden truths among the numbers in the process.

National newspapers are generally increasing their investment in data journalism. In 2009, the *Guardian* launched its data store, a part of its website dedicated to highlighting stories that can be told through various data sets. It uses various visualisation techniques to show trends, patterns and anomalies in publicly available data – and also encourages its readers to download, explore and experiment with some or all of the data in question. As *Guardian* data editor Simon Rogers (who has since joined Google) said at the data store's launch in 2009:

> We are drowning in information. The web has given us access to data we would never have found before, from specialist datasets to macroeconomic minutiae. But, look for the simplest fact or statistic and Google will present a million contradictory ones. Where's the best place to start?
>
> (Rogers 2009)

Data journalism, he said, has become an increasingly big part of the *Guardian*'s work, including significant interpretations of data from WikiLeaks to government spending. Here, the *Guardian* followed in the footsteps of the *New York Times*, which had launched its own data site in 2008. In a piece about Big Data, the mind-boggling information being made available about their digital lives by users of social media, *New York Times* writer Steve Lohr opined that data-driven insights would fuel a shift in the centre of gravity in decision-making, replacing the more traditional values of experience and intuition – 'more science and less gut feel':

Data, for example, is an antidote to the human tendency to rely too much on a single piece of information or what is familiar – what psychologists call 'anchoring bias.'

(Lohr 2013)

The web editor: a new power

In most newsrooms, the web editor generally started life as a kind of adjunct to the IT department. Eyed with suspicion by the rest of the newsroom, they were seen as 'geeks' – not really journalists, and probably not to be trusted. Even as late as 2004, the Telegraph Media Group's web operation was like the 'Guantánamo Bay' of the organisation – according to its digital director Edward Rousell, who joined the company in that year. Kept apart from the rest of the editorial team, on a floor where 'no newspaper executives ever ventured', it was very far from being integrated into the main part of the newspaper's operation. But just a couple of years later, when the group moved to its new headquarters next to Victoria station, producing content for the web had become an intrinsic part of the work of most of its reporting staff (Richmond 2009).

The digital first strategies of an increasing number of newspapers mean that the web editor is more powerful now than at any prior time. Martin Clarke, editor of the *Mail Online*, is one of the most senior figures at Associated Newspapers. He is a highly experienced print journalist and former editor of the *Scotsman*, the *Daily Record* and the short-lived *London Lite*. Such is the importance of the *Mail*'s online presence in global journalism, when the *Guardian* published its 2013 list of the top 100 powerful players in the media world, its members deliberated whether Clarke should appear above Paul Dacre, editor-in-chief of the *Mail* newspapers. They ultimately decided he shouldn't – but Clarke, nonetheless, appeared at number 18 in the list, ahead of every other national print editor and several chief executives of newspaper groups.

The social media editor: connecting with the audience

In May 2009, the *New York Times* became one of the first significant newspapers to hire a 'social media editor', not long after Reuters had hired Anthony de Rosa with the same job title. Very quickly the trend grew, and many newsrooms found somebody to take editorial responsibility for their social media strategies. But by early 2013, influential media website Buzzfeed was declaring: 'The social media editor is dead' (Fishman 2013). By any standards, that's a pretty short life cycle.

Buzzfeed's pronouncement may have been somewhat exaggerated. Plenty of newspaper organisations still employ them. Part evangelist, part trend-spotter, part gate-keeper, part news aggregator, the social media editor has generally been tasked with incorporating the social media platforms that make up what is sometimes known as the 'ambient wire' – Facebook, Twitter, Tumblr, YouTube and others – into the newsroom environment. But just as the 'web editor' (see above) started life as a lonely individual in an office separate from the main newsroom before becoming a central part of organisational thinking, so the social media editor's work has – or at least should have – made its way into the culture of the reporting team.

Another with a claim to be the first is Matthew Ingram, who was 'communities editor' at Toronto's *Globe and Mail* in Canada back in 2008. He says: 'The idea that being social or engaging with readers in new ways belongs to a specific subset of journalists reminds me of the bad old days when newspapers had a single "internet editor" or "web editor".' (Ingram 2013) Joanna Geary, the *Guardian*'s social and communities editor, left the paper in 2013 to join Twitter as news partnerships manager – helping media companies to engage with the platform more effectively.

At Associated Press, the social media editor's role is combined with that of user-generated content (UGC) editor, a role that looks after the growing deluge of user-generated content that arrives at newsdesks every day. Fergus Bell, the incumbent in 2013, has had notable successes in using user-generated content to cover stories including the Anders Breivik shootings in Norway in July 2011 and the civil war in Syria – where news organisations have found it particularly difficult to establish the veracity of clips uploaded to social media sites. This aspect of the UGC editor's job – analysing and verifying this type of content to separate what's real from the hoaxers, spammers and vested interest groups – is likely to become increasingly significant.

The programmer journalist: the geeks shall inherit the Earth

As the newspaper industry continues its bumpy journey into the digital future, the skill sets of the people it needs are evolving rapidly. Many of its most forward-thinking individuals now come from a background that might previously have prepared them for a career purely in computing. The term programmer-journalist has been around for a couple of years (Reeves 2010), and applies to the growing number of (mainly) young journalists who have at least rudimentary programming skills in one or some of the many computer languages that are being used to create websites and other digital products. But their acceptance into the newsroom has not been entirely smooth. Digital journalism pioneer Kevin Anderson blogged in January 2010:

> Prejudice towards digital journalists needs to stop. It sends a message to digital journalists that they are unwanted at a time when their skills are desperately needed by newspapers. Digital staff should not be the convenient whipping women and men for those angry and upset about economic uncertainty.
>
> (Anderson 2010)

Adrian Holovaty was another innovator who noted the difficulties faced by digital enthusiasts. Even if journalism schools started producing genius computer programmers, or if it were to become trendy for computer science majors to seek employment in the news industry, he said:

> Newspapers will need to change their attitudes, culture and resource allocation if they want these people to stick around. Otherwise, they'll pack their bags after a couple of months and go work for Google.
>
> (Holovaty 2006)

A few months after that was published, Holovaty packed his own bags to develop and launch Everyblock.com – a hyperlocal journalism project – with a $1 million grant from the Knight Foundation. It was later sold to MSNBC. But some newsrooms are embracing the challenge. The *New York Times* set up its Interactive News Technology Group in 2009 under the leadership of Aron Pilhofer. Profiled in *New York* magazine, Pilhofer explained: 'The proposal was to create a newsroom: a group of developers-slash-journalists, or journalists-slash-developers, who would work on long-term, medium-term, short-term journalism – everything from elections to NFL penalties . . .' (Nussbaum 2009).

His team continues to produce truly innovative journalism, using new digital techniques both in the gathering of news and in the way they present it to, and engage with, their audience. A couple of examples: their 'Health Care Conversations' feature was a creative way of encouraging reader debate and reaction to key issues on health reform, using what the team describe as a 'bento box' visual structure; 'Living With Less' was a crowdsourced feature in which readers shared their survival strategies for coping with the economic downturn; and 'Casualties of War' used a mass of data collated from the Iraq War to mark the 3,000th US military fatality there in a graphically stunning way in 2008.

The columnist: putting the 'i' into journalism

You know you've made it in newspaper journalism when your name is emblazoned across the top of a regular page. At the national level, columnists are among the highest paid journalists in the industry. In its 2006 list of the most powerful figures in the media, the *Guardian* reported that *Daily Mail* columnist Richard Littlejohn was being paid £1 million per year to write his twice-weekly diatribe. That was more than the basic salary of the editor who employed him, Paul Dacre. A couple of years earlier, Littlejohn had transferred from the *Sun* – a coup seen at the time as the equivalent of a move from Manchester United to Arsenal.

Columnists are considered so valuable by editors because of the intimate relationship they can engender with readers – for many of whom they become the voice of the newspaper. Their words are often accompanied by a head-and-shoulders picture or drawing of the writer to help 'personalise' this relationship further. Readers can come to love them – or hate them. The worst fate for a columnist is to be ignored. Yet, at the same time, as Christopher Silvester argues:

> A column appears in the same publication on a regular basis usually in the same position and with the same heading and by-line. The presence of the column is reassuring, therefore, not primarily because of what it has to say but because of its appearance in a particular spot, on a particular day or days and at an approximately predictable length.
>
> (Silvester 1994: xi)

Whether or not they are actually worth these astronomical sums remains open to question. As Marr (2004) muses: 'The best columnists are hugely prized by their editors, though there is no evidence I have ever seen that the loss of a writer visibly moves circulation at all.'

There are many forms of personal columns. They might be straight opinion, or involve a small amount of journalistic research. John Pilger's prominently displayed columns in the *Daily Mirror* in the lead-up to the 2003 invasion of Iraq carried powerful arguments against the US/UK aggression, but were always based on extensive research of the historical record.

Fashions in personal columns come and go. The 1990s, for example, saw an explosion of female confessional columnists, such as India Knight, Anna Blundy and Zoë Heller. Helen Fielding became the most famous exponent of the genre and her *Bridget Jones's Diary* went on to become a global best-seller. Suzanne Moore commented:

> As more and more people get their news from other forms of media, the role of newspaper journalism has become more interpretative and subjective. In these times of media saturation and its subsequent neurosis – information anxiety – columnists in their idiosyncratic ways wade through the mire of information about the world we live in.
>
> (Moore 1996: x)

Subsequently, we have seen a spurt in the growth of 'celebrity' columnists – given prominent newspaper space not for their ability to write, or even formulate a coherent view, but because editors hope that their profile in another field might bring new readers in. Thus television presenters, comedians and singers – the likes of Graham Norton, Russell Brand, Frankie Boyle – have all been given prominent columns in recent years. Not all of them last very long.

But, critics argued, instead of hard news and hard-hitting investigative pieces, frothy features full of the mindless musings of over-important, over-paid celebrity journalists were filling up the columns. According to Brian McNair (2000: 64):

The rise of the political commentator is a direct consequence of the commodification of the public sphere which makes it necessary for news organisations to brand their output (give it exchange value in a market place containing many other superficially similar brands).

Maintaining a constant stream of (ideally original) opinion is not easy. Indeed, according to Stephen Glover (1999: 290–291), the columnist's skill is 'in writing about matters of which one is ignorant'. Certainly, the columnist must be interested in, and reasonably informed about, a wide range of issues. Many journalists pick the brains of experts on their current subject – and then pass them on as if they were their own.

Keith Waterhouse (1995), the eminent Fleet Street columnist, provided his own 25-step plan for writing the perfect column, which included the following:

- Every columnist needs a good half-dozen hobby horses. But do not ride them to death.

- On cuttings, he suggests: 'Packing the column with other people's quotes is the columnar equivalent of watering the milk. Assimilate material and then discard it.'

- Never try to fake it. 'Nothing is so transparent as insincerity – pile on the adjectives though you may, false indignation has the ring of a counterfeit coin.'

- A column should not be used to pursue a personal grudge unless it is going to ring bells with most of your readers.

- Allow your readers only a few restricted glimpses into your private life.

- Columnar feuds are amusing to other columnists and may even yield them copy providing they don't mind living vicariously. The readers, or what Craig Brown describes as 'that diminishing minority of people who do not write newspaper columns', find them bemusing.

DIVERSITY IN THE NEWSROOM: SPECTACULARLY LACKING

In a piece for the *Guardian*'s Comment Is Free website, political journalist Anne Alexander recounts the visit a senior political adviser made to the lobby office at Westminster that she shared with five male colleagues. The adviser began introducing the journalists to someone who was with her: 'That's Frank from AFP, there's Ian from the *Manchester Evening News*, Bill from the *Lancashire Evening Post*, and this is Anne, their PA.' On being corrected of her mistake, Alexander reports, the adviser was horrified. '[I] have often wondered whether her assumption was based on my race (African-Caribbean origin), gender or my class (council estate, parents factory workers).' (Alexander 2013)

Alexander's experience neatly encapsulates a problem faced not just by British newspapers, but by the journalism industry in general: a spectacular lack of diversity. The 2012 Journalists at Work survey funded by the NCTJ spells out the facts:

> Journalists are less ethnically diverse than the workforce as a whole – 95 per cent are white compared to 91 per cent overall. This is particularly surprising given that we might expect journalists to have a higher proportion of non-whites because they are predominantly located either in London or other urban centres where the proportion of people from ethnic minorities is much higher. For example, the 2011 Census data suggests that 59.8 per cent of London's population is white, with 18.5 per cent being Asian/Asian British and 13.3 per cent Black/African.

The latter point was also addressed in a 2005 report for the Commission for Racial Equality, *Why Ethnic Minorities Leave London's Print Journalism Sector* (CRE 2005), which concluded from a series of face-to-face interviews and discussion groups that that there were many barriers to entry and promotion in the industry for ethnic minority groups, including:

- editors hiring and promoting from their existing networks, which mainly comprised people like them
- a reluctance among ethnic minority journalists to challenge discrimination
- stereotypes of black and minority journalists meant they were pigeonholed into doing stories about gun crime or 'black youth culture'
- many ethnic minority journalists cut their teeth on minority newspapers, which did not have a track record for being a route into more mainstream publications.

This and the Journalists at Work survey confirm what plenty of previous studies have also shown. A major report by Anthony Delano and John Henningham (1995) of the London College of Printing concluded that fewer than 2 per cent of British press, radio and television journalists were black or ethnic minority, while out of around 4,000 national newspaper journalists only two or three dozen were black. A 2002 study by the Journalism Training Forum (linking various media training bodies) similarly found just 2 per cent of journalists were from black or Asian backgrounds. And in October 2004, a report by the Society of Editors found just 28 ethnic minority journalists out of 634 on newspapers in 10 major English towns and cities (Preston 2004b). As black *Guardian* journalist Gary Younge commented: 'Editors tend to hire in their own image and thus reinforce the *status quo*.' (Keeble 2001: 74)

Against that gloomy backdrop, though, come some signs of progress. In the spring of 2013, Amol Rajan made history by becoming the first non-white editor of a

British national newspaper when he was appointed to the top job on the *Independent*. He told Indian television:

> British media as a whole has been restrictive for ethnic minorities but it is far better than it used to be . . . Newspapers though have lagged behind . . . If I can help play a small part in promoting ethnic minority representation in Fleet Street I'll be thrilled.
>
> (UK Asian 2013)

Welcoming Rajan's appointment in the *Guardian*, Joseph Harker noted the difficulty of the task ahead of him. There are plenty of senior people in the industry, said Harker, who would be happy to take any sign of failure as confirmation that a non-white editor – particularly one so young (Rajan was 29 at his appointment) – was not up to the rigours of the job. He also hoped that the appointment would make other newspapers look more carefully at their own recruitment and promotion practices to make sure they are not denying talented journalists the opportunity to take influential roles.

> Rajan has to . . . [get] beyond traditional narrow coverage to include a wider spread of stories across multicultural Britain – reflecting life as it really is for Britain's minorities, rather than just the typical shock headlines of terror, knife crimes and sexual grooming.
>
> (Harker 2013)

Jane Martinson, chair of Women in Journalism, wrote in her *Guardian* blog about the 30 per cent barrier that persists across all of public life (Martinson 2012). That's the percentage of women MPs, for example, and of women board members of British companies. But perhaps more shockingly, when Women in Journalism carried out an analysis of contributions to nine British national newspapers, women did not even make it to the 30 per cent mark. In fact, only 28 per cent of bylines belonged to female journalists, and of the 668 individuals quoted in the stories surveyed, just 16 per cent were women.

Finally, the impact of social class on an individual's chance of success in the industry is also of grave concern. In its 2009 report *Unleashing Aspiration* the Panel on Fair Access to the Professions found that the typical entry-level journalist will have grown up in a household that is better off than 75 per cent of the population. True, this trend may not be new: the report shows that the average professional born in 1958 came from a family that earned 17 per cent more than average; but by 1970 this had risen to 27 per cent, with journalism and accountancy the two professions showing the most dramatic shift in social mobility options.

The 2012 Journalists at Work survey shows that as entry-level journalism jobs have increasingly become the preserve of those with degree-level education, the likelihood has correspondingly fallen of those from underprivileged backgrounds getting a chance at the ground level. The survey report notes: 'There remains a concern that journalism is an occupation where social class impacts on the likelihood of entering the profession. As in 2002, young people entering journalism are likely to need financial support from their families.' None of these problems is new. What is perhaps most troubling is the industry's inability to act decisively to reverse them.

MONEY MATTERS: THE SCANDAL OF LOW PAY

Salaries for many in the newspaper industry remain scandalously low: for trainees they can be appalling. The Journalists at Work survey (see also Turvill 2012a) reported that the average journalist across all media earned £27,500 per year in 2012 – down 12 per cent in real terms over the previous decade. For newspaper journalists the average drops to £22,500. More alarmingly, the average debt for an entry-level journalist in 2012 was £15,000 – a figure that is only likely to rise in the coming years thanks to the leap in university fees that kicked in from 2012.

At the same time, top executives and columnists on national newspapers can earn significant six-figure sums (and very occasionally seven). Paul Dacre's baseline salary as editor-in-chief of the *Mail* titles, according to parent company DMGT's annual statement, was £1.75 million in 2012. His counterpart at the *Guardian*, Alan Rusbridger, was due to take home £457,000 in the same year plus a £150,000 pension contribution – although he volunteered a 10 per cent reduction in the former and a 50 per cent reduction in the latter in recognition of the cuts his company was having to make.

In contrast, for many freelances salaries have either stood still over recent years or dropped, while payments to them can take up to a year. Colin Sparks (2003: 47) argues that the media hierarchy, based around marked differences in status and salary, is 'a powerful mechanism of control'. 'In particular, the possibility of very substantial financial rewards for those who are professionally successful acts as a strong incentive on journalists and other creative staff to toe the management line.' The one crumb of comfort from the 2012 salary survey? Just 3 per cent of respondents said they did not enjoy their job.

GOING IT ALONE: THE FREELANCE

Freelancing is not for the faint-hearted. Nor, usually, is it for the journalist at the beginning of their career. A survey by the NUJ in 2004 found the average age of a freelance was 46, while 68 per cent had worked previously as staffers, typically for 11 years before going it alone. The overwhelming majority enjoyed being freelance, with only 30 per cent wanting to return to a staff job. Some 87 per cent rated producing high quality work as their most important motivation – even higher than getting paid (Leston 2004).

Just as there are many kinds of staff reporter, so there are many kinds of freelance. Some are the best paid and busiest writers. Others find life extremely difficult, with widespread cuts in newspaper journalists' jobs intensifying competition among freelances. When a newspaper's managing editor is looking for cuts in the editorial department, the freelance budget is usually the first in the line of fire.

There are clearly good and bad sides to the freelance life. To a certain extent freelances enjoy some 'freedoms' not permitted to staff writers. They can work from home, they are not forced to abide by a strict daily routine, they can avoid all the hassles of office politics. They may even be given the opportunity to pursue a specialism that no other journalistic route has allowed.

But freelances can rarely free themselves from the constraints of the market. You may be contemptuous of the capitalist rat-race of the newspaper world, but freelancing hardly provides a refuge from this. Freelances have to go where the money is. George Orwell, for instance, committed himself to small-scale, left-wing, literary journals and largely ignored the seductive appeal of Fleet Street. But until his last two novels, *Animal Farm* and *Nineteen Eighty-Four*, achieved global success, he lived in relative poverty. It was his ethical and political choice (Keeble 2000). If you are interested in progressive journalism, then secure a steady job (with a charity, progressive think-tank or pressure group) and build up your freelance experience on that foundation.

A freelance's working day is, in many respects, more demanding and stressful than that of a staffer. Not only do they have the problems of finding work, promoting new ideas and meeting deadlines, but they also have a range of other issues to worry about. They have to sort out taxation problems. They may have to chase finance departments to pay up. They have to negotiate rates and make sure all their equipment is maintained properly. Without the regular inflow of money enjoyed by staff journalists, freelances have, in short, to be far more financially organised. In the 2004 NUJ survey, 58 per cent of freelances reported having some or a lot of money worries.

On top of all this, the freelance has no job security. When jobs are on the line, they are invariably the first to suffer. Without the companionship that goes with a full-time job, the freelance's life can be lonely. Significantly, the NUJ survey found 64 per cent reporting depression and 47 per cent having serious drinking or smoking habits (Leston 2004).

Starting up

Launching into a freelance career is not easy. Many freelances are former full-time staffers who have developed a specialism, sent out linage (freelance copy paid by the line) to nationals and then, through either choice or redundancy, taken the plunge and gone solo or started a small agency. Sometimes a non-journalist professional may build up contacts and a specialist knowledge. They may have enjoyed close links with the media and even contributed occasional articles to the press. On this basis they may decide to switch to journalism as a career. The feature linking all these examples is a specialism that can be exploited journalistically. Very few freelances are generalists. As Stephen Wade comments:

> The besetting sins of writing freelance are over-confidence and naivety. Never assume that editors are clamouring for your work. The competition is massive and there is a lot of talent around. Do not be naive enough to think that you can compete immediately with the full-time professionals. You have to put everything into your first article and submit to a realistic market, with a good covering letter. If you are sure of why you are writing, then these will all be more attainable.
>
> (Wade 1997: 45)

Finding an outlet

Get to know the market for your specialist area of interest. Study the different writing styles, the lengths of sentences and articles in the different publications. Try to establish, by examining byline patterns, the amount of freelance work accepted and in which specific areas: it may be in celebrity profiles, in authoritative, fact-based comment or in timeless features. Read recent issues carefully to make sure you don't duplicate anything already done. It's not a good idea to ring a publication to gather this kind of information, or even their general views about freelancing. You are expected to do all the basic groundwork and then approach the publication with a potential article.

With a hot news story you will obviously contact the paper by phone. But with other kinds of story there are no rules. Some prefer contact by phone, others by email. Always direct your approach to the most appropriate person on the editorial staff. If you have a feature, ring the features editor (asking the switchboard operator their name before speaking). Expect to have to travel through a range of protective secretaries before speaking to them in person.

Explain the main point of your story and the likely length you envisage. In covering news, there is always a danger the paper will take down the details and then send out their staffer to handle it. Try to convey the story's importance and the fact that you have it ready to send over by phone, fax or email. Do not give too much away on the phone. Even if they use your call as a simple 'tip off' for a story they cover themselves, you are still owed a payment for that. If you are not known to the paper, they are unlikely to commit themselves to carrying a story on the basis of a rushed phone call. They are likely to say: 'That sounds interesting. Send in the copy but I can't promise anything.'

The perils of pitching

If you are pitching an idea for a timeless feature, explain your original angles, your main sources, the basic structure of the piece and wordage, why you are particularly suited to covering it and why you have chosen their particular publication. There are dangers here. The publication may steal your ideas and give them to someone else to follow up. And the freelance has absolutely no protection in law against this kind of theft. While written work can be copyrighted, an idea can occur to two people at the same time and can also be stolen. There is no easy solution to this problem. One approach is to hold back on the precise identity of key sources or case studies before the idea is accepted. Personal contact with the commissioning editor also helps in creating mutual trust and confidence. The best solution is to prove your abilities to the newspaper in a series of stories sent on spec or commissioned, so they will be concerned not to lose your work to other competitors. It is also worth emphasising that you are the only person with the unique knowledge, contacts, idiosyncratic viewpoint or desire to complete the article. Clearly, freelances have to develop special negotiation skills.

Always make sure you have a copy of all your submitted work. If it is rejected you may want to direct it to another newspaper or rearrange it with some new angles for a different outlet. Be persistent, but don't become a pest: remember *Gone with the Wind* was rejected 25 times before it was published, and *Zen and the Art of Motorcycle Maintenance* 121 times. There may be queries over the story that can be cleared up only with reference to your original copy; you may need to protect yourself against libel where the paper has subbed in a comment or error.

Once the idea is accepted

If the commissioning editor has said: 'OK, I'll be pleased to look at your story but I can't promise we'll use it', they are free to reject your story without incurring any financial liability. But if they have commissioned your piece and then don't publish it, they should pay you a 'kill fee' comprising part or all of the original amount agreed. But not all newspapers do. Many of the freelances in the NUJ survey complained of having their ideas stolen, or of not receiving responses from editors after spending hours preparing and submitting ideas.

How much should you expect to be paid for your hard work? Well, the NUJ draws up a list of minimum freelance rates which are regularly updated and will give you some idea of what to expect. It also provides useful guidance about working for day rates – either as writer or sub-editor – which can have implications for the way you are taxed, and for the copyright of your work.

Certainly make sure you also negotiate expenses when your piece is commissioned, since without that agreement you may end up using the payment simply to fund your research. And send in an invoice soon after the appearance of your copy.

Remember that, if you are a self-employed freelance, you own the copyright in your work: it is your 'intellectual property' whether submitted on spec or commissioned. Thus you are strongly advised to hold on to your copyright. This does not mean refusing further use of the material; you can licence it, giving permission for a specific use for an agreed fee. Many newspaper publishers include in their commissioning terms the right to store and display material on electronic databases and to authorise others to do the same. The reach of the web means that it's far more difficult for a freelance to sell a piece to multiple newspapers in different parts of the world.

CHAPTER 4

Journalism in the dock

Ethics, Hackgate and beyond

ETHICS AND THE PHONE-HACKING SCANDAL

You have been invited into the office of your local MP – a well-known government minister – to conduct an interview for your newspaper. He's talkative, although fairly guarded about any of the substantial issues you discuss, but you have enough material to write the piece your editor has commissioned. Towards the end of the interview, he is called out of the office briefly, leaving you alone at his desk. At the top of his in-tray you can see a letter with the distinctive headed notepaper of a top law firm. From where you are sitting, you can't quite see what the text says – it's a short note of just two paragraphs. But if you stood up and leaned over the desk, you would be able to read it. You clearly have time to do this without being spotted. What do you do?

When I offer this ethical dilemma to students on our journalism programmes, the reaction is generally mixed. Some take the view that the letter is private correspondence. It is not addressed to you, and has not explicitly been shown to you, so it would be wrong for you to read it. Others point out that you have been invited in to the office, you are known as a journalist, and if your interviewee has been careless enough to leave something on view, then that's his mistake. We bring up cases of government officials and police officers who have been photographed carrying documents on which the text can be read by zooming in to the picture. That's different, their opponents claim. They were in a public place; you are not. Another group say that the contents of the letter might be completely innocuous – but you'll never know unless you take a peek. Others suggest that perhaps he has left the room deliberately in order to 'leak' some important information, knowing that you would spot it.

We then look at the relevant part of the Editors' Code of Practice. Section 3, part 1 says: 'Everyone is entitled to respect for his or her private and family life, home, health and *correspondence*, including digital communications.' [my italics]

Ah, but what if contents of the letter are so explosive that the public must know about it? After all, this is someone whose salary comes out of the public purse. There are several clauses for which an exception can be made if the story is in the public interest. I generally tell students at this point that my guess is that the vast majority of professional journalists would probably read the letter. I remind them of Allan Little's explanation of a reporter's primary purpose, to 'go and find something out' (see Chapter 5), and of the suggestion by the celebrated *Sunday Times* war correspondent Nicholas Tomalin (1931–73) that journalists should show a little 'rat-like cunning'. And so we move on to the next step of the dilemma.

You lean across and read the letter. Its contents are explosive. It says your interviewee is being sued by a well-known celebrity over a distinctly dodgy-sounding failed business venture they had set up together. You sit back down, and your interviewee returns to the office. What now? Do you confront him with the story? Do you ask him leading questions about the celebrity, hoping this will tease out the facts? Do you say nothing, but write the story anyway? Do you say nothing, but make a mental note to ask your editor for guidance?

Further heated debate ensues. Failure to confront him with the story is cowardice, some say. Others worry that if you ask him about it, he will try to prevent the story being published in some way. It should be your editor's call, says another group. One group says just write the story – it's factually true, so there's nothing to stop you. Why not wait until you're back in the office, and then call the celebrity to stand up the story independently? asks another.

It's usually about this time in the proceedings that I ask students to step into the shoes of Clive Goodman.

In 2005 Goodman, an experienced journalist, was the royal editor of the *News of the World*. It was a tough job in one of the most notoriously ruthless editorial environments on Fleet Street. The pressure was immense to deliver good, exclusive stories on his patch. At this time, mobile phones were in their relative infancy as a mass-market possession, and Goodman was far from the only journalist to realise that many users were still rather naïve about the way they handled them. In particular, it was widely known that the majority of mobile phone users did not know there was a 'factory setting' for a PIN code on their voicemail service. If that setting wasn't changed, anybody could pick up messages left on that voicemail simply by keying in the four-digit default code.

What Goodman did, in March 2005, was to use this loophole to listen to messages left on the mobile voicemail services of royal aides who worked at Clarence House and whose mobile phone numbers he knew. It gave him an insight into some of the lives of royal family members, and he based some of his stories on them. Furthermore, the practice of accessing messages in this way was widespread among some of his colleagues. He knew that it had been done on hundreds of previous occasions, both by journalists and by private investigators working on their behalf who were retained by the newspaper. So the question that I put to my students is this: if you chose to read the letter on your notional interviewee's desk, how different are you from Clive Goodman?

In both cases you have accessed information you know was not intended for you; in both cases you have taken advantage of someone else's carelessness to do it – they could easily have prevented you from doing so by being more vigilant. Of course, it doesn't take long for the crucial point to be raised that what Goodman did was illegal under the Regulation of Investigatory Powers Act 2000. There is also the fact that this was not some isolated incident, or Goodman stumbling across something he shouldn't have done by accident or mistake. It was a systematic invasion of privacy: Goodman admitted in court to making almost 500 calls to the message services of the aides in question.

The practice of phone hacking, or phone 'screwing' as it was widely known amongst its practitioners in the late 1990s and early 2000s, was not confined to one 'rogue reporter', as Goodman had been memorably dubbed by his employer. Under the headline 'Is Fleet Street screwed?', *Press Gazette* reported at the time of Goodman's arrest the view of several tabloid journalists that the practice had been relatively common on a number of red-top newspapers, and that even some broadsheet journalists may have indulged (Ponsford 2006). The practice may even have been common enough that some of those journalists may not have given much thought to the fact that they were breaking the law.

This ethical exercise is by no means intended to exonerate Goodman, or to suggest that there was anything acceptable about hacking phones, but it does help to demonstrate to journalism students that it may not take much to cross the line from acceptable journalistic practice to ignoring the Editors' Code and even breaking the law, particularly in the febrile and highly competitive atmosphere of a national newsroom.

Goodman was given a four-month prison sentence in 2007, along with private investigator Glenn Mulcaire, who had been paid by News International and pleaded guilty to the same charges. Their imprisonment was to prove only the beginning of a saga that would change newspaper journalism forever and bring the ethics of its workers right to the top of the news agenda.

A phone hack too far: Milly Dowler

Clive Goodman may have served his time in 2007 (and pocketed more than £200,000 in unfair dismissal compensation from the newspaper group that had employed him), but the issue of phone hacking was still largely a story discussed in media and political circles, rather than in the pubs and on the buses of Britain. It would take revelations of the hacking of another phone – one belonging to a murdered young schoolgirl – to raise it to a level that outraged the general public.

Following the Goodman case, News International had instigated a damage limitation exercise after it became clear that he was far from the 'rogue reporter' the company had originally suggested. As the police investigation into phone hacking at its newspapers ground on, it began to make out-of-court payouts to high-profile names whose phones had also been hacked by its staff, starting with Professional Footballers' Association Chairman Gordon Taylor (damages and costs totalling £700,000), and continuing with celebrities including Max Clifford (up to £1 million); Charlotte Church and her parents (£600,000 each); Jude Law (£130,000); and Sienna Miller (£100,000). Scores of other cases were settled for smaller and undisclosed sums.

By early 2011, Andy Coulson, the former editor of the *News of the World* who had become David Cameron's communications director, had resigned from his position at the heart of the Downing Street operation as the scale of the hacking operation under his editorship became clearer. (He had previously resigned from the paper immediately after Goodman was jailed.)

And there the story might have slowly burned its way out. But in July 2011, the *Guardian* revealed that a mobile phone belonging to murdered schoolgirl Milly Dowler had been hacked by *News of the World* journalists. Milly had gone missing on her way home from school in March 2002, and her frantic parents had been leaving increasingly desperate messages for her in the hours and days following her disappearance. But the message system could only handle a small number of messages, and once the limit was reached, they couldn't leave any more.

But then one morning, Milly's mother Sally found that she was able to leave a new message. Understandably ignorant that anybody other than Milly would be able to access these messages, she felt that the only explanation was that her daughter was still alive and had picked up some of the earlier messages that had been left. In fact, the cruel truth was that her daughter had already been murdered by her abductor Levi Bellfield, although her body would not be found for several months. The *Guardian*'s report claimed that *News of the World* journalists had been accessing Milly's phone in the days following her disappearance in an attempt to get a new lead on the story, and had deleted some of the old messages (Davies and Hill 2011). The story said:

> The messages were deleted by journalists in the first few days after Milly's disappearance in order to free up space for more messages. As a result friends and relatives of Milly concluded wrongly that she might still be alive. Police feared evidence may have been destroyed.

The effect was to give the phone-hacking story rocket boosters. Where there had previously been a limit to the sympathy the public felt for celebrity victims of hacking, particularly as many of them were getting eye-watering sums in compensation, there was now an outpouring of anger directed towards the callous and cynical actions of these tabloid journalists and their bosses. Lawyers for the Dowler family called the actions of the reporters 'heinous and despicable'. Advertisers started to pull out from the *News of the World* within hours of the story appearing. A Facebook page entitled 'Boycott the *News of the World*' was 'liked' by thousands of users of the social media site. Shares in the newspaper's parent company dropped nearly 5 per cent overnight.

In fact, a central claim of the *Guardian* story – that the *News of the World* team had deliberately deleted the messages – was wrong. In December 2011, it published a correction acknowledging that the police now believed it was unlikely the *News of the World* journalists had been responsible for the deletions. But by then the damage was already irreversible. On 7 July 2011, less than 48 hours after the original Dowler phone story broke, News International announced the closure of the title, which had been in print since 1843. If there ever had been a time when journalists could take the view that the ethics of their behaviour was something discussed only by earnest academics, that time was well and truly over.

The Leveson Inquiry: a political football

As the Dowler phone-hacking saga played out, Prime Minister David Cameron found himself in a tight spot. His judgement had already been called into question over the appointment of Andy Coulson as his communications chief and, despite the latter's resignation earlier in 2011, the spotlight was back on the relationship between senior government figures and News International executives. Several arrests, including senior journalists from the *News of the World* during Coulson's time in command, had been made under the Metropolitan Police's Operation Weeting investigation into phone hacking. Coulson himself was arrested on 8 July, just three days after the Dowler story broke, and would later be charged on several counts.

How much, people wanted to know, was David Cameron aware of Coulson's involvement in or knowledge of phone hacking? Indeed, had Coulson even been properly vetted before being given a job that would take him to the heart of government? And what of the relationship between Cameron and Rebekah Brooks, Coulson's predecessor as *News of the World* editor and subsequently chief executive of News International? Brooks herself would later be charged under two separate police investigations.

Cameron's response was to do what all prime ministers do when the flames of a scandal begin licking too close to the door of 10 Downing Street. He launched an inquiry. The inquiry he set up was to investigate 'the culture, practice and ethics of the press', and would be led by Brian Leveson, Lord Justice of Appeal. His terms of reference were to be in two parts. The first would look at contact between journalists and police officers, and between journalists and politicians. It would also examine regulation and whether previous warnings about media misconduct had been properly heeded.

The second part would specifically examine unlawful or improper conduct at News International and other media organisations; whether such conduct had been appropriately investigated by the police in the first instance; and whether improper or illegal payments had been made to police by newspaper executives or journalists. Despite concerns being expressed that an inquiry merely kicked the issue into the 'long grass' (Stevenson 2011), and that ongoing police investigations meant that key subject areas were off-limits to him, Leveson began hearing evidence in September 2011 and called his final witness on 24 July 2012.

In all, 337 live witnesses gave evidence, and the statements of nearly 300 others were read in. One by one, senior politicians and their advisers, newspaper proprietors and editors, senior journalists, police officers, the victims of phone hacking and their lawyers made their way to the Royal Courts of Justice in the Strand for their ritual grilling at the hands of Leveson's QC Robert Jay. The inquiry, with sessions streamed live on the internet and witness statements published on its own website (www.levesoninquiry.org.uk), set out to be the most transparent investigation yet into the behaviour of British journalists, and their relationship with the police and with politicians. It was part soap opera, part sitcom and part forensic investigation.

Celebrities who gave evidence included actress Sienna Miller, who described how intimidated she felt being chased by packs of paparazzi photographers; author J. K. Rowling, who told of her anger at finding a note from a reporter inside her daughter's school bag; singer Charlotte Church, who claimed she was offered positive newspaper coverage in lieu of a fee for singing at Rupert Murdoch's wedding; and actors Steve Coogan and Hugh Grant, both leading lights of a campaign called Hacked Off, who described how 'kiss-and-tell' stories about them were paid for by newspapers.

Political witnesses included Prime Minister David Cameron, who was quizzed about his close 'kitchen supper' relationship and the regular text messages he exchanged with former tabloid editor and News International chief executive Rebekah Brooks. Former PM Tony Blair also gave evidence, describing how he made a deliberate bid to win over Rupert Murdoch before his first election win, but insisting he did no deals involving cross-media ownership. Blair's successor as PM, Gordon Brown, revealed his own anguish when details of his son's cystic fibrosis were reported by the *Sun*.

There was also evidence from witnesses who had found themselves caught up in press coverage of extraordinary stories. Christopher Jefferies, the innocent landlord of murdered Joanna Yeates, told of his nightmare at being described as a sexual predator by newspapers during the police investigation. He successfully sued eight newspapers, two of which were found to be in Contempt of Court for their coverage.

The parents of Milly Dowler also gave evidence, as did Kate and Gerry McCann, whose daughter Madeleine disappeared from a Portuguese hotel room in May 2007. Kate McCann said she felt 'totally violated' when the News of the World published extracts from her personal diary without her permission.

Among the police witnesses was Metropolitan Police Deputy Assistant Commissioner Sue Akers, the senior officer responsible for the ongoing investigations into phone and computer hacking, and bribery of officers. She told the inquiry about a 'culture of illegal payments' at the Sun to public officials – including one who had received £80,000 in total from the paper for providing information. John Yates, the former assistant Met commissioner who was responsible for the early flawed investigation into phone hacking, had to contend with allegations that he was far too close to senior News International executives.

Witnesses from the press were generally given a fairly hostile reception. Rupert Murdoch took the stand, as did his son James, who was executive chairman of News International at the time of the phone-hacking scandal. Murdoch senior said he had never asked a prime minister for anything. He said he had 'huge regret' that the culture of the News of the World allowed it to be so cavalier about risk. At a parliamentary select committee hearing that took place at around the same time, he said it was 'the humblest day of my life'.

Andy Coulson, the former News of the World editor and government communications director, said there was no 'grand conspiracy' between the government and News International. And BBC Newsnight's Jeremy Paxman said that he had been told by former tabloid editor Piers Morgan how to hack a mobile phone's voice messaging system. For many of the general public, though, it was the idiotic suggestion from former tabloid journalist-turned-publican Paul McMullan that 'privacy is for paedos . . . privacy is evil' that was most memorable. A more rational suggestion came from Private Eye editor Ian Hislop: 'I wanted to put in a plea for journalism and the concept of a free press, that it is important; it isn't always pretty . . . and I hope this inquiry doesn't throw out the baby with the bath water.'

Leveson's findings: no consensus

Leveson delivered his eagerly anticipated report in November 2012. It was 2,000 pages long and made comprehensive recommendations to the government on a number of fronts:

- the establishment of an independent self-regulatory regime to replace the Press Complaints Commission (PCC)
- amendments to the Data Protection Act as it pertains to journalism
- a review of damages available in civil law cases involving data protection and privacy
- rules governing the relationship between police officers and the press

- rules governing the relationship between politicians and the press
- and the issue of plurality and media ownership.

The most controversial of these recommendations was the first. Leveson's suggested framework for the regulation of the press remains mired in the political swamp long after he made it. In very broad terms his proposals on regulation – there were 47 in all – were as follows.

- Newspapers should continue to be self-regulated – and the government should have no power over what they publish.
- The industry should create a new press standards body, with a new code of conduct, that encompasses all significant news publishers.
- The government should introduce legislation to ensure the regulation was independent and effective – in the form of a recognition body that would oversee the working of the regulator. This responsibility should go to Ofcom.
- The new regulator should comprise a majority of people who are independent of the press, and should not include any serving newspaper editors.
- It should have the power to decide where and how an apology should be published, and to impose fines up to 1 per cent of the turnover of the publisher to a maximum of £1 million.
- Any publisher not signing up to the new system should be open to exemplary or punitive damages in civil cases.

It was the third item on the above list – the recommendation that some form of legislation should be required to oversee the self-regulatory system – that caused the greatest stir, a point foreseen by Leveson in the summary of his report. 'Despite what will be said about these recommendations by those who oppose them, this is not, and cannot be characterised as, statutory regulation of the press', he said. As we shall see, the industry very quickly disagreed.

Solutions to the Leveson standoff: the rival charters

Immediately after Leveson's report was published, Labour and the Liberal Democrats rushed to back his proposals, which, they said, should be implemented in full. Prime Minister David Cameron, though, had 'serious concerns and misgivings' about the introduction of any form of legislation: 'It would mean for the first time we have crossed the Rubicon of writing elements of press regulation into law of the land.' Already, Leveson's hopes that cross-party consensus – which he acknowledged would be essential – could be achieved were looking shaky.

But, whatever the political parties felt, the newspapers themselves were clear they would not countenance anything that involved statutory legislation. Max Hastings summed up Fleet Street's view in the *Daily Mail*. The report, he said, constituted a 'rotten day for freedom . . . a tragic blow to liberty and the right to know' (Hastings 2012). A memo signed by all of the national newspaper editors agreed to 40 out of Leveson's 47 recommendations on regulation – but none of the seven that involved enshrining its oversight into a new law. Cameron, meanwhile, had given himself some short breathing space by asking editors to come up with their own solution to establishing a self-regulatory system that took Leveson's main recommendations into account without the need for statute. At the same time, the political parties continued to come under intense pressure from phone-hacking victims and Hacked Off campaigners to stand up to the industry.

What emerged in March 2012 – reportedly following a late-night pizza-fuelled meeting in Ed Miliband's office attended by members of the Hacked Off campaign (although its executive director Brian Cathcart (2013) disputes accounts of this) – was the suggestion that a Royal Charter could be used instead of direct legislation. Royal Charters have been around for hundreds of years; they pre-date modern parliament and have been used to establish organisations including the Bank of England, the British Red Cross, the British Council and the BBC. They are not required to be put before Parliament, but are drawn up by the Privy Council – another ancient institution, made up of a group of senior political advisers to the monarch whose membership is not widely publicised. Writing in the *Daily Telegraph*, Andrew Gilligan (2013) described the move as

> in effect, a state press law, one of the strongest in Europe, and the Rubicon has been definitively crossed.

Mr Cameron's proposed regulator, Gilligan said, may not be part of the state, but it would have to conform to fairly prescriptive criteria set down by the state. The fact that those criteria are written in a Royal Charter, not an Act of Parliament, was irrelevant:

> They will in practice be every bit as changeable as any law by future politicians who wish to restrict press freedom.

But within a few weeks, a group from within the newspaper industry had itself published a rival Royal Charter proposal to put before the Privy Council, which would use the same ancient device to establish the rules for a self-regulatory framework, but which differed in some of the detail. The key differences boil down to two principles: how a Royal Charter might be amended in the future; and how much influence the industry might have over appointments to the main regulator.

In the version drawn up by the politicians, the Charter could be amended only by two-thirds majority agreement in both Houses of Parliament – political control that was anathema to most newspaper executives. In the industry's version, amendments could be made only with unanimous approval of the new regulator, the recognition panel for the new regulator and four other industry bodies: the Newspaper Society, the Newspaper Publishers Association, the Professional Publishers Association and the Scottish Newspaper Society. The newspaper groups' proposed charter also allowed the industry to retain a veto on appointments to the board of the main regulator – in order to restrict the possibility of politically motivated appointments – and allowed former editors to sit on the recognition panel. But with the costs of any Royal Charter-backed structure estimated by some as £3.5 to £4 million per year, the burden of cost for an industry not in the rudest financial health was also likely to be a significant problem (Halliday and O'Carroll 2013).

By October 2013, the industry's Royal Charter proposal had been turned down by the Privy Council's sub-committee, which would now turn its attention to the cross-party version. But with the industry set against it, and muttering about a judicial review of the process that could hold up progress for months or even longer, it seemed unlikely that a resolution would be found quickly.

The Independent Press Standards Organisation: the PCC with teeth?

As the Privy Council was considering the possibility of a Royal Charter, the core group of newspaper publishers pushed ahead with the launch of their own self-regulatory plan that they said would not need to be underpinned by a charter. By the end of 2013 all of the major national newspapers, with the exception of the *Guardian*, had signed up to the principles of the Independent Press Standards Organisation (IPSO), a new body that claimed to be a 'complete break from the past' while still delivering all of Leveson's key recommendations. IPSO's creators promised to have fully implemented the new regulator by 1 May 2014. It would have the power to administer fines of up to £1 million, investigate complaints, operate a whistleblowers' hotline, and dictate the positioning of upfront adjudications and corrections. For its supporters it offered a truly independent self-regulated solution with 'very real teeth' (Cusick 2013). For its detractors, however, including Professor Brian Cathcart of the Hacked Off campaign, it was simply a rebranding of the discredited PCC, offering little other than 'cosmetic change' and a means of 'ducking the Royal Charter'.

THE IMPORTANCE OF INDEPENDENT REGULATION: WHY A TRULY FREE PRESS MATTERS

Why is agreement on a system for the regulation of the press so difficult? Partly because it's so important. The stakes are very high. Because, while it's easy to dismiss the furore as one in which commercial organisations seek to defend their right to make money, what's really at issue is a far more important principle: the right of an individual to speak his or her mind, in print, without influence or fear of reprisal, as long as they don't break the law in doing so.

In this country, the primacy of that principle has meant there has been no state involvement in news publishing since the seventeenth century (see below). In other mature democracies, too, it is a cornerstone. There is no press regulation in the US, where instead press freedom is chiselled into the Constitution.

It is also difficult because it's complicated. What goes on behind the scenes in producing a newspaper, like making sausages, is not pretty. And where the public might enjoy the final product, they tend to get a bit queasy if they look too closely at the ingredients. How do you regulate the truth? Newspapers, for all their bluster, are rarely able to deal in black and white – truth or lies. Because the world is painted in shades of grey. Let's imagine a front page news story that contains, say, a dozen statements of fact. If, at a later date, one of the less significant of those 'facts' emerges as being wrong – either through error, mistaken assumption or a deliberately misleading source – then clearly the record needs to be put straight. But should the correction appear on the front page? Occupying the same space as the original story? And anyway, as Tony Blair debated with the Leveson Inquiry when giving his evidence, one person's 'fact' is another man's 'comment'.

It's also difficult because the definition of 'the press' is so much more difficult to pin down than it ever has been. Let's look at three websites: those belonging to BBC News, ITV News and the *Guardian*. Each could contain broadly similar content, and yet be regulated by three entirely separate methods: the BBC by its Trust; ITV by broadcast regulator Ofcom; and the *Guardian* by a press regulator.

Then there's the significant issue of the cost of regulation. Who picks up the tab when a complainant says they are being harassed inappropriately and demands an investigation? If the investigation shows no evidence of wrongdoing, should the bill fall proportionately equally on the small independent *Newbury Weekly News* as it does on the corporate behemoth that is *The Sunday Times*? Or should the 'polluter pays' principle be applied? And how, when the industry is so dominated by a small number of powerful corporate groups, do we prevent them from having too much influence on a regulating body for which they are likely to have to pay most of the bills? The importance of getting this right can barely be overstated. With such high stakes involved, perhaps it's little wonder that such paralysis set in during 2013 in the search for a resolution.

A BRIEF HISTORY OF MOVES TO IMPROVE PRESS STANDARDS: SEVEN REPORTS IN SEVEN DECADES

As Lord Justice Leveson archly noted as he introduced the summary of his findings in November 2012, his was the seventh report in as many decades to be commissioned by a government concerned about the behaviour of the press. The first Royal Commission in 1947 arose out of concerns over growing monopolies, with

Lord Rothermere, Lord Beaverbrook and Lord Kemsley (see Chapter 1) coming under particular scrutiny. Its most significant recommendation was that a General Council of the Press be set up to safeguard press freedoms and encourage the development of a sense of public responsibility among journalists.

A second Royal Commission, set up in 1961, also followed mounting concern over monopolies. Chaired by Lord Shawcross, it criticised the industry over its poor response to the original commission's recommendations and stressed the importance of including a lay element on the General Council. Thus, the Press Council came into being in July 1963.

The Younger Committee on Privacy was established in 1970 to consider a wide range of issues, but decided against the introduction of a right to privacy law.

A third Royal Commission (1974–77) was critical of the performance of the Press Council, making 12 recommendations to transform its operating procedures. However, these were largely rejected and the council remained a weak body, lacking the confidence of both the managers and the National Union of Journalists (NUJ) (Robertson 1983).

In 1989, following a spate of controversies over press intrusions into private grief, Margaret Thatcher's government authorised a committee chaired by David Calcutt to investigate the possible introduction of a privacy law. The industry, however, reacted quickly to the call to set up a self-regulatory press complaints commission in place of the Press Council and so attempt to ward off legislation. The first of many versions of a Code of Practice was introduced.

In January 1993, Calcutt (by then Sir David) presented a second report focusing on press and privacy issues. The PCC was accused of being ineffective and too dominated by the industry, and Calcutt proposed new offences carrying maximum fines of £5,000 for invasions of privacy and for the use of surveillance and bugging devices in certain cases. Later that year, John Major's government proposed the introduction of a privacy law. The PCC responded to all this controversy by introducing new clauses to the code on bugging and the use of telephoto lenses, and a lay majority (though only of the great and the good) was created among its members.

The privacy issue hit a new peak of intensity after the death of Princess Diana in Paris in a car crash on Sunday, 31 August 1997 (Hanstock 1999). Blame initially fell on the paparazzi following the royal Mercedes, and on the press that had so mercilessly pursued the Princess (though it was generally acknowledged that she had exploited the press when it suited her). New guidelines on the use of paparazzi photographs were introduced; in revising the code, Lord Wakeham redefined 'a private place' as covering the interior of a church, a restaurant and other places 'where individuals might rightly be free from media attention'.

THE END OF THE PCC: NO LONGER FIT FOR PURPOSE

In its turbulent 21-year history, the PCC had endured many testing times. But it was the phone-hacking scandal that would prove to be the issue that would finally break it apart. When Clive Goodman and Glenn Mulcaire were jailed in 2007 after admitting to phone hacking, the PCC's response was confused and indecisive. It did not, for example, question Goodman's editor at the *News of the World*, Andy Coulson, on the grounds that because he had now resigned it would be 'no longer appropriate' to talk to him. Instead, it wrote to Coulson's successor Colin Myler and to other newspaper editors asking them about potentially intrusive practices. From this, it planned to publish a 'review of the current situation, with recommendations for best practice if necessary, in order to prevent a similar situation arising in the future'.

Furthermore, in its submission to a parliamentary select committee, the PCC essentially backed News International's line that Goodman was a single rogue reporter. 'What the Goodman case highlights is that unfortunately neither the law nor the Code can guarantee that a determined individual will never breach their terms', it wrote. Two years later, the commission dug itself yet deeper into the hole. When the *Guardian* published evidence that phone hacking was far more widespread and systematic at News International (Nick Davies 2009a), and that the company had already paid out more than £1 million to compensate and gag high-profile victims, the PCC reacted defensively. It published another report, in November 2009, largely reiterating what it had said two years earlier – that Goodman was a one-off – and congratulating itself that it had helped to raise standards.

The report said it was 'satisfied' that its work aimed at improving the integrity of undercover journalism had 'played its part in raising standards in this area', and that it underlined the importance of a 'non-statutory, flexible body' such as the PCC. The report added: 'It would be regrettable if the renewed controversy over the historical transgressions at the *News of the World* obscured this.' It even went so far as to effectively rubbish the *Guardian*'s stories, which it said 'did not quite live up to the dramatic billing they were initially given'.

All of which meant that when, in 2011, the Milly Dowler phone-hacking story blew the whole practice wide open, the PCC was left without a leg to stand on. It withdrew its 2009 report, which it said had been based on misleading information provided to it by News International. All three party leaders queued up to pour scorn on the PCC as an effective watchdog.

In March 2012, Lord Hunt announced that the PCC would wind down, with the expectation that a successor organisation would take over its responsibilities after the Leveson Report was published later in the year (O'Carroll 2012). Leveson himself summed up that 'it is almost universally accepted that the body presently charged with the responsibility of dealing with complaints against the press is neither a regulator nor fit for purpose to fulfil that responsibility'.

HACKER IN THE DOCK: THE 'TRIAL OF THE CENTURY'

Andy Coulson, the former *News of the World* editor whose appointment as David Cameron's communications director had sparked the Leveson Inquiry, finally went on trial for phone hacking in October 2013. Seven others were also in the Old Bailey dock on a variety of related charges, most notably Rebekah Brooks, his *News of the World* predecessor who had later become chief executive of News International.

It was a complex trial that lasted 138 days with total costs estimated at £100m, making it the most expensive criminal trial in history, and it included a number of startling revelations – not the least being the details of the affair between Coulson and Brooks, which had all the ingredients of a great *News of the World* splash.

The jury was shown 3,000 pages of evidence, including details of 5,500 'likely' and 'potential' victims of phone hacking at the newspaper.

For Coulson, though, it was the emergence of an email that he sent to one of his news editors that would prove the most significant. It said simply: 'Do his phone.' Those three words helped to undermine his case that he knew nothing about phone hacking, which he claimed was a secret practice confined to a small group of individuals in the newsroom. Four other *News of the World* journalists, chief reporter Neville Thurlbeck, news editors James Weatherup and Greg Miskiw, and reporter Dan Evans, had already pleaded guilty of conspiracy to hack phones along with private investigator Glenn Mulcaire, before the trial began.

The jury found Coulson guilty of conspiracy to hack mobile phones and he was jailed for 18 months. At his sentencing, trial judge Mr Justice Saunders said: 'Mr Coulson has to take the major blame for the shame of phone-hacking . . . He knew about it, he encouraged it when he should have stopped it.'

Thurlbeck and Miskiw were jailed for six months; Weatherup and Mulcaire were both given suspended sentences of four months and six months respectively.

Coulson and his former Royal editor Clive Goodman also faced a retrial on charges of conspiracy to bribe public officials for which the jury could not reach a verdict. Brooks along with the other six defendants were acquitted on all counts.

But although at time of writing the 'trial of the century', as some dubbed it, was over, the line could not yet be drawn under the saga. At least 60 individuals were awaiting trial on various charges, with around 30 more on police bail waiting to hear whether they would be charged. And further police investigations at other newspapers were continuing.

EVERYDAY ETHICS: DAILY DILEMMAS FOR REPORTERS

Until the phone-hacking scandal blew up, mainstream journalists were often sceptical about the value of ethical debate. As media specialist Raymond Snoddy (1993) commented: 'It certainly sets the British press apart from newspapers in the US where on the whole the word "ethics" can be uttered without hoots of derision.' Former *Sun* editor Kelvin MacKenzie, who edited the tabloid between 1981 and 1994, told the Leveson Inquiry: 'I didn't spend too much time pondering the ethics of how a story was gained, nor over-worry about whether to publish or not. If we believed the story to be true and we felt *Sun* readers should know the facts, we published it and we left it to them to decide if we had done the right thing.' According to Ian Richards, similar attitudes predominate in Australia. He writes (2004: x–xi):

> Many journalists give little if any consideration to ethical issues in their daily work. As a result, approaches to ethical dilemmas are often determined by individual decisions based on such immediate considerations as what was done last time, what a colleague suggests, what the editor wants, and what it is considered possible to get away with.

There were a number of reasons for this scepticism. Many journalists are profoundly idealistic, concerned about ethical issues and determined to improve standards. Yet the dominant attitude in the mainstream press prioritises 'getting the story' and the demands of the deadline above all else. Ethical and political concerns are secondary, if they are ever considered at all. Andrew Marr sums up this view when he suggests that the phrase 'responsible journalism' should be shunned (2004: 5): 'Responsible to whom? The state? Never. To "the people"? But which people, and of what views? To the readers? It is vanity to think you know them. Responsible, then, to some general belief in truth and accuracy? Well, that would be nice.' Linked to this attitude usually is the belief that the best way to learn reporting is 'on the job'. Practical training is tolerated, but theoretical studies are generally thought a waste of time.

More importantly, many journalists (in particular young ones) are deeply sceptical about the power they have as individuals to improve media standards. Newspapers seem too committed to entrenched routines and mythologies, too prone to stereotyping and crude sensationalising, too closely tied to the political establishment and to the rigours of surviving in a market-led economy. Most newspaper operations are hierarchically organised with power to those (usually white men) at the top. Many lower down the pecking order often see themselves as impotent (and largely dispensable) cogs in a much larger machine. There is much talk of press freedom, but little of journalists' freedom to influence the organisation for which they work.

Adding to this ethical malaise are the theatrical, unreal elements at the heart of the current debate. Major controversies developed during the 1990s over invasions of the privacy of celebrities, randy royals and sports personalities. Yet these issues confront only a relative minority of journalists for a small part of their time. Far more significant political issues, such as the impact of advertisers, or the role of the vast military/industrial complex on the coverage of wars, are marginalised. As John Wadham, former director of human rights group Liberty, stressed: 'The press has been guilty of blatant intrusion into the private lives of citizens but it is not the worst offender. Our government has developed an almost obsessive desire to gather and control more and more data on its citizens and we need legislation to curb its excesses' (see www.liberty-human-rights-org.uk/news/press-releases/liberty-reaction-culture-media-sport-committee-report-privacy-media).

THE ETHICAL TENSIONS IN THE INDUSTRY: THE FREE PRESS AND MARKET FORCES

Mainstream journalists' scepticism over standards is, in part, a consequence of the ethical contradictions within the newspaper industry. Its central position as a largely monopolistic industry in a profit-oriented economic system means business and entertainment priorities dominate. News becomes, above all, a commodity to be sold. Yet journalists' rhetoric promotes notions of the public interest, the right to know and the free press, which are often in conflict with the priorities of the marketplace. Moreover, while journalists stress the importance of 'objectivity' and 'truth' (news being a mirror of reality), these notions conflict with the actual production of bias, myth and state propaganda by the press.

Journalists' widespread scepticism about ethics is strange, given the importance of the job's moral and political dimensions. All journalists talk of news 'values'. Moreover, representations of good and bad, the just and the unjust/criminal, predominate in the media (Cohen 1980). Read any red-top tabloid and you will see stories about 'evil' rapists, 'monsters' who attack old ladies, 'wicked' mums who lead their children into prostitution. When Moors murderer Myra Hindley died in November 2002, Fleet Street almost in unison condemned her as 'evil'.

The 1991 Gulf conflict carried this reporting genre to its extreme with representations of President George Bush as 'good, pacific and heroic' engaged in a personal battle with President Saddam Hussein of Iraq, the 'evil, bully, Butcher, new Hitler of Baghdad'. During the Nato attacks on Serbia in 1999, President Slobodan Milosevic was also demonised as 'evil' and a 'new Hitler'. And in the run-up to the US/UK invasion of Iraq in 2003 and during the conflict, Saddam Hussein was predictably represented in the mainstream press as a 'monster' and 'global threat', allegedly with weapons of mass destruction (though they, predictably, turned out to be non-existent). Jostein Gripsrud (1992) relates this moralising dimension of newspapers to the emotional excesses of the nineteenth-century morality play. Today it is the press (and mass media in general) that provides moral tales, stories that give lessons in, and define what is, good and bad, normal and abnormal.

The notion of standards is also central to any concept of professionalism. This concept emerged in the latter half of the nineteenth century as the radical, dissident, partisan, working-class-based newspapers collapsed following the ending of the Stamp Tax in 1855 and mainstream newspapers becoming integrated into the market-led economy (Conboy 2002: 66–86; Curran and Seaton 2003: 10–37). Linked to this process of professionalisation came the stress on concepts such as objectivity, neutrality, fairness, accuracy and the separation of fact from opinion (Kovach and Rosenstiel 2003). The concern of unions and management since the Second World War to promote journalism training has been closely tied to notions of standards and professionalism.

THE POLITICS OF EVERYDAY JOURNALISM: STARVATION VERSUS SURVIVAL?

Many journalists challenge such notions as professionalism, objectivity and the free press, and stress the mainstream media's function as one of social reproduction in the interests of dominant groups and classes. Other critics highlight the complex influence economic structures and political contexts have on journalists' routines, values and meaning (Golding and Murdock 2000). As Brian McNair (2003: 33) comments: 'News is never a mere recording or reporting of the world "out there" but a synthetic, value-laden account which carries within it dominant assumptions and ideas of the society within which it is produced.' According to the investigative reporter John Pilger:

> Many journalists become very defensive when you suggest to them that they are anything but impartial and objective. The problem with these words 'impartiality' and 'objectivity' is that they have lost their dictionary meaning. 'Impartiality' and 'objectivity' now mean the establishment point of view.
>
> (Barsamian 2002: 5)

Journalists critical of dominant mythologies choose, for political and ethical reasons, either to work critically within mainstream media or for an 'alternative' outlet such as a leftist or gay newspaper, trade union or environmental campaigning publication. Valerie Alia comments (2004: 43): 'Ethical practice need not always mean a choice between starvation and survival, though it may sometimes mean a choice between basic economic survival and wealth – and, in the worst of times, between life and death.'

ETHICS AND TRAINING: INSTILLING GOOD PRACTICE

While the Leveson Inquiry was washing the industry's dirty linen in the most public way imaginable, its chairman requested further information from the industry on 'how ethics are taught and promulgated amongst journalists'. In fact Lord Justice Leveson asked 12 specific questions about training covering culture, practices, ethics, standards and the public interest. Having given evidence to the hearings, the National Council for the Training of Journalists (NCTJ) decided to take the opportunity to re-evaluate how ethics was taught by its accredited training centres.

Although it acknowledged that many of the universities, colleges and commercial trainers that delivered its courses were incorporating ethical considerations into their programmes, an independent report that it commissioned had found that this was 'patchy, random and implicit'. So at the same time as the Leveson Report was published, the NCTJ unveiled a new structure for its diploma – the qualification for trainee journalists that most editors use as a benchmark when appointing new staff. The new diploma includes an ethics module as part of its core structure (NCTJ 2012b). The module sets out to ensure that trainee journalists can:

- recognise where ethical issues may arise in their day-to-day work
- understand how their work impacts on people's lives
- understand how their actions and work can reflect on the integrity and standing of their employer
- recognise that rights will bring responsibilities
- demonstrate how to carry out challenging journalism in a legal, ethical and responsible manner.

SOME EVERYDAY ETHICAL DILEMMAS

Beyond these general observations, let us identify some everyday ethical issues that can confront journalists.

- Should journalists ever lie or use deceit in the pursuit of a story?
- Should they ever edit a direct quote?
- Is it legitimate to tape a conversation and not inform the interviewee of this?
- Should journalists accept freebies? Should they do so only on certain conditions? Are there any significantly different ethical issues in being offered a book for review, a free ticket to review a play and a free trip to the Seychelles for a travel feature?
- Which special considerations should journalists have when interviewing children?
- Is chequebook journalism (paying sources) justified? (Phil Hall, the editor of *News of the World*, said in November 1996 that for almost 10 per cent of stories, subjects were paid.)

- Is it legitimate to invade someone's privacy for a story? Do different standards apply to public figures and members of the general public?

- Is it legitimate ever to break an embargo?

- To what extent does newspaper language reinforce militarist and ageist stereotypes and how can journalists confront these issues?

- What ethical issues are raised by business sponsorship of newspaper editions?

- Are newspaper reports 'dumbing down', focusing too much on celebrities, royals, reality TV spin-offs, sleaze, trivia and sensation? (see Lloyd 2004).

PRINCIPLED OR POINTLESS: CODES OF CONDUCT

Journalists work under many constraints, from proprietors, advertisers, laws and so on. One way in which journalists have regulated their own activities, with the aim of improving ethical standards, is through codes of conduct.

Starting the ball rolling: the NUJ

One of the most enduring is the National Union of Journalists' code, drawn up in the late 1930s (accessible at www.nuj.org.uk). In February 1998, the NUJ agreed to an amendment to the code to outlaw misrepresenting news through digital manipulation of photographs. The new clause prohibits use of manipulated photographs unless they are labelled with an internationally recognised symbol within the image area. The 13-clause code relies on generalised statements of high principle. On one hand, this has clear benefits. As Nigel Harris (1992: 67) argues, detailed sets of regulations foster a 'loophole-seeking attitude of mind'. And Chris Frost, Professor of Journalism at Liverpool John Moores University and chair of the NUJ Ethics Council, comments (2000: 98):

> A short code has the advantage of being easier for journalists to remember and use. They are able to measure directly their performance against the principles contained in the code and quickly realise when they are straying from the straight and narrow.

On the other hand, the code incorporates principles broken every day all over the country by NUJ members. What is the point of having them if they are not backed up by any penalties? As Bill Norris (2000: 325) argues:

> Every story is different and every reporter is driven by the compulsion to get the story and get it first. To imagine that he or she is going to consult the union's code of ethics while struggling to meet a deadline is to live in cloud-cuckoo land.

Attempts to impose the code through a disciplinary procedure and, since 1986, an NUJ ethics council have proved difficult, but the union has set up an ethics hotline to advise those taking difficult decisions.

The Editors' Code of Practice

Following stern warnings from the first Calcutt committee that the press should clean up its act or face statutory regulation, the PCC drew up a detailed Code of Practice (accessible at www.pcc.org.uk). Before the PCC announced that it would be closed in the aftermath of the hacking scandal, the code had been amended more than 30 times.

Under the new self-regulatory regime of IPSO (see above), a new editor's code of practice is expected to be drawn up, with input from senior editors and members of the public. Until this happens, journalists are best advised to refer to the PCC's code of practice – adherence to which is written into many journalists' contracts – for guidance.

SEX MATTERS: COMBATING SEXISM

There are no easy answers to the many ethical dilemmas in journalism. Even when people agree on the importance of certain principles (such as anti-sexism, anti-racism, anti-militarism), differences may emerge over strategies for implementing them. While certain attitudes and routines predominate throughout the mainstream media, each newspaper still has its unique culture. What is possible at one will be impossible at another. Thus, in tackling sexism within the industry, there are many strategies available. For instance, once you have secured your first job, you may choose to lie low on ethical issues and wait until you have established your credibility before speaking out.

You may work on ethical or political issues through the NUJ. Your newspaper may routinely carry page three-type images of women and glorify macho images of men. In this context, you may choose to work discreetly, raising issues in discussions with colleagues, using any freedom you have in choosing features and sources to tackle sexist assumptions. Some journalists even opt out of mainstream media for ethical reasons. For them, working in the mainstream involves too many ethical compromises. They may see racist, sexist and class biases as too firmly entrenched. Constant confrontations over these issues can prove both exhausting and counter-productive. In contrast, they may find a culture away from the mainstream press more open to progressive ideas. Wherever you choose to work, a sense of humour and a willingness to subject your own views to searching criticism will always prove invaluable.

The questioning approach

Since ethical debate remains remote from the dominant journalists' culture, simply raising pertinent questions can become an important first step. Many ethical questions stem from the unjust distribution of power in society; they are, at root, political issues. The dominant questions focus on how discrimination and stereotyping – of women, children, elderly people, disabled people and ethnic minority groups – can be reduced. But is there not a danger here of focusing on these groups as victims (of oppression and consequent stereotyping), while the problem groups are really the oppressors – men, adults, the able-bodied, the dominant ethnic groups?

The question of sexism

Attitudes have changed somewhat since 1964, when the *Daily Mail* headlined the story 'British wife wins Nobel Prize' after Dorothy Crowfort Hodgkin became the first British woman to gain the honour. Yet research by the pressure group Women in Journalism (WiJ), published in 1996, revealed a 'pervasive and flexible strand of stereotyping through coverage of women in the news'. Newsrooms tended to be male-dominated and traditional sexist attitudes survived unscathed. WiJ concluded: 'It seems clear that sometimes news desks go on autopilot, trotting out clichés and stereotypes when, in fact, the woman in the story before them is unique.' A later report from WiJ, *Real Women: The Hidden Sex*, in November 1999, highlighted the sexist use of images of women to 'lift' pages (see http://womeninjournalism.co.uk/real-women-the-hidden-sex/).

Most political editors and lobby correspondents remain male. 'So', according to Harriet Harman (2000), 'political news is reported in a way that appeals to and interests men. Issues of particular concern to women are inevitably lower on the agenda. This reinforces the sense among women that politics is a male activity of no relevance to them.' Research has also shown the general bias in news reporting towards male sources (Allan 2004: 119–131). Margareta Melin-Higgins (1997) found that most of the female journalists she interviewed were concerned that the recruitment system was disadvantageous to women in an industry where an 'old-boys network loomed large'.

Concern of feminist critics focuses particularly on the coverage of sport. Women cricketers, footballers and golfers hardly get a look-in. And often when women do feature, their presence is heavily sexualised.

An NUJ survey in 2004 found that more than half the union's gay, lesbian and transexual members had suffered discrimination at work through having promotion refused, being verbally abused or bullied. Women journalists, too, often face ridicule from their male colleagues. Ginny Dougary (author of *Executive Tarts and Other Myths*) was criticised for being an 'ambitious girl reporter' (she was 38) after her revealing profile of Chancellor Norman Lamont was published in *The Times* magazine in September 1994. As Amanda Platell comments on the institutionalised sexism in the press,

> It's about a widespread and inherent belief by some men that women can't cut it, that newspapers are a man's world, that women are only good for one thing – 'features' – and that ritual humiliation is a way of keeping girls in their place.
>
> (Platell 1999: 144)

Try to combat the routine marginalisation of women's voices in the media. Reports and features, where possible, should reflect the gender (as well as the race, age and class) diversity of the society. Editors need to be convinced that women's issues should not be confined to special pages and soft features.

Men and sexism

All these issues 'problematise' women. Instead, let us focus on men (see MacKinnon 2003). To what extent are male roles stereotyped in the press through images glorifying macho firmness, violence, power, militarism, heroism and success? Do not reviewers have a responsibility to challenge such representations in films, plays and books? To what extent does the press encourage men to question their emotional unease, their career obsessions or their traditional roles away from the home and child-rearing? To what extent are men challenged over their responses to sexual violence towards women, or to the sexual harassment of women in the workplace?

To add further complexity to the debate, it can be argued that sexism sometimes works in favour of women. Women foreign correspondents often say the 'invisibility' of women in some cultures helps give them access to places where men would be banned or harassed (see Leslie 1999). Editors are sometimes said to favour women as profile writers since men are considered more likely to open up to a female interviewer.

Man-made language

The marginalisation of women in the press and the glorification of macho or laddish values do not usually come from any deliberate policy. They emerge within a political culture where certain attitudes are routinely adopted and certain questions are routinely eliminated. One area where sexism is most evident is in language. Very often the male bias of language can render women invisible (Spender 1980; Mills 1991). Or it can infantilise them. For instance, when the Labour victory of 1997 was accompanied by a large new influx of women MPs, they were immediately dubbed (in sexist terms) 'Blair's babes'.

As Margaret Doyle stresses (1995: 4–5) in her seminal text on sexist language: 'The struggle for control of language has always been a political and highly charged one.' 'Political correctness' has become a useful label for ridiculing an opposing viewpoint and for discrediting 'the legitimate aspirations of different communities and their desire for a language that includes rather than excludes them'.

Challenging this bias is no easy task. Some newspaper-style books avoid all mention of sexist language issues except in relation to the use of 'Ms', 'Miss' and 'Mrs'. Most newspapers now accept the use of 'Ms' where appropriate and avoid using 'he' when 'he or she' or 'they' (as a singular bisexual pronoun) is more accurate. Phrases such as 'the common man' and 'the man in the street' are also widely avoided. Discussions over style book changes provide opportunities to raise language issues. But style book revisions are often monopolised by an editorial elite. In certain situations, it might be appropriate to work with your colleagues in the NUJ to confront sexist stereotyping in language. To assist such campaigns, the union has drawn up an *Equality Style Guide* suggesting words to be avoided and alternatives.

Even where style books fail to acknowledge these issues, there is often a certain degree of stylistic freedom available to the reporter to use such language.

RACE AND ANTI-RACISM: NOT JUST A BLACK-AND-WHITE ISSUE

It could be argued that the British press is at its worst when engaging in racist, overtly xenophobic rhetoric. Attacks on 'scrounging asylum seekers', 'Arab rats', 'funny Frogs', 'boring Belgians' or 'lazy Irish' are commonplace in the patriotic pops (Searle 1989; Gordon and Rosenberg 1989). In March 2000, for instance, the *Sun* directed its venom at East European 'beggars' and 'gypsy scroungers', yet failed to turn its attention to proprietor Rupert Murdoch, 'who has managed to avoid paying corporation tax in this country for years' (Wheen 2000).

In August 2001, the NUJ chapel at the *Express* and *Star* significantly condemned proprietor Richard Desmond for the newspaper's 'hysterical and racist' campaign against asylum seekers. A report by the European Monitoring Centre on Racism and Xenophobia in May 2002 blamed the British mainstream media for using negative stereotypes of Muslims and portraying asylum seekers as 'terrorists' and 'the enemy within' following the September atrocities in the United States. In 2003, the human rights body Article 19 criticised reporting as 'characterised by the inaccurate and provocative use of language to describe those entering the country to seek asylum. Fifty-one different labels were identified as making reference to individuals seeking refuge in Britain, and included meaningless and derogatory terms such as "illegal refugee" and "asylum cheat"' (Article 19, 2003: 9). And in May 2004, a report by the Commission on British Muslims and Islamophobia blamed the media for promoting anti-Muslim attitudes.

Since racist oppression is historically rooted in Britain's imperial past, is it not inevitable that the press, operating essentially as the propaganda and ideological arm of the dominant economic system, should reflect this? As Simon Cottle argues (1999: 197): 'News values lead to the forefronting of images of ethnic minorities in terms of conflict, drama, controversy, violence and deviance. Such deep-seated qualities of "news" are professionally pursued as a matter of unconscious routine and contribute to a journalist's sense of what makes a "good" story.' Along with institutional racism goes the overt racism of some journalists and media proprietors. In April 2004, Richard Desmond, owner of the *Daily Express*, launched a tirade against Germans whom he accused of being Nazis as he goose-stepped around a boardroom.

Tackling racism

We have seen in Chapter 3 the problems the industry has in achieving a workforce that matches the ethnic mix of the general population. There are no easy answers. As Allan (2004: 168) comments: 'The ways in which racist presuppositions are implicated in the routinized practices of news production, from the news values in operation to "gut instincts" about source credibility, are often difficult to identify let alone reverse.' But there are some useful strategies. Language used uncritically can play a crucial role in perpetuating racism (van Dijk 1991). Thus be wary of using 'black' in a negative context. Should alternatives be found for blackspot (accident site) and blackleg (strike-breaker)? The NUJ has drawn up guidelines for race reporting and for covering racist organisations, which are worth consulting.

Should newspapers ban coverage of racist parties? In 2004, the *Argus* of Brighton banned the far-right British National Party from its pages. Other newspapers argue it is important to expose the BNP's policies and campaign against them – and they note that the disastrous appearance of the party's then leader, Nick Griffin, on BBC's *Question Time* in 2009 was largely seen as a disaster for him. Mainstream journalists certainly need to extend their range of contacts to incorporate ethnic minority groups. The *Washington Post*, for instance, has a diversity committee that reviews the ethnic and racial composition of staff, a correspondent dedicated to race relations issues and a series of informal lunches where staff and the ombudsman meet to discuss the way the paper reports race issues. All newspapers should develop strategies for recruiting, retaining and promoting ethnic minority staff and consider the appointment of race relations specialists. Similarly, journalists need to be far more aware of the major religions of the world and of alternative and ethnic media (such as the *Muslim News*, *Q News*, *Eastern Eye*, *Asian Times*, the *Voice*, *New Nation* and the *Jewish Chronicle*), their different ethical standpoints and their opportunities for offering alternative careers away from mainstream stereotyping – and of the anti-racist campaigns of journals such as *Socialist Worker*, *Searchlight*, *Peace News* and *New Left Review* (Keeble 2001: 71–83).

HANDLING DISABILITY: PEOPLE FIRST?

According to the leading campaigning body, the United Kingdom Disabled People's Council (www.ukdpc.net), the disabled are people with impairments who are discriminated against by society. Government research suggests there are 8.6 million adults with disabilities in Britain (including 23,000 deaf people and those with impaired hearing), meaning that one in five people of working age are disabled. Yet they are too often marginalised, rendered invisible or stereotyped in the press and throughout the media. Scope (www.scope.org.uk), the organisation that fights for equality for people with disabilities, in a survey of press coverage of disabled people, concluded: 'There remains an imbalance between the reality of people's lives, hopes and aspirations and the way they are written about. Too often stereotypes are used and false assumptions indulged' (see http://www.holdthefrontpage.co.uk/2007/news/charity-s-attack-on-press-coverage/).

Covering people with disabilities poses a number of ethical issues for journalists that have been highlighted in a campaign 'People First' by the NUJ and the Campaign for Press and Broadcasting Freedom (with leaflets available for partially sighted people, in braille and on tape). The campaign suggests that, as a reporter, you should never assume that your audience is able-bodied. When advertising events (in listings, entertainment reviews, travel and eating out features), newspapers have a responsibility to identify the provision for access by disabled people. Similarly, traditional news values which marginalise the concerns of people with disabilities and confine them to specialist columns and publications need to be challenged.

The campaign also raises some other pertinent questions: how often are the voices of disabled people represented in the press by 'able-bodied' experts? How much is coverage of disabled people over-sentimentalised? Too often, stereotypes of disability promote the idea that charity can solve their 'problems', while marginalising the view that political and economic changes are needed to end the discrimination they confront. Similarly, disabled people are often associated with being courageous, tragic victims, eternally cheerful, grateful, pathetic and asexual. How often is it recognised they may be black or lesbian or gay?

Language

As a number of style books point out, it is better to refer to 'disabled people' rather than 'the disabled', which depersonalises them and focuses entirely on their disability. Words such as 'cripple', 'deaf and dumb' and 'abnormal' should be avoided. Negative words and phrases should not be linked with disabilities, as in 'lame duck', 'blind stupidity' and 'deaf to reason'. 'Physically challenged' is not generally accepted as a substitute for 'disabled'. Use 'wheelchair user' but not 'wheelchair bound'.

CENSORSHIP AND SELF-CENSORSHIP

It might seem strange to journalists on a small weekly to raise the issue of censorship. The problem at their newspaper might not be censorship, but the opposite: finding enough material to fill the next edition. Proprietorial interference may be non-existent. As for the advertisers, they might take up more space than is ideal – but that's reality in a market-driven economy, isn't it? Yet, for all journalists, censorship issues are relevant. At the most basic level, the dominant news values prioritise certain sources and perspectives and marginalise or eliminate others. In a way, isn't that a form of censorship?

The impact of advertisers

The impact of advertisers on the press is enormous. Occasionally they will put pressure on editors to highlight favourable stories and downgrade or remove others. Freesheets, entirely dependent on advertisers, are particularly vulnerable to this. As Donald Trelford (2000), former editor of the *Observer*, commented: 'There are certainly some parts of newspapers, usually in consumer areas such as travel, motoring and property where the choice of subject and the editorial treatment dance to a tune set by the advertisement department.' But in general, the pressure is far more subtle. Within the general economic environment, advertisers promote the values of materialism and consumerism as well as a conservative respect for the *status quo.*

Curran and Seaton (2003: 29–37) argue that the emergence of an advertisement-based newspaper industry in the late nineteenth century helped stifle the development of a radical press. Even as late as 1964, the Labour-backing *Daily Herald* closed with a readership far larger than that of *The Times* and *Financial Times* combined. It had crucially failed to win the support of the advertisers.

The impact of proprietorial intervention: the Maxwell factor

The film *Citizen Kane* captured all the mystique and romance that surround the media mogul in the cultural history of the West. Men like the American media tycoon William Randolph Hearst, on whom Kane was based, and Northcliffe, Beaverbrook, Rothermere, Rowland, Murdoch and Maxwell have cultivated images that have made them seem almost larger-than-life: eccentric, egocentric, super-powerful, super-rich. There are many accounts of these proprietors interfering in the day-to-day operations of their newspapers.

Editorials have been written or rewritten, layouts have been altered. Partisan politics (largely right-wing and belligerent during crises and wars) have been promoted. Favoured journalists have risen through the ranks; others have been sacked or pressurised into leaving. The now-disgraced former proprietor of the *Telegraph*s, Lord

Black, would write critically to the letters columns of his newspapers if he objected to a certain line. Newspapers end up being not public watchdogs, but press lords' poodles (Leapman 1983; Bower 1988; Shawcross 1992). Fleet Street's history is often portrayed as a fascinating saga revolving around these figures (Wintour 1990).

Most serious has been the cumulative impact of these devout defenders of the free press on narrowing the consensus in British newspapers. Given the links between the major media throughout the UK, censorship has seriously distorted news values, even in the provinces.

In particular, the integration of the media barons' empires into the world of international finance and industry has given rise to a host of potential no-go areas for newspapers. Understandably, newspaper proprietors are reluctant to have reporters probing into their more murky activities. *Mirror* owner Robert Maxwell managed to keep the scandal of his pension fund rip-off secret during his lifetime through a mixture of intimidation, a merciless use of the courts and libel laws and exploiting journalists' desire for the quiet life (Greenslade 1992; Davies 1995).

Moreover, media moguls inevitably have promoted their own financial interests through their newspapers. Tiny Rowland's *Observer* campaigned against the Al Fayed family following their purchase of Harrods. Maxwell constantly publicised himself and his many 'charitable' and political activities. Murdoch has promoted his television, publishing and internet interests through his many outlets, and has opposed the BBC at every opportunity.

All the same, there is a danger of exaggerating the power of the proprietors. All have been, or are, colourful personalities. But virtually every industry today is led at local, national and international levels by a small group of companies. Media moguls are merely the newspaper manifestations of this trend: typical monopoly holders within advanced capitalism. Stressing their power serves to boost their egos while exonerating journalists from some of their worst excesses.

CHAPTER 5

Standing the story up

Reporting basics

GO AND FIND SOMETHING OUT

Of all the many pieces of advice and guidance given to journalism students at the University of Kent by industry professionals in the past five years, one simple sentence stands out. In one of our regular masterclass sessions, Allan Little, a BBC special correspondent, was urging undergraduate students not to get too hung up on the fancy digital bells and whistles that they have access to. 'Technology is driving change really fast', he told them. 'And in all that it's easy to forget the core purpose. The core purpose is this: go and find something out.'

Go and find something out. There are no five better words to describe what newspaper journalism is ultimately for, and the reporter is the individual that really makes this happen. But where to start? Even the smallest 'patch' – the community of people assigned to a particular reporter for them to cover – might contain many hundreds of people. So how do you set to work discovering what's going on? Where do these stories all come from?

SOURCING THE NEWS: CULTIVATING CONTACTS

At the heart of journalism lies the source. Becoming a journalist to a great extent means developing and cultivating contact with people who are going to be able to provide information or authoritative views that your readers will care about. It's very rare indeed to have a story that doesn't require 'standing up' with the input of third parties.

Yet media research suggests journalists use a remarkably limited range of sources (McQuail 1992: 112–59; Manning 2001: 139). The components of the hierarchy will differ from newspaper to newspaper. Television soap stars and showbiz celebrities feature far more in the national tabloids than in the broadsheets, for instance, yet there exists a remarkable consensus over news values and sourcing routines throughout the mainstream press. Some sources will be prominent, others marginalised or generally covered in a negative way. Moreover, this consensus over news sourcing is reinforced by the growing centralisation and secrecy of government and the increasing consensus between the three major political parties.

Gans (1979) suggested that the relationship between reporter and source was like a tango in which 'sources usually lead'. Then there is the number of sources used. O'Neill and O'Connor (2008) studied nearly 3,000 news stories in four west Yorkshire newspapers over a period of one month. In 76 per cent of cases they found that just one source was quoted. In the same year, Nick Davies published *Flat Earth News* (Davies 2008a), which set out to show how journalism's 'tendency to recycle ignorance is far worse than it was'.

He commissioned research from Cardiff University in which more than 2,000 UK newspaper stories were analysed from the four quality dailies (*The Times*, the *Daily Telegraph*, the *Guardian*, the *Independent*) and the *Daily Mail*. For each story, researchers tried to trace the origins of their 'facts', and discovered that only 12 per cent of the stories were wholly composed of material researched by reporters. With 8 per cent of the stories, they couldn't be sure. The remaining 80 per cent, they found, were wholly, mainly or partially constructed from second-hand material provided by news agencies and by the public relations industry. When they looked for evidence that the provided 'facts' had been thoroughly checked, they found this was happening in only 12 per cent of the stories.

Davies makes liberal use of the term 'churnalism' – apparently coined by BBC Scotland journalist Waseem Zakir in 2004 – to describe this phenomenon of news as an industrial process whose workers have lost sight of their real purpose: 'No reporter who spends only three hours out of the office in an entire working week can possibly develop enough good leads or build enough good contacts. No reporter who speaks to only 26 people in researching 48 stories can possibly be checking their truth. This is churnalism.' But these numbers come from a single anonymous source (reliance upon which Davies purports to despise) – a reporter on a regional daily newspaper. Former *Guardian* editor Peter Preston (2008) puts another case in his review of Davies's book. He notes that when he finished editing the *Guardian* in 1995, the editorial staff was 260 or so. The 2008 figure (excluding internet-only staffing) was 430. *The Times* had increased its staff of journalists by 100 in a decade to about 450. Similarly, the *Telegraph*'s newsroom is better staffed than its old one.

> Fewer people? No: that's wrong. And more space to fill? Actually, the same Cardiff calculators claim that *The Guardian* only carries 20 UK stories a day, and *The Times* 24. From staffs of 400-plus, that doesn't sound exactly overstretched.

Further context can be added by the Journalists at Work survey commissioned by the National Council for the Training of Journalists (see Chapter 1), which also looked at productivity, asking its respondents how many stories they typically worked on during a day. Half of all respondents worked on fewer than four stories a day, with a small minority (6 per cent, presumably mainly those in management roles) saying they worked on none; nearly a quarter (24 per cent) one to two stories; and a fifth (20 per cent) three or four stories. The median number of stories worked on per day is three, the mean is eight, though again the mean value is skewed upwards by a small number of high values.

Yet, though Davies's approach might be questionable (particularly in its treatment of Press Association copy as being equivalent to public relations press releases), his central theme does hold some resonance throughout the industry. One effect of the concentration of ownership has been that remote managers place far more emphasis on productivity than the family-run businesses of old ever did. This undoubtedly feeds down to editors and the reporters who work for them. It will be down to these reporters – the editors of the future – to find a way to ensure the sources and contacts they use are robust and diverse enough to fulfil journalism's civic purpose.

WHERE SOURCES COME FROM

Diary and off-diary stories

All journalism organisations worth their salt have a newsroom diary. Usually looked after by the news editor, it's the place where a record is kept of upcoming events – press conferences, court hearings, performances, sports fixtures, anniversaries, election dates, etc. – that are public knowledge. And from this font of public knowledge springs the diary story. By definition it is not going to be exclusive. But it affords the reporter the opportunity to plan their coverage in advance. Doing the background research. Lining up potential sources. Thinking about possible picture treatments. Planning infographics.

The classic diary story in a regional newspaper's newsroom, for example, is the date in February when district and borough councils meet to discuss and set their spending plans for the next financial year. The business desk of a national newspaper will have a diary that includes dates when FTSE 100 companies are obliged to file their annual reports to the Stock Exchange. The fashion desk will keep notes of when top and upcoming designers are showing their new season's designs, and so on.

Reporters should not rely solely on the newsroom diary. The best practitioners keep their own personal news diary too. This might include more niche events related to your own patch, but is also a good place to remind yourself of follow-up stories. So if a local councillor promises immediate action on something, make a note to call them again in a week or a month's time. Anniversaries of big news events that you have covered are worth noting in the diary too. The 'One/Five/Ten Years On' feature can provide great copy.

The off-diary story is not so straightforward and, therefore, tends to carry greater kudos for the reporter that brings it in. It can come from almost anywhere – a passing remark in a pub, an ill-judged tweet from someone you follow, a strange smell on your way to work, a plume of smoke visible from the office window. Occasionally a reader might even ring in to the newsdesk with a tip-off about something they have heard or seen (which is why you'll see the news editor's blood pressure skyrocket if you allow a phone to ring more than three times). But the best reporters are the ones who can be proactive in bringing in off-diary stories. That means doing what Allan Little suggested: go and find something out. It means keeping in the loop, calling your contacts for a simple 'what's going on' chat, making check calls to emergency services, hospitals, union officials. It means working your sources.

Journalism and the PR industry: best of enemies?

The research for Davies's book led to a paper published in *Journalism Practice* by Cardiff University's Justin Lewis, Andrew Williams and Bob Franklin (2008), which attempted to take a more measured view of the influence the PR industry has on the news agenda. Their conclusions are a 'depressing confirmation . . . that much newspaper content now derives wholly or in substantial part from news agencies or PR materials, while only a small proportion of news articles make little or no use of such material'. It suggests, they say, 'an increasing reliance on pre-packaged material at all levels of British journalism'.

Let's put aside that awkward conflation of the work of news agencies, staffed by independent, professional and highly regarded journalists, with that of PR agencies, whose job and standing among newspaper journalists is 180 degrees opposite. It is undoubtedly true that the PR industry is more powerful and pervasive than ever before. In 1979 just 14 of the country's top 50 companies employed a PR agency. By 1984 this had risen to 49 out of 50. By the turn of the new century even the smallest organisations had started to employ communications experts either directly or indirectly to project a positive image (Balmer 1998).

Not all of these are sinister practitioners of the dark arts, personified by government spin doctor Jo Moore whose notorious email ('It's now a very good day to get out anything we want to bury') was sent to colleagues less than an hour after the second World Trade Center tower had been hit by a hijacked plane in September 2001. What it means in practice is that reporters have to ask themselves some fundamental questions when examining a press release. Is it true? Is there any real news value to it? Is it hiding a deeper, more powerful story? Is it only telling me one side of a story? Who else can I speak to, to give it more balance or credibility? And of course the most important of all: *Cui bono*? Who benefits?

Horror stories abound of journalists failing to do this. In 2011, a company purporting to be a Canadian firm called ApTiquant sent out a press release for a story which it said was based on a survey of 100,000 self-selecting web users who had completed an IQ test. The release said that these IQ results had been matched against the internet browsers used by the survey group, and concluded that those using Microsoft's Internet Explorer were of generally lower intelligence. The *Daily Mail* and the *Daily Telegraph* both ran the story. As did the BBC website, CNN and other high-profile news organisations. The problem? None of it was true. ApTiquant's website had only been created weeks earlier, and was a crude replica of a site belonging to another, entirely reputable company.

Nick Davies unearthed others in *Flat Earth News*, including the 2006 story run by dozens of newspapers and websites across the world about England football fan Paul Hucker, who had insured himself to the tune of £1 million against the emotional trauma of his national team getting knocked out of the World Cup. Again, untrue. A simple Google search revealed that Hucker was a PR agent who was listed as working in the insurance industry, among others.

Social networks as news sources: connecting with the masses

If Facebook were a country, it would be the third most populous on the planet. With 1.15 billion active users (as of March 2013), only India and China have greater numbers of people – and at the current rate it won't be long before it overtakes both of those. We'll look more closely at the impact that social media is having on journalism in Chapter 7. But the sheer amount of personal data that is shared by such a gargantuan user base makes Facebook – and other social networks – an obvious place for journalists to go in search of stories and sources. But it's equally clear that there are pitfalls awaiting the unsuspecting reporter who doesn't think clearly about their strategy for using social networks as a research tool.

First among these is the reporter's own privacy. As we will see in Chapter 7, there is a balance to be struck between having a visible presence – engaging with readers, soliciting responses and promoting your organisation's work – and giving too much away about your private life. Facebook, for example, has a 'Friends lists' feature which allows you to control what level of information is made available to different Facebook users – your close family and friends will be in a list with higher access privileges than your professional contacts. Your readers probably would be on a list with only very restricted information about you. Keeping multiple lists can be a good way of filtering wall posts and news updates from a large number of sources to make them more manageable. In the same way, there are several Twitter-based applications that allow you to group the Twitter accounts that you follow into specific communities or subject areas – making it more realistic to follow large numbers of accounts.

Some journalists feel uncomfortable about sending or accepting Facebook 'friend' requests, or LinkedIn network requests, to and from their sources as a reporter. A political reporter, for example, might feel that accepting a Facebook friend request from a local Labour councillor could compromise their objectivity in the eyes of Conservative or Liberal Democrat readers. For that reason, some journalists prefer to set up an entirely separate Facebook page for their professional life. This has the effect of keeping the professional and the private entirely separate – and allows a friend request to look less like some kind of endorsement. There are other privacy settings that the unwary journalist can fall foul of. Facebook's commercial strategy, for example, means that it likes to put adverts on your pages based on your own Facebook activity – visiting pages and buying items, for example. For the sake of your objectivity as a reporter, make sure your privacy settings are adjusted so that these ads do not appear.

Facebook as a directory of potential sources is a pretty compelling notion. Its 30 million UK users are likely to include a good proportion of your readers. That's where the company's new Graph Search function comes into its own. Described by the company as a 'rolodex of a billion sources', the service allows you to find individual Facebook users based on their interests, employment and location – provided they have made that information publicly visible. So, for example, if you need to find a source for a story about a particular organisation, Graph Search enables you to do that (but beware the pitfalls of 'digital doorstepping' – see Chapter 7).

It could also be valuable as a way of teasing out trends. So, for example, you could use Graph Search to find 'books liked by journalists' or 'songs liked by people from Manchester' across a specified date range, to give you a snapshot of popularity among one particular audience. The creation of 'interest lists' on Facebook is another way to use the power of the network to take the cultural temperature, by creating custom feeds of postings by users based on defined topics of interest.

One word of caution when fishing in the social networks pool for stories and sources: not everybody uses them. And of those who do use them, not everybody uses them equally (there's more discussion on the law of 'inequality of participation' in Chapter 7). In other words, don't assume that what you find on Facebook is a genuine reflection of the wider world.

The contacts book: a prized possession

One of the most treasured possessions of any journalist is their contacts book, in which sources' phone and mobile numbers, addresses, email and website details are listed. David Conley (2002: 164) describes the contacts books as the reporter's bible: 'It is a reporter's lifeline to the community; a bridge to news stories'. The diligent reporter takes a note of every single number they ever use, however obscure the contact might be. It's surprising how often a minor source from a small story can later be useful for something much meatier.

Today's contact book is perhaps more likely to be kept and maintained in electronic format. But a few words of caution are necessary here. For many reporters, the handiest place to keep an electronic record might be on their office computer, perhaps using a program like Microsoft Outlook. But transferring these records, when you change job for example, is often not as straightforward as you might think. And bear in mind that if your contract ends abruptly (it happens), you might not get the chance to collect 'your' data.

Another handy place is the contacts section of your mobile or smartphone. Again, you should always keep security in mind. Such devices are easily lost or stolen. Have you kept an automatic backup (using a service such as Apple's iCloud)? Have you password-protected your contacts from prying eyes? There are other electronic solutions too. Online contact book services such as Plaxo (www.plaxo. com) or eGroovyContacts (www.egroovycontacts.com) are free to use, but caution is advised here too. If you can't access the web (it happens) they are not a lot of use. And online services come and go. If they go out of business, your contacts might disappear overnight. A professional disaster.

Which brings us back to the good old-fashioned paper book. The best reporters painstakingly cross-index entries (so a local MP might be filed under the letter of their surname, the letter M for MP, and the letter C for Conservative Party, etc.) and make regular photocopies of the pages in case the original gets lost. Reporters investigating particularly sensitive issues (national security, spying, the arms or drugs trade, financial fraud) tend to keep details of important, exclusive sources separate from their main contacts book. They might use encryption to protect this data, or even just commit the details to memory. Police have been known to raid the homes and computers of journalists involved in sensitive areas, and revelations by former US National Security Agency analyst Edward Snowden in 2013 indicated mass surveillance of internet communications by the intelligence agencies of the USA and UK – thus every step should be taken to preserve the anonymity of such contacts.

PHONE VERSUS EMAIL: A ONE-SIDED CONTEST

Many students setting out on the first steps of their training in journalism are surprisingly reticent when it comes to picking up a telephone to make or answer a call. This seems counterintuitive, given that most of this particular generation have grown up with a mobile phone in their pocket or handbag. Yet ask them to make contact with a source, and their primary instinct is often to send an email or a text message. There are a number of reasons why this instinct has to be challenged. The first is immediacy. The phone is simply quicker. At the Centre for Journalism we occasionally have source races: one student attempts to get a quote for a story using only a phone; another by using only email. The winner almost every time is the phone user. Emails are often ignored altogether, or can be put off until later.

A ringing phone is harder to walk away from. And if your phone call goes unanswered, just move on immediately to your next target.

The second is the element of surprise. With an email approach, you have to give away some basic details about the story you are working on. This gives your source time to consider their response – which might well be to attempt to put you off the scent. By composing an email message, your source is very unlikely to let something slip that they didn't mean to say. With a phone call you have more chance of catching them off guard.

The third is flexibility. A telephone conversation can flow in the way that an email exchange can't. You can follow up your original questions, press for more detail or challenge answers. With an email exchange, this could take hours.

The fourth is the quality of the quotes. The vast majority of people don't speak in perfectly constructed sentences or soundbites. The transcript of a phone conversation or a face-to-face interview will sound far more natural – and therefore carry more credibility with your audience – than an email exchange with the same person.

Of course, if you are making these calls, you will need to be able to make an accurate note of what the other person says – which also goes some way towards explaining the reticence of new students. True, it's fairly easy to record phone conversations these days – there are plenty of smartphone apps available, and recording devices for landlines are inexpensive – but that opens up a legal and ethical can of worms.

It is not illegal to record a conversation for your own use (under the Regulation of Investigatory Powers Act 2000), but if you are planning to publish or broadcast any of the conversation, you would have to inform the other party in advance of the call, unless there is a reason of public interest why this might not be appropriate. So by far the best way of recording your conversation is to use shorthand, which, as we will see in the following section, remains more than ever one of the reporter's most fundamental skills.

THE IMPORTANCE OF SHORTHAND: A MODERN NECESSITY

Shorthand is arguably the single most important skill a modern journalist can learn. And what's more, it's even more valuable now, in the digital era, than it was before the first electric typewriter was invented. As with much in journalism, it boils down to speed.

Let's put two journalists side by side at an important press conference, whose main subject speaks for 10 minutes. One has 100 words per minute shorthand. The other has a digital audio recorder. Which of them will be first to post the key quotes, accurately, on their website or Twitter feed? The note-taker will win every time, because he or she doesn't have to rewind back through the audio file to find the right bit to write down. They can simply flip to the relevant page in their notebook and away they go.

There are good legal reasons, too, why shorthand is essential. The courts in England and Wales do not allow recording equipment while hearings are under way, and neither do some councils, so without shorthand a reporter simply couldn't write accurately about the case. Furthermore, as we have seen in the previous section, if a story becomes legally contentious, you may not be allowed to produce an audio recording of a telephone conversation in court as evidence. You will always be able to produce your shorthand notes – as long as they are legible and substantial. Finally, the ability to write shorthand confers a useful degree of professionalism on any reporter. Your sources will take you more seriously when they see you taking Teeline notes.

All of which explains why shorthand is a core component of the National Council for the Training of Journalists (NCTJ) diploma – in 2013 the NCTJ produced a video in which frontline reporters explained its importance – and why the vast majority of mainstream news organisations insist on 100 wpm shorthand, in some cases even for students wanting to do work placements with them.

IMMEDIACY AND NEWSINESS: PRIMARY AND SECONDARY SOURCES

Sourcing conventions help provide the news dimension of many stories. An issue may be long-running, but new information or opinion from a source will bring it into the news. The state of the national economy is an issue of constant concern. The Chancellor of the Exchequer warning of further 'inevitable' bankruptcies over the next year becomes news, just as the release of a report by a group of Cambridge University economists highlighting the plight of small businesses is newsworthy.

Some theoreticians divide journalism sources into two major categories: primary definers and secondary definers (Aitchison 1988). At the local level, councils, Members of Parliament and of the European Parliament, courts, police, fire brigade, ambulance service, hospitals, local industries and their representative bodies, trade unions and trades councils, and the local football and cricket clubs are defined as primary sources. Schools and colleges, churches, local clubs and societies, army, naval and air force bases, local branches of national pressure groups and charities are secondary sources. Other contacts in this category in rural areas may include village postal workers, publicans and hotel keepers, agricultural merchants, livestock auctioneers, countryside rangers or wardens. In coastal areas they include coastguards, harbour officials and lifeboat station personnel.

The stress on primary and secondary sources reflects the hierarchical assumptions underpinning conventional news values. Significantly, the definition marginalises a wide range of sources loosely termed 'alternative'. These might include representatives of religions other than Christian, ethnic minority groups, members and representatives of political parties other than the dominant three; feminist, lesbian and gay groups; pacifist, environmental and animal rights campaigning groups.

Journalists' sourcing routines tend to reflect the distribution of power in society: representatives of leading institutions and public services dominate, having easier access to the press. Representatives of 'alternative' bodies are consequently largely absent from the local and national press, which reinforces their relative powerlessness in society. Women and ethnic minorities are marginalised by the political system, just as they are marginalised in the press (Allan 2004: 119–70).

PROFESSIONAL ROUTINES: INSTITUTIONALISED SOURCING

Sources are often defined according to their relation to journalistic routines of news gathering. Thus, on-diary routine sources on a national newspaper will include the government, Parliament and select committees, the major political parties, the Confederation of British Industry (CBI), Church of England Synod meetings, prominent court cases, press conferences arranged by prominent bodies such as campaigning groups (e.g. Amnesty International), companies, the police, trade unions and charities.

At the same time, a system of 'calls' institutionalises this sourcing routine. The news editor, news desk member or specialist correspondent will contact by phone at regular intervals (as often as every hour) such bodies as the police, ambulance service or fire brigade to check on any breaking news. Such bodies are increasingly providing taped news updates, so local reporters will often 'call in' for a chat to help personalise the contacts.

Similarly, a local reporter will meet at regular intervals locally important people (such as vicars, business leaders, prominent campaigners and trade unionists) for informal chats, from which news angles may or may not emerge. Bob Franklin and David Murphy (1991), in a study of 865 stories in the local press, found local and regional government, voluntary organisations, the courts, police and business accounted for 66.7 per cent of the total. Such groups and individuals are described as on-diary sources, since details of their activities are listed in diaries, traditionally in book form supplemented by dated files, but increasingly now on screens.

REPRESENTATION: WHO CARRIES THE WEIGHT?

Linked to journalists' sourcing routines are certain notions about representation. A source, other than a celebrity in their own right, tends to assume a significance for a journalist when they can be shown representing not just their personal views, but those of a larger group or institution. Thus, usually accompanying the name of a source is their title or other description. Ms X may have believed Tony Blair ought to have resigned from the premiership over the illegal invasion of Iraq in 2003. But her views will mostly be of interest to a journalist if they can be shown to represent a larger group such as the local Labour Party, of which she is the treasurer.

Journalists are sometimes tempted, because of sourcing conventions, to invent a title when none exists. During the early 1980s, when the Greenham Common women were protesting outside the US airbase near Newbury, journalists often represented the relatively few people they quoted as 'spokeswomen' for the camp. In fact, the women sought to challenge traditional hierarchical notions of representation. Each woman spoke for herself. The group did not have representatives as such. By describing them as 'spokeswomen', journalists were failing to understand or respect an important political dimension of their struggle.

CREDIBILITY AND AUTHORITY: HARDENING THE STORY

Accompanying journalists' sourcing routines, and linked closely to views about representation, are notions relating to credibility and authority. The views of party politicians tend to be prominent in the national and local press because they are seen as having been democratically elected to represent certain widely held views. Along with that representative element goes authority and credibility.

Ms A may have very strong views about abortion. But on what authority does she speak and how credible are those views? Those short titles or descriptive phrases accompanying the name of the person quoted will answer that kind of question. Ms B might be described as having 'launched a campaign against abortion at her parish church'. This immediately identifies her commitment to the cause and her authority as a source. Similarly, when someone is described as 'an eye-witness to a road accident', their authority is established (though they may be mistaken and must not be seen to allocate blame). Inclusion of such details immediately 'hardens' the story. In the same way, the presence of 'ordinary people' (without any title or representative function) 'softens' the story.

BIAS AND NEUTRALITY: BALANCING THE STORY

Reporters use sources to distance themselves from the issues explored. Rather than express their views on a subject, reporters use sources to present a range of views over which they can appear to remain objective and neutral. The title or descriptive phrase accompanying the quoted person clarifies the bias. But this is the bias of the source, not the reporter. Sourcing routines also reinforce notions of balance. A campaigning group accuses a local authority of inadequate provision.

It is the responsibility of the reporter to contact the authority to balance the report with their response to the allegations. But such a process eliminates a range of other views. Indeed, many media theorists question journalists' notion of balance, and locate the construction of the notion of objectivity historically (Schudson 1978; Tumber 1999: 285–392). Considering the highly selective process of news gathering, the financial, political and legal pressures on newspapers, and the absence of any neutral language, they argue that objectivity is unattainable and a myth.

EXPERTS

Experts are often sought by journalists as sources. They play a crucial role as authority and independence are associated with their views. Journalists often use experts such as academics, think-tank members and pressure group campaigners (sometimes even fellow reporters) to provide background information, which is not necessarily used in copy, and ideas for future, more newsy contacts. But they can also use them more subtly to add extra weight to a view they (or their proprietors) wish to promote. The *Sun*, for instance, often quotes psychiatric 'experts' on the alleged insanity or otherwise of people in the news (such as 'madman' Saddam Hussein and Tony Benn of the 'loony left'). But experts can be wrong.

PROFESSIONAL STATUS

Journalists enjoying close contact with people at the top of the sourcing hierarchy tend to have a high professional status. On a national broadsheet, the parliamentary correspondent enjoys high status, just as a posting as a foreign correspondent (with all the contacts with presidents and other VIPs it involves) ranks as a journalistic top job. At the local level, the journalist whose everyday contacts are councillors enjoys high status; the journalist dealing with the Women's Institute reports or the children's page is usually low on the professional ladder. As Bob Franklin (1994: 19–20) comments:

> Journalists are conscious of being sited in a finely graduated hierarchy which influences their access to politicians . . . Acknowledging and exploiting to the full the advantages which their position in the hierarchy bestows is a precondition for journalistic advancement.

Journalists' reputations can be built on the ability to extract good quotes from sources. 'Did you get any good quotes?' is often asked by colleagues when they return from an assignment. Professionalism as a construct generally implies a certain objectivity and neutrality towards sources. In reality this is difficult to maintain. Many argue that journalists often get too close to their sources. Journalists' regular contact with elite sources means they are often accused of disseminating a range of conflicting elite perspectives. Journalists tend to be part of the same social milieu as the political elite, they speak the same language and often come from a similar social and educational background.

PRESS POACHERS: THE MEDIA AS A SOURCE

All journalists spend considerable time each day going through the media. They have to know what is going on, what is being covered and, more particularly, what is not being covered. They become 'media junkies'. As US broadcaster Dan Rather warns: 'Be careful. Journalism is more addictive than crack cocaine.' (Burrell 2004) Whatever your feelings about the heavies or the popular press, it is important to read (in hard copy or on the internet) as many papers as possible. You may despise the red-tops for their blatant racism and sexism, but they have the power to set the national news agenda and need to be watched. Similarly, you may find the heavies tedious and long-winded, but (while their omissions are often more significant than their content) they carry masses of important national and international news which might spark ideas for follow-ups.

Don't concentrate all the time on the nationals and your mainstream locals. They are just one (though the most powerful) ingredient of a diverse range of journals available. Look at the lively ethnic press (*New Nation*, the *Voice*, the *Caribbean Times*, *Asian Times*, *Eastern Eye*), the religious press (*Q News*, the *Jewish Chronicle*, *Methodist Recorder*, the *Catholic Herald*, *Church Times*), the left, social movement press (*Tribune*, *Socialist Worker*, *Morning Star*, the *News Line*, *Lobster*, *Peace News*) and the gay media (*Gay Times*). It is worth looking at these alternative publications (in hard copy or online) for a number of reasons.

- They often carry articles by specialists, raising issues and perspectives marginalised in the mainstream press and that can be followed up.
- The listings of meetings, conferences, demonstrations, vigils and visits to the UK by potentially newsworthy figures can be followed up.
- Journalists on them are useful contacts and their journals could provide outlets for freelance work (if your contract permits).
- They can prove rewarding places for student work attachments.

Newspapers published outside England and easily accessible via the internet, such as the *Scotsman*, the *Herald* (Glasgow) and *Irish Independent*, should not be ignored. The *International New York Times* (formerly the *International Herald Tribune*), carrying a compilation of reports from the *New York Times* and sold in 135 countries, is essential reading for anyone wanting an insight into elite opinion in the United States. For more dissident perspectives, see *Mother Jones* (www.motherjones. com), www.tomdispatch.com, www.counterpunch.org and *Z Magazine* (www. zcommunications.org/zmag). Most journalists will either speak, or want to speak, a second language and follow the press in that country. Comparisons with foreign newspapers on elements such as editorial bias, content, use of pictures, design and questions of taste can all throw up interesting insights into the UK press.

As a reporter, your own newspaper can provide a rich source for news. Letters to the editor can provide the basis for a follow-up (but should not be converted into interviews), while an advert asking for sources on a particular topic can often produce good results. For instance, *The Sunday Times* has a regular column in which readers ask former chief inspector of schools Sir Chris Woodhead his view on their education problems. One column (22 September 2013) included a question from a worried mother whose daughter's A-level results apparently included one freakishly low mark. An alert section editor passed the story on to reporter Sian Griffiths, who made the requisite calls and turned it into a front-page news story about exam mis-marking headlined 'Fateful paper dashes Oxford dream'.

CUTTINGS: KEEPING UP WITH HISTORY

Most newspapers have their own cuttings library (now mostly online), which is a crucial resource. Journalists also create their own filing system. For a freelance without regular access to a cuttings library, it is an essential. Most journalists, especially freelances, develop specialist areas, and tidy filing of cuttings, magazines, internet printouts, photocopies, notes from books and internet sources, and jottings of feature ideas can prove enormously useful and time-saving during research. But reporters can get details and quotes wrong. Unless cuttings are treated critically, there are dangers of reporters repeating each other's errors. In its March 1992 report, the Press Complaints Commission criticised journalists' over-reliance on cuttings: 'Cuttings are an essential part of newspaper research but too many journalists now seem to act in the belief that to copy from 10 old stories is better than to write a new one with confirmation by proper fresh enquiry.'

Following up items in the news is a constant feature of newspaper coverage. As controversy emerges in the national press, a local paper will 'do a follow-up' carrying the views of relevant local people and providing local information on the issue. Similarly, a report in a local paper, say about an education controversy considered sufficiently sensational, unusual or with wider implications, will be followed up by a national with new sources and new information.

Newspapers routinely record selected radio and television news programmes, build up stories from interviews on these media and perhaps do follow-ups on others. A great deal of the coverage in the Sunday heavies comprises follow-ups on the main stories of the previous week. On Mondays (following the relatively dead news day of Sunday), nationals are in the habit of carrying reports on interviews given by prominent politicians on weekend television and radio programmes (McNair 2000: 100–102). Investigations by Sunday newspapers can be followed up by the national press. Sometimes a reporter will 'lift' a story from another newspaper, rewording it slightly, perhaps adding only a few original pars.

Columnists on both national and local newspapers often base some comment on an event or opinion highlighted in a national. Journalists will also habitually use other reporters as sources. Sometimes a specialist in the field will be contacted by other reporters new to the area for contacts and ideas. It is a matter for the individual journalist how far they cooperate with such requests. The issue is complicated when the questions come from a friend or colleague on a competing paper. Some journalists say no to all such requests. Others supply basic information and contacts, and keep to themselves special sources gained only after considerable effort.

Journalists are often used as 'hard sources' for media-related stories. And in foreign stories, the views of local journalists are often considered informed and authoritative.

REINFORCING THE CONSENSUS

As competition between newspapers intensifies, pressures to conform to the dominant news agenda grow. Rather than feeling confident and pursuing their own news values, newspapers constantly look over their shoulder to see what their competitors are up to. Consequently, the range of views and experiences expressed narrows, and newspapers become increasingly predictable (Herman and Chomsky 1994). The media's over-reliance on the media also promotes a passive form of journalism.

Investigative reporter Tom Bower (1992) has spoken of the 'culture of inactivity'. Reporting becomes a reactive activity, requiring little imagination and courage. Office-based, it becomes a glorified form of clerking. Former editor of the *Independent* and the BBC's former political editor Andrew Marr agrees. He writes (2004: 98):

> . . . stories about ordinary life in Britain are being pushed aside by stories that are easier to write in the office – stories about new products, new consumer trends – and about brief celebrities. A deadly idleness has gripped journalism.

Disinformation dangers

Histories of the secret services show the extent to which newspapers are used for misinformation, disinformation and propaganda purposes (Bloch and Fitzgerald 1983: 134–41; Pilger 1998: 492–9; Keeble 2004). As Roy Greenslade, former editor of the *Mirror*, commented: 'Most tabloid newspapers – or even newspapers in general – are playthings of MI5. You are the recipient of the sting' (quoted in Milne 1995: 262). For instance, a contrived story alleging various atrocities by a certain anti-US movement may be planted in a foreign newspaper, perhaps financially backed by the secret service. It may then be picked up by the major international news agencies. That first report provides the authenticity and credibility for the ensuing coverage.

Combating censorship

Sometimes journalists send copy unsuitable for their own newspaper to another outlet (say *Private Eye*). Media in one country can be used to break through censorship regulations in another. In 1986, the Israeli anti-nuclear campaigner Mordechai Vanunu used *The Sunday Times* to reveal details of the secret Israeli nuclear programme that lay hidden behind a rigid censorship regime. (He was later captured by Mossad, the Israeli secret service, sentenced to 18 years in jail and only finally released in 2004. Then, in November 2004, Vanunu was re-arrested by Israeli soldiers 'on suspicion of passing classified information to unauthorised parties'.)

During the lead up to the Gulf conflict of 1991, after details of the 'allied' strategy were stolen from a Defence Ministry official's car, a D-Notice banning newspapers from reporting the event was issued by a special government committee. News of it leaked to an Irish paper. Thus it became public knowledge and London-based papers went ahead and carried their own reports. National security did not appear to be seriously damaged.

ON AND OFF THE RECORD: THE CURRENCY OF TRUST

The basis for any good contact between a journalist and source is trust. When that trust is broken, the source is lost. Most news is given on the record. A press release is issued; someone talks to you on the telephone, or face to face, or by email; you report a conference. All this information and opinion you gain on the record.

An off-the-record briefing is completely different. Information is given but, because of its sensitive nature, it should not be reported. If the off-the-record undertaking is broken, trust is lost. At the same time, such an undertaking leaves the journalist free to try to acquire the same information from another source who might be prepared to go on the record. Public meetings are on the record. If someone says during one, 'Oh, incidentally, that comment was off the record', you have no obligation to treat it as such. Similarly, private conversations are on the record unless established otherwise. Though it is tempting for students to submit copy to their lecturers drawn from off-the-record interviews (with the interviewee presuming no publication is intended), they will be indulging in an unreal form of journalism – which should be avoided.

Probably the most famous off-the-record source was 'Deep Throat', who fed information to the *Washington Post*'s Watergate duo, Carl Bernstein and Bob Woodward. In April 2003, their papers (which included 250 spiral notebooks, tapes, transcripts, scribbled jottings, internal memos and notes on discussions with editor Ben Bradlee) were sold for $5 million (£3.2 million). But, significantly, 'Deep Throat' remained secret. Then, in May 2005, Mark Felt, former assistant director of the FBI, revealed himself in an article in *Vanity Fair* to be the original 'Deep Throat'. But was there more than one 'Deep Throat'? The debate goes on . . .

Unattributable or background comments: sources close to the palace

Halfway between off-the-record and on-the-record comments lie unattributed or 'for background only' comments. Reports can carry these quotes but attribution is deliberately vague to conceal identities. During the 1992 saga of the Prince Charles–Princess Diana split, such phrases as 'sources close to Buckingham Palace' or 'sources close to the Princess' were prominent. By 2004, the use of anonymous, unattributed quotes was running out of control on Fleet Street, dominating the reporting of politics, journalism and 'human interest' gossip around celebrities. For instance, most of the over-hyped spat between the Blairites and Brownites in the government was reported via unattributed sources such as 'a senior Labour backbencher', 'a senior cabinet minister', 'a veteran Labour MP' and so on. In December 2004, coverage of the 'nannygate' scandal surrounding the affair of home secretary David Blunkett was saturated in quotes from 'friends of Kimberly Quinn', 'the Blunkett camp', 'informed sources' and so on. How can the reader trust that all of this is not simply made up? Similarly, much of the reporting of the 'war on terror' since the 9/11 atrocities in the United States has been based on anonymous (and competing) intelligence sources.

The reasons for all this secret sourcing are clear. As newspaper sales dip, editors' demands for exclusives feed the process, blurring the distinctions between fact and fiction. At the same time, the secret state has grown, with intelligence moving to the centre of power in Blair's cabal. As the power of the intelligence services advances (both in Britain and the USA), and Fleet Street hacks' links to the spooks deepen, so the culture of anonymous sourcing will spread.

Yet off-the-record, unattributed briefings potentially can benefit both source and journalist. The reporter can be informed on complicated details of which they may have no specialist knowledge and will learn of the source's bias. Sources often speak more openly at these meetings. And for the source, the briefing provides an opportunity to impress their perspective on the journalist. As Rodney Tiffen comments:

> Covert manoeuvres are commonly deployed to shape interpretations of public events, of success and failure, of intentions and portents. In complex or technical developments, briefings can highlight the 'essential meaning' of the details, to provide what journalists will welcome as a short-cut through the maze, but by doing so affording the briefer convenient scope for convenient selectivity. The meaning of opinion polls and some election results, of economic reports and indicators, of international agreements often pass into the news after the filters of briefings.
>
> (Tiffen 1989: 112)

Dominant groups, individuals and institutions have the power and access to the press to organise such briefings and the chance to attempt to influence the news agenda. Weaker groups and individuals have much-reduced opportunities for such manoeuvring. Campaigning journalist John Pilger (1996) offered this advice: 'Beware all background briefings, especially from politicians. Indeed, try to avoid, where possible, all contact with politicians. That way you find out more about them.'

FACT, FICTION OR FACTION? WHEN A LIE BECOMES THE TRUTH

Unattributed and anonymous comments can also blur the distinction between fact and fiction. For instance, the *Sunday Express* ran an exclusive in 2000 headlined 'Isabella: the blonde tipped to be Prince William's wife'. It was pure fantasy. It started with a jokey story in the December 1999 *Tatler* about Isabella Anstruther-Gough-Calthorpe, 'tipped to be a fairytale princess'. *GQ* and the Edinburgh University student paper followed up the prediction. By the time the *Sunday Express* carried it, a jokey 'tip' had become a 'fact' supported by anonymous sources: 'Royal insiders say the 19-year-old blonde has formed a close bond' with the Prince, it reported. In fact, Isabella and the Prince had never met.

Similarly, most national newspapers faithfully reproduced the warnings by Prime Minister Tony Blair and the intelligence services about Iraq's weapons of mass destruction (WMD) before the invasion in 2003: no such weapons existed.

KEEPING IT CONFIDENTIAL: PROTECTING KEY SOURCES

There are other occasions when journalists will legitimately want to protect the identity of a source, as in the following examples.

- Given the high unemployment figures, people are reluctant to criticise their employer for fear of the consequences. Nurses may not dare to speak out on the impact of financial cutbacks on the health service – some who have spoken to the press have been intimidated. Teachers may be reluctant to put their name to protests over the radical education changes of recent years.
- Interviews with people who talk about intimate aspects of their lives, such as sexual problems, illnesses and domestic violence, often carry a fictitious name. Relevant places, ages and descriptions are either changed or omitted. The newspaper ought to indicate this style at the start of the article. If it is left until the end, the reader may feel cheated.
- When an investigative journalist has acquired information without disclosing their professional identity, the newspaper does not then normally carry the sources' names. For instance, Esther Oxford (1992) explored the world of

rent-a-male agencies that provide women with escort and sexual services. She contacted the agencies and described her experiences. Clearly, she could not take her notebook. All quotes and place descriptions had to be written from memory. But the paper left until the end the short disclaimer: 'The names of the men have been changed.'

LEAKING IN THE PUBLIC INTEREST

According to Rodney Tiffen (1989: 96–7), a leak can be broadly defined as the unauthorised release of confidential information. However, this umbrella covers many variations – that release may come from a dissident but also from someone in authority seeking political advantage; that confidentiality ranges from the very sensitive to the innocuous, from what was intended to be forever secret to the about-to-be announced.

Leaks and the use of anonymous quotations by compliant journalists can be manipulated to launch 'trial balloons' or to 'fly a kite'. Government officials may release proposals anonymously through leaks to test responses. If an outcry emerges, the government can denounce the plans they drew up, though only reporters pledged to confidentiality will know this. Leaking can lead to institutionalised lying.

Leaks by brave whistleblowers can also be used to expose corruption – as auditor Paul van Buitenen found at the European Commission in 1998 (but he was sacked for his pains). In 2003, Katharine Gun was sacked from the top-secret government eavesdropping centre, GCHQ, after leaking to the *Observer* details of a US 'dirty tricks' operation to win UN Security Council support for the use of force in Iraq. The government controversially dropped her prosecution under the Official Secrets Act in February 2004 after it was put under pressure to reveal the legal advice that took Britain to war. Gun (2004) went on to help form the Truth Telling Coalition to support those engaged in public-spirited whistleblowing.

Leaks can also be used to discredit opponents. Histories of the Harold Wilson administration (Leigh 1989; Dorril and Ramsay 1991; Porter 1992: 210–27) show the extent to which secret service leaks to sympathetic journalists in national newspapers were used systematically to smear the prime minister and some of his close associates before his unexpected resignation in 1976. Because of the aura and glamour surrounding secrecy, information drawn from such sources can be overvalued, with an accompanying devaluation of information drawn from other sources. The desire to gain exclusives through privileged access to secret sources can lead to a critical dependency between source and journalist. The lure of the 'exposé' can also make a reporter more reluctant to explore alternative perspectives.

The launch of the WikiLeaks website in 2006 turned the debate about leaking into an international issue. There's a fuller discussion of this in Chapter 10. And in the UK, the scandal of parliamentary expenses may never have been exposed quite so spectacularly in 2009 had it not been for a leak – albeit in exchange for some serious money – by a disgruntled insider who felt that the public interest had not been served with so much detail being 'redacted' from records requested under the Freedom of Information Act.

EDITORS' GUIDELINES

Following the publication of the Hutton Report into the events surrounding the alleged suicide of arms expert Dr David Kelly, on 30 January 2004 the *Guardian*'s editor, Alan Rusbridger, issued new guidelines to staff on the use of anonymous sources. BBC *Today*'s Andrew Gilligan had sparked a massive controversy (and ultimately the Hutton inquiry) after using a secret source to back a claim the government had 'sexed up' WMD allegations against Iraq against the wishes of the intelligence services. Not surprisingly, Rusbridger advised staff to use anonymous sources sparingly and to avoid using unattributed pejorative quotes – unless in exceptional circumstances. Yet on that day alone, in the *Guardian* there were 31 cases of the use of anonymous quotes. In the United States, attribution rules tend to be tighter than in Britain. Guidelines provided by the editor of the *Cincinnati Enquirer* to his staff included the following (Greenslade 1995).

- The identities of all sources must be verified and confidentially disclosed to the editor.
- Misleading information about the true identity of a source may not be used in a story, even to 'throw off' suspicion.
- Information supplied by an unnamed source should be verified independently or confirmed by at least one other source. An exception may be made for individuals who are sole possessors of the information or whose integrity is unassailable.
- The motive of an anonymous source should be fully examined to prevent [journalists] being used unwittingly to grind someone's axe.
- Information attributed to an anonymous source must be factual and important to the story. Peripheral information or a 'good quote' aren't good enough reasons for anonymity.

HOAXES: THERE BUT FOR THE GRACE OF GOD . . .

Journalists' over-reliance on unattributed sources can make them vulnerable to hoaxes. Some hoaxers, such as Rocky Ryan and Joe Flynn, make a profession of fooling the press. On 17 May 1992, the *Independent on Sunday* revealed that 'one of Fleet Street's most prolific sources of information', particularly about the aviation business, was a conman. He claimed to be a highly placed source within British Airways. He was nothing of the sort. One of the most famous hoaxes of all was when *The Sunday Times* printed what it believed to be the diaries of Adolf Hitler. This was only after they were sold to *Stern* magazine by three German businessmen for £2.5 million, and Sir Hugh Trevor-Roper, author of *The Last Days of Hitler*, said that he believed they were genuine.

After the US/UK forces occupied Baghdad, in April 2003, the warmongering *Daily Telegraph* ran a report claiming that George Galloway MP was in the secret pay of Iraqi President Saddam Hussein. But the documents discovered in the Iraqi foreign ministry on which the claims were based were all forgeries and so, on 2 December 2004, the *Telegraph* was forced to pay damages of £150,000. The newspaper had rushed into print and taken no steps to verify the claims. And in November 1996, Stuart Higgins, editor of the *Sun*, fell victim to an elaborate hoax involving a video that supposedly showed Princess Diana cavorting with a lover. In May 2004, the *News of the World* paid model Lucie Clark £6,000 to reveal that *EastEnders* actor Chris Parker was a 'superstud'. It was all lies, promoted by the actor (see *Private Eye* 12–25 November 2004: 3).

Local papers are by no means no-go areas for hoaxes. New sources, particularly in controversial areas, should be routinely checked and their views and information corroborated by another reliable source. Journalists should be particularly wary of hoaxes just before 1 April.

The world wide web also makes the art of hoaxing considerably more accessible and tempting. For instance, Kaycee Nicole narrated her brave struggle against leukaemia in a widely reported daily online diary for two years. In 2001, it was revealed to be an elaborate hoax by 40-year-old Kansas housewife Debbie Swenson. In 2011, a widely followed blog purporting to have been written by a gay woman in Syria describing the growing unrest in her country was exposed as a hoax by an American man living in Scotland.

Journalists should also be on their guard for fake emails, tweets and Facebook pages – all of which are relatively easy to make appear convincing.

LOBBY CHANGES: THE ULTIMATE INSIDERS' CLUB

One of the most famous institutional manifestations of the briefings session is the parliamentary lobby. Every day on which the House sits, Downing Street gives two briefings to accredited lobby correspondents, of whom there are around 210 men and 30 women (out of 312 correspondents based at Westminster). The first meeting is at Downing Street at 11 am; the second in the House of Commons at 4 pm. In addition there are Friday briefings for Sunday journalists, a briefing on Thursdays by the Leader of the House on the following week's business and a weekly

Opposition briefing. There are also briefings by ministers or their mouthpieces to groups and individual lobby journalists.

The lobby was launched in 1884 – just five years before the first Official Secrets Act became law. All lobby members were pledged to secrecy, never attaching a name to any information. Instead, phrases such as 'sources close to Downing Street' or 'government sources' or 'members close to the Labour leadership' were used. As Michael Cockerell, Peter Hennessy and David Walker say in their study of the lobby:

> The paradox was that as Britain was moving towards a democracy by extending the vote to men of all classes (women still had 40 years to wait) mechanisms were being created to frustrate popular participation in government and to control, channel and even manufacture the political news.
>
> (Cockerell *et al.* 1984: 34)

Over the years, the lobby has raised enormous passions, pro and anti (see also Chapter 13). For a number of years while Bernard Ingham was Margaret Thatcher's press secretary, until October 1991, three high-minded newspapers – the newly launched *Independent*, the *Guardian* and the *Scotsman* – together with *The Economist*, withdrew from the system. Ingham used the lobby for blatant disinformation campaigns on political issues and against individuals both inside and outside the cabinet (Harris 1990). His immediate successors did not adopt similar tactics, and the decision by Christopher Meyer, John Major's press secretary, in 1995 to allow off-the-record briefings to be attributed to Downing Street marked the beginning of changes which were to transform the operations of the lobby.

Finally, Alastair Campbell, Tony Blair's press secretary (or spin doctor in the jargon), on 13 March 2000, ruled that he could be named as the source of his briefings (rather than the 'prime minister's official spokesman'). During the previous month, the twice daily briefings for journalists were put on the Downing Street website, allowing anyone to gain access to the discussions just hours after they had finished.

What are we to make of these seemingly radical changes? Was a new spirit of openness racing through the corridors of Westminster? Or was it more an attempt by the government to bypass media 'spin' and communicate directly with the electorate via the internet? Soon after Campbell's announcement, Fleet Street heavies printed verbatim versions of a lobby briefing and Fleet Street began mourning the death of the lobby. 'If local reporters in Darlington can access the Downing Street line, what's so special about being in the lobby?' asked one lobby correspondent (McCann 2000).

Most of the important business is still being conducted behind the scenes in informal, bilateral contacts between journalist and politicians. As former lobby correspondent Andrew Pierce (2000) commented: 'Ministers, their special advisers and senior Labour Party workers are still being wined by political journalists in fashionable restaurants within the shadow of Big Ben.' In April 2004, proposals to introduce daily televised lobby briefings, in a review of government communications chaired by Bob Phillis, chief executive of Guardian Media Group, were welcomed by No. 10. But there were concerns that such briefings would be dominated by journalists sympathetic to the Blair clique, with few opportunities for provincial reporters.

But the plans were never realised – even though a working group was set up in 2009 after a House of Lords committee had recommended the move to daily televised briefings.

CONTROVERSIES OVER CONFIDENTIALITY: DEFENDERS OF THE PRINCIPLE

Non-attributable briefings are vital to the journalist on many occasions, and the Code of Conduct (Clause 7) of the National Union of Journalists (NUJ) calls for journalists to preserve the confidentiality of sources. Yet the journalists' right to this confidentiality is not enshrined in law (as it is in most other European countries and the USA), and under Section 10 of the Contempt of Court Act 1981 courts have the right to demand that journalists reveal sources if 'disclosure is necessary in the interests of justice or national security or for the prevention of disorder or crime'. As legal expert Dan Tench (2004) advises: 'A journalist about to publish an article which reveals official secrets would be prudent to consider destroying all material which would lead to the identity of a source.'

In 1984, the *Guardian*, under pressure from the courts, handed over material which helped reveal that civil servant Sarah Tisdall had leaked information about the delivery of cruise missiles to Greenham Common. Tisdall was jailed. Then Jeremy Warner, of the *Independent*, was ordered in 1988 to disclose the source of a story on insider dealings and shady takeover bids in the City. He refused, and was ordered to pay a £20,000 fine and £100,000 costs in the High Court. His paper paid up for him and received good publicity in the process. He later commented: 'I quite enjoyed it, to tell you the truth. It's a great thing for a young journalist to become a *cause célèbre*.' (Lashmar 2000)

In 1990, William Goodwin, a trainee reporter on a weekly trade magazine, the *Engineer*, was fined £5,000 for contempt after refusing to hand over notes of a phone call which revealed confidential information about a computer company's financial affairs. He thus escaped becoming the fourth journalist in the twentieth century in Britain to be jailed for contempt. In 1963, Brendon Mulholland, a *Daily Mail* reporter, and Reginald Foster, of the *Daily Sketch*, were sentenced to six and three months, respectively, in Brixton jail for refusing to disclose sources in the Vassall spy tribunal, presided over by Viscount Radcliffe. In 1971, Bernard Falk refused to tell the court whether one of two Provisional IRA men he interviewed for the BBC was a man subsequently charged with membership, and went to prison for his pains.

However, pressure on the government to enshrine in law a journalist's right to protect the identity of sources intensified after Goodwin took his case to the European Commission of Human Rights. In September 1993, the commission ruled that Goodwin's case was admissible and called on the government to negotiate a 'friendly settlement'. Three years later, the European Court of Human Rights ruled that Goodwin had been right to protect his sources. But still the Lord Chancellor refused to change the Contempt of Court Act.

Earlier, Dani Garavelli, then chief reporter for the *Journal*, Newcastle, was threatened under the contempt law for refusing to name a source after being subpoenaed to give evidence to a police disciplinary hearing. Her 20-month battle ended in 1996 when a High Court ruled against the attempt by two chief constables to jail her. A judge's decision to throw out a Norfolk Police application for the *Eastern Daily Press* and reporter Adrian Galvin, who was backed by the NUJ, to name a source was lauded as a 'landmark judgement' by editor Peter Franzen. Judge Michael Hyman ruled: 'There is undoubtedly a very formidable interest in a journalist being able to protect his sources.'

In September 1999, Ed Moloney, northern editor of the Dublin-based *Sunday Tribune*, faced imprisonment for refusing to hand over notes (dating back 10 years) of interviews with a loyalist accused of murdering a Catholic solicitor. Moloney's ordeal ended the following month when Belfast High Court overturned an order by Antrim Crown Court that he should hand over the notes. Then, in April 2000, the *Express* overturned a High Court ruling that it had to reveal the source from which financial reporter Rachel Baird obtained confidential documents about a High Court action involving Sir Elton John.

The Prevention of Terrorism Act has also been used by the state in an attempt to intimidate journalists into revealing confidential sources. In 1988 the BBC was forced to hand over footage of the mobbing of two soldiers who ran into a funeral procession in Belfast. Following a *Dispatches* programme, 'The Committee', by independent company Box Productions in 1991, alleging collusion between loyalist death squads and members of the security forces in Northern Ireland, Channel 4 was committed for contempt for refusing to reveal its source and fined £75,000.

Subsequently a researcher on the programme, Ben Hamilton, was charged with perjury by the Royal Ulster Constabulary. Though the charge was suddenly dropped in November 1992, the police retained all items seized from Hamilton. They included his personal computer, all disks, newspaper cuttings and notes of telephone calls and meetings with other journalists interested in the programme. Another journalist involved in the programme received death threats and was forced to leave his home and live incognito at a secret address.

Changes to the terrorism legislation also provoked serious concerns among civil rights campaigners and journalists. The Terrorism Act 2000 extended the definition of terrorism to mean: 'The use of serious violence against persons or property or the threat to use such violence, to intimidate or coerce a government, the public or any section of the public for political, religious or ideological ends.' Journalists covering direct action could be caught by Clause 18, carrying a five-year sentence, for failure to report information received professionally that could lead to a terrorist act (Zobel 2000). Moreover, the Anti-terrorism, Crime and Security Act 2001 gave the police alarming new powers of surveillance (see www.liberty-human-rights. org.uk).

CHAPTER 6

Learning the language of news

The language of news today is the product of centuries of linguistic evolution. It is not a natural form of writing. It is a particular discourse with its own rhythms, tones, words and phrases (van Dijk 1988; Fowler 1991). It has to be learnt. As with all evolutionary systems, it is also subject to continual change. And with the advent of the digital age, new conventions and technical innovations are producing such a significant impact on the way news is written and consumed that its very essence is under review.

Take, for example, that most basic measure of journalism output: the story. In the traditional print version of a newspaper, the delineation of stories on a page in the news section is obvious. Each one has a headline, most have a byline, many have a picture and all are clearly laid out on the page to be read as discrete, individual elements – each edited and cut to fit exactly the space available, and each representing the facts as the reporter understood them at the moment when they filed the story in time for the newspaper be sent to print.

Newspaper designers will often talk about 'upping the story count': including more items on each page to give readers better perceived value for money. And news editors will still shout 'What's the story?' to the reporter arriving in the office from meeting a source. But once that package moves online, subtle and fundamental changes begin to occur. There is no longer a limit to how long the story has to be. Online users may not spend very long deciding whether to read beyond the first sentence, but once they do pick a story, they're more likely to read to the end than their print counterparts (Poynter Institute 2007).

Neither does the story have to be a snapshot whose contents are dictated by the logistics of getting a bundle of paper onto a van to reach the far-flung corners of the country. It can be continually updated – several times an hour if necessary – with fresh facts, augmented, corrected and 're-nosed' with new, more timely information at the top. It is also now, crucially, an interactive thing. The hyperlink means that the story is no longer a self-contained item. By adding links to a story, the reporter allows the reader to transport themselves with a simple mouse-click to an entirely different part of the web – where they can read or watch, for example, background details, source data, additional information or an opposing set of views.

And what about another fundamental question: who is this being written for? Where the newspaper story is purely designed to catch the eye of the page-turning reader, its online counterpart first has to make itself known to the web's search engines – since it's through these algorithmic filters that many human readers arrive at any given web page. All of these factors are having their own impact on the language of news, and we'll look at them individually in more depth later in this chapter. But before that, let's briefly get back, like John Major's cabinet, to basics.

THE ANGLE: WHICH WAY TO APPROACH THE STORY?

A single story can have many angles. Finding the right one is a skill that comes with practice and an understanding of your particular audience. Let's say a story breaks that there's been a helicopter crash in the north-east of Britain. There are a number of angles we might take in investigating this: the number of casualties and fatalities is the most obvious, along with the identities of the victims. The cause of the crash is another – was it pilot error, mechanical failure or terrorist attack? Did the weather have a bearing? If so, did meteorologists issue warnings? The purpose of the flight might lead to another angle: if it was carrying oil workers to a rig, say, there might be implications for production.

The selection of one or more of these angles for our story will depend entirely on the audience we are writing for. So our headlines might be:

- North-eastern regional daily: Scunthorpe rugby club team-mates injured in chopper crash.
- National daily: Safety fears after third Puma helicopter crashes on take-off.
- Insurance industry business website: Underwriters steel themselves for bad news on air policies.
- North-eastern regional weekly: Helicopter coma victim was due to wed this weekend.
- National Sunday tabloid: Scandal of snoozing air-traffic controllers as chopper headed for disaster.

Each of these is perfectly valid as an angle for the specific readership. Each will contain similar basic detail of the crash, but will amplify and prioritise different aspects of it. As an aside, the Aberdeen *Press and Journal* had long been the subject of an apocryphal story that its headline the day after the Titanic went down in 1912 was 'North-east man lost at sea'. It set the record straight 100 years later, by reprinting the original page showing the headline: 'Mid Atlantic Disaster: Titanic sunk by iceberg. 1683 lives lost, 675 saved' (Linford 2012b).

Finally, each of our stories will have a different top line.

THE TOP LINE: THE PUB TEST

I keep six honest serving men
(they taught me all I knew)
Their names are What and Why and When
And How and Where and Who.
                    (Rudyard Kipling, 1865–1936)

Among the questions that news editors will habitually bark at their young reporters (along with 'Why haven't you filed yet?' and 'Where's my coffee?') is this one: 'What's the top line?' The top line is, simply, the aspect of a story that your readers will find the most interesting at the specific time you write it. For that reason, it goes at the top of the story. Hence the name. It should contain information that's attention-grabbing, new and relevant to your audience – the place you would start the story if you were telling a friend in the pub. But note, too, that the top line changes as the story develops. The aspect that was the most interesting yesterday will no longer be new, and so should not be your top line today.

In a perfect world, the top line will answer all the questions posed by Kipling's six honest serving men: What? Where? When? How? Why? Who? Back to our air crash. Here's one top line:

Five rugby team-mates were injured this morning when the helicopter they were travelling in crash-landed at Scunthorpe Aerodrome in atrocious weather conditions.

Who? Five rugby team-mates

What? Injured

When? This morning

Where? Scunthorpe Aerodrome

Why? Atrocious weather may have been a factor

How? Helicopter crash

Of course, we don't live in a perfect world, and there will be plenty of occasions where the top line would be overloaded if it attempted to answer all six. It will be down to the judgement of reporter and news editor to decide which to choose. Journalists tend to feel most at home with the 'who', 'what', 'where', 'when' and 'how' of events coverage. The 'why' factors (the causal linkages) are often complex – and can be missed out, or handled superficially or stereotypically. Liz Curtis, in studying the coverage of Ireland, comments:

> The British media's emphasis on 'factual' reporting of incidents, concentrating on 'who what where and when' and leaving out background and significance, appears to be objective and straightforward but is, in fact, very misleading. This type of reporting provides the audience with details of age, sex, type of incident, injuries, location and time of day. But such information says nothing about the causes of the incident making violence appear as random as a natural disaster or accident.
>
> (Curtis 1984: 107)

THE MAIN CLAUSE OR 'NUT GRAF'

In our helicopter crash intro above, the story begins with the main clause. It contains all the essential detail for our readers to understand the story. But it won't always be the case that our main clause is the same as our intro. In some cases, the detail of the 'how', 'where' and 'why' would get us too bogged down if we try to get it into the top line. This is often true in 'developing' or 'running' stories, where the key information may already be known to the audience. It can also be true in news features where the reporter has more leeway to use a creative intro – more of which later in this chapter (and see also Chapter 8, which deals with feature writing).

Here's an intro from the *Derby Telegraph* of 14 November 2012, by Robin Johnson – business and finance writer of the year in that year's Regional Press Awards (see Figure 6.1 for full page).

> A LONE employee leaves the Celanese plant on a bridge which once saw 20,000 workers walk home after their shift.
>
> The scene yesterday was in stark contrast to thriving times at the factory which was once Derby's biggest employer.
>
> Today, after almost 100 years, the machines at the Megaloughton Lane plant will fall silent and the final production worker will walk out of the factory gates.

So here we see page layout and text working nicely together. The two intro sentences refer us directly to the pictures, leaving paragraph three as the main clause. The Americans, with their love of obscure jargon, sometimes call this the 'nut graf' – as it's the paragraph that contains the 'kernel' of the story.

Derby Telegraph

WEDNESDAY, NOVEMBER 14, 2012   CAMPAIGNING NEWSPAPER OF THE YEAR 40p

Day the machines fell silent

1920s: Thousands stream home from their jobs at Celanese

2012: The same route and a lonely walk home as the final production shift ends

Last workers leave Celanese Acetate today as city plant closes down after almost 100 years

BY ROBIN JOHNSON

A LONE employee leaves the Celanese plant on a bridge which once saw 20,000 workers walk home after their shift.

The scene yesterday was in stark contrast to thriving times at the factory which was once Derby's biggest employer.

Today, after almost 100 years, the machines at the Megaloughton Lane plant will fall silent and the final production worker will walk out of the factory gates.

It is the end of an era for the company, for Spondon and

most of all, for the generations of people who have worked at the site.

The writing has been on the wall for Celanese ever since April, 2010, when its American owner, Celanese Corpor-

Farewell to Celanese, Pages 2,3,4&5

ation, first announced plans to close the site, which makes acetate tow and flake, used for cigarette filters.

Today, those plans will finally become a reality when the last 130 production staff vacate the factory.

Last night, one employee, Ian Hawley, who has worked there for almost 25 years, said: "Celanese has been a massive part of people's lives. To think that this is finally the end of almost 100 years of production is very sad."

The workers left behind will gradually wind down the plant over the next 18 months, cleaning equipment in readiness for disposal and, ultimately, demolition of the buildings.

Celanese, which is closing the plant due to soaring energy prices, said it was grateful for the "professionalism and dedication" of staff.

REPORTING LOCAL LIFE SINCE 1879   www.thisisderbyshire.co.uk   **WEATHER:** TODAY'S MAX 12C/TOMORROW'S MAX 9C

FIGURE 6.1
Derby Telegraph front page, 14 November 2012

Who?

News often tends to focus on the human angle. Thus, if you were a news agency reporter covering the IRA attack on the Conservative Party conference in 1984, it would have been poor to write: 'The Grand Hotel, Brighton, was rocked today by a Provisional IRA bomb attack during the Conservative Party conference but Mrs Thatcher escaped unhurt.' The focus needed to be on the fate of the prime minister. The angle could not wait until the end of the first sentence: 'Premier Mrs Thatcher narrowly escaped an assassination attempt today after the Provisional IRA bombed the Grand Hotel, Brighton, where she was staying for the annual Conservative Party conference.'

Given the choice between the structural damage to a hotel and the fate of the prime minister, the second provides the better angle.

When?

News is rooted in time, the more up-to-date the better. Thus the 'when' element ('yesterday', 'last night', 'earlier today', 'next week') is crucial in many hard news intros. This emphasis on newsiness is commercially driven. The hotter the news, the more sellable it is. But intros hardly ever *begin* with the basic 'when' words such as 'last night'. Occasionally, when the timing is significant, it should be highlighted, as here from the *Guardian* of 25 October 2004:

> And finally, after 50 matches, 542 days and claims of invincibility, Arsenal have been beaten in the Premiership.

Usually it isn't necessary to be precise over the 'when' in the intro. Do not say: 'Mrs Gandhi, the Indian prime minister, was assassinated by Sikh bodyguards at 2.59 am today.' Sufficient to report 'earlier today'. The precise detail can be added later.

Weeklies often eliminate specific 'when' references, as phrases such as 'last Wednesday' and 'early last week' can reduce the news impact and be confusing for readers who might not read the story on the day of publication.

Where?

Local papers will often include the 'where' element prominently in the intro, as it stresses the local angle. Thus the *Lincolnshire Echo* (20 June 2012) had this as its splash by Mark Williams – 2012's weekly reporter of the year.

> A county councillor has claimed £23,000 in allowances over three years despite attending just 19 council meetings – and living in Cambridgeshire. Now furious residents are calling for Conservative Sara Cliff to quit her seat.

National papers may sometimes delay mention of the 'where' to add an element of vagueness and encourage everyone from all over the country to read on, as here in the *Daily Mail* (23 September 2013):

> A woman referee fled a match in tears after a spectator said she needed 'more testosterone' to do her job.
>
> Shelby Davis, 21, abandoned the under-15s fixture after being told that she 'needed a handbag' and that it was 'a man's game'.

Only in par 4 is the 'where' element ('in Hampshire') revealed. However, as we shall see in the next chapter, the 'where' can be an essential factor in search engine optimisation – if our story is to appear as high as possible in the page rankings of Google and others. So for online stories there is often good reason for putting geographical location within the opening paragraphs. The intro to the online version of the same *Daily Mail* story appears thus in *Mail Online*:

> A female referee was left 'in floods of tears' at a youth football match after a player's father launched a 30-second tirade of sexist abuse at her, telling her to 'get her handbag and go home'.
>
> Shelby Davis, 21, called off the game in response to the sexist comments, made at half-time in a Youth Cup game between the Wyvern Youths and Pirelli Pirates Youth in Southampton.

Most foreign stories carry the 'where' prominently, as here in *The Sunday Times* from a piece by the late Marie Colvin, posthumously garlanded as Foreign Reporter of the Year in 2012, the year she was killed reporting from the Syrian front line:

> They call it the widows' basement. Crammed amid makeshift beds and scattered belongings are frightened women and children trapped in the horror of Homs, the Syrian city shaken by two weeks of relentless bombardment.

SIMPLICITY: MAKING EVERY WORD COUNT

Brevity. That's one of the keys to effective news writing. Ernest Hemingway famously won a bet to prove he could write a story in six words ('For sale: Baby's shoes. Never worn'). And while a news editor might not be impressed if you filed that as a lead for page five, the principle still holds that every word has to count.

'Kiss (keep it short and simple) and tell' could be the journalist's motto. Complex sentences overloaded with long subordinate clauses should be avoided. Use short, precise sentences. As the left-wing novelist and journalist George Orwell advised:

> A scrupulous writer, in every sense he writes, will ask himself at least four questions, thus: 'What am I trying to say? What words will express it? What image or idiom will make it clearer? Is this image fresh enough to have an effect?' And he will probably ask himself two more: 'Could I put it more simply? Have I said anything avoidably ugly?'
>
> (Orwell 1984 [1957]: 151–2)

Many factors lie behind the creation of this concise news language. The arrival of the telegraph and telegram during the nineteenth century put a clear cost on elaborate language. Victorian newspapers were the souls of brevity. In the early nineteenth century, the generic term for a single piece of journalism was 'paragraph', and this necessity to condense was jealously enforced by editors. Contributors to the *Daily Universal Register* (later to become *The Times*) were advised to write paragraphs as 'long essays are seldom read' (Liddle 1999).

With the competition today between advertisers and editorial for space in newspapers, every reported word involves a cost. Economic language helps provide economies in production. Speed is the essence of newspapers. Sentence structure and page design are influenced by the need to help readers move through the newspaper quickly. And online readers are generally 'time poor'. The average reader's daily engagement with a national newspaper website is less than five minutes.

Newspaper and website design also influences language and sentence lengths. Long paragraphs – large, grey blocks of type – discourage readers. So reporters divide stories into bite-size chunks that are easy to read (Fedler 1989: 28). Online, that tends to be even more pronounced. Most major news websites – even those aimed at the more serious end of the market – adopt a style of a single sentence per paragraph for news copy. News reporters use clear, direct English to prioritise the most important facts and to tell the story in the most straightforward manner.

LIVELINESS: MAKING THE PACE

Keith Waterhouse, a newspaperman never short of the right word, had this to say about descriptive language in newspapers:

> Adjectives should not be allowed in newspapers unless they have something to say. An adjective should not raise questions in the reader's mind, it should answer them. Angry informs. Tall invites the question, how tall? The well-worn phrase: 'his expensive tastes ran to fast cars' simply whets the appetite for examples of the expensive tastes and the makes and engine capacity of the fast cars.
>
> (Waterhouse 1981a)

Popular tabloids tend to heighten the sensational, emotional content by adding adjectives and adverbs. Take this intro from the *Sun* (30 September 2013):

> Terrified tourists leapt for their lives into the Thames yesterday after an inferno engulfed an amphibious 'duck' bus.
>
> Kids as young as three were aboard the packed sightseeing craft, which travels London's roads and river, when it erupted in flames.
>
> The skipper beached it on the north bank as families scrambling to escape choking fumes took to its roof and clung off the sides.

The choice of verbs – engulfed, leapt, erupted – helps give the story its drama, as does the noun 'inferno', while the adjectives 'terrified', 'packed' and 'choking' all aim to add impact to the intro. Compare this with the *Guardian*'s more sober approach to the same story:

> Thirty people have been rescued after an amphibious bus caught fire on the river Thames opposite the Houses of Parliament in central London. Firefighters were alerted to the blaze on the London Duck just before midday yesterday and a fireboat was dispatched. Many of the 28 passengers on board jumped into the river to escape the flames and were rescued by police, the fire brigade and a passing boat.

While always remaining true to the style of your publication, be as bright as possible. Try to use active verbs and strong nouns. Take this intro from the *Nottingham & Long Eaton Topper* (22 December 1999): 'Revellers', 'splash out', 'big way', 'snub' and 'celebrations' all carry impact.

> Revellers across Nottingham are all set to splash out on Christmas in a big way – and snub turn of the century celebrations.

QUOTATIONS: KEEPING IT REAL

Quotations are the life force of the news story. They bring direct human impact into what otherwise runs the risk of becoming a dry series of factual statements. They also prove to the reader that we are doing our job as journalists – namely, getting out and talking to the people who are affecting, or being affected by, the stories we have found.

Since a lot of reporting is likely to be based on direct conversations with sources, we then have to decide which parts of those conversations to quote directly, and which will simply inform the factual content of the story. Lively and controversial comments provide material for many intros. But convention has it in British newspapers that hard news stories hardly ever begin with direct quotes. (Such a convention is not universal. In France, hard news stories commonly begin with direct quotes.)

The quotes convention is also broken in the UK from time to time. Here, for instance, is the *Socialist Worker* (20 November 2004) opening its report on the US assault on Fallujah, Iraq:

> 'WE HAVE liberated the city of Fallujah,' crowed General John Abizaid of US Central Command last Sunday.
>
> Fallujah, a city of 300,000 people, had been cut off from the world for six days, and subjected to a massive bombardment and invasion.

Now look at this intro from Joshi Herrmann in the *Evening Standard* (1 November 2012):

> WOMEN are being frozen out of an 'Old Etonian clique' around David Cameron, one of Whitehall's most senior figures has explosively claimed.
>
> Dame Helen Ghosh said the Prime Minister surrounded himself with a male-dominated 'network of friends', including members of the notorious Bullingdon Club at Oxford University, that was 'difficult' for women politicians to penetrate. Her comments, in a talk to students at Cambridge, will fuel controversy about Mr Cameron's leadership style – and claims by some critics that he has a problem dealing with women.

Here the reporter has picked out some of the most incendiary words and phrases from a speech and used them to construct a dramatic intro. The fuller quotations of the sentences containing those words come later in the story to make a strong back-up to the intro, expanding on the opening theme.

Sometimes individual words or short phrases have inverted commas around them without being attributed. This happens usually when colourful/significant words or phrases conveying opinion which the inverted commas imply will be attributed later. Inclusion of the attribution in the intro would overload it. For instance, the *Independent* (23 September 2012) reported:

> A 'final assault' was under way last night to lift the siege of Nairobi's Westgate mall, where terrorists belonging to the Somali militant group al-Shebab had been battling Kenyan security services.

Later on in the report, these highlighted words are attributed to police sources in Kenya.

Attribution: who said what?

Opinion is nearly always attributed clearly if it forms part of the structure of the intro paragraph. Thus *The Times* (26 September 2013) reported:

Cycling and walking schemes risk being starved of funds after the next election as local transport authorities focus on building new roads at the expense of sustainable transport, campaigners warn today.

Without those final three words, the intro would read like an assertion by the reporter.

Concise attribution (such as 'it emerged today' or 'it was reported yesterday') can also give a newsy angle to a report of an event, as in this *Telegraph* intro (20 November 2012):

Makers of the last typewriter to be built in the UK will donate the machine to a museum, it was revealed today, bringing to an end the 130-year history of the machine in Britain.

Clear attribution is particularly important when covering allegations and counter-allegations in court cases. Thus the *Independent*'s Jonathan Brown (2 September 2013) reported:

A *Coronation Street* star raped a young girl as she clutched a teddy bear, telling her that if she told anyone about the abuse 'you'll die and the evil will come over you', a court has been told.

It is legally vital that this report clearly identifies the fact that the allegations were made during an ongoing court hearing. In this case the actor was later cleared of all charges.

Casualty figures following disasters usually need to be clearly attributed, as here from the *Independent*'s report of the Nairobi shopping centre terrorist attack (23 September 2013):

The death toll had climbed to 68, according to Kenya's Red Cross last night, with at least 175 injured and many more bodies feared still to be inside, strewn around among the wreckage of what had been Nairobi's plushest shopping centre.

TENSES: THE PAST, PRESENT AND FUTURE OF NEWS WRITING

News is generally written in the past tense – understandably enough, as we are explaining things that have already happened. That's why quotations are generally attributed as 'he said' or 'she said' within news sections. In features, however, styles can vary. Many interviewers, for example, will use 'he says' throughout an interview feature to bring a greater sense of immediacy to the writing – to put us in the room with the interview subject (see Chapters 8 and 9).

But even within the news pages, there are occasions where tense is important.

A news update on the *Jewish Telegraph* site (www.jta.org) on 26 October 2004 reported:

> The era of infighting within the Russian Jewish community is over, the incoming president of the Russian Jewish Congress said.

Normally with such words as 'warned', 'said', 'declared' or 'criticised' the accompanying clauses follow the rules of reported speech and move back one tense into the past. An intro is one place where these rules are often ignored. This gives an extra sense of urgency to the report. Similarly, headlines and picture captions are usually in the present tense, though they report on past events. The future tense can also be used, as here in the *Financial Times* (24 September 2013):

> Ed Miliband will today announce plans to raise corporation tax if Labour wins the next election, as he seeks to put the party on the side of smaller companies rather than corporations and banks.

BOIL IT DOWN: CUTTING OUT THE WAFFLE

Never use two or three words when one will do. As Matthew Arnold put it succinctly: 'Have something to say and say it as clearly as you can. That is the only secret to style.' (see Humphrys 2004a: xiii) Words and phrases such as 'at the present time' (use 'now'), 'in the region of' ('about'), 'in view of the fact that' ('because') and 'strike action' ('strike') are all cuttable. Prefer short to long words: 'about' rather than 'approximately', 'show' rather than 'demonstrate', 'after' rather than 'following'. Avoid tautology and the over-wordiness of adjectives and adverbs: 'totally destroyed', 'root cause', 'important essential', 'past history', 'invited guest', 'best ever', 'broad daylight', 'close proximity', 'final outcome'.

'Very', 'quite' and 'rather' are meaningless modifiers, eminently cuttable. Beware unnecessary prepositions as in 'divided up', 'circled around', 'fell down', 'raise up', 'revert back' (Humphrys 2004b). Try not to repeat a word in the same sentence, or any striking words close together, unless a specific effect is intended.

The word 'that' can often be cut, as in: 'He admitted that he was guilty of stealing a pen from the office.'

Use language precisely. Don't confuse decimate/destroy, less/fewer, luxurious/luxuriant, affect/effect, it is/its. Beware 'homophones': words pronounced in the same way but differing in meaning or spelling or both – as in bear and bare, sort/sought, diffusing/defusing, censor/censure, rites/rights, yoke/yolk, draws/drawers. Generally try to avoid using 'thing'. It is vague and ugly. (For useful sections on wasteful and commonly misused words and redundancies see Bagnall 1993: 4–11.)

ACTIVE BEATS PASSIVE

'Dog bites man' is more compelling than 'man bitten by dog'. (And of course, as the old adage has it, both are beaten by 'Man bites dog'.) Construct your sentences using active verbs wherever possible. Rather than: 'A meeting will be held by TUC leaders next week to discuss the government's new privatisation strategy' it is better to say: 'TUC leaders will meet to discuss the government's new privatisation strategy next week.'

VARIETIES OF HARD NEWS INTROS

News writing might conform to a formula, but that's not to say that the writing has to feel formulaic. There are plenty of subtly different ways to write a news intro – the most important part of the story. Here are just a few of them.

Clothesline intro

So-called because everything hangs on it. For instance: 'Lady Godiva rode naked through the streets of Coventry today in an attempt to cut taxes.' This contains all of the six basic ingredients: 'who', 'what', 'where', 'when', 'why' and 'how'.

Single element intro

This, the most common of all news intros, picks a single point and sticks with it. So from the *Sun* (19 September 2013):

> The Ministry of Defence has put down 288 military dogs in the past three years, the *Sun* can reveal.

Immediate identification intro

Used where the person concerned is so important or newsworthy that their presence is a main part of the story. Many sports stories, in particular, start this way. Such as this one from the *Sun* (24 September 2013):

> Luis Suarez returns from his 10-game biting ban tomorrow with boss Brendan Rodgers insisting: He's hungrier than ever.

Delayed identification intro

Used where the event is more newsworthy than the identity of the person involved. Here's an example from the *Daily Mail* (27 September 2013):

> An elderly man suffering from dementia yesterday admitted killing his frail wife in a row over their central heating.
>
> Douglas Bailey, 79, snapped and beat his wife of 50 years Hazel, 82, to death with his walking stick in the bedroom of their bungalow last autumn.

Summary intro

This is used when the reporter, faced with a number of competing angles, none of which stands out, settles for a generalised intro. Thus:

> Former US President Jimmy Carter presented a revolutionary package of disarmament proposals to a historic session of the United Nations General Assembly yesterday.

Bullet or staccato intro

This is used where the main point can be covered very briefly. For instance, the *Independent* (10 November 2004) reported:

> Dubliners are in shock: Bewley's is closing the city's two most favourite cafes, for decades iconic fixtures of its social and cultural life.

Personalised intro

Generally news excludes the 'I' of the journalist. It suggests too much subjectivity. The personalised intro subverts that convention and places the 'I' (or 'we') at the centre of the action. The journalist's actions or witnessing of an event carries its own newsworthiness. Thus when *Daily Mirror* journalist Ryan Parry secretly worked as a footman at Buckingham Palace to expose a 'shocking royal security scandal', he reported (19 November 2003):

> The horse-drawn carriage came to a halt outside the Grand Entrance to Buckingham Palace. I jumped off, opened the heavy carriage door and lowered the blue-carpeted steps.
>
> It was a grand occasion for the occupants – they were about to have an audience with Her Majesty the Queen.
>
> Moments earlier I had stood proudly on the rear of the black and gold carriage as hundreds of tourists and royal watchers saw our convoy clatter up The Mall.

Or here is Anthony Lloyd's front page piece in *The Times* (19 September 2013) on an encounter with al-Qaeda fighters in Syria:

A teenage foreign fighter stepped out into the dusty road before us. Turbanned and wild eyed, he stared into our car with a gun in one hand, jabbing a finger in repeated accusation with the other.

Comment intro

News often has the appearance of objectivity when, in fact, it is the journalist commenting. For instance, the *Daily Express* (17 July 2003) reported:

Women graduates will have to spend half their working lives paying off their student debts if Labour ploughs ahead with its hated top-up fees.

Here 'ploughs ahead' and 'hated' convey the newspaper's opposition to the scheme.

The *Socialist Worker* (10 July 2004) had this overtly biased news story:

BLAIR'S FIVE-year plan for education will haunt ordinary parents and school-children for generations to come.

He wants to drive another nail into the coffin of comprehensive education.

His education secretary, Charles Clarke, is announcing the creation of around 500 independent schools with even greater freedom from state control.

Wordplay intro

Puns and wordplay are important in newspapers, particularly those at the popular end of the market. They are playful with language and its many-faceted meanings. Some can be forced. But their contrivance is part of their appeal. A certain wit is needed to construct them, just as they can convey a certain humour (Fiske 1989). Their humour contributes to their overall hedonistic appeal.

Take this example from the *Sun*'s Goals pullout section (25 September 2013), with a playful reference in each of the opening three paragraphs to the pay-off in paragraph four.

Aston Villa were certainly caught short by Spurs in the Capital One Cup last night.

A Jermain Defoe double plus goals from Paulinho and Nacer Chadli sealed it for Andre Villa-Boas' men, who looked the nuts as they eased into the fourth round.

And even when Villa did trouble Tottenham, the visitors had a cheeky way of stopping them.

Niklas Helenius thought he was clear only for defender Jan Vertongen to unintentionally drag him back in the area – by pulling his shorts down.

The plug intro

Newspapers often like to publicise their own investigations in intros, as the *Sunday Telegraph* (9 June 2012) reported:

> DRAMATIC IMAGES from Guantánamo Bay, of shackled men said to be the world's most dangerous prisoners, are revealed by the *Sunday Telegraph* today.

SOME INTRO ERRORS TO AVOID

Questions

Hard news intros do not normally start with questions, just as question marks do not normally occur in hard news headlines. Intros are for informing readers, not interrogating them. Occasionally questions can open features and 'soft' news stories.

The 'There is/was' cliché

Avoid beginning stories 'There was' or 'There is' or 'There will be'. This is dead copy delaying the appearance of the real news. So don't report 'There was a riot in Bow, East London, last night in which four policemen and two youths were injured.' Better to say: 'Two youths and four policemen were injured in riots in Bow, East London, last night.'

Label intros

Label intros are drab sentences showing no news sense. A good intro will do more than say 'a meeting was held', 'a speech was given'. 'Barack Obama, president of the US, gave a long speech at the United Nations in New York yesterday covering issues as diverse as the threat to the rain forests and nuclear disarmament.' A better angle would be more specific: 'President Barack Obama of the US yesterday called on the world community to introduce a 50 per cent arms trade tax to fight poverty in the Third World. In a wide-ranging, 50-minute speech to the United Nations in New York, he said . . .'

Present participles

Intro sentences starting with the present participle are to be avoided: 'Referring to the humanitarian crisis in Kurdistan, Noam Chomsky . . .' Better to say: 'A humanitarian crisis is engulfing Kurdistan, Noam Chomsky warned.'

Unidentified pronouns

Opening with a subordinate clause is particularly poor when there is an unidentified pronoun, as in 'With what his colleagues described as a clarion call to the party, Barack Obama . . .'

Negatives

There is always a way to avoid using negatives. For instance, instead of 'The Foreign Office would today neither confirm nor deny that two British pilots had been released by North Korea', say: 'The North Koreans are reported to have freed two British pilots but the Foreign Office would not comment on the news.'

Numerals

Sentences never begin with numerals. Don't say: '11 people were injured after a bus collided with two stray pigs in Bognor Regis last night.' Instead: 'Eleven people were . . .' One way round the problem is to avoid precise figures and say 'More than . . .' or 'Fewer than . . .' as Rob Waugh of the *Yorkshire Post*, daily reporter of the year in the Regional Press Awards, did (20 February 2012):

Nearly £16,000 was spent on a trip to the US by a chief constable and three other public officials, the *Yorkshire Post* can reveal today.

SOFTENING THE NEWS

As we saw in Chapter 2, the 'hard' news story might be the newspaper industry's stock-in-trade, but there are many other types of news story too: news features, 'colour pieces', news analysis – and plenty more besides. These 'softened' news stories generally have the news element at or near the opening – or they may be packaged in such a way that they link directly (either visually on a printed page or dynamically on a website) to an accompanying hard news piece. But the writing is often treated more colourfully and some of the rules of hard news reporting outlined above are broken to provide a 'softer' feel to the copy. Here we'll look at a few intro options for softer news pieces.

Direct quotation intro

Starting with a direct quote softens the story, as here from the *Socialist Worker* (10 July 2004):

'Choice is the political buzzword this week, but up until Respect was formed voters had no real choice. We offer that choice and the reception we are getting is brilliant.'

This is how Respect candidate Yvonne Ridley described the parliamentary by-election campaign in the Leicester South constituency as around 200 Respect supporters mobilised over the weekend.

The question intro

Beginning with a question also softens the impact of a story, and adds variety, as here in the *Guardian's* news blog (14 April 2009):

Could this be the most expensive break-up in world history? That's the question being asked today after Mel Gibson's wife filed for divorce, citing irreconcilable differences.

Delayed drop intro

Delaying the main angle (also known as the 'buried lead') is difficult to achieve and needs to be handled with caution (see Conley 2002: 82). But it does have its place in both national and local newspapers. It works by arousing the reader's sense of curiosity and will fail if the reader is not curious to know how it all ends. It is best used when something unusual or eccentric is being reported and the reader is kept in suspense before being let into the secret. Here, from the *Daily Mail* (5 May 2012), David Jones begins his investigation into designer babies:

Above a cheap mobile phone shop in a chaotic street in north Delhi, there is a grimy apartment whose peeling walls are decorated with photographs of adoring mothers nursing their babies.

The woman cooing at her child in the biggest portrait is beautiful, white and affluent-looking – in stark contrast to the flat's five residents, four of whom are pregnant, while the other is being pumped full of hormones in the hope she will soon conceive.

They are all uneducated, bare-footed, dirt-poor Indian women from outlying villages – and given the emotional turmoil that awaits them, one would have thought the very last thing they would wish to do is spend their enforced nine months of confinement here gazing upon images of maternal bliss.

Nominally, this forlorn place is a care home for surrogate mothers – at least that is how it is described by the company that runs it, Wyzax surrogacy Consultancy, which is cashing in on India's booming new babies-for-sale business.

It boasts of being the country's first 'one-stop shop for outsourced pregnancy'. In truth, though, it is nothing less than a baby factory; the end of a grim production line on which children are being designed to order for wealthy couples, mainly from Western countries including Britain, as if they were custom-built cars.

Offbeat intro

A variant of the delayed drop intro, it creates interest and surprise by highlighting an unexpected, obscure aspect of an event or person. Here, Tom Knowles in *The Times* (26 September 2013) focuses on the strange detail of a court case:

> It was surely the first time a court has been told about the antics of Whangdoodles, Hornswogglers and Snozzwangers. However, as two men were sentenced for attacking two others while dressed as Oompa Loompas, the prosecutor reminded them that the Roald Dahl creations are supposed to be peaceloving.

Eye-witness intro

Putting the reader at the heart of the events you are about to describe can be an effective opening gambit. Here is an example from the world news section of the *Independent* (1 October 2013):

> Gangs of drunken English-speaking men stand on tables stripped to the waist and bawling out drinking songs to the beat of a Lederhosen-clad Bavarian brass band. As they clink foaming tankards, their similarly beer-bloated girlfriends slip out for a quick pee on the grass outside – welcome to Munich's legendary Oktoberfest.

KEEP IT FLOWING, KEEP IT CLEAR: STRUCTURING THE NEWS STORY

News stories, whether of 5 or 35 pars, are formed through the linking of thematic sections. The reader progresses through them in order of importance, except on those few occasions when the punchline is delayed for dramatic reasons. The journalist's news sense comes into operation not only for the intro, but throughout the story. Who is the most important person to quote? Who is the next most important person? What details should be highlighted and which left to the end or eliminated? How much background information is required and where is it best included? All these questions are answered according to a set of news values held by the reporter.

Structure

Speed is the essence of news reading just as it is of news gathering. Information should flow logically and easily through copy, the structure being so refined it is invisible to the reader. Only when a story is badly organised with confusing chronology, say, or jumbled up quotes, does the reader become aware of any structure.

Opening section

Intro pars tend to highlight the news angle. Second and third pars can expand on intro angles, giving extra information. There is an urgency about hard copy which should be maintained throughout the story but particularly in the opening pars. Unnecessary background information, comment and description should not be allowed to delay the dramatic flow of the copy.

Later sections: the inverted pyramids concept

Traditional analysis of news stories stresses the notion of the inverted pyramid with the most important elements at the top and the least important (often defined as background) briefly at the bottom (Pöttker 2003). This notion is useful for stories based mainly on one source. For the vast majority, it oversimplifies the writing process. News values operate throughout the individual sections while background can occur anywhere in a news story. Sometimes, when a story is unintelligible without background information, it will occur high up.

News stories are never neutral or objective. An overall 'frame of understanding' influences the choice of content, sources, language and quotes used. Within this context, they are usually made up from a mix of quotes (in direct and indirect speech), factual details, background information and occasionally brief analysis. Each of these elements usually comprises a separate thematic section. News values are applied to each section: the most important comes first, the least important last. Thus, instead of a single inverted pyramid, it is more useful to think of a series of inverted pyramids within an overall inverted pyramid (see Figure 6.2).

DESCRIPTIONS AND TITLES

People in the news are always accompanied by a title or description. The reader needs to know on what authority or on what basis they are speaking. Thus the *Medway Messenger* (3 May 2013), under a headline 'Sappers build a bridge to remember', describes its two main sources as 'John Laverty, regional director of the Institute of Civil Engineers' and 'Lt Col Gareth Baker, commanding officer of 1 RSME'.

With sources for whom a job title is inappropriate in the context of the story, such as eye-witnesses to a road crash, it is more common to use their address as the descriptor. For example: 'Joan Edwards, of Chevening Crescent, saw what happened.'

People with long titles provide problems for intros. They can clutter them up with words. For instance, 'Mr Doug McAvoy, former general secretary of the National Union of Teachers, yesterday claimed'. One way round this problem is to use a phrase such as: 'The former leader of a teachers' union yesterday claimed'. Then

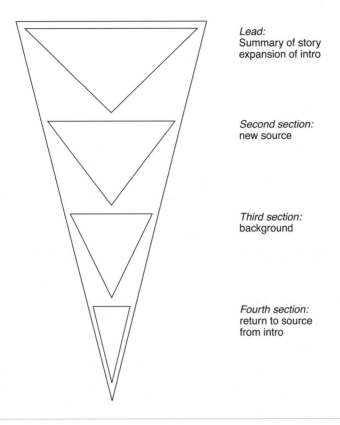

Lead:
Summary of story
expansion of intro

Second section:
new source

Third section:
background

Fourth section:
return to source
from intro

FIGURE 6.2
The inverted pyramids concept

in the next par or sentence you may give the name or title. The description of the person in the news does not have to be a formal title such as secretary, MP, councillor or director. It can be looser, for instance, 'of the Green Party' or 'who was a close friend of the victim'.

CLICHÉS AND HOW TO AVOID THEM

Clichés for Fleet Street columnist Keith Waterhouse (1991) count as no.1 among his 'seven deadly sins' of writing. There are thousands of clichés and they come in many guises. For instance, there are alliterative phrases such as 'safe and sound', 'slow but sure', 'chop and change', 'share and share alike', 'petticoat protest', 'followed in the footsteps', 'few and far between'. They appear as meaningless, over-dramatic adjectives such as 'driving rain', 'miraculous escape', 'tragic accident', 'brutal murder', 'coveted title', 'sudden death', 'horrific injuries', 'sweeping reforms', 'heated argument', 'proud parents', 'bare minimum', 'shock/major/hard-hitting report', 'mercy mission'. There are metaphors gone stale with overuse: 'blanket of snow', 'pillar of strength', 'tower of strength', 'tip of the iceberg', 'sweep under the rug', 'local boy made good'. Some single words, such as 'fairytale', 'viable', 'ongoing', 'crisis', 'situation', 'scandal', 'tragedy', 'disaster', 'fury', 'fuming', 'angry', 'shock', 'outrage', amount to clichés.

Amongst those listed by John Humphrys (2004a: 230) are 'on hold', 'up for grabs', 'calm before the storm', 'explore every avenue' and 'conspicuous by its absence'.

One of journalism's biggest clichés is 'exclusive', which is constantly devalued through overuse. Investigative reporter Phillip Knightley (1998: 44) argues that newspapers, in any case, give 'exclusives' the importance they don't deserve. 'Scoops are a journalist's way of assessing his or her colleagues and of interest only to journalists.'

Celebrating heroism in a post-heroic era

Every day the popular press, in these post-heroic times (when machines and technology have taken the place of humans in so many fields – scientific exploration and warfare to name but two), recreate clichéd images of heroism. During the Gulf conflict of 1991 the press was full of images of 'Top Gun heroes'; the British hostages (sudden 'victims' caught up in the drama of history) were all transformed into 'heroes'. In the *Sun* of 13 November 1999, a child suffering from leukaemia was described as a 'brave angel'. The Bradford *Telegraph & Argus* won a Newspaper Society award in 2000 for its campaign to honour local 'heroes'. Throughout Fleet Street and the local media, all the British medal-winners at the Athens 2004 Olympics were celebrated as national 'heroes'. When Paula Radcliffe broke down in the marathon, the *Mirror*'s front page splash of 23 August read: 'Tears of a hero'. And during the London 2012 Olympics, newspapers were, predictably, awash with reports about the 'heroics' of Team GB. Typically, the *Daily Mail* headlined on 28 August 2012: 'Olympics heroes to be honoured with victory parade through London where hundreds of thousands will line the streets.'

The mindless militarisation of language

One of the most prominent clichés revolves around metaphors of violence and warfare. 'Hit out at', '(bitter) battle', 'under siege', 'fight', 'massacre', 'blast', 'axe', 'mount a defence' are everywhere. There are many factors behind this militarisation of language. It reflects the militarisation of culture with the enormous expenditure on the weapons of war and the industrial importance of the arms trade. In addition, there is a high social status enjoyed by the military, the ever-presence of war toys, violent computer games and the media's glorification of violence and macho 'firmness'. Just as the culture is brutalised, so is the language of news.

Many stories are built around the drama of conflict, and warfare is an obvious metaphor for this. Moreover, as the media are driven to extremes to capture attention, constantly 'bombarding' readers with sensationalised trivia, so the language of violence is used to carry out this 'bombardment'. Politics and sport are the two areas most afflicted by this form of cliché. Thus, on 16 February 2004, the *Independent* reported under the headline 'Kerry takes war to Bush as candidates gather pace': 'Senator John Kerry was raising his defences against attacks from the Bush White House this weekend.' On 19 June 2004, the *Sun* reported under the headline 'Croat war': 'Croatia's plans for Monday's crucial clash with England have been rocked by a war of words.' 'Beef war', 'trade war', 'banana war', 'spice wars', 'tabloid wars' are all common clichés. On 1 July 2004, the *Lincoln Target* reported a gardener battling it out in 'the war of the roses'.

To simplify the historical record and highlight its confrontational dimension, the press often resorts to categorising. Doves and hawks, hardliners, loony/soft/cuddly/hard left, unilateralists and multilateralists, militants, extremists, moderates, realists, pragmatists and reformers are constantly 'doing battle' in the press.

Euphemisms: how job cuts become rationalisation

Journalists stress their commitment to writing plain English and so it is not surprising that euphemisms (bland expressions) are considered to be out. Never write that so-and-so 'passed away' or 'slipped away calmly' – they died. Philip Howard (1984) describes euphemism as the 'British linguistic vice': they are part of the air we breathe. It is impossible for journalists to avoid them. Thus, instead of the emotive sounding 'slump' we have the euphemistic, abstract Latinism of 'recession'. In business, 'rationalisation' and 'restructuring' mean job cuts. Hospitals often describe people seriously hurt as 'comfortable'. The 'spikes' for the tramps of Orwell's day are now the (equally appalling) 'rehabilitation centres' for down-and-outs.

'Wars' today are no longer declared. Bombings of cities are described as 'humanitarian'. People are no longer killed in them (except 'by mistake'). 'Targets' are hit by 'precise', 'clean', 'surgical' missiles. A whole lexicon of euphemistic nuke-speak, such as 'independent nuclear deterrent', 'flexible response', 'collateral damage' (for civilian deaths) and 'strategic sufficiency' has emerged to acclimatise our minds to the unspeakable horror of the nuclear holocaust (Aubrey 1982; Chilton 1985). In his spirited critique of 'junk language', broadcaster John Humphrys reports (2004a: 124) journalist Bernard Levin as believing all euphemisms are lies. 'He admired the writer Marghanita Laski, who translated "simple, inexpensive gowns for the fuller figure" into "nasty, cheap dresses for fat old women".'

Jargon: getting rid of gobbledegook

One of the biggest challenges young journalists face is to cast aside the academic trappings of their background and the jargon that accompanies it. Each social grouping (local authorities, education, the military, law, computers, librarians, Trotskyists, Conservatives) has its own in-language/jargon and acronyms as a communication aid and 'shorthand'. Academics, with their often mind-numbing abstractions, are in no way peculiar. General Norman Schwarzkopf contributed this piece of military nonsense during the 1991 Gulf conflict: 'It's not yet possible to get clear BDA in this area of KTO. The continued presence of Triple A means a constant risk of allied personnel becoming KIA or WIA.' With jargon such as this, language becomes a kind of fetish, not serving as a communication tool but reinforcing the group's special identity – and excluding uninitiated outsiders. And Donald Rumsfeld, the American defense secretary during the attack on Iraq in 2003, uttered this mumbo-jumbo classic (see Humphrys 2004a: 214):

> Reports that say something hasn't happened are always interesting to me because, as we know, there are known knowns: there are things we know. We also know there are known unknowns, that is to say we know there are some things that we do not know. But there are also unknown unknowns – the ones we don't know we don't know.

The reporter's task, often, is rapidly to learn the jargon of a group and translate it into terms comprehensible to a mass readership. It's not easy, particularly when spoken at speed. Journalism has its own jargon. Many of the clichés of journalism (journalese), such as 'probe', 'axe', 'boost', 'jibe', 'shock' and 'blast', all have a currency that bears no relation to their use in conversation. Martin Conboy (2003: 47) highlights the popular press's constant use of such words as 'hunks', 'fellas', 'the Beeb', 'shocker', 'pervert', 'plonker', 'stunna', 'beauty', 'fiend', 'groper', 'nut' and 'love cheat'. And he suggests this process 'constitutes a narrowing of cultural and linguistic reference. It is cultural compression, a set of allusions to the way the world works. One might say that in its compressed style of debate any rational political debate has imploded.'

CHANGING *TIMES*

One way to examine the newspaper language of today is to see how *The Times*'s style has changed over the years, just as it will, no doubt, change in the future.

(Joseph Sturge (1793–1859) played an important part in the fight to abolish slavery. He was also a member of a deputation from the Society of Friends which went to Russia in 1854 to carry their protest against the Crimean War to the Tsar.)

Notice how the language is influenced by the news sense applied. 'Spoke . . . on the subject of war' is too generalised and carries no dramatic weight according to today's news values. The second sentence fails to carry a verb, merely listing the 'three notable members' of the first sentence. Current newspaper style would be stricter on the coverage of the names. Mr Joseph Sturge carries the necessary first name while Bowly and the other Sturge are given only their initials. Today this would be considered an unfortunate disturbance of style. The repetition of Society of Friends is unnecessary.

The 'Friends on the War'

Three notable members of the Peace Society, and of the Society of Friends, spoke at a Christmas meeting of workmen in Gloucester, on Thursday night, on the subject of war. Mr Joseph Sturge, one of the deputation from the Society of Friends to the Czar, Mr S. Bowly, the peace and temperance advocate, and Mr T.M. Sturge, of Gloucester.

Mr Joseph Sturge, after alluding to his mission to St Petersburg, with the view of bringing about a termination of hostilities, expressed his firm belief, notwithstanding all that had been said against the Emperor of Russia, or whatever might be the evils existing in his Government, that there was no man in Europe who more earnestly desired a return of peace than that monarch, provided it could be done consistently with what he regarded as the honour of his country.

He also alluded to certain accusations which had been made against him in a letter that had been published, he having been accused of a desire to promote the war because it kept up the price of grain, and, in another part of the same letter, he said he was charged with wishing to put an end to the war, simply because it interfered with his trade.

Providence had, however, placed him in such a position that personally he should not feel the effect of the war further than now being unable to obtain grain from where he could formerly procure it, but he was unable to give employment to as many men as formerly, and he feared matters in this respect would grow worse.

At the present time when wheat was, in England, worth about 10s a bushel, whereas in Russia it could be bought for 2s; and thus, as a pecuniary question, it was desirable that the war should be terminated, apart from higher ground of the Christian duty of putting an end to such fearful scenes of bloodshed as were now taking place in the Crimea. He did not wish to say on whom the blame of the war rested, but he was desirous that each of his friends would use his influence to promote peace, should an opportunity of so doing present itself.

Mr Thomas Sturge recalled to mind the horrors of the wars of the French empire during which period it was computed by the most credible historians that 5,000,000 human beings were slaughtered. During the seven years of the Wellington campaigns 70,000 British lives were destroyed; and at the battle of Waterloo, where there were under 40,000 British engaged, no less than between 800 and 900 officers, and upwards of 10,000 soldiers, were destroyed. And he was of the opinion that if the war in the Crimea continued there would be an equal loss of life.

The second par is a monster by modern standards – 80 words with 5 subordinate clauses. There is an over-expansive, literary feel to the par 'Alluding to', 'with the view of bringing about a termination' and 'notwithstanding' today have an archaic air.

The third par is also long – 67 words, with repetitions of 'war', 'letter' and the awkward 'accusations/accused'. As well as being cluttered with subordinate phrases, it has such unnecessary embellishing words as 'certain' and 'simply' and phrases such as 'a letter that had been published' (better to say 'published letter') and 'to put an end to the war' (better to say 'to end the war'). The letter is contradictory (and probably drew laughter from the audience) so hardly worth reporting.

The fourth par has 59 words – still long by today's standards. The next sentence has 63 words. The following two are short in comparison: 38 and 32. The final two are 41 and 21. Notice how the explicit words 'slaughtered' and 'destroyed' are used to describe deaths in battle: there's none of the euphemistic 'collateral damage' jargon of today that aims to hide the horror of warfare. It is also interesting to see that though the report covers a speech, there are no direct quotes, probably because of the reporter's lack of a confident note (and with no shorthand). Converted into the news language of today, the report would read something like:

The Russian Emperor urgently desires peace in the Crimea, Joseph Sturge, who has just returned from a meeting with the Tsar, said on Thursday.

But any peace for the Tsar has to preserve the honour of Russia, he told a meeting of workers in Gloucester.

Mr Sturge, who met the Tsar in St Petersburg on a peace mission for the Society of Friends, said the war had interfered with his buying of grain and he had been forced to lay off some workers.

In England, wheat cost 10s a bushel against 2s in Russia. So it was not only his Christian duty to seek an end to the bloodshed, but such a move was needed for financial reasons.

No side could be blamed for the war, and he urged everyone to do their best to promote peace.

Thomas Sturge, also of the Peace Society, said 5 million people had been slaughtered during the wars of the French empire. Some 70,000 Britons had died during the seven years of the Wellington campaigns, while at the battle of Waterloo between 800 and 900 British officers and 10,000 soldiers had been killed.

He feared there would be an equal loss of life if the Crimean War continued.

This *Times* report (18 January 1940) shows how language and sentence structure were becoming shorter, though the copy still lacked the directness of journalism today.

(Finland was invaded by Russia in November 1939, and in spite of heroic resistance was compelled to surrender in March 1940.)

| January 18 | **ON THIS DAY** | 1940 |

FINNS' NEW SUCCESS
Unequal Struggle in the Air

From Our Special Correspondent

Helsinki, Jan. 17

ALTHOUGH THE weather is the coldest for 35 years, the Finnish ski patrols are still active and are distinguishing themselves in the Salla area, where the Russians have been driven back some 12 miles, and are still retreating, pressed by Finnish troops. Today's communiqué states that there was patrol activity north-east of Lake Ladoga between forces of similar strength, in which the Finnish troops routed an enemy company, which lost 70 killed, two tanks, and about 100 rifles.

While the strictly military results of the Russian air raids have been comparatively small, even when attacks were made with 400 machines, the sufferings of the civilian population have been great. Although most of the houses in the provincial towns are still standing, bomb explosions have smashed thousands of windows over wide areas, so that each day more and more houses become uninhabitable in this Arctic winter with temperatures which are exceptional even for Finland.

In the village of Ryttyla, where there are no military objectives, Soviet airmen machine-gunned a funeral procession.

The size of Finland is such that it is impossible to keep the whole of it, or even the most densely populated southern and central districts, adequately supplied with anti-aircraft guns and bomb-proof cellars; but considering that even now Finnish airmen, with rather slow machines, have been able to bring down a good number of enemy aircraft is evidence that a sufficient force of quick, modern fighters is the best means of checking and ending the attacks on civilians. The need for aircraft from abroad is at present the most urgent and decisive issue, the Finns declare.

One example will show the spirit in which the nation is meeting the horrors of air warfare. In a large industrial centre, where there have been frequent air raids, the management of a certain factory asked the employees whether they would be willing to continue to work during air-raid alarms to save time and increase the output of this important factory. The men were offered an extension of their summer holidays in exchange. They answered that they agreed to work during the raids, but would not accept the reward offered them. 'We are doing this,' they said, 'because the Russians must be defeated.'

US paratroopers send Saddam a dramatic message

Catherine Philp in Harir

THE long-awaited northern front was finally opened yesterday after US troops parachuted into Kurdish-controlled northern Iraq under cover of night. They were the first of thousands expected here in the coming days to launch a ground assault towards the key cities of Kirkuk and Mosul.

About 1,000 American paratroopers were dropped into the tiny Harir airfield in an operation marking the beginning of a new phase in the war. The troops spent yesterday preparing the airfield for the arrival of thousands of reinforcements accompanied by light artillery, tanks and armoured vehicles.

'We're ready to give Saddam Hussein another front to worry about,' an American special forces commander said.

Along with several hundred special forces soldiers already in the area and thousands of Kurdish fighters under their command, the force's task will be to punch through an estimated 100,000 Iraqi troops stationed along the heavily fortified 'green line' separating the northern Kurdish enclave from the rest of Iraq.

There was a dramatic escalation in airstrikes along the green line in preparation for a ground invasion by a force much smaller and lighter than was originally envisaged.

At Chamchamal, on the road to Kirkuk, Iraqi troops fled their frontline bunkers after two days of intensive bombing, pulling back more than ten miles. Huge explosions were seen on the high ridge at Kalak, where the road to Mosul runs under Iraqi guns.

Commanders hope that the opening of the northern front will alleviate pressure on forces in the south. While the northern force's first job will be to secure oilfields around Kirkuk and Mosul, they will also be well placed to march southwards to encircle Baghdad.

The Pentagon had hoped to open a northern front at the same time as the assault from the south, but Turkey balked at allowing 62,000 troops from the US Army 4th Infantry Division to launch an invasion from its soil.

That forced the US to opt for a lighter, smaller force drawn from the army's 173rd Airborne Brigade, based in Vicenza, Italy.

Commanders said that they had decided on a parachute landing for speed and to circumvent difficult weather and ground conditions, but also for its theatrical value. 'It sends a dramatic message to the whole region that the Americans are here,' the special forces commander said.

Warplanes circled overhead to provide cover for the landing as bombing raids were stepped up on Iraqi positions and artillery to the south. Helicopters accompanied the airdrop, swooping in to land on the small airstrip.

Cargo planes dropped several light Humvee vehicles on to the airfield, which landed with a thud in the deep mud. Paratroopers spent much of the next morning retrieving them from the swampy field as others dug trenches and built defensive positions.

One paratrooper was caked from head to foot in mud from his marshy landing. 'It's cold but it's good to be here,' he said. 'The peshmerga were excited to see us.'

> The Kurdish fighters turned out in their hundreds to guard the airfield and welcome their new allies.
>
> A few soldiers suffered minor injuries on landing but commanders said there were no serious casualties. One soldier assembling a machinegun at the edge of the field fingered a badly swollen lip from where he had fallen on rocks. Villagers assembled at the top of the hill the next morning. 'I wanted to run down and welcome them but the peshmerga wouldn't let me,' Hassan Ali said. 'We are very happy they are here. We have waited a long time. Now Saddam will be gone soon.'
>
> Others, however, fretted that the presence of US forces might put them in danger.
>
> 'I'm worried that Saddam will try to bomb them and hit us instead,' Ahmed, another villager, said.

Of the first five sentences, four begin with subordinate clauses. Newspapers now adopt the opposite style, starting with the main clause except occasionally for variety. Sentence lengths are still long: the first six have 43, 37, 31, 44, 17 and 79 words.

The first par opens without any impact on a subordinate clause about the weather. If the Russians have been driven back, the phrases 'are still active' and 'are distinguishing themselves' are redundant. The second sentence focuses on the communiqué 'stating' rather than on the more dramatic 'routing' of the enemy. The next par also reflects the passive, low-key coverage. Rather than the active '400 planes attack' it says 'attacks were made with 400 machines'. Similarly, instead of 'civilians have suffered greatly' it says more passively 'the sufferings of the civilian population have been great'. The next sentence repeats the point about the winter coldness made at the start.

Note the bias of the coverage. The Finns, fighting the Nazis, are represented as heroic and the sufferings of innocent civilians are highlighted. In contrast, the enemy Soviets are portrayed as ruthless warriors, even machine-gunning a funeral procession. Coverage of the Soviets was to change dramatically once they changed sides following the Nazi invasion of their country.

In 2003, Britain was again at war, backing the US-led attacks on Iraq. Notice how the language and sentence structure have changed. Focusing on the first pars of this 861-word report of 28 March 2003, see how much shorter, in general, the sentences are than in the previous examples: 20, 25, 24, 22, 17, 48, 28, 25 and 19.

Precise language and structure

Most sentences begin with the main clause, the language precise and dramatic. The opening par sets the main news theme (the opening of the northern front) with the second par expanding on this point and providing figures of troop numbers. Adjectives and adverbs are used only sparingly in broadsheet/compact hard news; different criteria apply in the red-top tabloids. Here only 'long-awaited' and 'finally' stand out at the start (articulating the views and sentiments of the western elites determined on 'regime change'). 'Tiny', in the second par, provides striking detail, contrasting with the enormity of the military machine being assembled by the US.

Language, propaganda and the impact of dominant sources

The language of the news is profoundly influenced by the language, biases, jargon, tones and rhythms of the sources quoted. Notice how the warring, colloquial rhetoric of the American special forces commander takes over par three and appears again in par 10. And see how the jargon of the military (militaryspeak), such as 'punch through', 'intensive bombing', 'pulling back', 'opening up the northern front' and 'stepped up bombing raid', is unproblematically appropriated by the journalist in her supposedly 'objective' report.

Language tone and contrasts in human interest bias

The tone is mainly dramatic rather than emotional and sensational. The main early focus is on the activities of the US troops and the commander's quotes. Predictably, he represents the 'enemy' as 'Saddam Hussein'. This hyper-demonisation of the president of Iraq (beginning during the 1990–91 crisis and continuing until his death in December 2006 and beyond) by the military, politicians and mainstream media has served to simplify an enormously complex situation and direct blame to one man (thus clearing the West of responsibility for any ensuing atrocities).

Similarly, Nato leaders throughout the Kosovo war of 1999 constantly referred in their propaganda to the president of Serbia, Slobodan Milosevic, as Hitler, and to the Serbs as Nazis. At the same time, the roles of US/UK imperialism and militarism, of the International Monetary Fund and World Bank strategies to destabilise the Balkans, of Croatian and German nationalism in provoking the conflict, were marginalised (Chossudovsky 1998; Chomsky 1999; Keeble 1999).

Even the two 'villagers' quoted later on in Philp's report focus on 'Saddam' as their 'enemy', thus reinforcing (and in a subtle way legitimising) the military's rhetoric by giving it the appearance of 'common sense'. Other quotes support the positive tone of the piece: a paratrooper stresses how 'it's good to be here' with the peshmerga 'excited' to see their advance, while Ali says they are 'very happy'. Yet all around them, innocent Iraqis are being slaughtered. 'Bombing raids' are reported but no consideration is given to the human consequences: the deaths, the trauma, the homes and hospitals destroyed. In this way, the unthinkable horror becomes normal. As Edward Herman wrote in his landmark essay 'The Banality of Evil': 'Doing terrible things in an organised and systematic way rests on "normalisation" ... It is the function of the experts and the mainstream media to normalise the unthinkable for the general public' (see Pilger 2004b).

Significantly, during the Gulf War of 1991 outrage was expressed in the press only once: over the BBC's coverage of the US attack on the Amiriyah shelter in Baghdad, which killed more than 1,000 women and children (Keeble 1997: 166–73). But consider the outrage that would have been expressed if a long-range Iraqi missile had landed on Tony Blair's home.

Notice also Philp's use of descriptive colour and the close attention to eye-witness detail, as in: 'One paratrooper was caked from head to foot in mud from his marshy landing' and 'One soldier assembling a machinegun at the edge of the field fingered a badly swollen lip from where he had fallen on rocks.' In this way the reporter is adopting a typical war-story narrative style that serves essentially to celebrate the heroism of 'our' men at war.

Language and the simplification process

The language of news also seeks to simplify events, to make the complex dynamics of history intelligible. Here the personalisation of news and the narrative style (pitting 'good' Americans and Kurds against 'bad' Saddam and Iraqis) are part of this process.

News language is concrete and non-abstract

On a more fundamental level, there is simply not the space to explore the complexities and abstractions of historical factors. News language, as here, is concrete, dwelling on 'facts', colour, quotes and narrative, and is very rarely abstract.

WORDPLAY

One of the most fascinating features of journalism is the way it records society's complex language shifts and at the same time creates new words (neologisms) and new meanings (see Beal 2004: 14–34; Dent 2004). Many hundreds of new words are recorded and invented every year in newspapers and magazines – and a growing number of them now have their roots in emerging online cultures.

For instance, new words added to *The Oxford English Dictionary*'s online edition in 2013 included 'omnishambles' (a situation that has been comprehensively mismanaged, characterised by a string of blunders and miscalculations); 'selfie' (a photographic self-portrait, usually taken with a mobile phone camera); and 'digital detox' (a period of time away from screen-based devices connected to the internet). Lake Superior State University, Michigan has been compiling (with appropriate humour) since 1976 a list of new words which it claims should be 'banished from the Queen's English for Misuse, Overuse and General Uselessness'. It's worth exploring at www.lssu.edu/banished (see Merritt 2003).

Many new words emerge from play with well-known prefixes or suffixes. Thus the 'Euro-' prefix may provoke 'Euro-wimp' or 'Euro-chic'. The suffix 'mania' has given birth to 'Gorbymania' and 'Spicemania'. The suffix '-ite' has provoked 'Trotskyite', 'Thatcherite' and 'Blairite' (but significantly not 'Cameronite'). Following Watergate, there has been a flood of '-gates': 'Mirrorgate', 'bananagate', 'zippergate', 'Shaylergate', Janet Jackson's 'nipplegate', 'plebgate' and even 'gategate'.

Just as George Orwell coined the words 'doublespeak' and 'newspeak', so they have spawned endless variations: 'nukespeak', 'massacrespeak', 'quangospeak', 'Reaganspeak'. The 1990s saw a new breed of neologism emerge alongside the internet explosion. Virtually any noun could be preceded by 'e', 'dotcom' or 'cyber': so, for instance, 'email', 'e-commerce', 'e-university', 'e-tailers', 'dotcom economy', 'dotcom advertising', 'cyber-players', 'cyber-verse'. A special e-commerce jargon (or cyberslang) emerged including 'buzzword compliant' (meaning literate in the latest internetspeak), 'incubators' (companies hatching dotcom start-ups) and 'bizzdev' (business development stage of an internet start-up).

DOING IT IN STYLE?

All newspapers have a view about good house style. This is outlined in a document called the style book (occasionally editorial handbook or sheet), though it is increasingly carried on screen. It will tend to focus on such elements as spellings, punctuation, abbreviations, the use of capitals, titles, Americanisms to avoid, the handling of quotations. Ethical issues, such as the handling of anonymous quotes or AIDS, can also be covered. That is the theory. The reality is very different. As Keith Waterhouse notes, style books are unfortunately 'often peppered with the random idiosyncrasies of editors and proprietors past and present'. Moreover, there is an enormous variation in approaches to house style throughout the industry. Some newspapers even manage to survive without a formalised style book.

The *Guardian* has made its style book, following debates with readers, available on its website (www.theguardian.com). On 'Direct speech' it comments: 'People we write about are allowed to speak in their own, not necessarily the *Guardian*'s style, but be sensitive: do not, for example, expose someone to ridicule for dialect or grammatical errors.' Under a section on 'Disability' it suggests that 'wheelchair-bound' and 'in a wheelchair' should be avoided: better 'wheelchair user'. Rather than 'backward', 'retarded' or 'slow', say 'person with a learning disability'. Under

'Gender issues' it says: 'Phrases such as career girl or career woman are outdated (more women have careers than men) and patronising (there is no male equivalent).' It also recommends special care in handling mental health issues. Terms to avoid because they stereotype and stigmatise include 'victim of', 'suffering from', just as 'a person with' is preferable to 'a person suffering from'. Under 'Clichés to avoid', it includes 'boost (massive or otherwise)', 'dropdead gorgeous', 'luvvies' and 'politically correct'. Other newspapers, such as *The Times* (www.thetimes.co.uk) and the *Independent* (www.independent.co.uk) have published their style books, while Keith Waterhouse's *Waterhouse on Newspaper Style* (1981a) is a lively critique of the tabloid's style.

While the subeditors (those who still exist) are usually regarded as the ultimate 'guardians' of style (see Chapter 3), staff reporters, freelances and student journalists should always be aware of the importance of following style and the journalistic disciplines involved. If there is no house style covering an issue, then make one yourself. Thus, if in copy you use 'jail' on first mention, it should be spelled the same way throughout. If you spell the former president of Libya 'Col. Gaddafi' at first mention, it should not later change to 'Col. Khadafi' or 'Col. Qaddafi'. And so on.

PRESENTATION OF COPY

It is vital that all copy, whether for your college, newspaper or freelance outlet, is immaculately tidy and follows basic rules. Untidy copy is simply spiked (thrown away). Freelances should particularly bear this in mind. Copy layout rules differ slightly from paper to paper, but the essential principles remain the same throughout the industry. Copy is written on screen, transferred to subeditors working on screen and appears in 'hard' form only when printed out in the newspaper. When hard copy is presented (say by freelances, accompanying a computer disk or email attachment), it is always typed in a standard font such as Times New Roman on one side of a white A4 sheet. Hand-written copy is never accepted unless from a big Fleet Street 'name' who can get away with such archaic eccentricity.

All freelances should work on Macs or PCs. And while conventions on copy layout have relaxed considerably in recent years with the emergence of electronically transmitted copy, it is still worth bearing in mind these points.

Byline

Use the 'header' facility on your word processing program to put on the top, left-hand side of the first page your name. Unless otherwise stated, this will be the name on any byline accompanying the story. Then comes an oblique stroke followed by the name of the publication.

Dateline

In the centre goes the date of publication, not the date of writing. This is particularly important for weeklies or monthlies. When using words such as 'yesterday' or 'tomorrow' it is advisable to put the day in parentheses afterwards to avoid confusion.

Catchline

At the top right-hand corner goes the catchline. This will usually be one word that clearly identifies the story. Page one of a story about Chelsea Manning will be catchlined 'Manning 1', page two automatically 'Manning 2' and so on. Avoid using such words as 'kill', 'dead', 'report', 'story', 'must', 'spike', 'flush', 'splash', 'header' or 'leader', which have specific meanings in newspaper jargon. When covering a crash, council meeting or fire, don't use the obvious catchlines such as 'crash', 'council' or 'fire'. Similar events may be covered by other journalists and to avoid duplication, words identifying the story's uniqueness should be used.

Copy

Your copy will begin some way down the first folio (page). Copy typed on newspaper computers will be formatted appropriately, but freelances should normally present their copy with double-spaced lines. Leave wide margins on both sides of the copy and clear spaces at the top and bottom of the page. Never hyphenate words between lines. Never let a sentence run from one folio to another.

At the foot of each folio except the last (in the 'footer' facility) should be 'more' or 'mf' (short for 'more follows'), usually centred. The story finishes with 'end'. Bylines, publication, date of publication and catchline will be produced at the top of each folio. Normally no large space is needed between the headers and copy on the second and any subsequent pages.

Copy should always be carefully checked before submission. Never delete the file of your story on disk. Copy can be lost or mislaid. Sometimes you might need to refer back to a previous story. If you send a disk through the post, always make a copy. Whenever there is an unusual spelling, such as 'Smythe' instead of 'Smith', or a name with possible variations, such as 'Dennis' or 'Denis', 'Maryline' or 'Marilyn', put 'correct' in square brackets afterwards. The sub should then delete it. Convoluted foreign names should be treated similarly to make clear to the sub that you are aware of the spelling issue and confirming its correctness. The sub should double check anyway.

If submitting copy as a freelance, it is usually advisable to attach a covering letter, reminding the editor of any necessary background to the commission, the payment agreed and giving daytime details, address and phone number along with home details. In some cases, a brief outline of your special credentials for writing the story might be appropriate. A word count is also invaluable to editors. If you are including photographs, remind the editor of payment agreed for these – and any expenses, too.

CHAPTER 7

News reporting in the digital age

The digital newspaper reporter serves many masters. There will usually be a news editor or section editor breathing down their neck to supply copy for the print pages; a web editor wanting updates on a running story for the main site's news section; they may well have their own blog to keep up to date; there's probably a Twitter account to maintain; a podcast they've been asked to contribute to; they may have to take their turn reading the hourly video bulletin. The modern news machine is a complex beast with many heads, all of which need feeding, and it's the reporter who has to supply the sustenance.

But it's not simply the workload and the need to learn new media skills – more of which throughout this chapter – that have changed the reporter's life so dramatically over the past decade. There are even more fundamental changes afoot. Perhaps most significant of all is the change in the relationship between a journalist and his or her readers. In theory, the reader has always been the most important person in a newspaper reporter's working life. In practice, the relationship was for a long time somewhat cold and distant.

In *Stick It Up Your Punter*, the classic inside story of life on the *Sun* in the 1980s, Peter Chippendale and Chris Horrie (1999) recount the tale of editor Kelvin MacKenzie grabbing the phone to speak to a reader who had dared to ring in complaining about a story. 'You're banned from reading the *Sun* ever again,' MacKenzie informs the astonished complainant and slams down the receiver. Minutes later, so the story goes, the telephone goes again. It's the man's wife wondering if the ban extends to her too. Such a dismissive approach may not have been typical (or even anything other than apocryphal), but it certainly was true that the readers did not have much say in the content or editorial agenda of the newspapers they read. And with the trend in the 1990s for local newspapers to close their town centre offices for cheaper out-of-town properties, even the slim chance of readers popping into the office with a tip-off diminished further.

But then, as news publishers began experimenting with their early websites, strange things started happening. In 1997, the nascent BBC News website – which at that stage was dedicated almost entirely to news and analysis of the general election – found itself deluged by readers emailing tributes to Princess Diana in the hours and days immediately following her death on 31 August (Allan and Thorsen 2010).

One direct result of this was the decision to launch a properly resourced site covering a full news agenda. But the other, in some ways more significant, realisation of the BBC web team was that there was a social aspect to news consumption. People wanted to be able to share their thoughts, to feel they could participate in the process and to express their opinions on the way it was being delivered (Hermida 2010). Participatory journalism has come a long way since those early readers' emails, and we will take a closer look at some of its current effects later in this chapter. But for now, let's concentrate on what the new relationship with readers means for the reporter.

NEWS REPORTING AS CONVERSATION: FROM PRODUCT TO PROCESS

In previous chapters we have looked at news stories largely as discrete products. We've examined the sources that inform them, the decisions made to create them, the conventions of language and structure that help the reporter to bring them to life and some of the production processes that enable them to be delivered to an end user. And it remains the case that, much of the time, a reporter will deliver that product and move on to creating the next one.

But a new school of thought has emerged in recent years which suggests that digital journalists should think of news stories less as products and more as ongoing *processes* – a development foreseen by John Fiske (1989) even before the dawn of the internet: '[Reporters] should not disguise their processes of selection and editing, but should open them up to reveal news as a production, not as transparent reportage.' Furthermore, those processes used by journalists to gather and publish information should be presented in such a way as to encourage the involvement of readers at every stage.

In the *Online Journalism Handbook*, Bradshaw and Rohumaa (2011) describe the 'conversation loop', a kind of virtuous circle that can be formed when a journalist involves their readers right from the early stages of a story:

> You could argue that the distinctions between conversation and publishing in an online medium are being eroded ... Conversation itself has become

publishing. A journalist in this context, then, needs to become a professional conversationalist: a mix of the ideal party guest and the ideal party host, taking part in – and stimulating – conversations in a number of ways.

These, they suggest, should include opening your work up to allow others to contribute editorially – presenting work in progress on a blog, perhaps, and encouraging others to help you fill in any gaps or correct inaccuracies. This concept is also sometimes labelled 'open source journalism', a term coined by the headline on a 1999 piece in the online magazine Salon.com (Leonard 1999), and whose roots lie in the computing movement that publishes the source code of software programs to allow other coders to help improve them. It's an idea that's not been without controversy. Some critics have argued that this open approach leaves the journalist vulnerable to the story being hijacked by special interest groups or professional PR campaigns, or to losing editorial control (Deuze 2001).

The idea requires an escape from the 'us-and-them' mindset of what is sometimes referred to as top-down journalism, and for the reporter to embrace a 'we' collaboration. Here are my four 'V's that underline the usefulness of involving readers in an appropriate way.

- Visibility – putting yourself at the heart of an online community raises your profile. It means you find new ways of reaching your audience, and of your audience reaching you.

- Veracity – allowing, even encouraging, your readers to correct errors and spot flaws should mean the final outcome is closer to the truth.

- Vulnerability – a more open and transparent approach helps to build trust. It shows you are not above criticism when you get things wrong.

- Variety – involving the community brings more voices, particularly those from 'outside the Rolodex', into your work.

LINKING AND LINK JOURNALISM: ONE GIANT LEAP

The concept of the hyperlink – the ability to join two pieces of otherwise unrelated data – pre-dates the web by a couple of decades, but it is one of its fundamental building blocks. Without it, the web would not really be a web at all. Strange, then, that many newspapers were pretty reluctant to use links, particularly links to websites other than their own, very much at all in the first wave of sites that they built. Partly this was down to a mindset, developed over decades of intense print competition, that steadfastly refused to acknowledge even the existence of rival newspapers within the pages of your own. And partly it seemed intuitive that publishers should want to keep readers within the confines of their own website, because that was what advertisers were paying for.

Publishers wanted their content to be 'sticky' – as a popular internet buzzword of the time had it – so they were not about to give readers the option of a mouse click to take them elsewhere. But by 2005, forward-thinking digital enthusiasts were beginning to doubt the sense of this approach. Blogger Dave Winer put it succinctly:

> Now the fundamental law of the internet seems to be the more you send them away the more they come back. It's why link-filled blogs do better than introverts. It may seem counter-intuitive – it's the new intuition, the new way of thinking.
>
> (Winer 2005)

Winer's example was a site that existed only to send its users away, a site that would become the biggest on the planet: Google. And by 2008, even the big newspaper publishers had started to catch on, as readers' online behaviour was studied more closely (Stelter 2008). Now it's widely accepted that if you give your readers the opportunity to link out to another piece of relevant related content, even if that takes them to somebody else's website, they will in the long term reward you with their loyalty. As long as you consistently link to useful and valid content, they will see you at least partly as a trusted resource, a curator or aggregator of other great content.

Former newspaperman-turned-digital journalism guru Jeff Jarvis has another way of thinking about this (2007). The traditional newspaper model, he says, has been to try to be all things to all readers, even if that often meant duplicating work that other organisations had already carried out. Furthermore, he points out that however good you are as a journalist, however diligent you have been in your research, there will always be experts out there who know more about a given subject than you do, and other specialist websites that publish more detailed information than you are able to. Jarvis says you should embrace their existence by linking to them as a service to your readers. His simple tenet is this: 'Cover what you do best, and link to the rest.'

Meanwhile, Jonathan Stray (2010b) explains four noble journalistic principles for the humble link: they are good for storytelling because they can remove the need for complicated explanations of background detail; they help keep your audience informed about other stories that you don't have the resources to cover; they are a currency of collaboration, a way that organisations or individual journalists can add value to each other's work; and they enable transparency by allowing a more direct way of attributing source material.

Scott Karp (2008) takes it one step further: 'Links aren't just a fundamental element of the reporting. Links can BE the reporting.'

LINEAR AND NON-LINEAR REPORTING: PUTTING THE READER IN CHARGE

Perhaps the most significant effect on journalism of the hyperlink is that it introduced the possibility of entirely new ways of structuring stories. Stories written purely for print, radio or television require, by definition, a linear structure. The reader, listener or viewer starts at the beginning and follows the story through to the end in whatever way the reporter has dictated. With online journalism, the possibility of non-linear reporting emerges. Stories can be constructed in such a way that multiple text, audio and video elements are organised to give the reader a significant degree of control over how they are consumed.

This is sometimes called 'chunking' – the breaking down of a story into parts or chunks, all interlinked. Each individual item might be linear in its own right, so the collective experience is sometimes described as multilinear. Furthermore, different angles and conflicting points of view can be layered in to the story or examined in more detail. Remember, too, that the nature of the web means you can't be sure which element of the story your reader is going to arrive at first. The chances are they will have landed on one of the elements of your story via a link from a search engine or a social networking recommendation. That means that each element of the story must work hard to explain the story succinctly, without becoming repetitive.

It's worth noting here that not all online or multimedia stories have to be non-linear. The 'author-driven' (as opposed to 'reader-driven') digital story can still be essentially linear in format, leading the user through a series of linked items in a specific order – an audio slideshow is one simple example. Segel and Heer (2010) analyse some interesting examples of digital storytelling forms in their research on narrative visualisations.

What becomes clear is that true online reporting can require a very different mindset of the reporter from the very beginning of their newsgathering efforts. And although the reality of many newspaper organisations means that the majority of content is still written first with the print product in mind, then repurposed (or remediated, or reversioned) for the website, these cultures are changing. Digital first strategies, such as those at the *Guardian* and the *Financial Times* (see Chapter 3), mean that non-linear forms are likely to become increasingly significant in journalism storytelling. As he or she researches each aspect of the story, the reporter should be considering a number of important questions.

- Is this a multimedia story? Not all stories are – particularly if face-to-face access to your sources is restricted. But that doesn't mean the structure has to be linear. You might give your readers background briefings, analysis of specific angles, source documents or timelines, for example, as separate linked items.

- Do I have the time and the opportunity to exploit the multimedia possibilities? Video and audio journalism can take a lot more time to get right than writing copy. If time and resources are against you, straight text might be your only option.

- Are there some aspects that would be best served by video? Or audio? Some stories are more visually compelling than others – there's no point in shooting video just for the sake of it. Not all your interviews need to be recorded as audio either. But if one of your sources makes a particularly forceful or emotional point, it can greatly help the story if you can include that impassioned audio clip.

- Are any of my story elements redundant? Don't repeat great chunks of the story in different media. The items should complement each other.

- Are there any other digital storytelling techniques that might help the story? Interactive maps, databases that users can interrogate, online polls – all these and many more might be appropriate in different story treatments. And in many cases these require early planning.

- Should any of these elements be published inline – as part of the main narrative flow of the story – or as standalone items that work entirely in their own right?

With more complex stories, wireframing or storyboarding are likely to be valuable exercises. This means mapping out all the elements of the story and examining how they link or interact with each other. It helps to clarify the possible pathways a reader might take to navigate through the story. There are many online tools to help with wireframes and storyboards (gliffy.com, for example) but often a pen and paper are just as effective.

IN SEARCH OF TRUTH: 'TRANSPARENCY IS THE NEW OBJECTIVITY'

Unlike their broadcast counterparts, who are governed by a statutory obligation, newspaper journalists do not have to be impartial. Provided their reporting stays on the right side of the laws of defamation, they can be as one-eyed, subjective, biased and skewed as they (or their bosses) like with their presentation of the facts. But that's not the intention of the vast majority. They would tell you that their aim when embarking on their research for a given news story is to find the objective truth. The important distinction here is between news reporting and comment – areas that are generally clearly delineated within a newspaper's pages.

But objectivity can be a slippery concept. Michael Schudson (1978) defined it thus: 'Objective reporting is supposed to be cool, rather than emotional, in tone . . . According to the objectivity norm, the journalist's job consists of reporting something called "news" without commenting on it, slanting it, or shaping its formation in any way.' And Gaye Tuchman (1972) describes the 'strategic ritual of objectivity' in which reporters absolve themselves of responsibility for any conflicting versions of a story that might appear by attributing them correctly to the sources that provided them.

Yet for Fiske (1989), objectivity was 'authority in disguise'. Facts, he said, always support particular points of view and their 'objectivity' is simply part of a power play. The very notion of objectivity discouraged audience activity and participation because it was presented as something that could not be challenged. 'Reporters should be less concerned about telling the final truth of what has happened, and should present, instead, different ways of understanding it and the different points of view inscribed in those different ways.'

Fiske was writing before the advent of the internet age. The logistics of print and traditional broadcast news meant that it was very difficult to realise his ambitious ideas of warts-and-all coverage of a story from all possible sides. But now, hyperlinked journalism perhaps allows us to get closer to his idea. And there is a school of thought that instead of hiding behind a veneer of flawed objectivity, it might be more honest for the modern reporter to be up-front about their own points of view, while linking extensively to counter-arguments and alternative agendas. David Weinberger (2009) made the case compellingly in a blog post entitled 'Transparency is the new objectivity':

> Transparency puts within the report itself a way for us to see what assump-
> tions and values may have shaped it, and lets us see the arguments that the
> report resolved one way and not another. Transparency – the embedded ability
> to see through the published draft – often gives us more reason to believe a report
> than the claim of objectivity did. In fact, transparency subsumes objectivity. Anyone
> who claims objectivity should be willing to back that assertion up by letting us
> look at sources, disagreements, and the personal assumptions and values
> supposedly bracketed out of the report. Objectivity without transparency
> increasingly will look like arrogance. And then foolishness. Why should we trust
> what one person – with the best of intentions – insists is true when we instead
> could have a web of evidence, ideas, and argument?

WRITING ONLINE: NEW FORMS FOR OLD STORIES

The basic principles of constructing an online text news report are not dramatically different from those we discussed in Chapter 6. We are still attempting to keep Kipling's six noble servants – who, what, where, when, why and how – occupied in as engaging and informative a way as we possibly can. We are still trying to write in lively, active sentences. We are still keeping the most important facts at the top of the story before expanding into more detail further down. But there are additional aspects that make writing an online news story different from its print equivalent.

One is paragraph structure. Take a look, for example, at any news story on the BBC News website and you'll see that the vast majority of paragraphs are a single sentence. Almost none is more than two sentences. The same policy applies for most news publishers, for two reasons. One is that most computer screen resolutions are not sufficiently high to display dense columns of text readably; the second is that readers are increasingly using their mobile devices – which have smaller screens – to consume news. A more significant consideration for the online reporter's writing style starts with a simple-sounding question: Who am I writing this for? The answer might sound obvious enough: you are writing for your readers, the audience. But many of your readers will arrive at your story only because it has appeared in a list served up by a search engine such as Google. And as most of us know from our own behaviour, we are far more likely to click a link from the first few entries of the first page of Google search results than we are to drill down into subsequent pages of results.

So it's in our interest as news writers to find a way of getting our stories towards the top of Google's search page when a user keys in certain search terms. This is the dark art of search engine optimisation (SEO) that was for a while somewhat controversial among print purists. Most search engines are highly secretive about the computer algorithms they use to decide which pages appear highest up on their results pages for any given search terms. But it's clear that the use of key words – particularly in the headline and first paragraph of text on any page – have a significant impact on its search ranking and, in turn, a significant effect on a user's decision whether or not to click through. As Shane Richmond (2009) pointed out in the *British Journalism Review*, resistance still lurks on the bank benches.

> For many a print journalist such tinkering amounts to butchery, and the insistence on keywords renders copy dry and formulaic. On top of this there's a resistance – seems like snobbery to me – to the idea that we are somehow reduced to writing for computers rather than for people.

Added to that comes the suspicion amongst some critics that SEO techniques (such as recognising the popularity of 'top 10' lists among web readers) will start to have an impact on editorial agendas. If certain keywords always produce good traffic – thereby pleasing advertising departments – won't managers start to insist that more of such stories are written, regardless of their editorial merit? Richmond also concedes that well-honed writing conventions such as the delayed drop intro (see Chapter 6) are 'an SEO nightmare'.

It's worth remembering too that good SEO in your writing will only get you so far. An arguably more important factor in the search engines' algorithms is the overall 'authority' of the website on which the story appears – measured by how many other sites link to it. That authority only comes from producing regularly compelling content. And lots of it.

Structuring the online story

As we have seen from the section above on non-linear storytelling, our online reportage might include several elements. Let's say, for example, that our story includes a textual narrative of events, a video interview we have conducted with one of the key sources, a 'backgrounder' explaining detailed information about one aspect of the story, some audio 'vox pops' of public reaction and an interactive timeline showing the historical context.

Already, we have some decisions to make. One option is that we create each of these elements as an individual item in our content management system (see Chapter 2), and make sure that we provide prominent links to each of the other items – giving our readers the option of how far they 'drill down' into the story, and in which order they choose to consume it.

If we choose this method, there's a vital consideration to bear in mind: if they find our story after being referred by a search engine, we don't know which element they will arrive at first. Much as we might like them to read our carefully constructed narrative first, we can't be sure that will be the case. Which means that each individual element has to explain the overall story in sufficient detail for them to know what's going on.

A second option is to include some of the elements 'inline', as part of that main narrative piece. So we might take our audio vox pops and drop them into the text at the relevant point so that the sound clip can be played without the reader having to leave the page. We might do the same with a short clip of the key quote from our video interview – while also including a link to a longer version, for those readers who want a deeper understanding of the story. Each element makes our overall story structure more complicated, so always bear in mind the user's experience. The aim is to make it as engaging and seamless as possible.

Blogging: a new voice

The blog (originally 'weblog') is a very flexible writing form that gives the newspaper journalist a number of additional options that the traditional news story, with its formulaic structure and rigid conventions, does not allow. Although it is a relatively new phenomenon, blogging has quickly become established as a fundamental part of the digital media landscape. In 2000, it was estimated that there were around 130,000 blog sites, a figure that had risen to 10 million by 2004 (Hargrave 2004). By 2012 there were 181 million (Nielsen 2012).

The secret to its success is simplicity and flexibility. A blog is extremely easy to set up, even for the most technically challenged amateur, and allows its owner to give voice to their thoughts and to publish them, with pictures, sound and video if they so wish, to the world. There are bloggers covering every conceivable aspect of modern life from almost every conceivable standpoint. And there are blogs making pretty serious money. The Huffington Post, for example, launched as a comment and news aggregation blog in 2005, and was sold seven years later to AOL for more than $300 million. In 2012, it even won a Pulitzer Prize for its 10-part series on wounded military veterans. Statistician Nate Silver recently moved his FiveThirtyEight blog from the *New York Times* to ESPN, in the blogging equivalent of a big-money football transfer.

There are countless UK examples: Paul Staines (aka Guido Fawkes at order-order.com), Pete Cashmore (mashable.com) and Susie Bonniface (aka Fleet Street Fox) are among the many who have shown that an individual blog can grow into a huge business, or lead to book deals and other spin-offs. BBC business editor Robert Peston famously used his blog on the corporation's website to break the initial news of Northern Rock's travails before going on air with the story. Yet the newspaper industry still has, generally speaking, a rather curious relationship with the blogosphere that is at least partly rooted in its past.

Most national newspaper websites, for example, have a blogs section, but in many cases what appears there is little more than an online extension of their comment pages. Take the *Daily Mail*, whose website is the most visited of any newspaper in the world. Yet as I write this, the vast majority of the writers who are named on the RightMinds blog section of the site have not updated their blogs for nearly 12 months. And when they did, their output tended to be based on the newspaper columnist's approach: a trenchant opinion of a current issue that attempts to cover a debate definitively, and generally containing few external links. the *Telegraph* has lots of blogs throughout its site, and aggregates them in a 'blogs' section accessible from its home page.

The *Guardian*, meanwhile, launched its Comment Is Free blog site as a direct answer to the Huffington Post's success, but also has blogs sprinkled liberally through other sections of the site. The more successful newspaper bloggers use the platform more comprehensively than purely as a soapbox. They spark debate, they link comprehensively to other sources (see the section on linking above), they engage with their readers and with other bloggers covering similar subjects. They put themselves at the heart of their online communities.

Frederick Filloux (2012), on the Monday Note blog site, examined how mainstream newspapers were using their blogs, noting how different in quality and quantity some of the offerings were. The *Guardian*, for example, published 61 regularly updated blogs; the *New York Times* had 68; and the *Washington Post* 102 blogs (of which 13 were focused on religion). *Le Monde* had 61 'home-grown' blogs, 26 guest blogs and 30 readers' blogs. The *FT*, meanwhile, had 14. Quantity, he pointed out, was no guarantee of quality. He gave a set of requirements that he thought were necessary for a successful newspaper blog:

- a byline – readers want a recognisable name in which they can invest their trust, even if it's a pseudonym
- a dedicated writing style – a blog should be more intimate in style than a newspaper column
- a concept – the overall purpose of the blog should be explainable in a single sentence
- an insider's view – a good blog takes readers into the heart of a community.

What a blog shouldn't be, according to Filloux, is a 'dump of disorderly news contents . . . random bursts of disorganized thoughts, or a receptacle for journalists' frustration'. For student journalists a personal blog has become almost a necessity. In a competitive jobs market, it might make the difference between a job going to you or to another similarly qualified applicant.

Liveblogging: back to the future

An extension to the traditional blog is the liveblog, a stream of posts that update readers on a breaking story or an ongoing event on a minute-by-minute basis.

Newspaper organisations are increasingly using this technique to cover key parliamentary debates, sports matches, even television shows. A liveblog can be run by a single reporter or may be an aggregated reporting effort incorporating input from a number of reporting staff covering different aspects of the story. The countdown to the publication of the Leveson Report in November 2012, for example, was an event that was widely liveblogged by newspaper teams. There are various third-party tools to help the liveblogging task. CoveritLive (coveritlive.com) is one. It's also possible to use Twitter as a liveblogging platform (see this chapter's section on Twitter).

But the idea is, in fact, nothing new. As the *Guardian*'s research department spotted in 2013, the newspaper's coverage of the 1923 election featured a column headlined 'Hour by hour', which bears a remarkable resemblance to the liveblogs it currently runs on a variety of subjects (Owen 2012).

Facebook and journalism: sociable sources

The internet may have been designed as a place where we could find out about the world, so the adage goes, but instead it's ended up as a place where we tell the world about ourselves. Of all the disruptions to newspaper industry economics since the turn of the twenty-first century, Facebook stands out as one of the most significant. From a standing start in 2004, it took the social media platform less than a decade to become the most popular website on the planet. It has more than 1 billion users, and was valued at $104 billion dollars when it went public in 2012, the largest ever valuation for a newly listed company (Caulfield 2012).

But it's not just its sheer size as a media business, nor the value of the advertising it has started to take, that make it so significant for traditional publishing businesses; it's also the site's ability to engage its users. According to web metrics organisation Alexa, the average Facebook user spends nearly half an hour per day on the site. Compare that with the figure for BBC News online, the UK's most engaging UK news site, whose users tune in for fewer than five minutes per day, and you begin to see how much of a challenge it is for newspapers to attract and keep the attention of an audience online.

But social media sites are more than just a threat to the attention spans of potential readers. They also offer journalism organisations, and the reporters who work for them, great opportunities for their reporting, the distribution of their work and their ability to reach new readers and viewers. By the middle of 2013, according to the Pew Internet and American Life Project survey, more than 72 per cent of all adult internet users had a social media profile – with Facebook by far the most common. In the UK, there were 30 million Facebook accounts in 2012 – more than half the adult population, making the country the sixth most active user base for the platform.

With so much of the population connected, it therefore makes sense that Facebook can be a potentially rich source of research for the reporter, and an equally rich seam of potential readers for a publisher in search of an audience.

Web statistics analysts Statista looked at which social sites were sending web traffic to mainstream news organisations in the US, in the first quarter of 2013, and found that Facebook was the most significant (Richter 2013). The *Washington Post*, for example, gets almost 10 per cent of all of its web traffic from social media sites, with Facebook contributing close to 6 per cent. What's more, in almost every case that proportion of traffic that comes to mainstream publishers from social media is growing sharply – while the proportion coming from search engines is beginning to fall.

A supply of traffic, though, is only one measure of the influence of social media. Another significant impact on newspaper publishers of sites such as Facebook has been a loss of control over where discussion of their work takes place. Where previously a reader might leave a comment on the publisher's website, they are now just as likely to open their own channel of debate with their own circle of friends via one or more social web spaces.

News-tracking platform Newswhip, which monitors social media sites to see which news stories are being shared most widely, published a table to show which mainstream sites were most influential in sparking conversations and other inter-actions on Facebook during the month of September (Buchanan 2012). It showed that the Huffington Post was clearly at the top, with 2,531 stories over the month that had more than 100 Facebook 'interactions' – in other words users 'liking', 'sharing' or commenting on them using their Facebook profile. The *Daily Mail* was second on the list, followed by Yahoo, the BBC, the *New York Times* and the *Guardian*.

A more academic study by Baresch *et al.* (2011) examined the sharing habits of a sample of around 300 Facebook users to shed some light on the type of stories they were passing on to their friends. It found that 21 per cent of shared links were from the 'general interest/news' category, followed by products (17 per cent), commentary (10 per cent), satire/comedy (9 per cent), features (7 per cent) and all others (15 per cent). In a paper for the academic journal *Journalism Practice*, Ju *et al.* (2013) examined the social media readerships of 66 major US newspapers to see what impact they were having, if any, on their newsprint or web editions. They found that Twitter was more effective than Facebook in extending audience reach – on average, newspapers had more than twice as many Twitter followers than they did Facebook 'likes'. But they noted that visitors who arrived at mainstream newspaper websites from social network links were not as engaged – measured by higher 'bounce rates' and lower page views – as those referred from other sites. 'Therefore, an important question to ask becomes: Are newspapers repeating the same "mistake" by giving away content for free to SNS [social networking site] users and by granting audience access to aggregators?'

Facebook continues to work quite hard to find ways of allowing journalists and news publishers to integrate their social media strategies with their main digital publishing operations. So, to give one example, Facebook Connect allows users to use their Facebook login to sign in to news sites that use the service – making it easier for them to leave comments without having to create yet another online account (see the section in this chapter on reader comments). Another is the 'Subscribe' feature, which allows Facebook users to follow the postings of individual reporters or entire newspapers without having to add them as a friend. For reporters looking for stories, Facebook's new Graph Search function is also proving highly valuable as a resource (see Chapter 5).

One word of caution here. While for many people Facebook *is* social media, it's worth remembering that web users are notoriously fickle. It's not so long ago that MySpace was the web's most popular destination – but once users decided it was no longer cool, the downward momentum proved unstoppable. Facebook's ubiquity may not last forever.

Digital doorstepping: privacy in the age of sharing

Here's an ethical dilemma I sometimes give to students on our undergraduate and postgraduate programmes. You meet a woman during your work as a reporter, and in the course of your brief interchanges with her, she accepts you as a Facebook friend. Several months later, she suddenly becomes a key source on a breaking news story entirely unrelated to your original reason for your contact – because her ex-boyfriend is wanted by police in connection with a serious crime. Because she has you as a Facebook friend, you are able to see all the messages she shares with her small circle of other Facebook friends. You can also see that she has her privacy settings so that only those friends can see her comments about her ex – which you know would be dynamite quotes for use in your report on the breaking story. Your editor is very keen for you to use the quotes in your story for the newspaper. What do you do?

The nub of the argument here is about expectations of privacy. On one hand, the internet is a public space. On the other, her privacy settings indicate that she doesn't want everything she says visible beyond her own circle. But she knows you are a journalist and has accepted you as a friend – so does that carry an implicit approval for you to use the quotes?

The concept of 'digital doorstepping' is as new as the social networks from which it springs. It became widely used for the first time following a murderous shooting spree on the campus of Virginia Tech – most of whose victims were students who had online profiles. Journalists raided these for information about the victims, and for details of their friends, whom they then chased for comment. As Alfred Hermida (2007) points out: 'This content is both private and public at the same time. It is private in the sense that it was intended for a specific audience of friends. But it is also publicly available online. This is a new ethical area for journalists.'

In some cases, journalists were believed to have set up online Facebook tribute pages to some of the dead in order to attract quotes from people who knew them. But that's not to say that all Facebook activity is off limits for reporters. In 2012, the Press Complaints Commission rejected a complaint against the *Farnham Herald* after it used pictures and details of an assault that had been posted on the social network site (Turvill 2012b). In that case, the victim himself had uploaded pictures and details of the assault, but had left the settings as 'public' (albeit unwittingly, according to him).

In our earlier example, the wise thing to do would be to contact your Facebook source directly – which has the double solution of ensuring she's happy to be quoted, and of getting something exclusive for your publication. If she's not available, or doesn't respond in time for your deadline, then it becomes an ethical judgement call. Talk it through with your editor. But don't be pressurised into doing something you feel is ethically wrong.

Twitter and journalism: news in 140 characters

Curious though it may seem now, in its early days the world wide web was not particularly up-to-date – not in the journalistic sense, anyway. For example, before about 2004, a Google search would produce a snapshot of web content that could be up to 24 hours old – because it could take that long for new content to be indexed by the company's technology at the time. For journalists, that made it useful for archive research, but not a lot of use for breaking or rolling news stories, or for updates on what was happening at that moment.

Today, we have what's often referred to as the 'real-time web', in which updated content is indexed and available on feeds as it happens. Right at the forefront of that movement has been the microblogging service Twitter, in which users post short updates of 140 characters or fewer. Launched in 2006, its growth as a business and a cultural phenomenon has been rapid. In 2013 there are more than 200 million active users, who collectively send more than 500 million tweets every day – and the company was planning a public listing on the stock exchange that could value it at $10 billion (Cellan-Jones 2013). Key to its success has been its accessibility to mobile users; its surge in popularity coincided exactly with the arrival on the market of affordable smartphones that allow their users more or less constant connection to web data, and the brevity of tweets makes them particularly attractive to that group.

Journalists have been pretty quick to recognise Twitter's value for newsgathering and for the digital distribution of their work. Most newspaper newsdesks today have a dedicated Twitter account which they use for sending out information on breaking stories – often, but not always, linked directly back to their main web pages.

For reporters, the social media aspect of Twitter is particularly compelling. By 'following' selected Twitter accounts, a reporter can keep up-to-date with news and comments from key sources within their community (see Chapter 5). Furthermore, they can use their own accounts to take the temperature of their audience's reaction to unfolding events, or seek eye-witnesses at the scene of a news story. The use of hashtags – a simple keyword filter used widely by Twitter users to group story trends together – is also very useful for reporters following a specific story or development.

Lehmann *et al.* (2013) identified a group of Twitter users they defined as 'news curators' – individuals whose interest in a particular topic could make them very useful sources to reporters and news editors. Some reporters use Twitter as a liveblogging tool (see earlier section) to post rolling updates to council meetings, sports matches or other set-piece events. Such has been its impact on journalism, Twitter's enthusiasts have been able to claim a number of notable 'scoops' for the service (Mackey 2009).

- One such was the first picture of the Airbus jet that crash-landed in New York's Hudson River in 2009, tweeted by J_nis Kr_ms. Half an hour after sending his tweet he was being interviewed on network television as an eye-witness.

- When terrorist gunmen attacked a string of hotels in Mumbai at the end of 2008, Twitter was used by many news organisations as a source of eye-witness accounts of the confusing and dramatic unfolding events.

- When mass murderer Anders Breivik ran amok in Norway in 2011, Associated Press's social media editor was alerted by unusual activity on

Twitter that something was amiss, and used the site to monitor the ongoing horror as some of the students involved tweeted what they had seen (see also Chapter 3).

- The Haiti earthquake of 2010 was the first significant international disaster where Twitter played a notable part. The first tweet was published seven minutes after the earthquake hit, and several thousand followed during the period when only two foreign correspondents were in the country and there was an insatiable demand for information from news organisations everywhere.

Like all technologies, though, Twitter comes with a series of health warnings that reporters should take seriously. The Iranian uprising of 2009 was, at the time, labelled the 'Twitter uprising' on account of the fact that much of the information about it was circulated via mobile social media. With western journalists banned from the country, and the authorities determined to shut down access to radio and television, many newspapers used Twitter as a source for some of their reporting. As Nic Newman (2009) points out, though, this was problematic for two significant reasons. Firstly, a large amount of rumour and false information circulated through Twitter, leading to several examples of erroneous stories being reported as fact. A large proportion of tweets that purported to come from within the country were later shown to have originated elsewhere.

Secondly, the balance of reporting became skewed. The majority of Iranians who had access to the technology that allowed them to tweet and post online were from the middle classes who supported one particular party. But the country's voting majority are typically from poor, rural areas – which meant the online debate simply did not feature their voices.

Finally, like any digital technology, Twitter is not entirely secure from hackers and hoaxers. In 2013, several mainstream news organisations, including the *Guardian*, the BBC, Reuters and Associated Press, had their accounts hijacked – in the latter case to send out false news that the White House had been attacked. Newspaper reporters have found similar problems in reporting fast-changing events such as the London riots in 2011 and the Boston Marathon bombings of 2013. Now it may well be true, as Clay Shirky suggests (2009), that the collective wisdom of the crowd will tend to correct these errors quickly, but reporters should remain vigilant about checking Twitter sources just as rigorously as they would any other second-hand piece of information.

They should also beware that their own tweets could lead them into murky waters. Several journalists were among those caught out by the disastrous *Newsnight* programme in 2012 which alleged that an unnamed senior Tory was involved in allegations of child abuse. Twitter was awash with speculation that this was Lord McAlpine. But the story was wrong, and well-known journalists including the *Guardian*'s George Monbiot (Halliday 2013) had to issue grovelling apologies and reach compensation agreements.

Also in 2012, a reporter from the *Great Yarmouth Mercury* was sacked after retweeting on his personal account jokes linking a well-known celebrity to a police investigation into sex abuse. In those situations, the disclaimer 'views are my own' on your account will not save you.

User-generated content: participatory pitfalls

For more than a century of mass-market newspaper publishing, the best that most readers could do to get their voices heard was to send a letter to the editor in the hope that a severely truncated version of it might appear in print several days later. What digital publishing has revealed is that readers' appetite for involvement in the debate, and even in the newsgathering process, is in fact far greater than many in the industry had ever imagined.

As we have already seen, the BBC's realisation of this came with the flood of emails it received to its nascent news website following the death of Princess Diana. Dan Gilmor (2004) wrote about a similar effect for American newspapers following the attack on the World Trade Center towers – an effect which saw what he describes as the 'former audience' beginning to play a significant part in framing public understanding of an unfolding news event.

Today, more than a decade later, that former audience has a wide array of sophisticated tools at its disposal with which to get involved in almost every aspect of the news process. Many of them have devices in their pockets or handbags that can take pictures of publishable quality, shoot and edit simple video sequences, and capture decent-quality audio – all of which can be uploaded to a publisher's web platform within seconds of it happening.

On several high-profile stories, material gathered by members of the public has turned out to be some of the most compelling. The tsunami that hit several countries in south-east Asia at the end of 2004 was notable in a news sense for the fact that no professional news cameras were there to capture the devastation as the waves hit – but many holidaymakers carrying video cameras were. The following year, when London was hit by a series of coordinated bombs that exploded on tube trains and a bus, it was passengers carrying mobile phones in the inaccessible gloom of the underground tunnels who were able to capture some of the grim aftermath of the explosions. The BBC alone received 22,000 emails and text messages, 300 photos and several videos on the day (Douglas 2006).

And in 2009, when innocent bystander Ian Tomlinson was violently shoved to the ground by a Metropolitan Police officer during protests at the G20 summit in London, it was footage from the mobile phone of another passer-by, discovered and published by the *Guardian*, that led to an inquest, a criminal trial, a High Court claim and eventually an apology from the force (Taylor 2013).

User-generated content (UGC as it is known in the industry) takes many forms, and is now an essential part of the newsgathering process. In a report for the BBC, Wardle and Williams (2009) identified five different types of UGC:

- audience content (pictures, audio, video footage and eye-witness accounts)
- audience comment
- collaborative content (produced with professional assistance)
- networked journalism (organised with the help of large crowds to gather specific data)
- non-news content (such as pictures of pets or weather).

Most modern newsrooms will have systems in place for acquiring, encouraging and (crucially) verifying contributions from their audiences – some even have UGC editors (see Chapter 3). So, for instance, in the summer of 2013, when more than 100 cars were involved in one of the UK's worst ever road pile-ups on a fog-bound Sheppey crossing in Kent, the *Kent Messenger* newsrooms were able to react quickly to the footage it was being sent from motorists caught up in the chaos. Their pictures and eye-witness accounts of mangled cars and massive traffic jams helped to give the *Kent Messenger*'s website its highest ever traffic – and were used widely on national television bulletins throughout the day.

Non-professionals have a range of reasons for wanting to play their part in the news machine – among them a desire for fame; a need to feel part of a community; and the feeling that they have to share something important. Bradshaw and Rohumaa (2011) identify several different types of UGC contributor, including:

- the brain – an expert source with detailed knowledge of a subject
- the voice – a commentator who is able to write lively comment on a variety of subjects
- the ear – someone with a particular insight into a specific community
- the accidental journalist – someone who stumbles on a story as an eye-witness, for example
- the technician – a web technology enthusiast who takes some existing detail or data and does something interesting, such as constructing a digital map
- the value adder – who adds additional detail, or links, to a story.

Hermida and Thurman (2008) investigated British national newspapers to see how far their web strategies went towards integrating UGC into their newsgathering and publishing efforts. Their survey showed a dramatic increase in newspapers adopting UGC policies between 2005 and 2006, but a degree of uncertainty remained as to their overall value to the newspaper brand and to the cost benefits they represented. Several contributors to the survey pointed out how time consuming it can be, for example, to moderate readers' comments – either pre-publication or reactively – to root out 'spam' and abusive, legally suspect or irrelevant posts. The study additionally highlights a crucial consideration for any journalist wanting to use UGC as any sort of bellwether for overall public opinion. Comments on stories on the BBC's website come from just 0.05 per cent of the daily audience on a typical day, while the *Guardian* reckons its UGC contributors represent between 1 and 5 per cent of its overall audience.

So, for any kind of participatory journalism, it's worth bearing in mind the 90–9–1 rule of online audience participation (described by, among others, Ochoa and Duval 2008). Sometimes also called the 'participation inequality' rule, this states that for any online community, 90 per cent will only observe (or 'lurk'), 9 per cent will make minimal contributions and 1 per cent will make extensive contributions. Wikipedia's community is a very good example of this in action. As Adrian Monck succinctly puts it:

> People very often don't want a conversation. People's interest in media is very often as background. The earliest investigations into media going back to the foundation of Gallup indicate that people are not as absorbed in media as the creators of media.
>
> (cited in Newman 2009)

Crowdsourcing: getting the audience to do the work

Here's a cautionary tale. In April 2013, several bombs exploded near the finish line of the Boston Marathon in Massachusetts, killing and maiming runners and spectators. In the days that followed, a massive manhunt for the bombers swung into action. The FBI released images from CCTV cameras around the bomb site showing two individuals whom they were keen to find, and thousands of amateur sleuths pored over their computer screens trying to identify them – many from an online community using the social network recommendation site Redditt.

Within hours, two names were circulating widely, one of which was Sunil Tripathi, a university student who had disappeared several days earlier. And when a Redditt user then claimed to have overheard a police message in which Tripathi's name was mentioned, the news spread like wildfire on the site, and on to other platforms including Twitter. Excited social media fans everywhere celebrated their success in identifying a suspect in one of America's most shocking crimes. A typical tweet trumpeting the triumph of the wisdom of the crowd came from Greg Hughes (@ghughesca): 'Journalism students take note: tonight, the best reporting was crowdsourced, digital and done by bystanders.'

Except that it wasn't. Sunil Tripathi was never a suspect. Neither was the other name that was widely circulated. As far as anyone can tell, Tripathi was never mentioned by police in connection with the bombing. His family, already overwhelmed by fear of what had happened to their missing son, had to endure messages posted on the Facebook page they had set up in a bid to find him, linking him to one of America's worst crimes. His body was found some days later in a park in Rhode Island.

Crowdsourcing, a term coined by Jeff Howe in *Wired* magazine (2006), is certainly one of the more compelling concepts of participatory journalism, and we'll look at it in more depth in Chapter 10. Johanna Vehkoo (2013) defines it as a task in which a network of readers are invited to take part in data collection or processing for a specific task – as distinct from simply collecting user-generated content or encouraging online comments. The idea that a journalism organisation can tap into the collective expertise of a group of engaged readers to achieve a task that would be impossible for an individual reporter is clearly appealing. And some newspapers have enjoyed notable crowdsourcing success stories.

- As we have already seen, the *Guardian* used it to find footage of the incident that led to Ian Tomlinson's death. It did a similar job to track down witnesses to the death of Jimmy Mubenga, restrained by security guards on a deportation flight to Africa in October 2010 (Taylor and Lewis 2013).
- The *Mercury*, a newspaper in the US state of Pennsylvania, used the Pinterest website to post pictures of crime suspects wanted by the police, and asked readers to identify them. The result was a 57 per cent increase in arrests (Daly 2012).
- And Finnish newspaper *Helsingin Sanomat* used its readers to crowdsource data about stockbrokers' secret trading bonuses.

Vehkoo (2013) identifies five important factors characterising successful crowd-sourcing projects for journalists:

- breaking down tasks: divide complex projects into achievable chunks
- motivation: make it fun or appealing to take part
- verification: make sure you can check the truth or validity of their input
- community building: make contributors really feel part of the investigation
- openness: don't frustrate your community by holding back important details.

She also identifies three important misconceptions about it. Crowdsourcing is not about random groups of people; it's not about replacing journalists with amateurs; and it's not about getting other people to do your job for you. Done well, crowdsourcing can be used to shine a light into areas of darkness and help perform vital functions of public service journalism. Left alone to run amok without proper verification processes, as Sunil Tripathi's family found to their great dismay, it can sow dangerous confusion and do great harm.

CHAPTER 8

Feature writing

Painting pictures with words

There's only one golden rule of feature writing and it's this: be interesting. Whereas readers will happily browse through the news section of a newspaper, moving on when they feel they have absorbed enough detail of a particular story, reading a feature requires a greater investment of their time. They will not forgive the feature writer who beckons them to join a compelling-sounding voyage, but who then fails to deliver a sufficiently entertaining experience.

Features tend to contain more comment, analysis, colour, background and a greater diversity of sources than news stories, and to explore a larger number of issues at greater depth. It is the extra length that accounts for many of the distinguishing elements of features.

And many of the conventions that apply to news writing – such as (often) not writing in the first person – are torn up when it comes to features. A feature may argue a case, and the personal views of the writer may be prominent. Where the objective of news is to convey a sequence of facts as efficiently as possible, in features the writer is often trying to provoke an emotional response. Readers should feel shocked, angry, delighted, outraged, moved, inspired. But never bored, baffled, lost or diffident. Or that they know more about the subject than you do. By the time they have finished, you want them to feel like writing a letter to the editor, haranguing their MP or sharing the story with their friends. That means the structure of the feature – which usually does not follow the more formulaic 'inverted pyramid' of the news story – needs to take the reader on a journey. There needs to be some kind of narrative arc.

The layout of a feature is often more colourful and imaginative than that of a news report. The headline, the standfirst (those few words that accompany most features summarising or teasingly hinting at its main point/s and carrying the byline), the intro, the picture captions and sometimes the graphics are worked on together by the subeditor to convey the overall message of the piece. It helps, then, if the reporter is able to think visually while composing the feature. Adding extra, linked features to the package (such as a profile, a vox pop, a background chronology) will also help improve the overall display.

PAINTING PICTURES WITH WORDS: KEY INGREDIENTS

Every feature has an angle: a particular aspect of a wider issue that can be investigated in some detail to help illustrate a broader picture. This might require a focus on specific communities, individuals, ideas, companies, regions or demographic groups. There are other key ingredients too. A good feature is likely to contain several of these elements:

- facts
- quotes
- descriptions
- stories
- anecdotes
- opinions
- analysis
- data
- conflicts
- trends
- case studies.

The skill of the chef is to mix them in the most compelling way possible.

The peg

Most features do not start with the five Ws and the H of the traditional news intro (see Chapter 6). Nonetheless, there has to be a peg – sometimes referred to as a 'hook' – which explains why this particular piece is relevant to the audience, and why it is relevant *now*. Many feature pegs come from following a current news story and focusing on a particular aspect of it. But there are plenty of other places to look for them: anniversaries of key events; life experiences of interesting characters; trends observed among your friends; dramatic personal experiences – all of these can give you a peg on which you can hang your research to build up a feature.

Intros: an infinite variety

The intro is the feature's single most important paragraph. It establishes the tone and voice of the writer, and sets the scene for the reader, hopefully compelling them to go deeper. There are an infinite number of ways to begin a feature, which is part of their great appeal. We can define some very broad categories.

The case-study intro

The vast majority of feature stories have a human angle. They are interesting to an audience for precisely this reason. You, as the writer, are helping to put that audience into the shoes of an individual or a group of people who are intensely affected by an issue. Often, the best way to do that is by way of case studies: the personal stories of the ordinary people caught up in your story. Sometimes, particularly in newspaper magazine layouts, these case studies will be treated as 'boxouts', separate from the main narrative flow. But in other cases they can also make effective intros.

Like this one from the *Daily Mirror*'s Tom Parry (20 March 2012):

> HANDS clasped together in prayer, Kyoko Sato wipes away a tear for her best friend – one of 74 pupils at Okawa Elementary School killed by the tsunami.
>   The 12-year-old trembles as she stands before a shrine by the crumpled building where she has just placed a symbolic stick of incense.
>   This is her weekly pilgrimage for her pal Airi, who was 11 when she was washed away by the tidal wave.

Quote intro

Most news intros (as we have seen in Chapter 6) do not start with a direct quote. In contrast, features can often begin with striking quotes: they set the scene and tone effectively and concisely as well as conveying the human dimension. As here in *The Sunday Times* (19 February 2012) at the start of a feature on young people imprisoned after the summer riots of 2011, British Press Awards feature writer of the year David James Smith opens with:

> 'What is your relation to the prisoner?' the uniformed officer asked. 'Friend,' I said. Even though we had never met, Jamie Counsel needed a friend and, more importantly perhaps, he needed to be heard.

Or here, in an *Observer* report (26 October 2004) on police racism:

> 'There's no Pakis round here,' spat the teenager. 'This is a white town.'
>   The youngster was right: Llandudno's Asian community was nowhere to be seen. Inside the pubs of Mostyn Street, the patrons are exclusively white.

So, too, are those flitting among its string of shops. Maybe this is what drew PC Rob Pulling to the popular Edwardian seaside resort, a place he felt his hateful intolerance could be shared without reproach.

Eye-witness intro

Gaith Abdul-Ahad, along with several other intrepid foreign correspondents, makes something of a trademark of his eye-witness accounts for the *Guardian*. Here's one from 26 August 2012, as he reports on the bloody conflict in Syria:

> The rusting green Mercedes truck could have been mistaken for a removal lorry. It was parked in a narrow street outside a luxurious villa a short distance from the Turkish border, and the arms and legs of chairs and tables protruded from the tarpaulin that covered the back. Beneath the furniture, however, were 450,000 rounds of ammunition and hundreds of rocket-propelled grenades destined for the Syrian rebels in Aleppo.

The news intro

Occasionally a feature will begin in a news style but then break away to cover the issues in a less formulaic way. For instance, the London *Evening Standard* (23 February 2000) began a feature on acquaintance rape with a straight news angle, but moved on to carry the verbatim accounts of two women at length:

> Acquaintance rape is Britain's fastest growing crime, according to recent Home Office research. But the rising figures could well be the tip of an iceberg, women's groups believe, because many such attacks – where the woman knows, no matter how briefly, her attacker – go unreported.

Historical background intro

A focus on the past can often throw a particular light on the news of today. Thus a few opening pars focusing on historical background can be an effective way of leading into the main angle, as here in Paddy Shennan's intro for the *Liverpool Echo* (12 September 2012):

> **APRIL 15, 1989 to September 12, 2012.** Twenty-three years, four months and 28 days. It's a scandal that it has taken this long to get to this point but, of course, the Hillsborough families and survivors know all about scandals. And cover-ups. And a lack of accountability. And the denial of justice. Today though, the covers were off with hundreds of thousands of documents having been dusted down and distilled into a near 400-page report.
>
> It may take days and weeks to fully absorb the weighty words carefully crafted by the diligent members of the Hillsborough Independent Panel.

But to help people take on board some of their key findings, members of the panel addressed family members and survivors this morning before facing the media this afternoon.

There it was, in black and white, after all this time. All this campaigning. All this waiting. And my God, it was even worse than many of us had thought.

The shocking lies and shifting of blame. The abhorrent and appalling attempt to denigrate the dead and survivors. The rank amateurism and ineptitude of the emergency service response. All of this is laid bare in this astonishing report, with sickening revelations coming thick and fast.

Striking contrasts intro

Highlighting striking contrasts in descriptive language can be an effective way to inject urgency and special interest in the intro section. Here, in the *Guardian* (31 March 2003), Alfred Hickling, through vivid, colourful writing, contrasts a deprived Leeds suburb with the area around West Yorkshire Playhouse to highlight Mark Catley's background:

> The south-Leeds suburb of Beeston is barely a mile from West Yorkshire Playhouse but it may as well be in another country. Situated on a windy hill overlooking Leeds United football ground, Beeston is one of the city's most deprived urban areas. Its most famous landmark is the desecrated grave-yard featured in Tony Harrison's poem *V*. Many of the red-brick terraces are boarded up and abandoned; the only business that seems to be thriving is the bookies.
>
> Nobody from Beeston ever goes to the Playhouse, including, until recently, the 32-year-old writer Mark Catley.

The personalised intro

In news intros the 'I' of the reporter is only rarely prominent. But the tone of features can be far more personal, putting the reporter into the heart of the action – as with this opening on a piece about scientology from the *Evening Standard*'s Joshi Herrmann (11 July 2012):

> Twenty minutes into my visit to Saint Hill Manor last week, a Georgian house on the edge of East Grinstead and about an hour on the train from Victoria, a uniformed man with a dog approached me, and he wanted to check a few things.
>
> 'You are a Scientologist?' he asked, with a Polish intonation.
>
> 'No, I'm just having a look around.'
>
> 'So you are a guest,' he said. 'We like to know who is here.'

Question intro

Questions rarely begin news reports. But in features they are OK. As, for instance, in this quirky report by Tanya Gold in *The Sunday Times Magazine* (25 March 2012):

> What happens when money runs out, Mother, and bills are unpaid? The bailiffs come and take your stuff, child. Every year bailiffs collect £600m in debts in Britain. They are the first to see when banks stop lending; the first to see the recession roll in. They are the monsters that haunt the nightmares of a consumer society and, because I am always intrigued by those who are mysterious, I ask Marston, the biggest bailiff company in England, if I can follow its officers for a week and observe our bonfire of the vanities.

The narrative intro

Sometimes, features can begin in story mode: a familiar territory for most readers. Here Gareth Davies, of the *Croydon Advertiser*, sets the scene for a feature on the first anniversary of the riots that devastated the town in August 2011:

> Binu Mathew had been pinned against his shop window and repeatedly punched in the face in front of his terrified wife, then looked on helplessly as hooded youths destroyed the business they bought with their savings.
>
> But as the couple fled down London Road in their van, Mr Mathew, blood pouring from his face and his shirt ripped from his back, did something almost unbelievable. In the middle of a full scale riot, surrounded by hundreds of menacing figures breaking into businesses and attacking people on sight, he stopped at a red light.
>
> Before the signal turned amber, he and his wife Lisy George, 39, were surrounded, dragged from the van, beaten and then robbed.
>
> Their ordeal summed up the events of August 8 – decent law-abiding people falling victim to wanton criminality.

Intro pitfalls

A good intro will avoid:

- too much detail
- too little detail
- being too rambling
- being too obvious – particularly when asking a question
- asking too many questions
- being too hypothetical.

THE BODY OF THE TEXT: THEMATIC STRUCTURE

While colour, description, opinion, analysis, narrative, quotes, dialogue and historical contextualising may be important in a news feature, they are all still built on the cement of factual detail and a sharp news sense. Just as, in news stories, the most important information comes first with the details declining in importance thereafter, so the same is true of news features.

At the same time, the writing style of features can be far more colourful and varied than that found in news stories. Emotional tones (angry, witty, ironic, condemnatory, adulatory) can vary along with the textual rhythms. Before launching into your writing, along with establishing the structure, it is crucial to identify the emotional core of your piece. Take these opening pars from a feature by Paddy Shennan in the *Liverpool Echo* (11 September 2012; see Figure 8.1), which helped him to win feature writer of the year at the Regional Press Awards:

> IT WAS the day that changed everything – the 20th anniversary of the Hillsborough disaster and a memorial service like no other. A record-breaking attendance of around 30,000, more than double the previous record of 14,000 for the 10th anniversary service, gathered at Anfield on a day marked out by its raw emotion, passion – and anger.
>
> Many in the stadium had simply had enough of being fobbed off – and Andy Burnham, the then secretary of state for culture, media and sport, was about to feel the full force of their frustration.
>
> He may be a Scouser and a football fan – on April 15, 1989, he was at Villa Park supporting Everton in that day's other FA Cup semi-final – but on April 15, 2009, he was a member of a Labour government headed by a Prime Minister who had ruled out the possibility of a fresh inquiry into Hillsborough, just as the then-home secretary Jack Straw had done months after Labour swept into power.
>
> Liverpool-born, Cheshire-raised Mr Burnham had been invited to speak by the then Lord Mayor of Liverpool Steve Rotheram, now Labour MP for Walton, and he provoked much applause – not least when praising those fans who helped the dying at Hillsborough and saluting Merseyside's sense of community, spirit and solidarity.
>
> But there was also booing, barracking and cries of 'hypocrite' which, after the minister had sat down, prompted Hillsborough Family Support Group president Trevor Hicks to apologise.
>
> Yet today many may say the ends justified the means, as the call for full disclosure of the unseen Hillsborough files gathered pace that day – Mr Burnham has stressed that he and Garston and Halewood MP Maria Eagle had already been working on this. Today, recalling the 20th anniversary, Mr Burnham said: 'I agonised about whether I should go. My main worry, and it seems strange saying this, was getting through my speech without crying.'

FIGURE 8.1

Paddy Shennan's award-winning feature for the *Liverpool Echo*

Use of parentheses

Parentheses are rarely seen in news stories: they break the urgent flow of the copy. But given the more flexible rhythms of features, they can work. For instance, Jonathan Glancey, in his *Guardian* report (10 January 2000) on the newly restored Pompidou Centre in Paris, wrote:

> Below shop and cafe are a children's rumpus room (the sort of mimsy you expect to find at Ikea) and a bookshop twice as big as before.
>   At the centre of this space is a stunted tree growing from a huge cube of earth rising from the basement (where four new performance and lecture spaces, including a second cinema, have been shaped) and a shoulder-shrugging information desk. (Don't try to speak a foreign language and, whatever you do, don't attempt your school French: this will only make matters all the more degrading for you.)

The final flourish

A hard news story carries information in order of news value. The last par is the least important and can be cut without destroying the overall impact. A news feature can be different (Hennessy 1993; Adams 1999: 82–5). News values still apply, but the final section often carries its own importance. A feature may explore a range of views on a subject and conclude by passing a comment on them; another may argue a case and come to a conclusion in the final section. A final par may raise a pointed question; it may contain a striking direct quote or summarise an argument. Feature subs have to be particularly sensitive to this. Writers often include the words 'Must par' in brackets before a final sentence to stress its importance to the sub (who will not feel obliged to follow the advice).

NEGOTIATING THE SUBJECTIVE: THE EYE-WITNESS

Journalists often attend sporting events, not to record the happenings and results from a specialist perspective, but simply to describe the experience of being there. As Lynne Truss (1999: 127) commented: 'Uniquely in journalism, its appeal to the reader is entirely in the presentation of the simple fact: "I was there; I saw it with my own eyes; it happened once and it will never happen again."' The journalist becomes the outsider looking in. Such an assignment presents a varied challenge. You will need to extract a range of factual details relating to the event and highlight any news elements. It will provide you with opportunities for descriptive colour, eye-witness reporting, the development of sources and the use of quotes, and for the exploration of your subjective response.

The experience of attending an event as an 'ordinary member of the public' is very different from being a reporter there. As a journalist, you are likely to have a notebook and tape recorder to record any interesting sights, interviews and facts. You are on the look-out for the unusual, perhaps even the slightly bizarre, the newsworthy. You need to keep all your senses alive to collect a mass of details, quotes and impressions that will go towards creating your article. You are unlikely to provide a simple chronology of your experience: arrival, watching spectators, the highlights of the event, results and departure. Instead, special journalistic values should come into play. You may want to intro on a lively quote or a striking incident that happens towards the end. It may be good to start with a colourful description of a participant and then pan out to take in the overall event.

Eye-witness writing is always overtly subjective. It should never be self-indulgent. If you are describing an underwater hockey match, the reader doesn't need to know at length your fears of underwater swimming originating in some early childhood trauma in Lake Ontario. This constraint does not apply to celebrity writers. Their own subjectivity is often, in journalistic terms, as interesting as the event they are describing, so their self-indulgence is legitimate. But, in general, subjectivity works best when handled delicately. It is not easy striking the right balance between egotism and sensitive, effective subjectivity.

Eye-witness features within this genre are usually aimed at non-specialist readers. So you may need to explain the rules of the game, if it is an unusual one, and the level of support in the UK. Evidence of class, race and gender bias runs through whole segments of British life and is prominent in sporting activities. Certain sports are more distinctly working class (football, ten-pin bowling, rugby league, darts) than others (polo, hunting, grouse shooting). There may be opportunities in your feature to explore these aspects.

Unusual sports are played all over the UK: it is a challenge to search them out in your own area. Don't worry if you have never seen them played before. The newness of the experience will make it all the more intense for you. All the same, it is advisable to prepare as far as possible before covering the event. Consult local libraries for contacts and information; ring the relevant national sports council or consult its website. Type your chosen sport into a web search engine and see what comes up. Ask friends and relations if they have any background information.

You may find the event boring and unintelligible. That merely poses the challenge of conveying that dullness in an interesting way. Always try to stay true to your feelings. Given the many pressures and constraints on journalists, that is not easily achieved. Try never to transform what you experience into a cliché you hope to be accepted by your news desk; try never to transform the 'dull' into something lively simply to 'beef up' your copy. It will inevitably appear inauthentic. Tone will be an important ingredient of your piece. Humour, irony, wry self-criticism, mock chauvinism: any of these may be appropriate. But the tone has to emerge from your own experience. The eye-witness piece will work only if that tone is genuine.

JOURNALISTS' DILEMMAS: THE ORWELL SOLUTION

To what extent can and should journalists remain outsiders? How much do journalistic notions of neutrality, objectivity and balance conflict with inevitable feelings of sympathy, compassion, alienation, confusion and solidarity? George Orwell grappled with such dilemmas by going to live the experience he wanted to write about (Inglis 2002). He became a *plongeur* (a dish-washer in a hotel kitchen) and a tramp before writing *Down and Out in Paris and London* (1933); he fought alongside the Republicans in the Spanish civil war and wrote of his experiences in *Homage to Catalonia* (1938).

Later, Orwell (often considered one of the twentieth century's greatest journalists) largely ignored the prestigious Fleet Street outlets for his journalism and concentrated his attentions on small circulation, left-wing and literary publications. But even the 'Orwell solution' is not without its problems and paradoxes. The best journalists can do is seek to understand their own histories, their own subjectivities, as well as the broader political dynamics of their society. It is perhaps a tall order – but worth striving for.

PAINTING A PROFILE

Open a newspaper and you are likely to find a profile somewhere. People, according to Harold Evans, former editor of *The Times* and *The Sunday Times*, are news. The profile (in French, *portrait*), the drawing of a portrait with words, is the archetypal manifestation of this 'people/human/interest bias' in the media. It need not be only of a person: organisations, buildings, cemeteries, roads, parks, schools, Father Christmas, even weapons (rather obscenely) can be profiled. But people profiles are the most common. Profiles succeed in satisfying a wide range of interests.

- *Readers*: profiles are immensely popular. They feed people's curiosity about other people. What makes them tick, what hurdles have they overcome, what is the person really like behind the public face, what accounted for their downfall? This kind of questioning has great appeal. The ToT (triumph over tragedy) story, in which people talk about their success against tremendous odds, is a particularly popular genre. We become voyeurs into private or professional lives.

- *Reporters*: writing profiles is fun, challenging and can often help a journalist to build up contact with a useful source. Reputations can be made on the strength of profile writing.

- *Editors*: profiles often appear in series that guarantee a certain space being filled each week. Readers like the series format also, perhaps because they provide a feeling of continuity, stability and order. They occupy the same spot at regular intervals and so simplify the reading process.

- *Proprietors*: there is an important commercial aspect to profiles. In terms of cost-effectiveness they are particularly attractive to newspaper proprietors. An interview with an accompanying picture can easily provide half a page (broadsheet) or a page or more (tabloid or magazine). Compare this with the cost-effectiveness of investigative reporting. A journalist may spend hours, months even, investigating a story and get nowhere.

- *People*: being profiled can pander to their vanity. Profiles can help promote business. A writer, for instance, hopes the publicity will help sell more of their books. The PR industry is forever pressurising the press to profile their clients.

Types of people profile

There are many kinds of profile, and no standard format. There are no profile rules. The following lists a few styles within the genre.

- A short profile may highlight some newsworthy feature of the subject. A variation on this theme are the tiny portraits of people drawn in diary or gossip columns.

- A profile may focus on the person's views about a contemporary issue or experience, or highlight a recent achievement or failure.

- A longer profile will aim to provide an overview of a life. The person will be chosen probably because of a newsworthy element (a new job, a new book/film/television series/political campaign, or a visit to the local region) which will be highlighted.

- A person may be profiled because of some unusual feature of their life. They may have the largest collection of football or theatre programmes in the country, or an unusual job such as travelling around advising gypsies on educational matters. The news element here is not significant.

- There is a whole range of 'special focus' profiles that build a picture of a person around a specific angle. *The Sunday Times* has its 'Life in the Day' series and 'Relative Values', in which two members of the same family give their impressions of growing up with the other person.

- Becoming increasingly popular are question-and-answer profiles around various themes. The *Guardian Weekend* supplement has its 'Questionnaire', in which celebrities answer a standard series of questions, while the freebie *Metro* series has 'The 60-second interview'. Often these special-theme profiles are commentaries rather than interview-based features. The *Guardian*'s G2 has 'Pass Notes', in which the subjects are dissected through a jokey, conversational style of questioning.

Preparing the paint

Focus

The journalist has to be aware of the particular kind of profile sought by their publication. Is it to be an overview of the life, or a focus on the latest achievements or affairs, or a 'life in the day' (very different from a 'day in the life')? In every case, the focus will influence the questioning. The journalist tends to indicate to the subject during their initial contact the kind (and possible length) of profile envisaged.

Background research

Absolutely crucial. Quite simply, the more knowledge of the subject and their special area you bring to the interview, the more respect they will have for you, and the more likely they are to open up. Thus, if you are interviewing a writer/film director/television producer or sports personality/local council leader/political campaigner, you should be aware of their previous achievements. People featured in *Who's Who* will not expect questions about fundamental details of their life. The challenge is very different when the subject is unknown. Then, the journalist needs to convey an interest in their subject and their specialist area.

Before (and, if possible, after) the interview, ask other people about your subject. You may want to include some of these views in your profile. Consult the cuttings; check out Google, other search engines and their website (official and unofficial); consult the celebrity site www.celebritiesworldwide.com – but don't presume details are accurate without checking. Immerse yourself in your subject.

Place of interview/s

Most profiles are built on the basis of one-off interviews. Describing the time and place of the interview might provide colour to the piece. Good journalists use all their senses. Sometimes, the profile is the result of a series of interviews. On one occasion the subject may be relaxed, on another completely different. They may be extremely busy; describing snatches of conversation in various places can convey a sense of their hectic lifestyle. The journalist may meet the interviewee before the formal meeting by accident – and describe the experience in their copy. Occasionally a person is so famous they are extremely difficult to get hold of. Describing the hunt can provide colour to the profile. If the hunt ends in failure, the non-story can become the story. Again, some people are very shy of interviews. When they finally agree, the rarity is worth highlighting.

Sometimes personalities are unwilling to be interviewed. Profiles of them are still written, often containing comments about the person by other people. The person may have revealed something about themselves in a rare television interview, and quotes and details from that may be used. Occasionally a profile might be built around a press conference, but then the copy loses the feeling of intimacy that a face-to-face interview provides. Increasingly, profiles are amounting to nothing more than rewrites of cuttings with some newsy element in the intro, and concern is growing over the power of PR departments to shape celebrity profiles. According to Tad Friend (1998): 'Most profiles are almost scripted by the PR agency.'

Constructing the profile: those important brush strokes

The influence of the news

Profiles need not begin with the newsworthy aspect. They might seek to highlight a particularly significant or unusual event in the past. They might open with a particularly revealing quote. They might be descriptive, focusing on the appearance of the person or the environment in which the interview takes place. But many profiles are influenced by the news agenda, and in these cases their news aspect will never be buried in copy. It will be near the start. Take, for instance, this profile of Nia Long by Elsa O'Toole, in the *Voice* (1 November 2004), which focuses, in chatty style, on her role in the recently released film remake of *Alfie*:

> Let's face it, most women would not require the Dutch courage of a stiff drink before bedding Jude Law. Even if it was on a pool table, with 30 hairy-arsed film crew members standing around ogling.
>
> For Nia Long, however, it's all part of the day job, so when it came to shooting love scenes with Britain's hottest hunk, alcohol was foremost in her mind.
>
> The film in question is the *Alfie* remake which stars Jude in the title role made famous by Michael Caine in 1966.

Other profiles, in contrast, are 'timeless', without a specific news angle. The person themself may simply be newsworthy, or there may be something particularly interesting about them.

The importance of quotations

Most profiles will carry the views of the person through the use of direct quotes. The importance of these to the profile cannot be overstated. Given that the profile is attempting to paint the most vivid portrait possible, the language of the interviewee is a vital ingredient of their personality. A profile in which all the views are in reported speech will be deadly dull.

Some profiles will carry snatches of conversation (sometimes remembered rather than noted) verbatim. This helps provide special insights into the subject as well as varying the rhythmic pulse and tone of the writing. As here, from Joanna

Coles's profile of the American novelist Joyce Carol Oates in *The Times* (7 April 2000): the novelist Edmund White, who has an office opposite at Princeton University, 'bursts in'.

> 'We're talking about the role of illusion,' says Joyce by way of introduction.
>
> 'She's being very modest,' I complain.
>
> 'Well she's great,' says White.
>
> 'Oh isn't that sweet,' Joyce giggles.
>
> 'Ever since I've been here, she's taken me under her wing and introduced me to everybody. She's incredibly sweet and has more energy than anyone I know,' says White. 'And she's also incredibly smart.'
>
> 'Oh my, *blush!*' cries Joyce.
>
> 'Very good, very good,' beams White sweeping up his raincoat and bustling out. 'See you later.'

Notice how Coles uses a range of attributive verbs ('says', 'complain', 'giggles', 'cries', 'beams'). Similarly, in her profile of Hollywood star Jamie Lee Curtis, Tiffany Rose (the *Independent*, 3 December 2004) used 'practically hollers', 'chatters away', 'rattles on', 'says wryly', 'shrugs', 'almost snorts', 'says, sighing'. That variety is typical of many features and profiles, but be warned – poorly handled, it can appear contrived.

Hard news hardly ever begins with direct quotes, but profiles quite often do. A striking phrase can encapsulate so much of a person's personality. Other profiles will merge quotes from a conversation into one long, direct quote, as the 'Life in the Day' feature in *The Sunday Times*'s colour supplement. The interviewee will often be consulted to see if they approve of the editing. Some profiles carry quotes from people about the interviewee, their personality and/or their work. This is particularly the case in 'authoritative' profiles which attempt to provide an overview of the person and their achievements.

Descriptive colour

Many profiles carry descriptions of the person, their appearance, their mannerisms perhaps, their asides, the environment where they live, work or are interviewed. All this adds colour and variety to the copy. Thus, to capture the personality of Italy's famed foreign correspondent Tiziano Terzani, Peter Popham (the *Independent*, 21 April 2004) described his home in detail:

> Tiziano Terzani at home in Florence is reminiscent of one of those 18th century English nabobs, returned after a lucrative spell with the East India Company laden with treasures of the East. The home is fabulous, a house high up on the hills above Florence, in a district justly named *Bel Sguardo* (beautiful view). A cherry tree is in bloom outside the front door. The home he shares with his

wife and frequent travelling companion, Angela, is full of the spoils of their journeys: an antique Chinese four-poster bed, chests and carpets, gleaming bronze buddhas, thousands of books.

Or take a look at the collection of marvellous profiles by drama producer and critic Kenneth Tynan. This is how he describes Noel Coward's home, with such clarity, colour, metaphorical inventiveness and meticulous attention to detail (Tynan 1990: 34):

> His house in Kensington is like a smart tavern in a market-town: hidden in a mews, with doors of glass and wrought-iron, and new-smelling panelling on the walls. A chic but quiet rendezvous, with a goods cellar, you might judge, until you enter the studio – a high, airy room which might belong to a landscape painter with a rich Italian mistress. There are paintings everywhere except on the floor, which is board as often as it is carpet; over the door, an excellent oil of the owner by Clemence Dane; deep, snug and unshowy armchairs; and two grand pianos on rostrums in opposite corners.

But do not be tempted to invent descriptive colour to brighten up a phone-based profile. In its 1992 report, the Press Complaints Commission criticised a reporter who said of the interviewee 'Watching her, sitting up in bed', though they had never seen her face-to-face.

Chronology

Only rarely do profiles begin at the beginning of a life and end with a focus on the present. That chronology will appear extremely dull, since it reflects no concept of journalistic values. Instead, profiles can highlight a newsworthy/specially interesting aspect of the person and then, in the body of the article, take up the chronological theme, finally returning to the main theme. But be careful not to make confusing chronological jumps (first talking about 1975, then 1965, then 1999, then 1962).

In his *Independent on Sunday* profile of Brian Keenan, held captive by Islamic militants in Lebanon during the 1980s, Cole Moreton begins by exploring his search for self-understanding (7 November 2004). Then, mid-way through the profile, Moreton offers a concise narrative of Keenan's life up until that fateful day in 1986:

> He was restless, in the first three decades of his life. After school in east Belfast he worked as a plumber's apprentice but then went on to university to read English literature. He kept returning to Belfast after working in Spain, Brussels and Scotland but at the age of 34 he decided to cut free of a city that was 'falling apart'. He took up a year's contract to teach English and Russian literature at the American University in the Lebanon, intending to travel on to Australia when it expired. One early morning in April 1986, after four months in Beirut, he was surrounded at the gates of his villa and bundled into a car.

Newspapers often carry the biographical details briefly in a box accompanying the article, leaving in the profile the space to concentrate on more up-to-date matters. Such 'fact boxes' are also useful for giving textual and visual variety to the page.

The presence of the reporter

In any representation of an individual there is bound to be a subjective element. Many profiles rely on an entertaining mix of quotes and background detail, the journalist subjectively selecting the material and remaining invisible in the copy. But some profiles exploit the journalist–interviewee relationship and make the journalist intentionally intrusive. Reporters may present their own views on the subject or on some of the issues raised in the interview. They may describe the dynamic in the relationship and how the interviewer responded to some of the questions (abruptly, hesitantly). This is how Miranda Sawyer, in the *Observer Magazine* (31 October 2004), describes actor Bill Nighy:

> When I say to him, I'd like to talk to you about your clothes, he almost whoops with joy, and we spend a good 20 minutes on suits, including which buttons to do up your jacket: 'Middle: always. Top: sometimes. Bottom: never. Younger men do this unbearable thing where they do all these buttons up, and you just want to kill them.'

Top interviewer Lynn Barber, in the *Independent on Sunday* (30 January 2000), was not afraid to admit her insecurities to her readers when profiling Jimmy Savile (revealed after his death in October 2011 as a serial paedophile). Notice how she makes no attempt to soften the impact of the question ('I hope you don't mind me asking, but'); she goes straight to the point:

> Still, I was nervous when I told him: 'What people say is that you like little girls.' He reacted with a flurry of funny-voice Jimmy Savile patter which he does when he's getting his bearings.

And in her *Independent* profile of Hollywood star Jennifer Tilley (19 November 2004), Tiffany Rose uses both her eyes and ears, observing her subject's droll reactions to passers-by:

> At our early-morning rendezvous in the lobby of the Sutton Place Hotel, Toronto, Tilly is glowing. She is oblivious to the admiring glances from onlookers who clearly recognise 'that face' but are having trouble placing it. 'They're probably thinking: "Did we go to college together? Were you a bridesmaid at my first husband's wedding? Or something"', she muses.

The bias of the newspaper

When newspapers of the left carry profiles, they often promote strong political points rather than the subjective bias of the individual reporter. As here, *Socialist Worker* (3 June 2000):

> Brian Souter, head of Stagecoach, has tried to pose as the voice of the people with his funding of the referendum over the anti-gay law, Section 28, in Scotland.
> Really, he is a shark who has spent the last 20 years building a multi-billion transport company by ruthlessly forcing other companies off the road.

The finishing touches

Profiles usually end on a significant note. Copy doesn't just die away meaninglessly. A common device is to end on a positive note, particularly if the subject has been open in the interview about their difficult times. Thus a profile of singer Russell Watson by Rebecca Hardy, in the *Daily Mail*'s *Weekend* section (20 November 2004), which has focused on his childhood difficulties and the 'hell' of his early career struggles, ends with this telling quote:

> 'I appreciate what I have because I did go through the mill,' he says. 'I'll never forget what it was like to have nothing.'

The tone

This is the most vital ingredient of the piece. Is it to be an affectionate piece? Is it to be respectful, gently mocking, a damning exposé, intellectually discursive, witty, 'neutral'? (Hopefully never sycophantic.) In each of these, the language used will be different. You may spend a couple of hours, even days, with your subject. They may offer you a meal. Some form of human contact is established. It is then very tricky to write a damning (though obviously non-libellous) profile of that person. Equally, there is a danger of solving this dilemma by lavishing praise on your subject. There can be no standard response. At all times, passing judgement should always be handled delicately. A crook, a racist or a sexist needs to be exposed. But the interview is an extremely artificial environment and the impression that the subject provides should always be viewed as partial and superficial.

CHAPTER 9

The art of interviewing

Interviews are what breathes life into journalism. The great *Express* editor Arthur Christiansen constantly told his reporters: 'Always, always tell the news through people.' The only way to do that is by speaking to them.

The dynamics of every interview are different. They may be 15 seconds or many hours long; they may take place in a busy street, a secluded hideaway, a packed pub or an airport lounge. Rex Reed once interviewed singer Bette Midler while she was sitting on a toilet in a gay bathhouse (Silvester 1994: 30). They may be friendly or confrontational. They may be about someone's sex life or about high matters of state. The controversial Italian journalist Oriana Fallaci often spent up to seven hours in her interviews (which she described as 'coitus' and a 'seduction') with famous people such as Golda Meir and Indira Gandhi.

Many interviews are unpredictable. Sometimes an interview can change your life. This happened to Fenner Brockway (1986), the late Labour peer, peace activist and journalist, who was 'converted' to socialism following his interview with Keir Hardie.

How then to write about such imponderables? One of the most eminent Fleet Street interviewers, Lynn Barber, formerly of the *Observer* and *Penthouse*, the *Independent on Sunday* and *The Sunday Times*, admitted: 'I've made various attempts at instituting a system for organising interviews but have come to the conclusion that, in journalism, panic is the system.'

Here are a few tips to help you traverse the fascinating territory of the interview. The best way to learn is to go out and do it. But always go about your journalism with a critical hat on. Watch colleagues, examine interviewers on television, listen to them on the radio. Notice how they can differ in their techniques. Seek all the time to improve what you are doing.

WHY INTERVIEW?

An interview is intentional conversation. But, as a journalistic convention, it has to be seen in its historical context. It is easy to imagine the interview as a 'natural', unproblematic activity. But Christopher Silvester (1994: 4–48) shows, in his seminal history, that the interview as a journalistic technique had to be invented. The interview between Horace Greeley, editor of the *New York Tribune*, and Brigham Young, the leader of the Mormon Church, in 1859 lays claim to being 'the first full-fledged interview with a celebrity, much of it in the question and answer format familiar to modern readers', as Silvester (1994: 4) comments. According to Jean K. Chalaby (1998: 127), the practice of interviewing spread to England in the 1880s, largely pioneered by W. T. Stead, the editor of the *Pall Mall Gazette*.

Journalists should always be aware of the interview's specific purposes: they may be seeking exclusive, new information or confirming established facts; they may be providing opinion or evidence of someone's state of mind. They may be investigating a subject and seeking to expose a lie or wrong-doing. Observing closely the work or home environment in which the interview takes place can help provide extra details to the picture of the subject being drawn by the journalist. For the source, the interview has a purpose too: they are seeking to convey an opinion or information, hide a secret or merely articulate their mood. But beware – the source may be:

- confused, yet afraid to admit this
- afraid to speak their true opinion; they could lose their job or face social or professional isolation
- lying, conveying misinformation or propaganda, or seeking revenge
- intimidated by the presence of a reporter and so not expressing their true feelings
- flattered by the interest of the journalist, and coming across as more extrovert and 'colourful' than they normally are
- forgetting or hiding important details
- speaking in a foreign language, and so unable to express what they mean
- making fun of the whole interview process.

The reporter's personality and bias, even their body language, are likely to affect the relationship with the source and the kinds of response solicited. A reporter may be afraid of their source (for instance, if he is a Balkan warlord) or may defer to someone they consider famous or powerful. A different reporter might draw out different answers. Someone may respond more openly to a female reporter, another may feel more relaxed with an older man. Research has shown that interviews by black and by white people draw different kinds of response.

But remember: relax. Louis (Studs) Terkel, the celebrated American interviewer, had this modest explanation for why people opened up to him so easily: 'I'm inept. I'm known as the man with the tape recorder but I'm inept. Often I press the wrong button. So people aren't in awe – they see this guy who's having trouble with a tape recorder.' (Burkeman 2002)

TYPES OF INTERVIEW

The quickie or grabbed interview

Many interviews are short. You may be covering a parliamentary select committee and want to follow up something said. You have time to ask just a few questions. You have a clear idea of your angle and need extra information and/or quotes to support it. You go to the MP, pen and notebook in hand (tape recorders are not permitted). There are just a few minutes before the MP is off on other business.

Vox pop

This is not about interviewing Madonna or Robbie Williams. It is the jargon term for the short interviews that journalists have with people on a given subject (*vox pop* is derived from the Latin for 'voice of the people'). Do you think a law should be introduced to restrain the press from invading people's privacy? That sort of thing. Local papers love vox pops: accompanied by mug shots of those quoted, they provide lively, easy-to-display, 'human interest' copy. Newspapers often build up a story around a series of short quotes drawn from street interviews (with a photographer accompanying the reporter to provide mug shots for the story) or from ring-arounds. A subject is identified and there follows a list of people with direct quotes attached to them. Or a vox pop can constitute part of a feature. The main story can dwell on the news, background and important details. A series of quotes highlights a range of views in an easy-to-read format. Sally Adams gives this advice on out-of-doors vox pops (2001: 11):

> The best way to find people likely to talk is to look for the journalistic equivalent of a captive audience: people who are already standing still, waiting for a bus, for instance, or in a queue to get into a club. Shopping centres and street markets can be productive areas.

Also be aware of the ethical issues involved: how important is it to reflect ethnic, age and gender diversity and range of viewpoints in your selection?

Doorstepping and ambush interviews

Occasionally journalists wait outside people's homes in the hope of gaining an interview. This 'doorstepping' technique is used particularly to gain access to celebrities. It can be abused, with the journalistic 'rat-pack' intimidating sources with their constant presence. Similarly, a journalist might suddenly swoop down on a source to ask them questions. The 'ambush' technique should be used only when all other means of gaining access have been exhausted and when the issues are serious enough to warrant such treatment. It is most commonly used by television investigative reporters, the ambush itself providing dramatic footage.

And beware of overstepping the line into harassment. Actress Sienna Miller's evidence at the Leveson Inquiry (see Chapter 4) evoked much public sympathy when she described being chased by a pack of photographers. 'I was 21. I would often find myself running down a dark street on my own with 10 big men chasing me. If you take away the cameras what have you got? A pack of men chasing a woman. That's a very intimidating situation to be in.'

The death knock

It's a rite of passage for many a young reporter. 'There's been a car crash', their editor tells them. 'A 16-year-old lad has died. I want you to visit the parents. See what you can get.' The death knock interview is one of the most demanding and emotionally difficult tasks a reporter will have to undertake. There is always uncertainty over the reaction to their appearance – it might be a torrent of abuse, but more likely will be a welcome understanding of the reason for the visit.

In 2012, Jackie Newton and Sallyanne Duncan surveyed 49 regional newspaper reporters and six senior executives who had responsibility for commissioning death knock stories. They also conducted interviews with 24 bereaved families, who were generally positive about their experiences with local journalists. One bereaved parent said:

> To me there's always a story behind the headlines and if that story is told in a proper manner with compassion and accuracy between the person with the pen and the person telling the story I think it's a good marriage. It's a good thing to do because it can also help families being able to talk about their loved one.
>
> (Newton and Duncan 2012)

But for the other side of the story, it's worth reading journalist Chris Wheal's less positive experience when there was a tragic death in his family (Greenslade 2010).

In a *Press Gazette* piece, Mary Stevens (2001) talked to a number of experienced reporters who gave sound advice on how to approach a death knock effectively. They include: be smart, polite and apologise for the intrusion; explain that it's an opportunity to pay tribute to the person who has died; don't say 'I know how you feel' unless you genuinely do. And finally, if a family makes it clear they don't want to talk to the press, leave straight away.

PHONEY JOURNALISM

Speed is the essence of journalism, and the phone or email provide the easiest and quickest ways of contacting a source. But as Christopher Browne (1996) comments:

> The speed and frequency of deadlines means that instead of meeting their sources face to face an increasing number of today's reporters and correspondents rely on mobile and standard telephones, faxes, pagers, teleprinters and computers to get their stories. This creates an artificial barrier between the newsmen [*sic*] and the news leading to errors, misunderstandings and reports that lack the inimitable freshness of human contact.

The advice is clear: whenever you have an opportunity to see a source face to face, take it. If you are to develop that source, you will need to meet them.

Phone interviews tend to be shorter than face-to-face contacts. Reporters have to be clear about the questions they want to put and the information they need. There is little time for waffle. Profiles are rarely conducted by phone: the contact between reporter and source is too superficial and impersonal. At the same time, reporters conducting phone interviews have to be extra sensitive to the nuances of speech: a hesitancy, an abruptness, a quivering in the voice all carry meanings which the reporter should be quick to note or respond to.

A reporter should also try to confront the impersonality of the phone and respond emotionally to the conversation. Facial and arm gestures can all help; if you are stressing a point, move your hands about; if jokes are made, laugh. Standing up can help provide extra confidence when making a particularly difficult call. Some journalists lodge a phone on their shoulder and type up the conversation at the same time. Not only can this practice lead to repetitive strain injury (RSI), but it can be also intimidating to the source, and the reporter may have to return to note-taking with a pen if no other solution is possible.

INTERVIEW PHOBIA

It is common for people new to journalism to find first contact with sources difficult. It is a challenge to ask a stranger questions (maybe in a foreign language) and maintain a coherent conversation while taking a note. Some find the 'distance' provided by the phone reassuring; others find face-to-face interviewing less intimidating. If you are not at ease on the phone, you are not alone. Communications specialist Dr Guy Fielding estimated in the 1990s that 2.5 million people in Britain suffered telephone phobia (Rowlands 1993). And despite the ubiquity of smartphones today, many student journalists are surprisingly reluctant to use them for voice calls in the early stages of their careers because they are so much more accustomed to using text messaging and email as a means of communication (see also Chapter 5).

In your first few months of reporting, it is a good idea to join up with a colleague during assignments. While journalism is an individualistic job, it can succeed only through people working in a team. Joint reporting in no way conflicts with journalistic norms. One of the most famous scoops, the exposé of the Watergate break-in, was the result of a joint effort by Carl Bernstein and Bob Woodward of the *Washington Post*. Investigative reporters often work in pairs or threes. It is safer, and while one asks the questions the other/s can observe reactions and the environment closely (K. Williams 1998; Spark 1999; de Burgh 2000).

If you are alone on an assignment in those early months, or at any other time, it is fine to ask someone to slow down in their talking. Don't hesitate to ask the interviewee to spell out a difficult word, or to repeat a strong quote or important information. Figures, names and titles are worth particular attention. Don't hesitate to ring back to check or extract new information. That merely reflects painstaking efficiency rather than incompetence.

THE ROLE OF PRESS OFFICERS

If you are contacting pressure groups, political parties or professional bodies, you are likely to come into contact with their press relations officer (PRO). It is important to establish good relations with this person. They can be a vital source for background information and sometimes good for a quote. They can provide contact numbers for other sources, and help in setting up meetings and interpreters if deaf people or foreign-language speakers are being interviewed.

But PROs expect a certain amount of background knowledge from reporters. A local government PRO would not expect to have to explain the intricacies of the community tax to an enquiring reporter. Official spokespersons are generally not referred to by name. They are described as 'a spokeswoman for such-and-such body'. They might also refer you to someone else in the organisation with specialist knowledge and responsibility in the area you are investigating.

IN CASE OF INTIMIDATION

Some people may feel intimidated by a phone call from a journalist. It might be their first contact with this awesome and seemingly powerful institution, the press, so capable of destroying reputations. You may decide to give them time to think about their responses. You could give them a few basic questions, which they can respond to when you ring back in, say, twenty minutes. You have established some trust and they may be more inclined to respond to other questions. If the source is a racist attacking Pakistani or gypsy homes in your area, you will adopt a different approach. As so often in reporting, political and ethical issues merge.

ARRANGING A FACE-TO-FACE

Be polite, stay relaxed and sound efficient. It is important straight away to establish the likely length of the interview. The source is likely to have their own diary of engagements to complete. PROs often organise the meetings for celebrities, and minor skirmishes are likely over arranging the time and place of the interview. Negotiating the time length is important since it provides a shorthand indication of the probable depth of the questioning.

Most interviews aiming to extract specific information can last for around half an hour; for a profile of any depth at least three-quarters of an hour is required, though they can last up to three hours (with a follow-up phone conversation as well). Lynn Barber (1999: 198) says that she refuses to do any profile interview for less than an hour. Ginny Dougary (1994), of *The Times*, says she spent two hours with Michael Portillo for her award-winning interview in which he revealed his gay past – and followed it up with a telephone conversation.

Give a brief indication of the purpose of the interview (whether for a profile, as part of a feature or an investigation) and, in general terms, the kind of questions to be put. Identify clearly the newspaper you are working for and, if you are a freelance, the target publication you are aiming at. In some cases a subject will be interviewed by a group of reporters. In that case, it is a good idea to spell out briefly how your approach is intended to be different. Indicate if you are to be accompanied by a photographer or (where relevant) an interpreter.

Fixing time and place

There are several potential locations:

- *Your territory* (newspaper office if you are a staff writer; your home/office if you are a freelance; college if you are a student). This is rarely adopted by reporters; offices lack the privacy and relative calm needed for interviews and can appear intimidating to members of the public.

- *Their territory* (home, particularly likely if the person is unemployed, office or shop floor). Journalists often visit the source's home when writing a profile. People tend to feel relaxed there and talk most freely. The home is an expression of their personality: the source might wish to display it. The reporter can certainly use their observations of it and the source's behaviour within it to provide colour in their copy. The reporter might also visit the home when the source considers it too sensitive to hold the interview at their workplace. Visiting homes is not without its problems. The source is extending their hand to the reporter, inviting them into their private territory. The reporter can find it more difficult criticising the source after developing this kind of contact. Investigative reporter Nick Davies (2000) advises reporters not to park outside their source's home. 'If they are prompted to look out of the window they will make decisions about you before you introduce yourself.' The source's office is a common site for an interview (factory shopfloor workers are rarely profiled given current news values). The environment can be made relatively free from distractions and relevant information and documents will be at hand.

- *Neutral territory* (a pub or restaurant): useful sites when you are building up contacts. Their informality promotes fruitful contact. The source is being 'entertained' and that helps the conversation flow. The journalist will always go with a specific intention, but the informality allows time for digressions, small talk, gossip and jokes. All this helps in developing a relationship. The journalist can express their own knowledge of, and views about, the subjects discussed and that, too, helps develop trust.

Reassuring the source

Sometimes a source will need reassuring that they are not opening themself to attack by agreeing to be interviewed. Members of progressive groups, such as peace activists, feminists, trade unionists, gays, lesbians and anti-capitalists, have been pilloried in the media, and their fears are understandable. Even in today's supposedly democratic Britain, a large number of people are afraid or unwilling to express their views to the media. In these situations it is important to explain whom you are writing for, and what you hope to extract from the interview. Edward Jay Friedlander and John Lee advise (2004: 146): 'If you detect reluctance on the part of the subject, try to find out what's bothering the potential interviewee. If the problem is something you can correct, correct it. For example, if the subject is concerned about the kind of story you intend to write, send a sample of a previous story you've written.'

Never speak to someone on the basis you are writing for one media outlet which they are happy with and then send the copy elsewhere without consulting them. Student journalists might win a difficult interview on the understanding it is not for publication. This makes for unreal journalism (since it is credible only in the context of a target publication) and so should generally be avoided. Certainly the student should resist the temptation to betray a trust and send the copy off to a newspaper.

Submitting questions in advance

Someone might speak to you only on the condition they see a list of questions beforehand. Many politicians and showbiz celebrities are now adopting this line. It is a practice which, in general, should be challenged. Journalists can end up clerical poodles pandering to the whims of the famous. But it is wrong to call for a blanket ban on this request for questions.

A journalist may be aware of the interviewee's views; they are more important as a source of information. Since speed is of the essence in journalism, the source might plead ignorance and essential information may go missing. They might need to do some research or consult colleagues before answering. At least sending questions gives them time. They cannot plead ignorance during the face-to-face interview.

It might be legitimate, when a crucial source is sought and no other way appears possible, to agree to send a list of questions. You may even suggest it. At least some response is gained, and there is the possibility the source will be impressed by your questions and invite you in for a face-to-face. An interviewee might first promise half an hour of their time, but then running through the previously submitted and impressive questions might easily last for an hour and a half.

At the opposite end of the scale from the media-shy person is the self-publicist. Every newspaper office will be harassed by someone desperate for coverage. Reporters need to be on their guard against this kind of person.

Preparing for an in-depth interview

Preparation is essential (Coleman 1993). If you are well informed, you are more likely to extract new and interesting information and to be sensitive to the source's bias. Read the cuttings, do the research, check the internet (particularly fan sites if you are covering a celebrity), talk to friends and colleagues about the subjects likely to be raised. An uninformed reporter becomes the pawn in the hand of the source: they can lie, they can hide crucial information, they can misinform, they can steer the conversation away from tricky subjects. Celebrity interviewer Ginny Dougary says that she prepares for an interview 'like a military campaign'. To help prepare for asking difficult questions, she psychs herself up with deep breathing, wears smart clothes and makes absolutely sure her tapes are working.

Most professions have their own stock of jargon, and there is a bewildering array of acronyms with which the reporter should have some familiarity. But sources used to handling the press have different expectations of journalists. The specialist is assumed to have more knowledge than the generalist and cub reporter. Never be afraid to express ignorance. Better to clarify a point than flounder or carry mistakes in your copy.

The question of questions

Journalists differ on the extent to which they prepare specific questions. To avoid 'drying up', some argue it is best to write down most of the crucial questions in a logical order and tick them off as the interview proceeds. But many find this can impede free-flowing conversation. Talk usually moves too quickly to allow this ticking-off. If a detailed list of questions is used, it should be on a separate sheet of paper and not buried in a notebook. In any case, interviews can often move in unpredictable directions, making it absurd to stick to a preplanned outline.

Another approach is to think through the interview beforehand, listing detailed questions in order. The act of writing helps the memory. For the interview, three or four vital headings are listed, and around this skeleton the flesh of the interview can be spread.

Dress sense

A journalist should be conscious of the messages put out by their dress. Informal dress will be appropriate on some occasions, such as when interviewing members of progressive campaigning groups or think-tanks; formal dress when meeting white-collar professionals or politicians. A journalist will always have at the back of their mind: 'If I dressed differently, would the source be more open to me and more trusting?'

Preliminary courtesies

First contact is crucial. The reporter should be calm and relaxed, polite but assertive. The greeting should be pleasant, with a firm handshake and some eye-to-eye contact. The reporter might need to make clear again the purpose of the interview (though during some investigations the real purpose might be hidden).

If the interview is off the record or unattributable for some reason, this needs to be established. Politicians and most PROs will be aware of the attribution conventions of newspapers. But many people are not. They may begin to answer questions and then try to designate them as off the record. A journalist should not be willing to permit that kind of arrangement automatically. A source may say something on the record that, in print, could damage them or someone else unnecessarily. In this case, the journalist will operate self-censorship.

If you are planning to use a tape recorder/Dictaphone, make sure this is fine with the source, who might choose to set up their own taping device, after all. You might not wish to bring out your notebook until you have relaxed into the conversation and passed the preliminary courtesies. The notebook should never be over-prominent.

THE ACTUAL INTERVIEW

Note-taking

In your first weeks as a reporter, you may find it difficult keeping a conversation going while making notes at the same time. Don't feel self-conscious about that. You may even say: 'That's an important point. Would you mind repeating that?' Selecting the useful information and quotes becomes an art. Sometimes all the notes will be used, usually just a part of them. The writer, confident in their powers of memory, might add more details or comments they remember but did not take down. This has to be handled carefully, particularly if the views are contentious and potentially libellous. Without any notes or tape recording, the journalist has little defence in court.

Presenting your personality

Dennis Barker (1998), former media correspondent and columnist on the *Guardian*, argues that journalists should ask 'questions which the Man on the Clapham Omnibus would ask if he were there' and should not follow their own agenda. But it is impossible to deny your personality in the meeting. The selection and bias of your questions, your manner and your dress will carry the stamp of your personality. The extent to which your personality more overtly intrudes on the interview will differ according to the circumstances.

In most interviews where the focus is on extracting views and information, the reporter's intervention is likely to be limited. An exchange of views and a joke or two are useful for varying the mood and helping conversation flow. In profile interviews, your own personality can come more and more to the fore. Someone confronted with a reporter who is nothing more than a blank sheet merely uttering concise questions can hardly convey their own personality.

But you should never dominate a meeting. Your views and experiences are of secondary importance, and should be revealed only to entice more out of your subject. Displaying some of your knowledge on the subject can also impress the interviewee and help build up trust. Never show off. And don't be too familiar: it is rarely appropriate to address your source by their first name.

Pacing the interview

Most journalistic training manuals advise reporters always to begin with the non-threatening questions establishing basic information and views. This helps to create trust, after which more sensitive questions can be raised. In practice, reporters respond in many different ways to the shifting dynamics of the interview. Some suggest it is best to throw in a difficult question near the start. As Lynn Barber (1991) comments: 'The subject's relief at having survived it so quickly and painlessly may pay dividends for the rest of the interview.'

Yet there is always the danger that the interviewee may call a stop to the conversation early on if this strategy fails. Barber (see Reeves 2002) says that at the start of interviews she makes a point of stressing the interviewee's right to refuse: 'Please don't be offended by my questions. If you don't want to answer them, just shake your head and I won't even put no comment.' Questions should be concise. But the interview is not likely to be all questions. It may be fruitful to exchange ideas. Formulate a mix of open-ended questions and specific questions, avoiding those that call for a yes/no answer.

Active listening

Most interviewers stress that active listening is one of the most crucial skills. Journalists can often be surprised at how open and talkative people are when profiled. Their vanity may be flattered. Here is someone taking an interest in them; however fleeting, a little fame is assured by the coverage. In some respects the press (and the media in general) have taken over the role of the church as the site of the confessional, where personal secrets are revealed. Every day the press carries the revelation of some secret: the secret of so-and-so's sex life; the leak of secret divisions in the cabinet; a secret arms sale.

Paradoxically, this is happening in a society where government and industry are becoming increasingly secretive and remote from democratic accountability. Given the willingness to talk, the journalist's role is to listen intelligently and help the conversation along with concise, clearly focused questions.

The flexible approach

Reporters should be relaxed and flexible, ready to abandon their list of questions and follow up more interesting ideas as they emerge. They should always be clear about what they want from an interview. It is dangerous to go into an interview with a vague brief hoping that something will come out of it. It rarely does; the reporter will end up with a lot of waffle. In contrast, continual evasive responses to key questions suggest to the reporter they are on to something important. There is a place for unstructured chat, say over a meal, between journalist and source. Contacts are being maintained and maybe something of interest will emerge. But chat is very different from an interview.

Power games people play

The distribution of power in many communication processes is complex and fluctuating. A source may seek to exploit the reporter to transmit their views, their misinformation or their propaganda. The reporter exploits the source as a 'quote giver' or 'information giver'. In this light, interviews can be seen as a contest. The journalist must be aware as far as possible of the dynamics of the interview and try to be in control, determining the flow. The interviewee should never take over. If they do, by rambling on some irrelevant point, for instance, the journalist should reassert their authority with a pointed question.

Body talk

Eye contact is important, but continuous contact is likely to appear intimidating. During profile interviews, other aspects of body language and non-verbal communication, such as sighs, shrugs, silences, coughs or shrugging of shoulders, will be closely observed by the reporter. Interviewing children poses special problems for the journalist. For instance, getting eye contact with them often involves crouching down (Hughes and McCrum 1998). Also, be aware of your own body language: is it helping to put the subject at ease?

Don't fear the silence

Any reporter who has listened back to the recording of an in-depth interview knows the feeling of horror at the sound of their own voice interrupting their subject at a crucial moment. It's amazing how often this happens. That's because it's easy to forget you are not taking part in a normal conversation.

It also means overcoming your fear of pauses and silences. Some of the most experienced interviewers know that if they don't attempt to fill the silence, their interview subject often will – and by doing so can often add telling detail or make revelations that they wouldn't otherwise have made.

Raising the emotional temperature

Another great tip from Lynn Barber is to be wary of interviews that seem to be going too well. It's not uncommon for a journalist to find, mid-way through the interview, that they are enjoying the company of their subject and have unconsciously relaxed into a social mode where they're no longer thinking as a journalist. This might feel like a more enjoyable experience for the journalist, but it usually doesn't make for particularly compelling copy.

Barber's trick when she finds herself in this position is to excuse herself and go to the bathroom, where she will 'psych' herself up to ask some more difficult questions and 'raise the emotional temperature' of the interview.

DEALING WITH THE DIFFICULT ONES

The hostile interviewee

An interviewee may be hostile for a number of reasons. They may have a poor opinion of the press in general, or have been criticised in the past. They may feel threatened or insulted by a particular line of questioning. They may simply dislike the sound of your voice or the colour of your jacket. As a result, you may have to reassure them about the standards you and your newspaper follow, and that you understand their sensitivity about a particular issue.

Whatever happens, keep cool. Never argue with an interviewee. Try to steer the conversation towards calmer waters. If the source is particularly important and reacts nervously to your questions, you may agree to show them the copy before publication. Lynn Barber (1999: 197) says 'the best interview ever' was Lillian Ross's profile of the novelist Ernest Hemingway. Ross sent him the article before publication: he asked for one deletion, which she made. Sometimes the source might walk out on you. That is their privilege.

It can also make for great copy in itself, like Janice Turner's 2013 interview with screen actor Rhys Ifans for *The Sunday Times*, which opens like this:

> I'm not sure where it started to go wrong with Rhys Ifans. A truly awful interview can catch you like a cloudburst in August. How quickly his answers escalated through disdain to disgust then mad-eyed vibrating hostility until he announced 'I am bored with you' and stalked out, leaving his publicist hand-wringing and ashen.

The over-hasty interviewee

This is the person who says: 'I don't have time to talk to you.' A good response is to say something like: 'I won't take up much of your time, but this is an important matter and I want to get it right.' Be sympathetic and straight to the point. They should thaw.

The silent interviewee

You don't seem to be going anywhere. They answer in dull, monosyllabic tones. Give them time to warm up, open-ended questions and lots of encouraging head-nods. If all else fails, fall silent and see what happens.

The 'no comment'

As veteran investigative journalist Phillip Knightley (1998) advises, never take 'no' for an answer. If the source is particularly important, be persistent but don't harass them. If they continue to say 'no comment', you could tell them this looks bad in print. Stress you don't want to write a one-sided story and need their comments, perhaps to correct inaccuracies. Ask why they cannot comment. Someone may try to delay you until the following day. Suggest the story is going to print and will be unbalanced without their quotes.

The dodger

They may claim ignorance of some major detail but be simply trying to avoid controversy. You need to be well briefed to cope. They claim to have been absent at a crucial meeting. 'Ah, but I have looked in the minutes of the meeting and noticed you were present.' That sort of comment should jog their memory.

The waffler

They may habitually be a raconteur and stray away from the main conversational issues. Or they may be trying to evade a delicate issue. Don't let them take command of the conversation. Keep it focused.

Ending the interview

Sometimes it is worth asking: 'Is there anything else you wish to mention?' Appropriate courtesies should be made: 'thanks for your time' and so on. And arrangements for checking and future contact (perhaps also by a photographer) can be made. If you have interviewed them at their office, it might be useful to have their home number and email details.

An interviewee might ask to see copy before it is published. You will then have to deal with that issue.

AFTER THE INTERVIEW

This is another crucial period. You might need to ring or email back to clarify some points. They might well contact you again. Often after profile interviews, it is courteous to write back thanking them for their time. Also try to transcribe the tape and compile your article as soon as possible after the event. If you wait, you are more likely to forget details, distort others and find your notes incomprehensible. When the interview is part of a feature investigation, it should similarly be written up as soon as possible and ideas for new interviews and issues to examine should be noted.

Direct quotes

These are best reserved for expressions of opinion. For instance: 'She said: "Tony Blair has already proved himself to be the worst prime minister of the century."' Direct quotes add a newsy element to stories and provide colour, immediacy, authenticity and the crucial human dimension to copy, hence their prominence. They can also add humour. Quotes also help personalise the news. It is always better to have an individual express a view than an impersonal institutional voice. Instead of 'the National Union of Teachers claimed', say 'a spokeswoman for the NUT claimed'. When using a press release, a phone call or email may be necessary to add this detail.

Lengths of direct quotes will vary. But take any book of quotations and see how short the majority are. Some of the most famous are a matter of a few words. Just as the heavies use longer sentences than the pops, so their quotes tend to be longer. But do people speak in shorter sentences to tabloid journalists?

It is a vexed question among journalists as to how much freedom they have to edit a direct quote. Most will agree that such phrases as 'you know', 'like I said' and 'er, er' slipped into conversation can easily be cut. Beyond that, some argue that a direct quote should never be changed. However, there is a case for editing when someone speaks ungrammatically. Nothing is served by leaving it in other than showing that the source is stupid. Thus particular care should be given when quoting people for whom English is not their first language. But nonsense is worth quoting when the subject of the piece requires it. For instance, newspapers have focused on the ungrammatical language used by a series of prominent US politicians (Reaganspeak, Haigspeak, Bushspeak), often in off-the-cuff remarks to journalists. Peculiar speech mannerisms and dialect can be quoted to convey the source's typical speech patterns. This has to be done sensitively, mostly in features.

Particular kinds of cliché, jargon and rhetoric do not make good quotes. Thus, 'The President said: "This historic meeting of the world's leading industrial states has achieved a lot and we have reason to be proud of what we have done this weekend"'; 'She was "very pleased" with the takings from the raffle for disabled children.' These are examples of clichés and rhetoric which can be easily cut.

Reported speech

The conventions of reported speech are simple. Following verbs such as 'said', 'informed', 'claimed', 'warned', 'demanded', 'alleged', 'hinted', 'added', the tense of the verb in reported speech takes one step into the past.

Direct speech	Reported speech
am/are/is	was/were
shall	should
will	would
may	might
was/were	had been
have been	had been
must	had to
could	could have

'Aneurin Bevan said: "I read the newspaper avidly. It is my one form of continuous fiction"' is using the direct quote. In reported speech it becomes: 'Aneurin Bevan said he read the newspaper avidly. It was his one form of continuous fiction.' It is wrong to say: 'Aneurin Bevan said he reads the newspaper avidly. It is his one form of continuous fiction.'

Thus: 'He said: "The trade union movement has been crippled by the Tories' punitive legislation and has little support from the Blair government"' becomes: 'He said the trade union movement had been crippled by the Tories' punitive legislation and had little support from the Blair government.'

Pronouns are affected by reported speech conventions. 'She said: "We may decide to emigrate to Iceland"' becomes: 'She said they might decide to emigrate to Iceland.' 'She told the council "Your attempts at promoting equal opportunities in this county are pathetic"' becomes: 'She told the council its attempts at promoting equal opportunities in the county were pathetic.'

Adverbs are also affected. Thus, 'He said: "We shall all meet here soon to plan next week's agenda"' becomes: 'He said they should all meet there soon to plan the following week's agenda.' For a longer exposition of reported speech rules, see Aitchison (1988) and Hicks (1998: 53–4).

Note the use of reported speech in this article in the *Morning Star* of 10 November 2004:

> A lesbian couple who wed in Canada can seek to have their union legally recognised in Ireland, Irish High Court Justice Minister Liam McKechnie ruled yesterday.
>
> Mr McKechnie said that lawyers representing Ann Louise Gilligan and Katherine Zappone had presented an arguable case that merited a full hearing, which is likely to take place next year.
>
> He predicted that the case would have profound consequences for predominantly Catholic Ireland.

In the first par, following 'ruled', 'can seek' is used (following the convention for intros) instead of the reported speech 'could seek' to maintain immediacy. In par two, after the verb 'said', notice reported speech 'had presented'. But 'is likely' is used (rather than 'was likely') since this was not said by McKechnie, but information inserted by the reporter. In par three, after 'predicted', note 'would have' ('will have' would be wrong).

Beware of making reported speech, say in a press release, into direct speech. A release that says: 'Former President Nelson Mandela accused the South African government of continuing to suppress black rights' cannot be changed into: 'Nelson Mandela said: "The South African government is continuing to suppress black rights."' There is no proof he said those words. The indirect speech might have been the paraphrase of a longer sentence or a combination of sentences.

Reported speech within a direct quote cannot be converted into direct speech. Thus: 'He said he would ask his wife if he should resign tomorrow' cannot become: 'He asked his wife: "Should I resign tomorrow?"'

Most reports of speech will combine direct and indirect speech. A report concentrating too heavily on indirect speech will lack immediacy and colour; a report almost exclusively in direct quotations conveys the impression the journalist has surrendered their role of selection and interpretation to the source.

Partial quotes

These are used to highlight particular words in sentences. Thus the *Yorkshire Post* reported (14 July 2003):

> Services aimed at tackling drug addiction in parts of Yorkshire are at 'complete meltdown', it was claimed last night

Journalists use partial quotes sparingly. They are most commonly used in intros, but become confusing if used throughout a story.

Quotation dangers

Two or more people rarely speak in unison. When reporting a public meeting it is strange to have two people identified with the same direct quote. Thus: '"The BBC should be privatised immediately," two Conservative councillors urged yesterday' is wrong. People can agree on an issue and be linked to a direct quote without any problem. Thus it is perfectly feasible to say: 'The BBC should be privatised immediately, two Conservative councillors urged yesterday.'

Be careful not to distort reports by over-selective quoting. Someone may devote part of a speech to conveying the pros of an issue, the other part to the cons. One side of the argument may be highlighted; it is irresponsible to eliminate all reference to the other side.

Journalists can let their imagination take over when quoting. The Press Complaints Commission went so far as to censure journalists for resorting too frequently to invention in the use of quotes. One of the most famous instances was the *Sun*'s invented interview with the wife of a Falklands war 'hero' killed in battle. (The woman journalist involved went on to edit a national newspaper.)

A variation on the invention theme is the 'words-in-the-mouth' technique. When an interviewee remains unresponsive, the journalist is tempted to feed them quotes. They may ask the interviewee: 'Do you think this scheme for Blackpool transport is outrageous and should never have been backed?' When the hesitant interviewee replies, 'Er, yes', the journalist is able to report: 'She said she thought the transport scheme for Blackpool was outrageous and should never have been backed.' Such a technique should be used sparingly.

But former *Sunday Mirror* reporter Wensley Clarkson (1990) tells of when he met ex-Beatle Paul McCartney in his car with his wife alongside him as he drove out of his country estate. Merely on the basis of a few grunts of the 'Yep, sure do' variety, Clarkson invented an 'exclusive'.

Along with invention can go exaggeration and sensationalism. Two residents are quoted as being opposed to plans for a shopping complex on a school sports site. The story reads: 'Residents are protesting' etc. The report gives a false picture of the strength of opposition for the sake of journalistic hyperbole. If one of the residents was a spokesperson for the residents, then you could intro: 'Residents are protesting' etc. When opposing views are expressed, 'rows' have not necessarily broken out, nor have 'wars', nor is one side necessarily 'up in arms'. Disputes at churches need not always be dubbed 'unholy rows'.

There is a danger of placing direct quote marks around a phrase and not making clear the source. Such 'hanging' quotes confuse. Always make the attribution of any quote clear. And be careful not to run two sections of a direct quote together when they were separated by sentences. End the first sentence with double inverted commas. Begin the next sentences with, say, 'She added'.

Punctuating quotes

Lynne Truss's surprise global bestseller, *Eats, Shoots & Leaves* (2003), usefully and humorously highlights the importance of correct punctuation to good prose (see also King 2000). Most newspapers adopt the following style. They will say:

> She added: 'I intend to vote for the Raving Loony Party.'

Notice the colon followed by a space, then inverted commas and a capital letter. At the end of the sentence the full stop is followed by the inverted commas.

Variations on that model are considered wrong. Avoid:

> She said, 'I intend to vote for the Raving Loony Party'.

and

> She said that 'I intend to vote for the Raving Loony Party.'

When a partial quote is used, the punctuation should fall outside the quote marks. Thus:

> He described the US-led attacks on Iraq as 'illegal and barbaric'.

> The rail strike is 'outrageous', according to Prime Minister Tony Blair.

If single quotes are used, quotes within them should be in double quotes, and vice versa. Thus:

> He said: 'The US/UK attacks on Baghdad are best seen as a "barbaric slaughter" of innocent Iraqi civilians.'

First words in partial quotes are not capitalised. Thus:

> Barbara Tuchman said war was the 'Unfolding of miscalculations'

is wrong. It should read:

> Barbara Tuchman said war was the 'unfolding of miscalculations'.

Square brackets are used in direct quotations around words inserted by the journalist to make the meaning clear. Thus:

> He [President Clinton] quite obviously backed the bombing of Iraq to deflect attention away from the controversy surrounding his affair with Monica Lewinsky.

Interestingly, American newspapers place square brackets around copy from agencies (such as Reuters or Agence France Presse) which is inserted into stories by staff reporters.

Put an ellipsis (. . .) in a direct quote to indicate irrelevant words are missing. But used more than once, it looks as if the reporter is struggling with a poor note or indulging in over-zealous editing. It is simpler to change the quote into indirect speech and remove the offending dots.

Attribution verbs

'Said' is most commonly used to convey attribution. It is short and neutral, and for these reasons is rapidly read over. To use 'said' on every occasion would be dull, and words such as 'replied', 'commented', 'pointed out', 'protested', 'warned', 'indicated', 'explained', 'added', 'hinted', 'revealed', 'claimed' and 'alleged', which have specific meanings, may be used, always carefully. They are most often placed in intros, where they convey extra emphasis and drama. They should never be used simply to provide colour in news stories, though more flexibility is possible in features.

'Claimed' should be used only for controversial statements of alleged fact when there is some reasonable doubt over them. When evidence is undisputed, the use of 'claim' throws up unnecessary doubts. When a newspaper reports: 'In its report which follows a detailed review of the operation of the 1976 Race Relations Act, the commission claims ethnic minorities continue to suffer high levels of discrimination and disadvantage' it is using 'claim' in a subtly racist way to dispute the fact of widespread discrimination.

'Admitted' should be used only when a source is confessing to an error, a failing, a limitation, charge or crime. Thus, the *Lincolnshire Echo* (20 October 2004) reported on a magistrates' court case in which a man was accused of hurling abuse at a police officer:

Bourke (40), of Gibson Close, Branston, admitted being drunk and disorderly on 18 October.

'Added' should be used only after a source has already been quoted. It is wrong to introduce a new source with the words: 'She added: " . . . .".'

'Revealed' should be used only when significant new information is being relayed. 'Stated' is archaic and generally avoided. 'Quipped', 'joked' and 'chuckled' are clichés and best avoided or confined to light features and diary pieces.

An effective way of conveying attribution is to use the phrase 'according to'. It is most commonly used in intros, as here from the *Hull Daily Mail* (23 June 2004):

Fake identification is openly for sale on the internet, according to a study out today. An investigation uncovered bogus proof of age, national ID and employee cards on offer from UK-based companies.

GETTING THE QUOTES DOWN: RECORDING TECHNIQUES

Shorthand

One of the essential skills of the journalist is recording notes effectively. The National Council for the Training of Journalists requires 100 words per minute (wpm) from successful candidates. Many training courses devote considerable time to shorthand, and most provincial newspapers will require good shorthand from applicants. The two most popular systems with journalists are Pitmans and Teeline, the latter invented primarily with trainee journalists in mind.

During the nineteenth century the emergence of shorthand as a special journalistic technique (with novelist Charles Dickens demonstrating particular skills) helped to develop the notion of 'professionalism'. As Anthony Smith (1978) argues: 'It meant that a man could specialise in observing or hearing and recording with precision . . . it gave the reporter an aura of neutrality as he stood between event and reader.'

Today there is a paradox that the higher up the greasy pole of journalistic success you go, the less likely you are to find shorthand competence. Not all Fleet Street writers possess it. Very few other journalistic cultures give shorthand the kind of importance that British provincial newspapers attach to it. Yet it is important for all aspiring journalists to do shorthand to at least 100 words a minute. Nobody regrets the effort put into the learning. For certain jobs, such as covering Parliament, select committees, courts and coroners' courts, where tapes are banned, and council meetings, good shorthand is essential. If reporters had better recording techniques, fewer errors would crop up and the habit of inventing quotes and facts would diminish.

Selective note-taking

Acquiring the skills of selective note-taking is crucial. It is not essential to record everything said. Over-detailed note-taking prevents profitable contact in interviews. The best shorthand writers are not necessarily the best writers. The good journalist knows when something of interest is being said. Their ears prick up and all attention is paid to getting down those facts, those views, that feeling. If you are not certain you have the quote correct, either double check or paraphrase the general meaning (if you are clear about that) and put it in reported speech. David Spark (1999: 47) offers this additional advice:

> If you are in the habit of adorning your notes with comments about the people you are speaking to give up the habit. In court, a rude comment can be construed as showing your evidence-gathering was malicious, not even-handed. In a libel case, malice invalidates a defence of fair comment or a claim to privilege.

Memory

In some cases, journalists don't take down notes at all. During a risky investigation a journalist may keep their identity hidden. At a particularly sensitive interview a journalist may consider the presence of a notebook impedes conversation and over-formalises the meeting. A source may be prepared to talk but find the notebook intimidating. On these occasions the reporter has to rely on memory. Only those with a good memory should adopt this approach.

Tidiness

Reporters usually use easy-to-handle notebooks that slip easily into pockets and whose pages flip over quickly. Notes should never be made on odd sheets of paper. These can be easily mislaid. A tidy system of keeping used notebooks is essential since back-referencing is sometimes needed. When complaints are made to newspapers over coverage, easy access to the relevant note is essential. The Press Complaints Commission warned newspapers over their increasing habit of losing important notes. When complaints were made, newspapers had little ground on which to base a defence.

Note-taking from written sources

For developing background knowledge of people, events and issues, written sources are vital. For research in libraries (using CD-ROM, cuttings, the internet, databases and other written sources), you may work with a quiet laptop or more usually with pen and paper. Always make clear the title of the book or article, full name of author, publisher, place and year of publication. These details are usually in small type on the imprint page, before the contents list. It is also advisable to identify the page number as you note the document. This can be important if you go on to write a project or book on the subject. Many journalists work on books in their spare time or on sabbaticals. So it is a useful habit to develop.

Make clear the distinction between a direct quote from a work and a paraphrase. To lift someone's words directly and not attribute them can lead to allegations of plagiarism.

Learn to use books, reports, articles and website features selectively. You will rarely read from beginning to end. There is not the time. Sometimes you will rapid-read a work and take detailed notes of the conclusions or recommendations. There may be a vital book or article which is worth reading three times to digest. Use book indexes to go straight to the material you need. Look at the bibliographies for other useful sources.

Recording devices: pros and cons

Many journalists are relying increasingly on audio recorders – especially as most modern smartphones have them built in. They are small and unobtrusive, and few people are intimidated by their presence. If a source challenges a reporter over a quote, nothing is better at ending the controversy than a recording providing the evidence. But courts are aware that recordings can be tampered with. Alastair Brett, a lawyer at Times Newspapers, advises: 'Tape everything you can, every word you utter or is uttered to you.' After a solicitor complained that a *Sunday Times* reporter had 'grossly misled' him, the newspaper had the whole conversation taped and was able to prove otherwise (Spark 1999: 45).

You should inform your source that you are using a recording device – unless you have agreed with your editor that subterfuge is a necessary part of the operation.

Never rely entirely on an audio recorder. Technology fails; the battery may run low; the microphone may pick up unwanted noises. If you put it on the centre of a table during a panel discussion, it might not register the voices at the end of the table. Always take a back-up note. The dangers of having a recording erased were highlighted in the case of Jason Connery vs the *Sun* in 1992, when the newspaper's defence failed after a tape that promised to provide crucial evidence was 'lost'. The only record remaining was a transcript of the conversation which the judge said had been 'embellished, added to and altered' (Leyland 1998).

For copy needed quickly, audio recorders can be a positive nuisance. There is not time to wade through the tape to find the relevant quotes and information. Recordings are best used for features and profiles when you have time to note and digest their contents. It is very rare that journalists transcribe all the tape. Take down the most important sections as soon as possible after the interview, then return to it for a more thorough run-through when writing up your story.

CHAPTER 10

Investigative reporting

The good, the bad and the ugly

Nick Nuttall

To paraphrase the novelist Jane Austen, an investigator into the human condition of sorts herself, it is a truth universally acknowledged that investigative journalism has a higher profile now and is held in lower esteem than at any period during the last decade. It is the ultimate irony perhaps that the former invariably accompanies the latter. The reasons for this do not reflect particularly well on journalism in general, nor investigative reporting in particular. Yet it should not be forgotten that, in the words of journalist and academic Stephen Berry: 'Investigative reporting produces work that usually reflects the best that journalism has to offer, and it often prompts change in society and in people's lives. It is how journalism should work when editors and reporters . . . want "to get it right".' (Berry 2009: 1)

For many investigative reporters the 'it' in 'get it right' is often the problem. What exactly is 'it'? Maybe it's just the story. Or could it be the methodology used? Or perhaps it's all about getting the right audience response. For any of this to make sense, however, we need to define investigative reporting – both as a genre and as a way of working.

DEFINING THE GENRE

In February 2012, the House of Lords Select Committee on Communications published its third report on the future of investigative journalism. The opening paragraph of the summary offers a succinct review of the genre at a time when the Leveson Inquiry into the 'culture, practices and ethics of the press', or the phone-hacking scandal, as it became known, was still to report:

> The role and practices of investigative journalism have received unprecedented scrutiny over recent months. Its long history of exposing issues that are not in the public domain and speaking truth to power has come under the microscope as the phone hacking scandal, perhaps the greatest political media scandal of a generation, has gradually unfolded, raising a plethora of questions surrounding the public interest, privacy and media ethics.
>
> (House of Lords 2012: 5)

That it has a long history is undeniable. As long ago as 1644, a new publication called the *Spie* announced that it planned on 'discovering the usual cheats in the great game of the Kingdome. For that we would have to go undercover' (Chapman and Nuttall 2011: 56). Nearly 300 years later, Alfred Harmsworth (later Lord Northcliffe) defined it very simply when he first published the *Daily Mail* newspaper in 1896. Such stories were his 'talking points' – designed to reflect readers' concerns on a day-to-day basis. They were stories that made the news, rather than relying on traditional newsgathering routines. In similar fashion, more recently the 'cash for questions' scandal (1994) involving two Conservative MPs and then-Harrods department store owner Mohamed Al-Fayed had nothing to do with the news agenda of the day until the *Guardian* broke the story. It's generally accepted now that this story, along with the 'arms to Iraq' affair (de Burgh 2000: 292–8) and the Jonathan Aitken scandal (1995), were all instrumental in the defeat of John Major's Conservative government in 1997. Such can be the power of good investigative reporting.

Despite these examples, there is still a need to identify the genre, at least from a vocational perspective, and to offer a more robust and forensic definition than Alfred Harmsworth's a century ago. Hugo de Burgh offers a straightforward definition in *Investigative Journalism: Context and Practice*: 'An investigative journalist is a man or woman whose profession it is to discover the truth and to identify lapses from it in whatever media may be available' (de Burgh 2000: 9). So now the 'it' referred to above might also reasonably be identified as the 'truth' of a story. In *Investigative Reporting: A Study in Technique*, David Spark suggests the following:

> Investigative reporting seeks to gather facts which someone wants suppressed. It seeks not just the obvious informants who will be uncontroversial, or economical with the truth, but the less obvious who know about disturbing secrets and are angry or disturbed enough to divulge them.
>
> (Spark 1999: 6)

Inherent in Spark's definition is the belief that journalists are not seduced by base motives. Hence his bald assertion that investigative reporting just seeks to gather facts which someone wants suppressed. Yet here Spark also touches on another important aspect of the genre. 'Obvious informants' are not always the best or most reliable sources of information. In his 2004 anthology of investigative journalism *Tell Me No Lies*, John Pilger recalls how Martha Gellhorn (1908–98), doyenne of female war reporters, explained her technique to him: 'All I did was report from the ground up, not the other way round.' (Pilger 2004a: 1) In other words, voices not normally heard are unearthed by intrepid journalists such as Gellhorn partly because such journalists understand that in any great organisation, whether public or private, you can probably learn more about what is really going on behind the scenes from the doorman rather than the CEO.

Today, there is added piquancy to the phrase 'obvious informants'. Many celebrities, and especially those who were phone-hacked by *News of the World* journalists, were blithely unaware they had become 'informants' at all, and it is probably reasonable to assume that they wished the sort of personal information gleaned from hacking to remain private. Apart from the illegal aspects of phone hacking itself, journalists were also faced with an awkward ethical dilemma. Was it in the public interest to publish such material, or was the material merely of interest to the public?

THE PUBLIC INTEREST – WHAT IT IS AND WHAT IT ISN'T

It is important then to distinguish between true investigative journalism and the bogus stuff that masquerades as the real thing. This bogus stuff often invades people's privacy without there being any real public interest in the resulting story. So what is the difference? Usefully, the Press Complaints Commission (PCC) (now deceased) fleshed out a concept of 'the public interest' in its Code of Practice. It provided a series of ethical standards journalists were expected to meet, especially in stories concerning privacy, harassment, children, children in sex cases, hospitals, reporting of crime and payment to criminals. However, there could be exceptions to these standards when the public interest is involved. Accordingly, the public interest includes, but is not confined to:

- detecting or exposing crime or serious impropriety
- protecting public health and safety
- preventing the public from being misled by an action or statement of an individual or organisation.

Furthermore, the Code of Conduct of the National Union of Journalists (NUJ) states in Clause 5: 'A journalist shall obtain information, photographs and illustrations only by straightforward means. The use of other means can be justified only by over-riding consideration of the public interest.'

One of the major debates surrounding investigative journalism inevitably, therefore, concerns the precise meaning of such phrases as 'the public interest' and 'of interest to the public'. According to the House of Lords Select Committee's report on the future of investigative journalism: 'Questions about the public interest, which in UK law is used to effect the balance between Article 8 and Article 10 of the European Convention on Human Rights, lie at the heart of these [media organisations'] decisions' (House of Lords 2012: 24, cl. 71). Article 8 states: 'Everyone has the right to respect for his private and family life, his home and his correspondence . . .'. Article 10 states: 'Everyone has the right to freedom of expression. This right shall include freedom to hold opinions and to receive and impart information and ideas without interference by public authority and regardless of frontiers . . .'. On the subtle differences between the two can hang the legitimacy of a reporter's methods when pursuing a story. It could be argued, for example, that the MPs' expenses scandal of 2009 (see below) was a story pursued in the public interest. Stories resulting from the phone hacking of celebrity mobile phones, on the other hand, might be of considerable interest to the public but could seldom be said to be in the public interest. However, the exposure of the underhand or illegal methods used by many journalists to obtain such information clearly is in the public interest.

THE STORY SO FAR . . .

According to the Committee of Concerned Journalists, a group of practitioners worried about the future of the profession: 'Like a theme in a Bach fugue, investigative reporting has swelled and subsided through the history of journalism but never disappeared.' (Chapman and Nuttall 2011: 56) Many pundits believe we are now in a period of 'subsiding'. No less a luminary than actor Robert Redford, interviewed before the inaugural Sundance London film festival in 2012, argued that 'documentaries have replaced newspapers as the media's main source of investigative journalism'. He went on say: 'I didn't imagine that it [morality and professionalism] would decline so steeply and drastically, that the rules that governed journalism – like you had to get two sources before you could quote them – would be gone.' (Gompertz 2012: 1)

On the other hand the 'swelling' lobby can point to any number of great investigative coups of the post-war years – particularly those carried out by *The Sunday Times*'s Insight team under the editorship of Harold Evans (1967–81) as evidence that investigative journalism has been, and continues to be, in rude health, listed below.

- The Profumo affair (1963), which destroyed the career of a cabinet minister and arguably helped bring down the Conservative government the following year (Knightley and Kennedy 1987).
- The Poulson scandal (1970), where politicians were bribed by architect John Poulson to award him lucrative building contracts. Paul Foot used *Private Eye* to highlight the work of local journalist Ray Fitzwalter in uncovering the scandal. It resulted in Poulson's bankruptcy and imprisonment and the resignation of then Home Secretary Reginald Maudling (Tomkinson 1973; Fitzwalter and Taylor 1981).

- The Insight campaign begun in 1972 on behalf of the Thalidomide children. Distillers, the giant drinks conglomerate, made the drug Thalidomide under licence and marketed it as a safe anti-morning-sickness pill for pregnant women. Yet the drug was not safe and worldwide some 10,000 children were born with Thalidomide-linked disabilities. As Phillip Knightley, one of the team assigned to the story, recalled in his autobiography, *A Hack's Progress*: 'Thalidomide crossed the placental barrier and with devilish precision sabotaged the developing limb buds of the foetus, so that children were born with hands emerging direct from their shoulders, and feet emerging direct from their hips and, in a few horrific cases, with both abnormalities.' (Knightley 1998: 156) Ultimately, Distillers compensated the hundreds of affected children in the UK to the tune of £28.4 million. Finally (in September 2012) the German maker of the drug, Gruenenthal, issued an apology, 50 years after the drug was withdrawn from sale in Europe (though its use to fight leprosy continues in some developing countries).

- The DC-10 Paris air crash (1974), which killed 346 passengers and crew. As Harold Evans noted in *Good Times, Bad Times*: 'They died violently because the DC-10 had a lie in it.' (Evans 1983: 27) The 'lie' was that a faulty door mechanism had not been modified adequately and the door blew off at altitude. Planemaker McDonnell Douglas eventually paid $62 million in compensation.

- The *Guardian*'s reporting of the 'cash for questions' scandal (1994), in which MPs were paid £2,000 a time to ask questions in Parliament. It effectively ended the careers of two MPs and arguably tolled the death knell of John Major's Conservative government (de Burgh 2000: 56).

- The long investigation by the *Guardian* into the expenses claims of government minister Jonathan Aitken (1994–9), which resulted in his eventual disgrace and imprisonment on perjury charges (Leigh and Vulliamy 1997; Spark 1999: 107–13).

- The *News of the World* splash on 29 August 2010 carried the headline: 'Caught! Match-fixer pockets £150k as he rigs the England Test at Lord's'. The newspaper's undercover reporters, posing as front men for a gambling cartel, paid the money to an agent who then arranged for no-balls to be bowled at certain times during the Test match – a practice known as spot-fixing. At the subsequent trial at Southwark Crown Court, three Pakistan players were convicted and jailed for spot-fixing offences. This was a typical sting operation that, for once, could be considered in the public interest.

There is much to be proud of in this long tradition, but the changing nature of modern journalism, its fragmentation, its cost-consciousness, its relentless pursuit of 'entertainment' as well as the possibilities inherent in digital technology, are probably to blame for two events or, to use the jargon, 'scandals' that have 'rocked' the news media to their very foundations. Both these events in their own way not only cast a light on the state of investigative reporting in the first decades of the twenty-first century, but also provide a 'stinging' commentary on the methods, ethical standards and in some cases the very morality of journalists themselves. The scale of these events and their likely far-reaching consequences requires us to examine them in a bit more detail.

EXPENSIVE EXPENSES

The MPs' expenses scandal of 2009 was triggered by the leaking of MPs' expenses claims to the *Daily Telegraph* rather than through any sleuthing by journalists. This has become a developing pattern of disclosure, mainly because of the use of electronic storage systems and databases. It is a good example, bearing in mind how simple it is to copy and transport digital information, whether on CDs, DVDs or flash drives, of how dangerous it can be to agglomerate vast amounts of information in one digital 'home'.

When the Freedom of Information (FoI) Act 2000 came into force in 2005, a number of journalists, and notably journalist and campaigner Heather Brooke, filed requests for the details of certain MPs' expenses to be released. The request was delayed because MPs were voting on an amendment to the FoI act which would have exempted them from its disclosure provisions. After much publicity and obvious public anger, the amendment was abandoned and the Commons announced that full details of MPs' expenses would be published on 1 July 2009. However, before this occurred the *Daily Telegraph* acquired a leaked, uncensored copy of MPs' expenses records which contained more than 2 million documents (Brook and Gillan 2009), and began a series of daily instalments on 8 May 2009. Publication was justified on the grounds that the official release would have omitted key information and it was in the public interest that all expenses details should be published.

The information was stored on a 'computer disk' stolen from the parliamentary fees office. A number of newspapers, including *The Times* and the *Sun*, were offered the information but turned it down. Eventually the *Daily Telegraph*, according to its assistant editor Andrew Pierce, paid £110,000 for the files. It was, he said, 'money well spent in the public interest' (Tryhorn 2009). It was later revealed that a former SAS man, John Wick, had acted as go-between, passing the details from an anonymous source in the fees office to the newspaper. 'Mr Wick said the version of the expenses which the Commons was due to release had lots of details removed and he felt the public had a right to know' (BBC News 2009). The 'mole' in the fees office has never been identified, and it is another facet of digital systems that downloading data can be carried out (with suitable safeguards) virtually anonymously, thus making detection almost impossible.

CROWDSOURCING

The *Daily Telegraph* caught the rest of the daily press on the hop. No one realised quite what a big story MPs' expenses would become. The *Guardian*, like all other newspapers, had no option but to wait for the House of Commons to publish the official set of expenses claims. But the newspaper then created a system to allow the public to search methodically through 700,000 expense-claim documents, producing a crowdsourced analysis. More than 20,000 people participated in finding erroneous and remarkable expense claims by MPs.

Such an investigative method broke new ground in the way huge journalistic tasks could be accomplished very quickly if a newspaper was prepared to be open about its processes. At the same time, it cut the cost of research while building and strengthening a newspaper's own community by engaging its readers beyond the normal reading and commenting interaction (Andrew Davies 2009).

For the investigative journalist, crowdsourcing provides a unique way of managing and categorising the huge amounts of data that are being retrieved from FoI requests. But it can require a lot of hard work and large resource capabilities, as shown by the *Guardian*'s experiment. It also works best on high-profile topics which readily engage public interest. As freelance journalist Michael Andersen (2009) points out: 'It really helps if users are pre-motivated to assist – with the public outcry about the expenses scandal providing a perfect scenario for such an approach.'

Crowdsourcing is clearly an investigative tool that is entirely dependent on computer technology. It is not adapted from earlier ways of working, and it replicates the 'large numbers' implicit in the input of computer data with the use of large numbers of people, as the name implies, at the output end of the process. It is early days to make any hard-and-fast rules for crowdsourcing success, but a number of journalists and researchers have suggested there are four basic requirements. Michael Andersen (2009) suggests the following.

- Workers are unpaid so it needs to be fun – the *Guardian*'s success was based on the understanding that the process had to have a 'fun' element. This was achieved through a simple four-panel interface for each page. Pages could be categorised as either 'interesting'; 'not interesting'; 'interesting but known'; or 'investigate this'. A progress bar on the project's front page gave people an idea of what had been achieved and how many pages were left to review. This gave the community a goal to share.

- Public attention is fickle so a fast launch is essential – this is true of most journalistic output. But with crowdsourcing people will only be interested in participating if it is a 'hot' issue. The MPs' expenses scandal caught the public's imagination from day one. According to the *Guardian*'s software architect Simon Willison: 'It became quickly clear on Thursday that it was a huge story, and if we failed to get it out on Thursday, we'd lose a lot of momentum.'

- Speed is mandatory so use a framework. Without getting too technical, a framework enables the creation of complex, database-driven websites. The *Guardian* used the custom web framework Django. There's no faster way to churn out content. It's the difference between offset printing and using moveable type and it enabled the newspaper to tabulate its results and publish almost immediately.

- Participation will come in one big burst, so have servers ready – it is essential that computing power is available from the outset. Simon Willison's team at the *Guardian* knew that 'they would get a huge burst of attention followed by a long, fading tail, so it wouldn't make sense to prepare *The Guardian*'s own servers for the task. In any case, there wasn't time'. Instead Willison used Amazon Elastic Compute Cloud (Amazon EC2), a web service that provided resizable computing capacity in the cloud. It is designed to make web-scale computing easier for developers. It reduced the time required to obtain and boot new server instances to minutes from the typical *Guardian* lead time of several weeks for new hardware to be up and running.

WikiLeaks and crowdsourcing

In many respects, WikiLeaks and crowdsourcing go together like peaches and cream. Although the website dumps thousands of pages of often classified information into the public domain, it requires a heroic effort in time and personnel to cull the best stories and exclusives from such huge data flows. At the same time, rather than fearing exposure and retribution by leaking directly to the press, whistleblowers can leak to WikiLeaks, which then leaks to the press for them. To that extent WikiLeaks and its founder Julian Assange have changed the game as far as investigative reporting is concerned.

For those who are unaware (few though they may be), WikiLeaks is a worldwide online organisation which regularly publishes submissions of secret information and files, news leaks and classified information from anonymous sources and whistle-blowers (http://wikileaks.org/About.html). Its website was launched in 2006 and its aim was 'to bring important news and information to the public'. It has the potential to turn anyone who so desires into an investigative reporter.

The website first came to wide public attention when it published a huge tranche of United States government documents leaked to it by a US army private, Bradley (now Chelsea) Manning. The material included 250,000 United States diplomatic cables and 500,000 army reports that came to be known as the Iraq War logs and the Afghan War logs. It was the largest set of restricted documents ever leaked to the public. Much of it was published by WikiLeaks or its media partners between April and November 2010. At the same time Assange collaborated with major global media organisations to release US State Department diplomatic cables in redacted format (Madar 2012; Leigh and Harding 2011).

Yet despite the advent of WikiLeaks, the most recent example of leaked government documents on a huge scale involved a traditional newspaper, in this case the *Guardian*. Edward Snowden was an American computer specialist who worked variously for the CIA and the American National Security Agency (NSA). In late 2012, he contacted *Guardian* journalist Glenn Greenwald and offered him a large tranche of classified US government documents. They included details of various surveillance programmes including PRISM (stored internet communications), NSA call database (more than 1.9 trillion telephone call records) and XKeyscore (search and analysis of internet data about foreign nationals). The *Guardian* also revealed details of Tempora, a British black-ops surveillance programme run by the NSA's British partner, GCHQ. Snowden fled to Hong Kong from Hawaii where he had been living. He then flew on to Moscow where he applied for asylum. The US charged him with espionage and the theft of government documents. On 9 June 2013, at his own request, the *Guardian* made public Snowden's identity. On 24 June 2013, Julian Assange confirmed that WikiLeaks had paid for Snowden's lodgings in Hong Kong and his flight to Russia.

There have been concerns that the casual dumping of so much data into the public domain, without any checks on whether it could impact on particular individuals, organisations or governments, is dangerous and displays a callous disregard for the security of individuals and nations. For others, WikiLeaks and whistleblowers such as Edward Snowden provide a long-overdue service by forcing governments in particular to confront and justify their behaviour to their citizens. According to Heather Brooke in *The Revolution Will Be Digitised* (2011): 'Exemptions for the disclosure of official information must be for two reasons only: Where it is in the public interest (not the nation's interest) or to prevent actual (not imagined) harm.' (Preston 2011: 27) Such statements raise almost as many questions as they answer, however. Who is to decide what the difference is between public and national interest? What is imagined harm? Which mind is it that does the imagining? What is certain, however, is that no one can turn back the clock. Media organisations and investigative reporters must acknowledge the new reality posited by a WikiLeaks world, and alter and adapt their ways of going about business to accommodate the opportunities it presents and the new ways of working it demands.

I SPY WITH MY LITTLE EYE

In *The Future of Journalism in the Advanced Democracies*, Peter Anderson and Geoff Ward summarise the current situation thus: 'Journalism is a much maligned profession. Politicians in the UK and elsewhere frequently accuse the media of sensationalism, trivialisation, narrowness of focus and straightforward factual inaccuracy.' (Anderson and Ward 2006: 13) Many journalists, of course, would aver that such an accusation is a close approximation to what they are actually doing even if it is not what they are supposed to be doing. Editors and reporters alike have defended this *status quo* for decades if not centuries, and most of the following examples of investigative journalism have been defended as being in 'the public interest'. Though typical of current offerings in the national press, few of them would pass the PCC and NUJ codes.

Sleazy does it – the story with no discernible public interest

In 1994, the *News of the World* ran a story about the new Bishop of Durham being conditionally discharged by Hull magistrates for a gay sex act 26 years previously. The information was obtained from court records, but it is questionable whether the public interest was served by running the story so long after the event. More recently, the French edition of *Closer* magazine, in September 2012, published pictures of the Duchess of Cambridge, Kate Middleton, sunbathing topless in the secluded grounds of a chateau owned by Lord Linley, the Queen's nephew. The pictures were taken with an extreme telephoto lens camera. The editor gamely attempted to use a public interest defence but few people believed this was anything other than a sleazy attempt to boost circulation and gain publicity.

Chequebook journalism – kiss-and-tell

Manchester United and England football star Rio Ferdinand had an affair with interior designer Carly Storey in 2004. She sold her story to the *Sunday Mirror* in 2010 for a fee of £16,000 negotiated by publicist Max Clifford. The paper headlined the article 'My Affair with England Captain Rio'. Ferdinand described the story as a gross invasion of his privacy and brought a legal action for damages and a worldwide injunction. The case turned on whether the *Sunday Mirror* could claim a public interest defence under Article 10 of the European Convention on Human Rights because Ferdinand was England captain and supposedly a 'reformed and responsible' character, or whether he was entitled to privacy in accordance with Article 8 of the European Convention. Mr Justice Nicol found for the defendant, Mirror Group Newspapers.

Similarly, in April 2004, David Beckham was the target of a 'kiss-and-tell' exposé by Rebecca Loos, his former PA. During his testimony to the Leveson Inquiry, former *News of the World* chief reporter Neville Thurlbeck said Loos was paid around £1 million for details of the alleged affair (Kelso 2004; Bowater 2011). More recently, Ryan Giggs's attempts to muzzle the media over his 'affair' with Big Brother's Imogen Thomas in 2011 were finally undone by the power of the internet – blogs, tweets and overseas online news sources 'outed' him as the footballer concerned despite Mr Justice Eady granting him a super-injunction gagging order preventing the *Sun* from naming him in their story of a 'six-month fling' with Thomas (O'Shea 2011).

The sting – an individual is set up for a fall

Sophie, Countess of Wessex was invited to a meeting in February 2001 with an Arab she hoped to do business with. Unknown to her the 'Arab' was *News of the World* reporter Mazher Mahmood (better known as the 'fake sheikh'), carrying a secret tape recorder and video camera. He recorded indiscreet comments about the royal family by the Countess, and 'Sophiegate' was born. Suggestions of her using her royal connections to further her PR business interests ultimately led to a change in royal protocol and the withdrawal of both the Earl and Countess from their private business interests. Once again there seems to be no public interest defence in this 'manufactured' story, just one example of many Mahmood stings (see Mahmood 2008; Burden 2009). Others include the Victoria Beckham 'kidnapping' plot (2002), and his entrapment of various celebrities for 'supplying' drugs – *London's Burning* actor John Alford (1997), *Blue Peter* presenter Richard Bacon (1998) and Radio 2 DJ Johnnie Walker (1999). But in 2006 Mahmood failed to con Respect MP George Galloway into making anti-semitic remarks. Galloway went on to place his image on his website, georgegalloway.com, and on the Respect party website, respectcoalition.org (see Brook 2006).

Undercover agent – the journalist assumes an identity to get the story

In November 2003, *Mirror* reporter Ryan Parry used bogus references to get a job at Buckingham Palace as a footman. He was there during President Bush's visit and this exposed serious flaws in the royals' security arrangements. A few months previously Parry had infiltrated Wimbledon as a Securicor security guard, again using false references. Within two hours of starting work he was 'protecting' championship favourite Serena Williams. In both these cases there was a clear public interest in the information seeing the light of day, although the assumption of a false identity still irks many traditionalists. More recently, in 2013, posing as a maid, Hsiao-Hung Pai (2013) infiltrated the murky world of the UK sex trade for the *Guardian*.

FACTS, FACTS, FACTS – THE CLASSIC INVESTIGATIVE STORY

In October 2004, John Pilger exposed the fate of the islanders of Diego Garcia, a British colony in the Indian Ocean, midway between Africa and Asia, in a report for the *Express* (which accompanied an ITV investigative broadcast on the same theme) (Pilger 2004c). In 1966, the islanders were forcibly shipped off to Mauritius to make way for an American military base. They have never been allowed to return. In 2000, the High Court ruled their expulsion illegal but the British government invoked a 'royal prerogative' decree banning the islanders from ever returning.

Pilger, describing the British government's actions as a 'crime against humanity', used information from files found in the National Archives in Washington and the Public Record Office in London as well as interviews with the islanders. Investigative journalism as a genre requires no further justification. Then, in May 2006, the High Court ruled the 'royal prerogative' unlawful.

THE DIGITAL DILEMMA

The past decade has seen a sea-change in the way computers and digital technology have become part of everyone's day-to-day life. Journalists are no exception. But for the investigative reporter digital technology can often be a two-edged sword. On one hand it enables journalists to access an almost infinite amount of information and also to connect with people in ways only dreamed of before emails, blogs, Twitter and Facebook came along. But on the other hand, in the process of pursuing access and interviewees, it's a stone-cold, slam-dunk certainty you will leave a trace of your activities online and thus leave you and your sources vulnerable to detection – whether by the authorities or by competitors. Needless to say, such detection can seriously undermine a reporter's ability to gather the necessary evidence to make a story stand up. This, if you like, is the digital dilemma.

The problem is compounded by the fact that, as noted by media lawyer Geoffrey Robertson QC, the law 'requires protection for journalists' sources for the very good reason that they would dry up if informants promised anonymity were to be exposed and prosecuted'. The European Court of Human Rights has 'held that the watchdog role of the media would be imperilled if government agencies were able to force disclosure of sources in order to subject them to reprisals' (Robertson 2011: 10). More prosaically, journalists can enable online protection for themselves by downloading free software such as Tor (which stands for The Onion Router, originally developed for the US Navy to protect government communications). According to its website (www.torproject.org/about/overview.html.en), journalists use Tor 'to communicate more safely with whistleblowers and dissidents'. It is reputed to be so effective at allowing organisations and individuals to share information over public networks without compromising their privacy that it has been implicated in criminal network activity and the distribution of child pornography. Significantly, revelations by the former NSA analyst Edward Snowden indicated that both the NSA and GCHQ (Britain's spying agency) had made repeated efforts to crack Tor (Ball *et al.* 2013). Perhaps journalists working on particularly sensitive stories from now on will have to meet sources face to face as much as possible to avoid the prying gaze of the state?

Despite anonymous surfing and various legal protections, governments are eagerly promulgating new laws that compromise journalists' freedom to investigate. 'Want to be an investigative journalist of the future?' asks journalist Charles Arthur. Well, 'you'll need a pen and paper, pay-as-you-go phone, and a motorbike' (Arthur 2009:

par 1). Counter-intuitive though they are, Arthur's tongue-in-cheek suggestions may become the new reality. Under regulations that came into force in 2009, telephone and internet companies are required to keep logs of what numbers are called and which websites, email services and internet telephony contacts are made. Given a judge's clearance, government departments, local authorities, the police or even quangos can access this data. Investigative journalist Duncan Campbell believes that 'investigative reporting is desperately threatened by what this government (Conservative/Lib Dem coalition) is doing' (Arthur 2009: par 3). What concerns journalists at the moment is that, if someone contacts them and they then write a story 'based on that information, the new regulations mean that the police – or intelligence services or local council – can work back from the database of all the contacts made to the journalist and figure out who the whistleblower is' (Arthur 2009: par 8).

The *Guardian*'s former investigations editor David Leigh says you need to 'step down a couple of technological rungs' to counter such a risk. 'Just send a letter – you know, snail mail.' He adds: 'When I've dealt with secret sources they take very great care not to communicate on any electronic medium.' (Arthur 2009: par 9) Such a precaution on its own may well not be enough, though. Duncan Campbell suggests that journalists need to do what drug dealers and terrorists do: 'Use pay-as-you-go phones and unregistered sim cards, bought with cash. Such closed rings are almost unbreakable – once you've met to swap numbers.' (Arthur 2009: par 10)

For David Leigh, however, the really troubling development is the automatic number plate recognition (ANPR) system. It is already in use by police to track vehicle tax evaders and criminals. At the moment it can only be accessed by the police and intelligence services and cannot be used in real time. But there is no reason to suppose it will not eventually be used as a matter of course and in real time. And 'when that moment comes it will be truly dangerous . . . ANPR is a greater threat [than internet and phone-logging] because it's tracking the physical movement of vehicles that are closely correlated to people', Campbell says. 'Unlike sim cards.' (Arthur 2009: par 19)

So Charles Arthur's tongue-in-cheek notions suddenly take on a more serious tone. As he concludes: 'We ponder solutions. Bicycles? Horses? Too slow. Motorbikes? Those usually only have a numberplate on the back – and the ANPR cameras focus on the front plate. Campbell and Leigh like it. Add it to the future armoury.' (Arthur 2009: par 20)

Computer-assisted reporting

Despite such concerns, journalists are divided on the dangers and benefits of using digital technology. Many now see it as inevitable, especially with the rise of computer-assisted reporting. Sometimes called 'reporting by numbers', it is all about harnessing the unique power of the computer to analyse and correlate large volumes of data to produce stories that might otherwise slip through a traditional reporter's net. Information is collected in databases, public records are analysed with spreadsheets and various statistical programs, political and demographic change can be monitored using geographic information system mapping. Interviews are conducted by email and background research compiled using the web.

Governments of all hues have stated that more and more information will be made available online and this will enable journalists to cross-reference data from a number of different sources, as well as compiling their own databases. Investigative reporter Cliff Levy, for example, 'frequently builds his own databases, plucking stats and information from his digitized documents into computer spreadsheets'. Levy is a digital convert. 'As for paper,' he says:

> 'I don't use it. Every document I get, I get it digitised,' he explains. To carry the project with him wherever he goes, he has found that a three-inch-long flash drive beats a briefcase . . . His electronic folders are divided into years, and within each folder he has a Microsoft Word file for every month of that year and all the notes for that month are entered in chronological order. That is like a master file, from which he creates 'summary files' and files that contain 'my best stuff'. Although the summary files are important, Levy says he also periodically reviews the longer monthly Word documents.
>
> (cited in Berry 2009: 150)

There is no doubt that journalists will have to make difficult decisions in the future about their investigative choices and *modus operandi*. The ubiquity of databases and computer-assisted reporting as used by Cliff Levy pose their own risks. But as Levy says: 'This is not complicated stuff. And I grit my teeth when reporters don't want to learn how to do this. You miss out on some really good reporting.' (ibid.: 151)

Regardless of a reporter's digital abilities, the internet has become indispensable to journalists and newsrooms alike. Used intelligently, it saves time and can occasionally produce spectacular results. For the investigative journalist there are a number of sites that can speed up research and offer a simple and inexpensive way of getting information that would otherwise require visits to libraries, government offices such as HMSO (Her Majesty's Stationery Office), Companies House or other specialist organisations dotted around the country.

Looking for Mr Right? People searches

Social networking sites such as Facebook can prove very effective in tracking people down. The problem for the investigative reporter is that his or her own identity will be compromised in the process. This can often be a handicap or sometimes even potentially dangerous. Yet it is important that a journalist maintains a high ethical stance when using such sites. The same rules apply to microblogging sites such as Twitter. Here users can send and read text-based messages of up to 140 characters, known as 'tweets'. It has over half a billion users and has become a favourite way to connect with celebrities – most of whom are on Twitter. For the investigative reporter it can be a way of finding stories by looking at what is 'trending'. This term identifies a word, phrase or topic that is tagged at a greater rate than others either through a concerted effort by users or because an event, the 2012 London Olympic Games, for example, prompts people to talk about it. More and more, it is being used by political protestors around the world because of its immediacy, simplicity and availability on portable devices such as smartphones. There are also many dedicated websites for tracing people. All have their limitations, but the investigative journalist can sometimes find that elusive person, or a specific piece of information about him or her, by using one of the following sites.

www.192.com
Lists full names, addresses, age guides, property prices, phone numbers, aerial photos, company and director reports, family records, and much more. Directory enquiry listings are free, and once you register you get 20 free searches every day. You will need a Premium Content credit package for full information such as electoral rolls, births, deaths and marriage indexes, etc. Credits last for six months. If you register, use an email address created specifically for the purpose.

www.friendsreunited.co.uk
A dedicated reunion directory to find old school friends, trace family members, etc.

www.missing-you.net
Formed in 1998, this is a free and instant online messaging service designed, as they say, to help you contact missing persons, old friends, distant relatives, former workmates, forces buddies.

www.internic.net/whois.html
Should reveal your target if s/he has registered an internet domain name. Click on the Whois tab if page does not come up automatically.

www.servicepals.com
For finding people who were in the armed services.

www.tracesmart.co.uk
People finder, address finder, database of all births, deaths and marriages in England and Wales between 1984 and 2006. Charges range from approximately £8 for six searches to £100 for 600.

www.direct.gov.uk/en/Governmentcitizensandrights/Registering lifeevents/index.htm
This is the Directgov website for births, marriages, deaths, adoptions and civil partnerships.

www.nationalarchives.gov.uk
For census returns, wills, military records and other similar material.

www.genesreunited.co.uk
This is another site that allows searches for people in a variety of ways – more than 550 million family history records, databases of births, deaths and marriages, the armed forces and the colonial service, electoral roll and census records, some newspaper archives.

As well as electronic sources there is still a wealth of paper sources available. It's a common yet nevertheless true dictum that you can never have too much information, and paper sources can be a useful starting point for background detail or as a way of adding authority to your interviewing technique. Many of them are also available on the internet, but usually a fee is involved. All the volumes listed here should be available in good reference libraries:

- *Who's Who* – biographies of some 30,000 individuals (the British 'Establishment')
- *International Who's Who* – ditto, but worldwide
- *Debrett's Peerage & Baronetage* – a who's who of all titled citizens of the UK and Ireland and the British royal family
- *Catholic Directory* – lists Roman Catholic clergy in England and Wales plus details of schools, colleges, religious societies, etc.
- *Crockford's Clerical Directory* – who's who in the Church of England, lists all clergy and their livings throughout the UK
- Family Record Centre at the General Register Office, 1 Myddleton Street, London, EC1R 1UW – this office contains all birth, death and marriage certificates from 1837 onwards and wills before 1859, copies of certificates are available for a fee
- Principal Registry of the Family Division, Family Division of the High Court, 1st Avenue House, 42–49 High Holborn, London, WC1V 6NP – this office contains copies of all wills lodged for probate in the UK from January 1859 onwards; a printed index is available locally at County Records Offices.

Looking for company? Organisation searches

Organisations, like people, leave traces of their activities. Commercial organisations produce a variety of information, from annual reports to new product blurbs. Public sector and voluntary organisations tend to be less 'in your face', aware that their activities often involve the expenditure of public money. However, voluntary organisations, public authorities, trades unions, etc. also set up companies whenever they wish to take advantage of the limited liability offered by incorporation.

For company searches the best place to start is Companies House. All companies with limited liability are required by law to deposit at Companies House a range of documents including articles of association, shareholder, director and member details, subsidiary and parent company information, and yearly balance sheets, profit-and-loss accounts and annual reports. The free search will provide basic company details, register of disqualified directors, insolvency details and history of company transactions.

Charities are similarly governed by statute. The Charity Commission website is the place to start looking. All registered charities are listed, as well as Inquiry Reports that give details of formal inquiries of charities carried out in accordance with Section 8 of the Charities Act 1993.

Local councils all have websites, and the Municipal Yearbook site is the best place to start looking for information. Online searches are by job function or council name. Your right of access to local government information is enshrined in the Local Government (Access to Information) Act 1985 (Northmore 1996: 116–32), the Local Government Act 2000 and the Freedom of Information Act 2000. Central government information is available from a myriad of sources, but a good starting point is the *Civil Service Yearbook*. The following websites are the main online sources available.

www.charitycommission.gov.uk
The website of the Charity Commission, established to regulate charities in England and Wales.

www.civil-service.co.uk
Extensive information on central government departments, the royal households, research councils, etc. Search by department name, job title or name. Subscription required for full service, but the book itself is usually available in reference libraries.

www.companieshouse.gov.uk
Companies House is a government agency. Its three main functions are to incorporate and dissolve limited companies; to examine and store company information delivered under the Companies Act and related legislation; and to make this information available to the public. The main office is in Cardiff and other centres are in London, Edinburgh and Belfast. You have to register online (the fee is £4 a month) to use the premium service, Companies House Direct. It contains documents filed since 1995 and charges start at £1 per document downloaded. There is no charge for basic information.

www.municipalyearbook.co.uk
Online searching for information on councils and local authorities. Search by keyword, job function, council name or interactive map. Hefty subscription needed for full information, but the book itself can be consulted in reference libraries.

www.statistics.gov.uk
UK national statistics from government departments.

www.justis.com/default.aspx
This is a full text online legal library of UK, Irish and EU case law dating back to 1163 and legislation from 1235. The service is not free, but anyone can register for a free trial.

As with people searches, there is a wealth of paper information available. The following list is by no means exhaustive but should provide a useful starting point.

- Annual reports produced by public companies. The information is often very detailed and helpful to potential management, professional and technical employees. This information can be obtained from the company's public relations department.

- The *Municipal Yearbook* (Hemming Information Services): an annual, three-volume publication which gives comprehensive details of all local authorities in the UK plus health authorities, emergency services, etc.

- *Who Owns Whom* (Dun & Bradstreet): two-volume directory that shows the relationship between parent companies and their subsidiaries in the UK. Volume one lists more than 7,000 parent companies; volume two lists all the subsidiary companies (over 100,000) and matches them with their parent.

- *Key British Enterprises* (Dun & Bradstreet): four-volume work giving financial data on turnover and capital, details of trade, trade names, trading styles and a full list of directors by name and function, of top 50,000 businesses in UK.

- *The Waterlow Stock Exchange Yearbook* (Caritas Data Ltd): provides a brief financial description of all quoted public companies on the London and Dublin Stock Exchanges.

- *Kompass* (Reed Business Information): published annually in three volumes. Volume One lists companies and gives basic facts on location, activities, staffing, directors etc.; volume two lists products and services; volume three lists industrial trade names.

- *Britain's Top Privately Owned Companies* (Jordan Information Services): a five-volume directory of major British companies providing trading and financial information. Alphabetically lists details of company address, nature of business, name and telephone numbers of chief executive.

- *International Directory of Company Histories* (Thomson Gale): detailed histories of more than 6,700 companies worldwide in 63 volumes. Full contact information, company history, key dates, etc.

- *Civil Service Yearbook* (The Stationery Office): gives details of all central and devolved government departments and key staff profiles.

- *Charity Choice UK: The Encyclopaedia of Charities* (Waterlow Professional Publishing): lists more than 8,000 charities with full contact details and areas of activity.

- *The Green Index* (Cassell): a directory of environmental organisations in Great Britain and Ireland – name, contact details, interest area, etc.

- *The Diplomatic Service List* (The Stationery Office): a yearbook that lists all diplomatic staff at overseas embassies, high commissions and consular posts. Biographical notes on staff and lists ambassadors, etc. for previous 20 years.

- *Aslib Directory of Information Sources in the United Kingdom* (Routledge): contains listings of more than 11,000 associations, clubs, societies, companies, educational establishments, institutes, commissions, government bodies and other organisations which provide information freely or on a fee-paying basis.

THREE STEPS TO HEAVEN

Investigative journalism is often expensive and time-consuming. The House of Lords Select Committee's report on the future of investigative journalism noted: 'We have taken investigative journalism to mean reporting which requires a significant investment, in terms of resource and/or funding; which runs a high risk of potential litigation; and which – most importantly – uncovers issues which are in the public interest but which were not hitherto on the public agenda.' (House of Lords 2012: 7) There is also seldom any guarantee of success. So what can you do to minimise failure? The superstitious may consult a fortune-teller, look for a four-leaf clover or buy a rabbit's foot, but we need a surer talisman, one that, without actually guaranteeing it, at least maximises our chances of success. Organisation and thoroughness are the keys.

Go backwards

Every effect has a cause. Find the cause by building a narrative of events, a timeline or something similar. Complex investigations may need multiple timelines – for example, one for each protagonist in the story. Watch how they intersect and diverge. At some point you should discover the pivotal moment of your investigation, the 'big bang' if you like of the universe you are briefly inhabiting.

Go public

In any investigation there will be a wealth of information in the public domain. Search in libraries, the National Archives, Companies House, the Land Registry and so on. Perhaps advertise in local newspapers, shop windows or internet newsgroups for people with inside information to come forward. Use Twitter, Facebook, blogs and any other digital interfaces to ask for information.

Go looking

Talk to everybody you turn up in your researches, regardless of how unimportant they might seem to be. Anyone who is central should be face-to-faced. Others can be contacted by phone or email.

DON'T FORGET TO REMEMBER

Apart from these working strategies, there are a number of basic ground rules that apply to investigative reporting, from those you need to consider during the research phase to those that are paramount during the writing phase. No set of guidelines can be all-inclusive, but the following seem by common consent to be the most important.

- Ensure that all significant facts are corroborated.

- Ensure that all documents germane to the inquiry are checked for authenticity.

- Tape all conversations wherever possible and date all entries in your notebook/laptop file. Sometimes these are your only defence against a potential action for defamation. In an ideal world you want a witness to everything.

- Visit the scene of the 'crime'. Neighbours talk, shopkeepers remember, employees divulge – but only if you talk to them face to face.

- Try to find sources who are prepared to be quoted, and don't quote people if you don't know who they are, or if their allegations seem too fanciful or outlandish.

- Protect your sources at all times, even if a refusal to divulge who they are constitutes a contempt of court. Prison might await, but hey! – if you can't be trusted to keep your word, you have no right to be an investigative reporter in the first place.

- Do not misrepresent who you are or what you are doing. This can often play badly if the lawyers are brought in. There are occasions when subterfuge is necessary, such as exposing criminal activity, but it should be just that – necessary – and not simply a wheeze or a sop to the reporter's vanity.

- Recent changes in the law, specifically the 'Reynolds qualified privilege defence', mean that your allegations should be put to the person against whom you are making them, before publication, allowing him or her the right of reply.

- If you are researching in a strange town, it's often a good idea to base yourself in the main library reference section. Virtually all the documents and books mentioned in this chapter are available there. You can usually access the internet, and the staff are highly skilled and always helpful.

- Develop your interviewing skills. Remember that you should attempt 'amiable conversations' rather than interrogations. Use open-ended questions and allow your interviewee to talk. In other words, don't interrupt all the time like a tyro on the Radio 4 *Today* programme.

- Be aware that a minor error can undermine a whole investigation because it casts doubt on the credibility of your sources, your methods or your argument.

- Never prejudge the quality or value of potential information sources. You can only reliably determine usefulness after you have looked up that written source, tracked down and spoken to that individual. Even if you have doubts, do it anyway.

- Finally, consider the ethical dimension of your story – how will it impinge on the privacy or other human rights of your quarry? Do you have a convincing public interest defence?

There is one further test that should be applied to the results of any investigation – have you presented the facts in such a way that readers can make up their own minds? As David Spark notes in *Investigative Reporting: A Study in Technique*, 'The facts should be allowed to speak for themselves without loose and exaggerated expressions of opinion which could be hard to defend in court.' (Spark 1999: 94)

According to Stephen Berry: 'Investigative journalism operates from the notion that society cannot make something better until its people know what is wrong.' (Berry 2009: 177) This, if you like, is the true reason why investigative reporters get out of bed in the morning. No 'wrong' is too small, or indeed too large, that it cannot be accurately dissected and examined. The results need to be displayed on the laboratory bench of society's collective conscience. For only then will people be moved to utter the timeworn phrase that is so often the beginning of action: 'Something must be done.'

CHAPTER 11

The wrong arm of the law?

Newspapers and legislation

If you are one of those journalists or students who might not have given your undivided attention to the legal aspects of your training, try this sobering fact for size: there were more journalists simultaneously facing trial in the UK in 2012 than at any time in the entire history of the newspaper industry. We may technically have a free press – or even, as Harold Evans, the legendary former editor of *The Sunday Times* (1967–81) once memorably described it, a half-free press (Evans 1974) – but that does not mean that journalists are in any way above the law.

Neither does it take much to argue that Evans's half-free press has been still further shackled by legislation that he could not even have dreamed of nearly 40 years ago when he made his address to the Guildhall in London. Of the more than 60 laws that might constrain a reporter's access to information, newsgathering activities or ability to publish facts, 52 went on to the statute books after that 1974 speech.

It would, of course, be totally paralysing if a journalist had to have a full understanding of each of those pieces of legislation. I doubt very much, for example, that many of those currently facing trial (in the wake of the Hackgate scandal) under the Computer Misuse Act of 1990, or the Regulation of Investigatory Powers Act of 2000, had much of a working knowledge of what was and was not permitted by them. But it is, nonetheless, vital that anybody involved in the news business has a decent grasp of some of the more important legal principles that govern what they can and cannot put into print.

It is beyond the scope of this book to provide a definitive guide to the law as it applies to newspaper journalism, but this chapter focuses on some areas that have come to be of particular concern in recent years – because they involve either new legislation, or new or worrying developments in the way they have been applied to journalism. Chapter 12 also contains more detailed discussion of covering the courts. But we'll start with those journalists' arrests and the police investigations that led to them.

THE POLICE INVESTIGATIONS

In the background of all this fevered debate around the regulation of the press, several police investigations were continuing. Not only did they hamper the Leveson Inquiry's discussion of some of the most contentious industry practices, for fear of jeopardising ongoing cases, they also provided a good reason – according to its sternest critics – for not having an inquiry at all. After all, they pointed out, the key elements of newspaper wrongdoing were already illegal. Any failures, therefore, were failures of enforcement rather than failures of regulation.

Operation Caryatid was the first phone-hacking investigation, launched at the end of 2005 when royal aides working at Clarence House became suspicious about stories appearing in the *News of the World*. The investigation led to the convictions of Clive Goodman of the *News of the World* and private investigator Glenn Mulcaire in 2007. But the investigation was not widened, despite investigating officers' belief that they had evidence to show more than 400 people's phones had been hacked, partly because Metropolitan Police resources were so stretched by anti-terrorism operations. The operation was reviewed in 2009 by Assistant Commissioner John Yates, following further revelations that there may be more than 3,000 victims of hacking. Yates dismissed these allegations very quickly – a decision he later described as 'pretty crap', and which ultimately caused his resignation (Mendick 2011). His friendship with *News of the World* executive Neil Wallis came under scrutiny – as did hospitality received by other senior police officers – during the Leveson Inquiry.

Operation Weeting was the second investigation into phone hacking, launched in 2011 when further details of the scale of the practice were revealed. By late 2013, the operation was ongoing and had led to the arrest of around 60 journalists from newspapers including the *News of the World*, the *Sun*, *The Times*, the *Mirror* and *Daily Star*. At that time, 24 of them had been charged and 10 had been cleared. Those charged include former *News of the World* editors Andy Coulson and Rebekah Brooks, former managing editor Stuart Kuttner, former chief reporter Neville Thurlbeck and former news editor Greg Miskiw.

Operation Elveden is the Metropolitan Police's investigation into illegal payments to public officials, launched as the phone-hacking investigation widened. Two police officers, April Casburn and Paul Flattley, were handed prison sentences in 2013. Casburn had offered to sell police information about the phone-hacking investigation to the *News of the World* (though she always denied this). Flattley had provided information to newspapers on Kate Middleton's security arrangements. Journalists to be charged as a result of the investigation included Brooks, Coulson and Kuttner (see above), Clive Goodman, former *Sun* chief reporter John Kay, *Sun* managing editor Graham Dudman and *Sun* picture editor John Edwards.

Operation Tuleta is the investigation into computer hacking that was formally opened in 2011. Like Weeting and Elveden, Tuleta was headed by Deputy Assistant Commissioner of the Metropolitan Police Sue Akers. She told the Leveson Inquiry that 57 claims of data intrusion by or on behalf of journalists were being investigated, and that officers were examining 4 terabytes of data. Former *Sun* journalists Ben Ashford and Nick Parker were the first to be charged as a result of this operation, in late 2013.

Operation Rubicon, opened as a result of investigations surrounding the defamation action taken by Scottish Socialist politician Tommy Sheridan against the *News of the World*, had led to two journalists being charged. Andy Coulson was charged with perjury in 2012, and former *News of the World Scotland* editor Bob Bird was charged with attempting to pervert the course of justice.

The BBC News website carries a regularly updated list of people arrested, charged and sentenced in relation to the Hackgate inquiries at www.bbc.co.uk/news/uk-12296392.

PRIVACY

'It is well known in English law there is no right of privacy, and accordingly there is no right of action for breach of a person's privacy.' Such was the often-quoted ruling of Lord Justice Glidewell after two journalists from the *Sunday Sport* blagged their way into the hospital room of sitcom star Gorden Kaye in 1990 after he had suffered terrible head injuries from a car crash. The judge was hearing an application for an injunction to prevent the newspaper publishing the fruits of the reporters' ill-judged mission – pictures of the seriously ill TV actor and a rambling interview with him. The Kaye story was one of the events of that year that led to Conservative minister David Mellor warning the industry that it was 'drinking in the Last Chance Saloon' and, in turn, to the creation of the Press Complaints Commission.

In the couple of decades since then, privacy has been at the heart of some of the fiercest debate. The arrival of the Human Rights Act in 1998, which enshrined into British law the principles of the European Convention on Human Rights, crystallised that debate into a battle between two competing clauses: Article 8 of the Convention, which outlines an individual's right to a private life; and Article 10, which guarantees freedom of expression.

Many of the key cases have involved celebrities: news presenter Anna Ford, premiership footballer Gary Flitcroft, DJ Sara Cox, Hollywood couple Michael Douglas and Catherine Zeta-Jones, and supermodel Naomi Campbell all fought significant privacy cases in the early 2000s with varying degrees of success. The Campbell case, in particular, demonstrated the confusion and uncertainty that surrounded the issue. She won modest damages of £3,500 after winning a breach of confidence action under the Data Protection Act against the *Mirror*, which had revealed she was attending Narcotics Anonymous meetings having previously been in an anti-drugs campaign. This was overturned by the Court of Appeal, but then reversed again when the Law Lords ruled three to two in Campbell's favour.

By this time, editors were feeling angry about the growing sensation that a privacy law was being created through the back door. In a speech to the Society of Editors, *Daily Mail* editor Paul Dacre argued that:

> The British press is having a privacy law imposed on it, which – apart from allowing the corrupt and the crooked to sleep easily in their beds – is, I would argue, undermining the ability of mass-circulation newspapers to sell newspapers in an ever more difficult market. The law is not coming from Parliament – no, that would smack of democracy – but from the arrogant and amoral judgements – words I use very deliberately – of one man. I am referring, of course, to Justice David Eady who has, again and again, under the privacy clause of the Human Rights Act, found against newspapers and their age-old freedom to expose the moral shortcomings of those in high places.

Headlining Dacre's list of Eady rulings was the one he made after Formula 1 boss Max Mosley, having been exposed in 2008 by the *News of the World* for taking part in sado-masochistic orgies, successfully argued that there was no public interest in the story, and that what consenting adults do behind closed doors has no place on the front page of a newspaper. He won damages of £60,000, plus his costs, in the High Court, and then took his fight to the European Court of Human Rights. There he claimed that UK law did not properly match its privacy obligations under the European convention. In particular, he wanted a requirement that a newspaper would have a duty to approach the subject of a story such as his before going into print – raising the spectre of 'prior restraint', long considered one of the most oppressive forms of censorship. Mosley lost his European action, but continues his battle. The Leveson Inquiry heard that search engine Google had removed 'hundreds' of URLs from its search indexes in the UK following applications from Mosley (Leveson 2012).

Breach of confidence

But, despite Dacre's warnings, the celebrities are not having it all their own way. England footballer Rio Ferdinand lost his privacy claim against the *Sunday Mirror* in 2011 after it had paid his former mistress to reveal details of their affair (Shaw 2011). The judge in that case ruled in favour of the newspaper on the grounds of public interest, given that the married footballer had been asked to captain the England team, a job that carried an 'expectation of high standards'. 'Overall, in my judgement, the balancing exercise favours the defendant's right of freedom of expression over the claimant's right of privacy,' he said. 'At one level it was a "kiss and tell" story. Even less attractively, it was a "kiss and paid for telling" story, but stories may be in the public interest even if the reasons behind the informant providing the information are less than noble.'

Another case was less satisfying for the newspaper industry, and brought sharply into focus the issue of privacy for traditional publishers in the social media era.

In January 2013, the *Sun* planned to print pictures it had found on the social networking site Facebook of the husband of actor Kate Winslett. The man in question, who was also the nephew of Richard Branson, had changed his name by deed poll to Ned Rocknroll. He obtained an injunction preventing the newspaper from publishing the photographs, even though they had been available to view by anybody with a Facebook account since 2010.

In more recent times, it has been the privacy of ordinary individuals that has come to the fore. A study in 2013 by legal publishers Sweet and Maxwell showed that the number of privacy cases reported in the UK rose by 22 per cent in 12 months, and that the proportion of those brought by high-profile individuals had dropped over the same period. 'There has been a sudden shift from privacy law being the preserve of wealthy, high profile celebrities to privacy law being used by a much broader cross-section of society,' Jonathan Cooper, editor of Sweet and Maxwell's *European Human Rights Law Review*, told *Press Gazette* (Turvill 2013).

Super-injunctions

There's legally no such thing as a 'super-injunction'. Yet in 2010 and 2011 they seemed to be everywhere. Or at least, so rumour had it. Because the most sinister feature of these shadowy obstacles to press freedom was that their very existence could not be reported. Let me explain by way of one of the best-known examples.

In 2006, a British oil trading firm called Trafigura arranged for a cargo of waste to be disposed of in the Ivory Coast, after which tens of thousands of local people complained of serious illness. The company quickly commissioned a report by lawyers Minton, Treharne and Davies to examine the likelihood of the illnesses being linked to the waste it had dumped. Although the report was never made public, Trafigura paid more than £30 million in legal costs and compensation to the victims in a 2009 out-of-court settlement.

Shortly before that settlement, the *Guardian* obtained a copy of the Minton report. Which is where the lawyers stepped in. The law firm Carter-Ruck persuaded a judge that the nature of the Minton report was confidential and obtained an injunction preventing the newspaper not just from revealing its contents, but even from revealing the fact that it existed. If this was not chilling enough, the judge also ruled that the injunction itself could not be made public – by the *Guardian* or by any other news organisation.

The case descended even further into Kafka territory when Labour MP Paul Farrelly tabled a question in the House of Commons referring to the serious danger to press freedom arising from the case. Carter-Ruck insisted that the injunction prevented the *Guardian* – or any other publication – from reporting anything about Farrelly's question. And lest the power of this be underestimated, it's worth remembering that the penalty for breaking an injunction order such as this is could include the directors of the newspaper being fined or imprisoned, and assets belonging to the newspaper being seized (Rusbridger 2009). Others to obtain so-called super-injunctions over the following few years included footballers John Terry and Ryan Giggs, and, in a particularly blatant case of hypocrisy, BBC journalist Andrew Marr – whose career was founded on his ability to quiz public figures about their actions. So why can we report these names now? The answer, at least partly, is because of social media.

In the Trafigura case, social media network Twitter was quickly alive with news of the heavy-handed nature of the injunction. So rapidly did the tweets spread that the details of its client so carefully defended by Carter-Ruck were circulating arguably more widely than if the story had been published to the *Guardian*'s circulation of readers. Add to that the outrage of MPs that the supremacy of Parliament was apparently being challenged, and the legal firm soon bowed to the inevitable and the injunction was lifted. See also the lawyer's view of the Trafigura case (Tait 2011).

The same Twitter storm also engulfed the injunctions that both Terry and Giggs were attempting to enforce – in the latter case, some estimates suggest the injunction was being broken 900 times per hour at the height of the media storm (Black 2011). Marr lifted the injunction himself after being challenged by the scourge of many a hypocrite, *Private Eye* (BBC News online 2011).

These cases, and others, may have forced some celebrities to abandon the notion that the super-injunction is a viable way to defend their privacy. Nonetheless, it remains a potentially powerful weapon, and newspapers must remain vigilant.

LIBEL

For an editor, particularly of a publication that doesn't have the deep pockets of a multinational company behind it, there are few feelings to match the cold dread of a libel letter arriving on your desk. I speak with some experience here.

The very fact of the letter's existence means you are going to be spending money. You will have to involve your own legal advisers, who will examine every dot and comma of the story you published, all the while with their hourly meter running. You and your reporter will have to justify every fact, every quote, every potential interpretation of every phrase. In the pit of your stomach is the fear that you got it wrong. Yet, even if you didn't, in the very worst of those cases you may find yourself having to agree to an apology, and even a payout, even though you remain convinced that what you published was right, because the expense of fighting an action is so great and the result so risky. Such is the chilling effect that the Defamation Act(s) can have on freedom of expression.

The trouble is that it's ridiculously easy to libel somebody. You simply have to lower their reputation in the estimation of other people – or rather, have a tendency towards that in the eyes of a reasonable person. There are other ways of transgressing: a defamatory statement can expose someone to hatred, ridicule or contempt; cause them to be shunned or avoided; or disparage them in their business or profession.

So if news is, to use an age-old definition, something that somebody wants to suppress, you're running the risk of committing a libel with virtually every story you publish. Which is why every journalist needs to be alive to the traditional defences against accusations of defamation, namely:

- that the story is true (the defence of justification)
- that it is an honest opinion, based on facts, made without malice (the defence of fair comment)
- that it is a fair report of Parliament, council meetings, court hearings or meetings of other public bodies (the defence of privilege)
- that it is in an honest attempt to report the truth in the public interest (what used to be called the 'Reynolds defence' – since it emerged following the case involving Irish Prime Minister Albert Reynolds and *The Times* in the early 1990s).

The Defamation Act 2013

But in 2013 a new Defamation Act (to add to those of 1952 and 1996) was passed that gave journalists greater protection from being sued for libel. This was one of those rare pieces of legislation to be viewed in a generally positive light by the media industry. For many years, London had earned a reputation as the 'libel capital of the world' thanks to various aspects of the defamation framework seen as being in favour of claimants: the burden of proof is on the defendant; the claimant doesn't have to demonstrate specific loss; damage awards have traditionally been high; and conditional fee arrangements (also known as 'no win, no fee') mean claimants do not risk financial loss themselves.

This led to the practice of libel tourism – known in legal circles as 'forum shopping' – becoming common, often with English courts as the final destination. So, for example, Prince Alwaleed, a member of the Saudi royal family, threatened in 2013 to sue US business magazine *Forbes* over a paragraph about him in its annual Billionaire's List. The action he threatened was through London's courts – even though he is not a UK resident and *Forbes* is not a UK publication. The new Act is designed to discourage this form of libel tourism and to make level the playing field between libel claimant and publisher. Its key aspects are as follows.

- Claimants must prove to the court that England is the most appropriate place for the case to be heard – unlikely in the case of the Saudi prince and other libel tourists.

- Claims will have to pass a 'substantial harm' test, demonstrating that the claimant's reputation has been seriously damaged by the publication.

- A new public interest defence means that, for the first time, journalists can win a case by showing they 'reasonably believed publication was in the public interest'. This effectively replaces the Reynolds defence.

- The defence of privilege is extended to include peer-reviewed journal articles, international academic conference proceedings, international court hearings and international government proceedings.

- The single publication rule is abolished. This means the 12-month time limit to bring a libel claim is based on the first date of publication, and not reset every time an article is accessed online.

- The court will have the power to compel a losing defendant to publish a summary of the judgement.

- A statutory defence for 'third party' hosts of defamatory comments. This means internet service providers – likely to include social media sites such as Facebook and Twitter – should not be liable for defamatory postings provided they act quickly to take them down after being notified.

- The removal of the right to have a jury hear libel cases.

Simon Singh, an academic who had been involved in a long-running libel dispute over a comment piece he wrote for the *Guardian* about chiropractic medicine, was among those to welcome the new legislation as something that will 'change the landscape of free speech in Britain' (Ponsford 2013b). But there were some dissenting voices. Brendan O'Neill (2013) wrote on the *Daily Telegraph* blog that the new Bill was a 'disaster for free speech', particularly because it removed the right for a jury trial. 'Public debate and freedom of speech are not experiments taking place in a lab – they are things that affect all of us, and which all of us should therefore have a say on, both inside defamation courts and in the court of public opinion.'

THE DATA PROTECTION ACT

The Data Protection Act (DPA) is one of the most misunderstood pieces of legislation on the statute book, particularly as it applies to journalism. Many a school head teacher has banned newspaper photographers from attending events because of it. And many a police officer has used it to explain why perfectly legitimate requests for information by reporters should be blocked.

At its inception, the DPA existed to protect members of the public from having information about them held by public or commercial organisations without their knowledge. But journalism was given special treatment. It would be inimical to a free press if crooks and corrupt politicians could derail a newspaper's investigation into them by demanding a release of that data. So there were wide exemptions for those involved in public interest reporting, meaning that reporters did not have to comply with the Act. The exemptions mainly fall under section 32 of the Act.

What actually happened was that there was a creeping misuse of the Act from both sides of the journalistic fence. So, for example, the Association of Chief Police Officers (ACPO) in May 1999 issued guidelines that names of victims and witnesses of road crashes or other accidents were entitled not to have personal details released without their permission.

From the other side, Operation Motorman demonstrated that journalists were employing some highly questionable tactics to acquire personal data about celebrities and others, often using private investigators as middle men. Operation Motorman was not a police investigation, but an investigation by the Information Commissioner's Office (ICO) into data being acquired by newspaper organisations in pursuit of stories. It was carried out in 2005, following an earlier discovery of documents belonging to a private investigator, John Boyall, showing misuses of data from the police national computer. The operation led to Steve Whittamore, another private investigator who had been employed on a freelance basis by newspapers including the *News of the World*, *Daily Mail*, *Mirror*, *Sunday Times* and *Observer*. More than 300 journalists were named in Whittamore's documents. He pleaded guilty, along with three others, of conspiring to commit misconduct in a public office, and was given a conditional discharge.

With hindsight, the revelations from Motorman, published in two 2006 reports by the ICO (*What Price Privacy?* and *What Price Privacy Now?*), should have been a wake-up call for newspaper editors that some of the 'dark arts' they were using to acquire information could yet blow up in their faces. Yet, as Leveson noted as he delivered his report: 'None of these revelations led to any newspaper conducting an investigation either into its own practices or into those of other titles. No newspaper sought to discover (let alone expose) whether its journalists had complied with data protection legislation.'

However, in his 2012 report into the culture, practices and ethics of the press, Lord Justice Leveson made proposals that would not only narrow the exemptions from the DPA, but would also introduce the spectre of prison for those journalists or their managers who failed to comply (Doyle 2012). Leveson's key data protection recommendations were that:

- personal data can be held only if it is 'necessary for publication', rather than simply with a view to publication
- any invasion of data privacy would be outweighed by the public interest
- Section 32 be narrowed in scope to remove several journalistic exemptions
- victims of data protection invasion can seek compensation for 'pure distress', not just financial loss.

In its official response to the Leveson Report, the ICO was somewhat cool on the recommendations. Information Commissioner Chris Graham was concerned about the 'chilling effect' they might have, and that the changes would effectively turn the ICO into a 'mainstream press regulator', a role it is 'not actively seeking' (Swinford 2013).

THE POLICE AND CRIMINAL EVIDENCE ACT

Among Lord Justice Leveson's more controversial recommendations – and there were plenty of those – from his 2012 report was that the Home Office should reconsider aspects of the Police and Criminal Evidence Act (PACE) that apply to journalism. In particular, he wanted a reappraisal of the section of the 1984 Act that protects journalists from having to hand over to the police evidence they have gathered as part of legitimate inquiries. As things stand, journalists are protected from being forced to pass evidence on to the police, even in circumstances where it may have been obtained illegally (see also the section on sources in Chapter 5, pp. 105–6).

But Leveson wanted the Home Office to consult on whether journalistic material should be considered confidential only 'if it is held or has continuously been held since it was first acquired or created subject to an enforceable or lawful undertaking, restriction or obligation'. Decode that and the suggestion is that journalists would need some kind of contract with the sources who provide them with details of information that might be of interest to the police. It doesn't take much to realise that many sources would run a mile in the opposite direction rather than come forward with information if there was a risk of them being named to the police.

The *Daily Telegraph*'s scoop on the scandal of parliamentary expenses is a case in point. The details of MPs' individual expense claims were passed to the *Telegraph* – in exchange for money – on a CD via a source who might well have broken the law by passing it on. Would that source have come forward if they felt details of their dealings with the *Telegraph* might end up in the hands of the police? Even the lawyers were a bit queasy on that one. Magnus Boyd was quoted in the *Telegraph* as saying:

> I think the relationship between a journalist and his source here is the cornerstone of investigative journalism, the cornerstone of public interest journalism. I think we would need to think very carefully before you put anything in place that fettered that. I'm a claimant media lawyer and I'm always having a gripe about journalists not having to disclose their sources, but the principle here is greater than any one case . . . You have to protect that relationship.
>
> (Johnson 2012)

COPYRIGHT

Most journalists could be forgiven for not having noticed the passing of the Enterprise and Regulatory Reform Act in the spring of 2013. And yet, particularly for photo-journalists, its implications may be significant. Partly designed to simplify the process by which creative works can be used online, the new Act allows the use of 'orphan' works – creative items such as photographs whose original creators cannot easily be identified – without explicit permission as long as a 'diligent' search has taken place.

The government said the Act was designed to 'support the UK's enterprise culture and help to make it one of the best places to do business'. It didn't take long for the new legislation to be dubbed the 'Instagram Act' (Orlowski 2013), after the online photo-sharing service which is notoriously aggressive in its treatment of copyright issues.

FREEDOM OF INFORMATION

> Freedom of Information Act. Three harmless words. I look at those words as I write them, and feel like shaking my head 'til it drops off. You idiot. You naïve, foolish, irresponsible nincompoop. There is really no description of stupidity, no matter how vivid, that is adequate. I quake at the imbecility of it . . . The truth is that the FoI Act isn't used, for the most part, by 'the people'. It's used by journalists. For political leaders, it's like saying to someone who is hitting you over the head with a stick, 'Hey, try this instead', and handing them a mallet. The information is neither sought because the journalist is curious to know, nor given to bestow knowledge on 'the people'. It's used as a weapon.
>
> (Blair 2010)

Tony Blair might have regretted his part in the enactment of the Freedom of Information (FoI) Act in 2000, but for many journalists it has proved a valuable tool in the battle to hold power to account. According to a report published two years after it fully came into force in 2005, the Act had accounted for more than 1,000 stories being published, on matters including:

> . . . significant disclosures about the Iraq conflict, the possible cause of Gulf war syndrome, assaults on public service staff, the state of civil service morale, compensation paid to victims of medical accidents, schools' efforts to inflate their exam results, hospital techniques for deflating waiting lists, the universities teetering on the edge of financial collapse, police officers with criminal records, government efforts to encourage gambling, lobbying by multinational oil, pharmaceutical and food companies, nuclear safety and other hazards, crimes

committed by offenders on parole, unpublicised prison escapes, the expansion of the national DNA database and innumerable reports about high expenses claims and dubious public spending.

(CFOI 2008)

It also, of course, played its part in the release of information about MPs' expenses in 2009 that reverberated throughout the country.

Neither is it only journalists who have felt the benefit of the legislation. In 2012, a parliamentary sub-committee undertook a post-legislative scrutiny of the Act. The first sentence of its report reads as follows: 'Freedom of Information has been a significant enhancement of our democracy and the Act is working well.' (Graham 2012)

Nonetheless, there remains concern following that sub-committee's report that the government would like to see the Act watered down. Its proposals, which went out for public consultation in 2013, would, for example, make it easier for public authorities to refuse time-consuming requests, campaigners fear. That's because the proposals would allow authorities to add in the time spent 'considering' the request and redacting any exempt information when calculating their costs. Under the current rules, they can only charge for time spent locating, retrieving and extracting the information.

Once the cost of processing a request reaches £600 (for councils; £450 for other bodies), that request can be turned down. Furthermore, the government was proposing that individuals and organisations should be limited to the amount of requests they can make over a three-month period – in order, they said, to prevent 'industrial' usage of the Act. As the Campaign for Freedom of Information pointed out, local newspapers, which cover a range of different issues involving their councils, would be the first casualties.

> A single request about school exam results might be enough to reach the cost limit. Thereafter the whole paper – not just the individual journalist – might be barred from making any further FOI requests to the authority for the next quarter, even on different issues such as child abuse, road safety or library closures.
>
> (CFOI 2012)

CONTEMPT OF COURT

The Contempt of Court Act 1981 is designed to protect jurors and members of the judiciary from reading material that may prejudice their view of a trial on which they are sitting in judgement. It applies to any case in which proceedings are 'active', and takes into account various factors including the content of the publication, its circulation footprint, the time between publication and court proceedings, and the location of the trial. But its enactment was at a time when the means by which the public could access such information – essentially newspapers and news broadcasts – were easily quantifiable.

The subsequent explosion of an online world in which the means of publication became almost unlimited may go some way towards explaining why, in the early part of the twenty-first century, the boundaries became somewhat blurred as to what was tolerated under the Act. An apparent reluctance by successive attorneys general to prosecute newspapers that apparently stepped over the line only helped to reinforce the view that, as Magnus Linklater put it in *The Times* (2006): 'The Contempt of Court Act 1981 is being torn to shreds by rapacious media and sanctioned – through his acquiescence – by Lord Goldsmith, the Attorney General.'

High-profile cases such as the Soham murders in 2002 or the so-called 'Suffolk Strangler' in 2006 saw newspapers, perhaps fearing they would be overtaken by commentators in the blogosphere, printing stories before the trials, which would have been unthinkable just a few years earlier – despite advance warnings by the Attorney General (Colman 2008). So, by the time the police began investigating the murder of Joanna Yeates in Bristol in 2010, perhaps newspapers had begun to get the sense they were almost untouchable when it came to reporting the arrest of her landlord, Christopher Jefferies. Jefferies was never charged but, nonetheless, endured a devastating vilification at the hands of a number of newspapers covering the investigation. Giving evidence to the Leveson Inquiry (see Chapter 4) in 2012, he said:

> I can see now that, following my arrest, the national media shamelessly vilified me. The press set about what can only be described as a witch-hunt . . . The incalculable effect of what was written about me by these highly influential tabloid newspapers is something from which it will be difficult ever to escape.
> (Leveson 2012)

In the event, the Attorney General did pursue two newspapers – the *Sun* and the *Daily Mirror* – and both were convicted under the contempt act. Jefferies won libel payouts from eight newspapers. Leveson's subsequent report included the suggestion (although not a full recommendation) that 'save in exceptional and clearly identified circumstances' – for example, where there may be an immediate risk to the public – the names or identifying details of those who are arrested or suspected of a crime should not be released.

Meanwhile, ACPO was drafting fresh guidance, which would eventually have to be approved by the College of Policing and chief constables, that people who have been arrested should not be named and only the briefest of details should be given. But this raised the spectre of 'secret arrests' where officers declined to confirm identities of those detained. Index on Censorship's chief executive Kirsty Hughes told the *Guardian*:

De facto anonymity for people who have been arrested would reverse the principle of open justice that we have in the UK and could lead to people being arrested and taken into custody without anyone knowing about it. Anonymity may be appropriate in certain circumstances, but sweeping powers for secrecy should not be the norm.

(Bowcott 2013)

The 'fade factor' is another area of contempt that is having to be re-evaluated in the light of changes in technology. In the days before internet archives, a newspaper could partly rely on the fact that there would be a long time between publication during a police investigation and any subsequent trial. Today, those original reports remain available and easily accessible through search engines. On at least one occasion, a High Court judge has written to newspapers requesting the removal of archive material for the duration of a trial.

THE BRIBERY ACT 2010

The Bribery Act came into force in July 2011 and is widely seen as one of the most stringent pieces of legislation of this type anywhere in the world (Pugh 2011). It was largely intended to address issues of business corruption, but it also has implications for journalists in various walks of life. Under the terms of the Act, it is a criminal offence to give financial or other inducements with the intention of making the recipient perform improperly a task that is expected to be carried out impartially or in good faith. Both parties to the bribe can be liable to prosecution: the recipient as well as the bribe-giver.

The implications for certain spheres of journalism were noted wryly by a fashion journalist who wrote anonymously in *The Times* about the volume of gifts she was routinely sent by the PR industry in the hope that she would write favourably about their clients:

> I am a magazine fashion editor, and this is our dirty little secret . . . we supplement our lower-than-you'd-think wages with thousands of pounds worth of free stuff . . .
>
> But, if everyone is to take Kenneth Clarke's new Bribery Act seriously, then my way of life is over.

As a result, many publishing companies introduced policies whereby their journalists are instructed to declare any PR gifts, which are often then distributed to charity. But the Act also has a more seriously chilling impact on some investigative journalism. Crucially, it has no public interest defence, which, according to the *Sun*'s investigations editor Brian Flynn, means that important stories are going unreported. He told the 2013 Society of Editors' Conference:

Every day *The Sun* turns away stories that are in the public interest because of the 2010 Bribery Act. With no public interest defence we cannot talk to whistleblowers who want compensation for the risk they are taking.

(Ponsford 2012)

CHAPTER 12

All human life

Covering the courts

Mark Hanna

The trials of those charged with serious crime – such as murder, rape or fraud – can become national news stories. A reporter can convey the intense drama in the courtroom when witnesses, overcome by what they must recall, break down giving evidence, or when an evasive defendant is undermined by a barrister's cross-examination.

The intensity in a crown court trial increases when, after the jury has deliberated for hours or days on its verdict, this is finally announced in court. It will convict or acquit the defendant, and so is greeted with elation or relief by one side in the case, and with despair or resignation by the other. In the court's public gallery there may be shouting and weeping among friends and relatives of the defendant or the crime's victim or alleged victim. Those hoping for justice may include the parents or spouse of someone murdered.

Occasionally, a journalist is personally part of the drama. In 2013, freelance John Davies was covering a case at Bradford Crown Court when the defendant, Karl Jones, 37, of King's Drive, Shipley, was told the length of his sentence for six armed robberies. 'Is that 12 years? . . . I can't do 12 years!' Jones shouted. He then leapt from the dock to try to flee the courtroom. Davies rugby-tackled him. The judge commended Davies and awarded him £250 from public funds for stopping Jones's escape (Loweth 2013).

It is the reporter's job to understand and accurately narrate the court's proceedings, whether dramatic or humdrum, and especially to relate what a crime's victim, and anyone bereaved by a homicide, has suffered. The public consumes the media's reports of court cases with horror or indignation at deeds or scenes described, and may gain satisfaction from justice being done when a criminal is convicted and jailed, perhaps for life. Where, how and why crime is committed, and how efficiently perpetrators are traced by police and dealt with by the courts, is always a matter of concern locally or nationally – because, obviously, we do not want crime inflicted on us or our loved ones.

Also, media scrutiny of how courts work is one safeguard against innocent defendants being convicted in miscarriages of justice.

THE OPEN JUSTICE PRINCIPLE

By reporting from the courts the media enable society to enjoy the benefits of open justice. What Lord Justice Watkins, the Lord Chief Justice, said in 1987 holds good (if allowance is made for the fact that a reporter is now less likely to be male):

> The role of the journalist and his importance for the public interest in the administration of justice has been commented upon on many occasions. No-one nowadays surely can doubt that his presence in court for the purpose of reporting proceedings conducted therein is indispensable. Without him, how is the public to be informed of how justice is being administered in our courts?
>
> (*R v Felixstowe Justices, ex p Leigh* [1987] QB 582)

One benefit of open justice is that a witness is less likely to lie if testimony can be reported widely. In a Court of Appeal case in 1998, the Lord Chief Justice, Lord Woolf, drawing on case law dating from 1913, listed other reasons why legal proceedings should continue to take place in 'the full glare' of open court:

> It is necessary because the public nature of proceedings deters inappropriate behaviour on the part of the court. It also maintains the public's confidence in the administration of justice. It enables the public to know that justice is being administered impartially. It can result in evidence becoming available which would not become available if the proceedings were conducted behind closed doors, or with one or more of the parties' or witnesses' identity concealed. It makes uninformed and inaccurate comment about the proceedings less likely.
>
> (*R v Legal Aid Board, ex p Kaim Todner*,
> *Court of Appeal* [1999] QB 966)

Government policy can be influenced by open justice – public and political outrage about a particular crime may lead to reforms in the law or police procedures if, for example, media reports of a court case show that a criminal escaped detection for a long time, committing further offences before he or she was finally caught.

However, the ideal that the media helps promote the benefits of open justice may not always be the reality. The way the media selects cases to report – with concentration on the worst crimes – may be a distorting factor, increasing the public's fear of crime, although to reach conclusions about 'media effects' is not easy (Greer and Reiner 2012: 261–2). Media coverage can also air or stoke controversy about what some crime victims see as 'lenient' sentencing. Many people tend to think that courts are 'soft' on offenders, and these opinions may fuel demands for tougher sentences. But the overall picture is that the UK prison population has risen in the past decade, and that the incidence of crime in the UK has been declining for some years (ONS 2013; Sentencing Council 2013).

In individual cases, insensitive reporting can aggravate what a crime victim suffers if the detail of evidence reported is humiliating, or can worsen the grief of anyone bereaved. There are ethical considerations, then, in how cases and their wider context are reported.

THE CASES COVERED

When making day-to-day decisions on which court hearings to cover, news editors rarely feel any duty to uphold the open justice principle. Their decisions are pragmatic, based on the limits of their resources to deploy staff reporters or pay freelances, and commercial, based on which cases will most interest audiences and so maintain or increase broadcast ratings or a newspaper's sales. When someone is charged with a newsworthy crime, the media keep track of the case's progress by sending reporters to preliminary hearings at court, or by ringing the police or the Crown Prosecution Service. A good reporter will sniff out other interesting cases by being personable, cheery and cheeky to gain tips from the court community about cases in the pipeline. Each courthouse has ushers (who fetch defendants and witnesses into court), court clerks, security guards, administrators and receptionists, and a network of lawyers who practise there. Word of a pending case with an unusual twist may spread quickly among them. Most cases, of course, go unreported in the media. It is often pot luck what is covered.

THE HISTORY OF COURT REPORTING

The seductive thrill of hearing or reading about some criminals' lifestyles, the frisson of fear engendered by crime reports and the comfort provided by reports of justice done have created much of the market demand in which our popular press evolved.

A multitude of crime 'pamphlets' flourished in the seventeenth and eighteenth centuries, describing – with great artistic licence – the lives of notorious thieves or murderers, to be sold at their execution or shortly afterwards. By the early nineteenth century, murder and execution 'broadsides' were so popular that one – the 'last Dying Speech and Confession of William Corder, murderer of Maria Marten', published in 1828 – sold 1,166,000 copies (Patricia Anderson 1991: 25).

In 1843, the first issue of the *News of the World*, a Sunday newspaper later to be dubbed a 'squalid recorder of squalid crime', included a front-page story headed: 'Extraordinary charge of drugging and violation' (Berrey 1933: 35; Bainbridge and Stockdill 1993: 13). The motto of Lord Northcliffe – who, in 1896, launched what is regarded as the first 'popular' daily newspaper, the *Daily Mail* – was: 'Get me a murder a day!' (Williams 1998: 56).

THE COURTS SYSTEM

This chapter refers, except when specified otherwise, to the laws and criminal justice system operating in England and Wales. Northern Ireland's legal system is similar. Scotland has its own distinct courts and laws.

There are around 1.6 million criminal cases in the magistrates' courts each year. Most offences are minor, punished by a fine. Only around 6 per cent of cases lead to trial by magistrates (Ministry of Justice 2012: 8). The rest involve sentencing after guilt is admitted, or are otherwise disposed of. Magistrates deal with more than 90 per cent of all criminal cases – for example, traffic offences, drunkenness and low-value thefts. The maximum jail term magistrates can impose is six months. In Scotland, the lowest tier is the Justice of the Peace courts.

The Newspaper Society (2013) has published data from 37 editors which indicated that 37 per cent of local newspapers send a reporter to cover a criminal court each day of the working week. But in many areas, reporters rarely attend the magistrates' courts. Her Majesty's Courts and Tribunals Service sends to local newspapers for publication the daily 'registers' from these courts, giving brief details of convictions, including who the defendants were and what punishments were imposed.

Virtually all criminal cases begin in the magistrates' courts. But the media are most interested in the cases – around 150,000 each year – sent by magistrates to the area's Crown Court. These involve charges too serious for magistrates to deal with. At Crown Courts, around 70 per cent of defendants plead guilty (Ministry of Justice 2012: 9). The rest are tried by a jury unless the case is dismissed for insufficient evidence or other reasons (in Scotland, juries are involved in some trials at the Sheriff Courts, and all trials at the High Court of the Justiciary).

LAWS TO ENSURE TRIALS ARE FAIR

Reporting from the courts is not a job for an amateur. Journalists need training to know the many laws that affect, and often restrict, what can be published.

When a case is heading for a Crown Court trial, laws restrict what can be reported from preliminary hearings – for example, when a murderer makes his first appearance at a magistrates' court. The media can report basic information, including the defendant's name, age and address, the charge/s, and whether bail was granted. But until the eventual trial is over, law usually bans the media from quoting references made in these early hearings to evidence, and from publishing any previous conviction/s the defendant has. These bans are to prevent prejudicial information being seen or heard by members of the public who may later be selected, from the register of local electors, for jury service at the Crown Court. Jurors will not normally be told during a trial if a defendant has a previous conviction, because they should try the charge only on the evidence presented to them. For the same reason, the bans aim to ensure jurors are not in a position to recall from media reports what evidence was referred to in preliminary hearings, because by the time the trial starts, the judge may have ruled that some of that evidence is inadmissible.

In 2012, the *Sun* was fined after it admitted breaching the ban on evidence being reported from preliminary hearings. It had quoted evidence from phone texts – 'gas pipe cut, . . . boom' – from a hearing in which Andrew Partington, 28, of Buckley Street, Oldham, faced charges of manslaughter and criminal damage. He was later jailed for ten years. The charges concerned an explosion caused by him cutting gas pipes when drunk to threaten his girlfriend, to whom he was habitually violent, that he would commit suicide if she left him. The blast flattened three houses and killed a neighbour's child.

When a trial begins, the media can usually report all the evidence immediately, as it is given in court. This reflects the open justice principle. But laws still apply, requiring the reporting to be fair and accurate and to exclude extraneous information which could improperly influence a jury. An unfair or inaccurate report of any court hearing can be regarded as a contempt of court, and therefore as illegal, if it creates 'a substantial risk of serious prejudice or impediment' to a later stage of that case or to a related case – for example, if a distorted account has potential to confuse or prejudice a jury. A media organisation which commits a contempt can be fined an amount unlimited by law and, in theory, its editor or the reporter responsible could be jailed.

The last time a UK journalist was jailed for a contempt was in 1949 – this was Sylvester Bolam, editor of the *Daily Mirror*. But several newspapers have been fined in recent decades in contempt prosecutions begun by the Attorney General. For example, in 2011 the *Daily Mail* and the *Sun* newspapers were found guilty of contempt after they published on their websites a photograph of Ryan Ward, who was being tried in Sheffield for murder. The contempt occurred because the photo, taken from a social networking site, showed Ward, 19, of Phillips Road, Loxley, posing with an automatic pistol. But the charge and evidence in his trial did not involve a gun – he had murdered a man by hitting him with a brick – so publication of the gun picture created a risk that jurors would be improperly influenced against Ward, because it made him seem a would-be gangster. This was the first time that online publication in the UK had led to a contempt conviction. Each newspaper was fined £15,000 and had to pay the Attorney General's costs of £28,117. The case illustrates how strict the law is, because there was no evidence that any juror actually saw the picture before it was removed.

LIBEL LAW

Defamation law, too, specifies that media reports of court cases must be fair and accurate.

A newspaper, TV channel or radio station may have to pay libel damages to some-one whose reputation is diminished by inaccuracy and unfairness. This is why reporters covering a trial should attribute direct and indirect quotes to the person making these statements in court. If there is no attribution, an allegation may seem to readers to be a fact, and so the report could wrongly suggest, for example, that the defendant is guilty or that a witness has lied.

When a defendant admits the crime, or is convicted in a trial, there is no longer any need to attribute the crime allegation to anyone. It is now proved. But care must still be taken to attribute any evidence or argument which goes beyond what is proved by an admission or verdict, especially any allegation which affects the reputation of people other than the defendant.

A major factor in a banker winning 'substantial damages' in 2013 in a libel action against the *Mail on Sunday* was its failure to attribute one paragraph of a report of two men being jailed for a £49 million fraud plot. It did not make clear that the judge had said there was no evidence that the banker – who was not a defendant or witness, but who was referred to by a defence barrister – was complicit in the plot (*Media Lawyer* 2012a, 2013a).

ACCURACY

As each court case involves damaging allegations, journalists cannot be slipshod in reports. The intro of a report of a trial can attribute the allegations by means of a tagged-on phrase – such as 'a court heard' or 'a jury was told' – if the next paragraphs quickly reveal who made the allegation. For example:

> An angry farmer shot his sheepdog when it would not stop barking, Heavytown magistrates heard.
> Joe Bloggs watched his collie Rover die in agony from the shotgun blast, said prosecutor Ronald Emery.

In a lengthy report, to attribute each statement directly (with phrases such as 'Mr Emery said', 'he added') can leave the copy clogged up stylistically. If one sentence is not attributed, but is sandwiched between other statements made by the same person which *are* attributed, this may be safe. It depends on the report's total effect. Attribution can be achieved indirectly by using the grammatical convention of 'reported speech'. This involves shifting the tense of the verbs back in time: for example, shifting a verb in the present tense into the past tense. Indirect attribution should not run over several sentences. Direct attribution must be inserted frequently to remind readers that trial evidence is not proved.

For example, a witness called Evans says:

> John Smith is always messing about, playing daft tricks on people when he is drunk, you know, if he has had a few or more than a few drinks. It's just his way, to muck about now and again, but it is all harmless. He never carries any kind of knife and, you know, he does not go around making threats to people. He is aggressive now and then in how he says things, you know, his tone, but as I just said, he does not threaten to do anything to anyone. He can lose his temper in the pub in arguments but he calms down quickly.

This can be reported accurately as:

> When drunk, John Smith played harmless tricks on people, Mr Evans said. But Smith never carried a knife and did not make threats. He was sometimes aggressive in tone. 'He can lose his temper in the pub in arguments but he calms down quickly,' Mr Evans added.

Use of direct (verbatim) quotes makes court copy lively if each quote has a sharp focus, adds a flourish or expresses the speaker's character. But verbose, rambling statements should usually be succinctly and fairly paraphrased, to keep the narrative brisk.

Journalists must be accurate when summarising charges. It may be libellous to report that someone is charged with *dangerous driving* when the charge is the lesser offence of *careless driving*. People found guilty of *drink-driving* – that is, driving when the alcohol in their blood or breath was above the legal limit – were not necessarily *drunk*, so this term should not be used unless there is evidence that they were.

A great danger of libel arises if a media report fails to include sufficient, available information to identify accurately the defendant and anyone else subject to defamatory allegations in the case. If you publish that 'John Brown of Rotherham' is accused of a sexual assault, anyone else called John Brown who lives in Rotherham may be able to sue you for the libellous suggestion that they may be a molester, if they can prove that acquaintances could reasonably think the report refers to the John Brown they know.

So media reports should include, as well as the defendant's name, their age, street address and occupation, as stated in the proceedings or as officially made available by the court. If you have gleaned such details merely from the magistrates' court's daily list of cases, check when listening in court that they are accepted as correct. Similarly, always use officially available details to fully identify in your report any other person or organisation mentioned by name in evidence (and it should be noted that the examples in this chapter of how reports should be written all rely on fictitious characters!).

MAKING DETAIL WORK FOR YOU

The intro of a court report should be a snapshot of the most newsworthy points of the case, with gripping detail to project a vivid, verbal picture. Which of these intros interests you the most?

> The crown court trial has begun of an 18-year-old Heavytown man who allegedly murdered his mother.

Or this one?

> A teenager cut off his mother's head with an axe after she complained his room was untidy, a jury has heard.

The latter version has stark detail and a chilling contrast – the immensity of the alleged violence compared with the mundane nature of the alleged cause. Ideally, an active construction is used in the intro's grammar – someone doing something to someone. An intro is weakened if overloaded with minor facts or subordinate clauses.

Imagine that the following story is a court report in the mythical Heavytown's daily paper.

> A pub landlord swindled £50,000 from his customers and squandered it on prostitutes and gambling, a jury heard.
> Jeremiah Tankard, posing as a gemstone expert, persuaded 18 of his pub's regulars to speculate in diamonds, Heavytown crown court was told.
> Tankard, entrusted with cash from their savings, claimed he was going to Amsterdam to buy the gems for them, but instead visited London brothels and casinos in a 'massive spending spree', said prosecuting barrister Alfie Heren.
> Tankard, aged 45, of The Sparkly Arms pub, Facet Road, Heavytown, denies 18 charges of fraud.

Notice how the intro hopes to seize the readers' attention. The allegations are then succinctly elaborated, with sufficient attribution in the third paragraph. Without slowing narrative pace, other details are filtered into the copy to state which court this is, who is being quoted, and what the charges are. The fourth paragraph makes clear that Tankard denies guilt. It accurately summarises the charges. The full wording of each charge, specifying the money allegedly obtained from each alleged victim, should be in the reporter's notebook, so he or she can justify this summary if necessary, or provide more detail as the trial unfolds.

It is usually a good idea after the intro and early paragraphs to relate the alleged events in their chronological order, to give the readers context. Hence, this story could continue:

> In 2011 Tankard arrived in Heavytown after buying the pub, Mr Heren said. Tankard had quickly grown friendly with local people, impressing them by running fund-raising events for the village school. He had been elected to the parish council.
> 'But Mr Tankard is really a charlatan without much conscience. Having won the trust of his village neighbours, he set out to exploit them with bogus talk of diamonds,' Mr Heren added.

This Tankard court story is constructed mainly from what would have been the prosecuting opening of such a case, in which – before any witness gives evidence – the prosecution barrister outlines the main allegations against the defendant, to help the jury gain quick understanding. But the need for fairness means that the media's reports should indicate what the defence case is, if this has been aired in open court so early in the trial. For example, the report could conclude:

> After his arrest Tankard told police that his customers had greatly exaggerated the amounts of cash they gave to him, and that he had lost the money – which he claimed was only £17,000 – when a prostitute stole his briefcase, Mr Heren said. The trial continues.

For many media organisations the convention is to deny a defendant any courtesy title – for instance, Mr, Mrs or Ms – unless and until they are acquitted.

BACKGROUNDERS WHEN THE CASE ENDS

After all verdicts in a case are announced, the media are free to publish or broadcast their 'backgrounders' – analytical features about the case and people involved. These can include material which the jury, for legal reasons, was not told in the trial. For a major case, to achieve immediate publication of its backgrounder a media organisation will have prepared two versions: one to be used if the defendant is acquitted – which may question, by referring to evidence, whether he or she could have been charged at all; the other if he or she is convicted. The latter, because conviction means the defendant has a reduced or no chance of success-fully suing for defamation, can assertively portray the defendant as dangerously sociopathic or stupid, seek to explain why his or her character evolved to be criminal and quote what the crime's victim, or those bereaved by the crime, think of the perpetrator.

In 2011, the *Daily Mail* published online, for about 90 seconds, the wrong version of a pre-prepared report of case's culmination. It said that an Italian appeal court had upheld the conviction of American student Amanda Knox for murder. In fact the court had found her not guilty. After a member of the public complained about the error, the Press Complaints Commission criticised the newspaper for this inaccuracy, and because the report contained a manufactured – because imagined – account of how this (falsely reported) verdict had been received in the courtroom, including that Knox had begun sobbing (PCC 2011).

AUDIO-RECORDERS AND CAMERAS ARE BANNED

To be accurate, reporters need to make fast and plentiful notes in court, and so shorthand is invaluable. The National Council for the Training of Journalists sets a standard of 100 words per minute shorthand for journalism trainees. Some achieve higher speeds.

The Contempt of Court Act 1981 bans the use of audio-recorders in court in most circumstances. People in the public gallery are not allowed to use them because a recording might help dishonest witnesses collude to produce matching evidence, or be used to intimidate or humiliate a witness by playing back to him or her, or to others, the testimony given in court. Courts have discretion to let reporters use audio-recorders. But shorthand is better because key quotes are easily marked and quickly found. In a courtroom there is seating for journalists – the press bench. Elsewhere in the courthouse building there is, or should be, a room for journalists to write their reports and ring their newsdesks.

In 2012, the *Guardian* won a landmark ruling in the Court of Appeal that its reporters should have been given access to case documents used in an extradition hearing (*R (on the application of Guardian News and Media Ltd) v City of Westminster Magistrates Court* [2012] EWCA Civ 420). This judgement established rights, now recognised in court rules, for journalists covering criminal proceedings to see such documents – for example, witness statements – to aid that coverage.

The Criminal Justice Act 1925 bans photography and filming in courts and their precincts. This is to prevent witnesses and defendants suffering additional pressure from the scrutiny of a lens. Some witnesses may be deterred from testifying if pictures or footage could be published of them reliving humiliating or painful experiences when giving evidence. For these reasons, the only media images of a trial that can be published are sketches made by artists, who memorise the scene in court and make the sketch elsewhere.

The Supreme Court, the UK's highest court, normally permits televising of its proceedings. Because these are appeals, they do not usually involve witnesses giving evidence in person, and any defendant present is not shown. In 2013 the law was changed to permit the televising of legal argument and judgments in the Court of Appeal. There are plans to permit the televising of Crown Court judges making sentencing remarks about a defendant. But there are no plans in England, Wales or Northern Ireland to allow the filming or photographing in courts of defendants, witnesses or jurors. The Scottish courts have, on a few occasions, allowed TV cameras to film proceedings, including defendants who consented to this.

'LIVE, TEXT-BASED COMMUNICATIONS'

In a major trial, reporters may file 'running copy' – a series of updates of what has been said in court – as quickly as practicalities permit. If a media organisation can afford to send two reporters to the same trial, the pair take turns in the courtroom, one making notes while the other, in the courthouse pressroom, writes up notes to file a story to her or his newsdesk. The Press Association news agency covers trials of national interest, so media organisations can use its 'copy' too, and that of freelances.

Using mobile phones to make or receive spoken calls in courtrooms remains banned, to preserve the dignity of the proceedings and to avoid disruption. A ringtone could interrupt and faze a witness already having difficulty giving evidence. But in 2011 the Lord Chief Justice gave a general permission for journalists to use mobile phones and laptops in court for 'live, text-based communication' in reporting cases, provided that use of such devices is silent and unobtrusive. This means reporters no longer have to ask in each case for the court's permission to email or text 'running copy' from the press bench, or to post updates directly onto news websites, or to 'tweet' from court to report the case on Twitter. These methods mean court reporting can now be almost 'live'.

ONLINE PUBLICATION INCREASES THE TASK

The internet's development has made the task of court reporters more complicated and onerous, leading one to complain: 'It's multi-skilling gone mad.' (*Press Gazette* 2012)

A reporter may be required to update a website by filing a polished article in the lunchtime break, then to update the site again at the end of that day's session and possibly to produce another, amalgamated narrative (unless there is a sub-editor to do this) to be printed overnight in the newspaper, or an audio or 'to-camera' piece outside the courthouse for broadcast or webcast. Throughout the hearing, he or she may also have to tweet or post as running copy on its website – for example, 30 times a day – each newsworthy piece of evidence, with his or her newsdesk monitoring whether rival organisations are breaking that news faster.

The new capability for 'live, text-based communications' places even more responsibility on reporters to be fair and accurate, and to obey any restrictions on what can be published. When a report is uploaded to a website, there may be no opportunity for a news editor or sub-editor to query or revise its content before the public can see it, and there will be no such opportunity if the reporter is tweeting. It must be right first time.

An example of what can go wrong occurred at the 2012 trial of Harry Redknapp, former manager of Tottenham Hotspur Football Club, in which he was acquitted of tax evasion. Sports journalist Jamie Jackson, working for the *Guardian*, tweeted a juror's name and information about legal argument taking place in the absence of the jury (*Media Lawyer* 2012b). Reporting jurors' names is potentially a contempt of court, and so is reporting, before a trial ends, what the judge and lawyers discuss in court when the jury is kept out of the courtroom – for example, to stop it hearing references to inadmissible evidence. The judge in Mr Redknapp's trial reacted by banning all tweeting from it.

Online publication means that reporting can gain an international audience. A journalist covering a court hearing in South Africa gained more than 40,000 Twitter 'followers' in five days, because of national and international interest in the case (Silverstreak 2013). The defendant was 'Blade Runner', the Olympic athlete and double amputee Oscar Pistorius, charged with murdering his girlfriend.

ANONYMITY FOR JURORS, JUVENILES AND SEXUAL OFFENCE VICTIMS

As noted above, media reports should not normally identify jurors. The general rule in the common law of contempt is that jurors should have anonymity, to minimise the possibility of a defendant or his or her supporters intimidating them to acquit, and the possibility of reprisals in the event of a guilty verdict. This law ensures that people are not deterred from serving on juries. In Northern Ireland, identifying a juror is banned by statute.

Statutory protection of juries also makes it illegal to attempt to interview any juror about how a verdict was reached, or to publish what a juror volunteers about this. In 2009, *The Times* was fined £15,000 and had to pay the Attorney General's prosecution costs of £27,426 because it published, after being contacted by a juror, a brief allusion to how the jury on which he served decided to convict a childminder of the manslaughter of a child. The juror was fined for what he told *The Times*.

Since 1933 it has been illegal in most circumstances for media reports to reveal the identities of juveniles (children aged under 18) concerned in youth court cases as victims of a crime, witnesses or defendants. In other types of court, magistrates or judges can use discretionary powers to grant a juvenile similar anonymity. But it does not apply to dead victims.

When such anonymity applies, it is illegal to publish any detail – not just the name – likely to identify the juvenile as being involved in the case. This includes any detail likely to betray his or her identity to any relatives, friends or acquaintances unaware of the involvement.

It is also illegal in most circumstances for the media to identify victims and alleged victims of sexual offences. In 2013 the *Luton Herald and Post* was fined £1,000 for publishing in a report of a trial details which, by their accumulation, identified such a victim. The report included her age and that she had come to the UK to study, named her home country, gave the approximate date and location of her arrival, named the institution where she was studying and referred to her living arrangements and professional aspirations (*Media Lawyer* 2013b). In the period 2011–13, the Press Complaints Commission issued 11 adjudications criticising newspaper or magazine editors for publishing detail that identified, or had potential to identify, sexual offence victims, including some children. This represents an increase in these adjudications, which is perhaps to some extent a reflection of how cuts in staffing levels in newsrooms mean there are fewer people to check copy or guide inexperienced reporters.

OTHER TYPES OF COURT

The legal and ethical principles of reporting from the criminal courts apply, in the main, to coverage of other types of court – for example, coroners' courts, the civil courts and family courts.

Coroners hold inquests into certain categories of deaths, including those caused by accidents or violence, and when the cause is not known. Coroners also hold inquests to decide if ancient objects found by the public should be classed as 'treasure', and so be offered to museums.

In civil cases, heard in the county courts or High Court, one party is suing another; for example, a former patient is suing a doctor after alleged medical negligence, claiming damages for suffering or injury allegedly caused. Again, allegations and evidence in these cases must be fairly and accurately reported. If the parties agree an out-of-court settlement – that is, to avoid more legal costs they agree a financial deal, so there is no need for a trial – it should not be reported as if the party sued accepts liability, unless this is true. Otherwise, there could be libel problems.

Family proceedings include intra-parental disputes after a divorce about where the children should reside, and cases involving intervention by social workers when a child is considered at risk of abuse in his or her home. The public are excluded from family cases involving children. Journalists who have a press card from the scheme operated by the UK Press Card Authority have a general right to attend. The presumption is that these 'accredited' journalists will know about the reporting restrictions which usually ban media reports of a family case from identifying any child involved, and therefore his or her family too, and ban the reporting of evidence unless the court permits this. But these journalists, too, can be excluded by these courts in circumstances specified by rules. These complex and controversial restrictions mean that cases in family courts are rarely reported. In 2013, Sir James Munby QC, president of the Family Division, made clear he wants to 'improve access to and reporting of' their cases, while retaining anonymity for families involved.

CONCERN FOR THE FUTURE OF COURT REPORTING

In recent years, cost-cutting reductions in the number of reporters employed by regional and local newspapers have undoubtedly led to fewer attending court cases. This has led police to consider how to publicise successful prosecutions, to help ensure the public has confidence in law enforcement. An initiative by the West Midlands police force involved its staff conducting a 'tweet-a-thon' one morning to report cases from Birmingham magistrates courts (BBC 2011). Data on the reduction of media coverage of courts remains scant. But a survey by the Press Association of senior clerks in magistrates courts found that 80 per cent of those who responded said that the number of cases reported had declined (Ponsford 2009), a finding broadly corroborated by other research (Holmes 2010). Editors, other experienced journalists and senior judges have also expressed concern that fewer cases are being covered, including in Crown Courts (Davies 2008b; Holmwood 2009; Lord Judge 2009; Rozenburg 2009; Holdthefrontpage 2010; Dacre 2011). This reduction diminishes journalists' ability to inform our society of the consequences of social division and policy failures.

Duncan Campbell (2013), a former crime correspondent for the *Guardian*, is among those who have warned that a valuable source of knowledge is being neglected: 'A morning in a magistrate's court will tell you more about the state of the nation in terms of education, class, family, employment, immigration, consumerism, honesty, addiction to drink and drugs, sexual politics, housing, health and alienation than a dozen think-tank reports.'

CHAPTER 13

Powerful information

Reporting national and local government

John Turner

Politics is about power, and information is power. Journalists are part of the information business and are crucial in a political process that involves the exercise of this potent force. People with power, whether they be cabinet ministers, senior civil servants or chief executives of local councils, have a vested interest, not only in protecting their own power, but also in obscuring the extent of their authority in the first place. The journalist occupies a pivotal position between those who make and implement important decisions and those who are often forced to comply with such decisions. Any democratic system depends on people being well informed and educated about politics by a media that gives a full and accurate account of news, encompassing a wide and varied range of political opinions.

The media in general have a large and growing significance in politics. However, the evidence regarding the nature and extent of this influence is unclear. The political impact of the media, and the press in particular, is difficult to assess, for various reasons.

- It is difficult to isolate the effect of the media from other influences such as family, education, work and economic circumstances.

- There is a complex of myriad mutually influencing factors which complicate the relationship between newspaper and reader. The political impact of a newspaper will depend less on what is being read than on who is doing the reading, and their level of knowledge and experience about politics in general.

- The media are fragmented, with television, radio and the national press having different effects in comparison with local coverage. A direct relationship between the media's influence on a political issue is therefore confused.

• Traditional media now have to live alongside multi-channel satellite, digital TV, cable, the internet and text messaging. New media offer wider and more diverse information and new ways of becoming politically involved.

• Similar messages are received and interpreted in different ways by different people, hence a claim that the media are being used for propaganda purposes cannot be verified because one cannot be sure of the intended effect.

Before turning to aspects of local and national politics, it is important to outline briefly three ways in which the impact of the media has been assessed.

Agenda-setting and primary definers

Here the media are accused less of telling people what to believe than of having a more pervasive influence on what people think about, and how they make judgements about, different issues. Agenda-setting involves a constant interaction between a newspaper and its readers. Newspapers also tend to take on board sources of information that control and establish initial definitions of particular issues. As such, a great deal of news coverage reflects the interpretations initially created by official sources.

Reinforcement and hegemony

Here the media are involved in not so much creating attitudes, but strengthening and reinforcing existing beliefs and prejudices. This can be linked to the notion of hegemony, whereby consent is sought for those ways of making sense of the world that fit with the perspective of those in power.

Independent effects

There is a growing view that the media have a more direct and independent effect on beliefs and behaviour. Again, evidence for such a view remains controversial. New media technologies have as much influence on attitudes and behaviour as the uses to which they are put.

Newton (1986) has pointed to a paradox in the media's impact on political awareness. Whereas political information is delivered faster to more people, nevertheless the mass tabloids contain only a little political content and what they report is personalised, trivialised, sensationalised and biased. Consequently, a large proportion of the public are provided with restricted news and knowledge of current affairs. This contradiction has been discussed by Seymour-Ure (1974) in his distinction of levels of readership between a mass public and an informed political public. An information gap has been created, with a small, well-educated public who use the media becoming better informed and a mass public who mainly read gossip columns and sports pages, and are therefore more readily influenced by biased news. The internet provides people with alternative sources of news and current affairs, often not mediated through large media organisations. It has accelerated the decline in newspaper circulation and allowed younger people to grow up without the habit of buying a newspaper.

Local papers do not work in a vacuum. They are as much a part of the political system and process as anyone, and journalists working for them have assumptions about the way in which the political system operates. There is far less of a division between local and national politics today. Local government increasingly has become simply an arm of central administration and, as in the case of education policy, it is difficult to disentangle separate national and local agendas. Equally, there is nothing inherently local about local newspapers. Much of what is considered to be national news is local in nature and source. Indeed, Britain's tradition of a dominant national press has imposed a kind of artificial parochialism on the local press, which has led to a number of criticisms about the rather narrow way in which local papers have covered local politics. The homogeneous and national nature of the British political system and political culture must not be underestimated in this respect. They have had an important effect on the way in which politics is reported by the local press.

THE BRITISH POLITICAL SYSTEM

Previous studies of the British political system have pointed to its strong civic culture, supported by a stable and cohesive system of politics (Almond and Verba 1963; Rose 1965). They pointed out the dominant values of moderation, toleration, respect for law and deference to authority. However, power in Britain is centralised and, unlike many other European democracies, it is concentrated in the cabinet in Parliament and Whitehall, supported by political conventions, the cohesiveness of political parties, Treasury control, ministerial responsibility and the Crown prerogative. This strong and cohesive model of British government has been accentuated by a period of prime ministerial dominance, without the safeguards of accountability which might be imposed by a bill of rights or constitution. Certain elements of the British political system can be highlighted.

A culture of deference

People in Britain have a remarkably deferential attitude towards the dominant political institutions (Kavanagh 1983). An appeal to tradition is used as a way of defending many of the institutions which have become a stable part of the political system. The monarchy, the House of Lords, the dominant role of the prime minister and pervasive secrecy are the ingredients of a political culture which has not been up-ended by revolution or war. Leigh (1989) has referred to the system as a huge mountain with abandoned monuments, with some still powerful and others forgotten. An example is the role of the royal prerogative in allowing ministers to make decisions without parliamentary debate or scrutiny. The powers of an authoritarian monarchy have been transferred to a modern executive, allowing ministers to declare war, make treaties and grant honours without parliamentary approval. A Ministry of Justice review of these powers took place in 2009, but little has changed.

Political participation

Such deference has made Britain a relatively law-abiding country. There is a general respect for authority and the law which complements a low level of political participation. Many social scientists were surprised that there were not greater social disturbances as a result of mass unemployment in the 1980s. However, the past 20 years have seen the rise of effective grassroots movements using protests, boycotts, internet campaigns and civil disobedience to further their causes. In the early 1990s, the anti-poll tax movement saw 4 million people in court for not paying their tax, and since then there have been protest campaigns against new roads, airports, animal exports, GM foods, fuel increases and, more recently, fracking. This seems to have been accompanied by a decline in voting at all elections. Since the 1990s turnout has fallen by 10 per cent. In 2001 only 59 per cent turned out to vote, 61 per cent in 2005 and 65 per cent in 2010, well below the level of participation of previous decades. Local election turnout has fallen to around 30 per cent, as low as 10 per cent in some mayoral votes. Today, only about 5 per cent of people are members of a political party, with only about 2 per cent being party activists (Hague and Harrop 2010).

Centralisation and concentration of power

In Britain's unitary system of government, decision-making power has been highly concentrated and centralised. Parliament, government, the administration, law courts, major companies and the BBC are all based in central London. Given the lack of a written constitution, save European law which Britain has had to sign up to as a member of the EU, Britain has failed to develop any notion of federal-style government. However, since 1997 Britain has a quasi-federal state, with a Scottish Parliament and Welsh Assembly and a system of directly elected mayors in London and other cities and boroughs.

Laissez-faire

The debt crisis and austerity measures imposed by the Coalition government since 2010 set off a debate about the extent of state involvement in the management of the economy. Some suggested the crisis had been caused by not enough regulation, others that regulation had become too tight. The Coalition's policies seem to suggest that by cutting state spending, the private sector will flourish. The *laissez-faire* assumptions about self-regulating and free competitive markets underpin George Osborne's financial strategy. It is the role of markets to distribute rewards, and the state should not redistribute resources towards a fairer society. The management of the structural deficit has become a euphemism for a return to *laissez-faire*.

Consensus and Coalition government

There has been a high level of agreement on the main areas of policy in British politics, including foreign policy in Afghanistan and Iraq; Northern Ireland; race relations and immigration; and the welfare state. The 2010 election was a landmark in that it failed to produce a parliamentary majority for one party for the first time since February 1974, and established the first long-lasting Coalition government. It also established a fixed parliamentary term of five years for the first time. The Conservative and Liberal Democrat parties agreed a programme of deficit reduction with support for George Osborne's spending cuts and increased taxation. The Liberal Democrats contradicted their firm election pledge not to triple university tuition fees as a price for staying in the coalition. They argue that without them, policies on NHS reform and the abolition of inheritance tax could not have been modified.

The major conflict between Coalition partners has been on electoral reform. The government held a referendum on the alternative vote (AV) electoral system to replace first-past-the-post in May 2011. The old system was supported by 68 per cent on a 42 per cent turnout, a crushing defeat for Liberal Democrat leader Nick Clegg. This was followed by defeats in local elections, and the Liberal Democrats lost many seats in the Welsh Assembly and Scottish parliamentary elections. In every case, it seems the Liberal Democrats were being punished for entering the coalition and reversing crucial policies. In retaliation for not supporting House of Lords reform, Clegg also refused to allow a reorganisation of parliamentary boundaries, which would have given the Conservatives many more seats at the next election.

Supranational politics

The 28-state European Union now has a fundamental influence on the politics of Britain. After joining the then European Community in 1973, Britain signed the Single European Act in 1986, establishing an integrated single market 'without frontiers'. In 1991, the Maastricht Treaty was signed, establishing a three-pillar structure including first, the old European Community which established the Euro single currency; second, a common foreign and security policy; and third, policing and immigration control. Britain has stayed outside the euro, and the euro crisis in Greece, Spain and Portugal has hardened attitudes against joining, even within the pro-European Liberal Democrats.

In 2004, the EU was enlarged by the accession of 10 countries, including some ex-communist states in Eastern Europe (such as Estonia, Hungary and Poland), and Cyprus and Malta, joined by Romania and Bulgaria in 2007 and Croatia in 2013. The 2009 Lisbon Treaty brought in a new European Constitution designed to reorganise all existing treaties. It has been a contentious issue for the Coalition government, made up of a more Eurosceptic Conservative Party and the pro-European Liberal Democrats. Prime Minister Cameron has promised a referendum on EU membership after the next general election in 2015. The Conservatives fear the rise of the United Kingdom Independence Party (UKIP), which could take anti-European voters away from the party. Some pollsters suggest UKIP may get most votes in the 2014 European parliamentary elections and may drain votes away from the Tories in the general election of 2015.

Quango state

In recent years, there has been a tendency to distance areas of administration from direct political control and public accountability by placing it in the hands of quasi-government organisations (quangos) which operate in a no-man's-land between central and local government. Quangos include public, private and voluntary organisations, or combinations of each. In Britain, examples include the Forestry Commission, British Council and BBC, Higher Education Funding Council and the Consumer Futures to be merged with the Citizen's Advice Bureau in 2014. A key issue for these bodies is the degree to which they are accountable to the public or to the political process of election. A further problem with the growth in quangos has been the role of patronage, as most posts involve some financial benefit. In 2010 quangos were responsible for about £50 billion of expenditure, and the new Coalition government set up a review under Frances Maude which recommended reducing their number from 901 to 648, with the abolition of bodies such as the Audit Commission, the UK Film Council and several health authorities and primary care trusts.

Privatisation

The process of privatisation has seen public utilities which were formerly nationalised industries sold off to the private sector. These private companies, such as British Telecom, British Gas and the electricity and water companies, are now huge monopolies which have been able to make very large profits for their senior managers and shareholders. In a number of cases, the problem of delivering public services in an efficient and cost-effective way by the private sector has raised issues of accountability. Privatised water companies have been criticised for failing to deliver services, and British Gas executives for paying themselves large salary increases. Regulatory bodies such as OFWAT and OFGAS have been powerless to interfere. New Labour continued to extol the virtues of the private sector over the public sector, going ahead with the privatisation of air traffic control, and rejecting completely any suggestion of the renationalisation of the railways following the train crashes at Ladbroke Grove (1999), Hatfield (2000) and Potters Bar (2002). Private sector funding also came from private finance initiatives (PFI) in the building of hospitals, roads, schools and prisons. Such investment is paid for by the public over a 25-year period, and is useful for governments because it provides new finance without increasing public borrowing. Under the Coalition government, the latest privatisation has been the Royal Mail. In 2013, it was sold at a share price of 330 pence, but in subsequent weeks this price rose to 560 pence, suggesting the government had undervalued the company by some £2 billion.

Secrecy

Linked to this centralisation of power is the secrecy that pervades British politics. Recent public commitments to more open government belatedly recognise how less than open governments have been in the past. Britain's culture of secrecy is buttressed by harsh libel laws, weak rights of access to official information, the Official Secrets Act and the D-Notice system. Since 11 September 2001, British and other western governments have taken on additional powers to counter terrorism. After the terrorist attacks in London in 2005 and Glasgow in 2007, there has been a sharp focus on the balance between national and internal security and civil liberties and freedoms. The erroneous use of intelligence to justify war in Iraq in 2003 saw the security services being used by government as an arm of its public relations and news management. There are concerns that the lack of open government and a written constitution in Britain have strengthened restrictions on civil liberties, as in the use of detention without trial, control orders, phone tapping, security cameras and identity cards.

In 2013 the Snowden leaks from the US National Security Agency indicated that Britain's GCHQ and other European spying agencies were colluding to intercept phone and internet communications across the world. Direct taps were being made into optic cables with the tacit agreement of telecommunication companies. Different countries were being used so agencies could bypass their own laws on civil liberties. The Freedom of Information Act became law in 2005, but gives fewer rights to official information than those enjoyed by people in the USA, Australia, Canada, New Zealand or the Irish Republic. It was, however, directly responsible for the revelations that led to the parliamentary expenses scandal in 2009 (see Chapters 10 and 11; also see www.cfoi.org.uk).

However, in 2010 Tony Blair declared that freedom of information had been a mistake and governments had disclosed too much. Anti-terrorism legislation puts journalists at risk and in danger of arrest when covering the activities of campaigning groups such as pro-hunt activists, road protesters, animal liberationist or environmentalist groups. Terrorism laws and surveillance imposed to fight organised crime have been used to arrest and detain protesters (see www.gchq.gov.uk). The Regulation of Investigatory Powers Act 2000 also threatens journalists' sources and confidential information, with the state able to intercept email and telephone calls across private networks 'in the interests of the economic well-being of the United Kingdom'. For local government, the new executive cabinet system of decision making has reduced public scrutiny of local government decisions over issues such as education, social services and planning. Decisions are increasingly made in party groups, behind closed doors and not even in council buildings. Most decisions are made within the executive, and scrutiny committees are presented with policies already made.

Party politics

In the past, Britain has been described as a two-party system, and since 1945 in nearly every general election either the Conservative or Labour Party held a majority of seats in parliament. The whole narrative of political reporting has assumed a two-party system of government and opposition, of cabinet and shadow cabinet, two sides of a parliamentary chamber divided by two sword lengths. However, the dominance of the two parties has been as much about the nature of the first-past-the-post electoral system, which has discriminated against smaller parties and those with more diffused support across the country. Labour and Conservative parties have relied on their safe seats with built-in majorities in urban and rural areas, respectively. However, as Figure 13.1 indicates, support for the two parties has been in decline, their share of the vote at elections sliding from about 90 per cent in the 1950s to 60–70 per cent today.

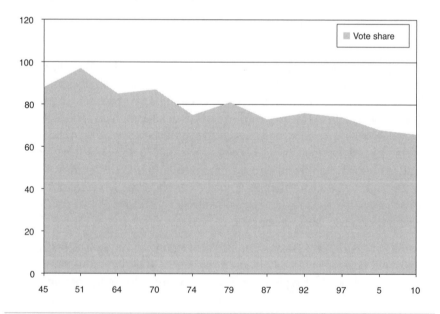

FIGURE 13.1
Decline in support for two main parties (General Elections 1951–2010)

LOCAL GOVERNMENT

Local government has two principal roles in the British political system. First, there is a political role as democratically elected bodies representing local people and giving legitimacy to local political demands and interests. Second, there is an administrative role in implementing policy, including the delivery of services, which have often already been determined by central government. Over the past 30 years there has been a slow, but persistent battering of local government by central government, which has had an opportunistic habit of relegating the role of local government to an administrative arm, delivering policies decided and funded from the centre. If policies fail or are unpopular, then usually it has been local government that has been blamed. Over the years, governments of all parties had a vested interest in undermining the legitimacy of local government to preserve its power and control over policy. Potential conflict between central and local government persists, but it is less ideological and confrontational than in the 1980s, when local Labour-run councils saw themselves as a last bastion against the policies of Thatcherism. The relationship between central and local government is characterised by the following.

- *Partisanship and polarisation*: local government became increasingly politicised in the 1980s and much subsequent legislation has been motivated by a need to curb local government attempts to challenge successive governments.

- *Centralisation and privatisation*: two clear responses have involved the transfer of many functions away from local government. It has lost control of key services and decisions to central government, other public agencies, the voluntary sector and private companies. Private firms now delivering services are not necessarily local, but are subsidiaries of national or multinational organisations, with no direct responsibility to local people.

- *Economic cuts*: in the 1980s a central plank of central government financial policy was to cut local government spending and its ability to raise taxes (rates, poll tax and council tax). In 2013 austerity measures, following the debt crisis, have profoundly affected local government finances and the services they can provide.

- *Electoral turnout*: turnout at local elections has continued to decline over the past decade, falling to about 36 per cent. Poor turnout has often reflected the lack of resources and publicity put into local campaigns by the national parties. It has been used as another argument to interfere in local government to reinvigorate it and make it more accessible to ordinary people.

- *Accountability and transparency of decision-making*: a persistent criticism of local authorities has been that they make decisions behind closed doors and through procedures in committees that are not readily understood by local people. Central government has intervened several times to change the internal organisation of authorities, and continues to do so.

Powers removed from local government

Successive governments have adopted a 'small carrot' and 'large stick' policy, determined to take away services from councils that fall short of agreed standards. Over their years in power, New Labour under Blair and Brown made a sharp distinction between 'how services are funded and how they are delivered'. This included taking 'failing' schools away from local authorities and putting them into the hands of the private and voluntary sectors, for example, the government sending in so-called 'hit squads' into Hackney. The carrot took the form of beacon councils, identified as centres of excellence, and consequently given extra discretionary powers over capital investment and the way services were managed. Sheffield City Council received beacon status for delivering cleaner air, and Bristol City Council for tackling antisocial behaviour (Wilson and Game 2006).

In 2000, New Labour also introduced the Private Finance Initiative (PFI) which allowed private firms to bid to build and run capital projects like roads and schools. Between 1997 and 2004, more than 600 PFI deals were organised. Labour went further in wanting the private sector to become involved in the delivery of services. Spending was increased but it was more closely linked to performance targets and league tables. The resulting schools were given freedom from local authority control. Labour also brought in Academy Schools, with autonomy from local education authorities, and after 2010 the Coalition government introduced 'free schools', directly funded by central government and open to personal and private funding. Free schools were allowed to set their own pay, employ teachers without qualifications, determine their own admissions policy and set their own length of terms and the school day. Free schools operate independently of local authorities and outside the community of schools around them.

Enabling councils: towards the outsourcing of services

As enabling authorities, local councils have to negotiate and collaborate with a network of different organisations at multi-levels of decision-making. This may involve lobbying in Brussels for European Union (EU) money, like the Regional Fund and Social Fund. Councils will also have to comply with EU directives. In Scotland, Wales and Northern Ireland, councils will have to negotiate with their own national parliament and assembly. The local network of stakeholders may involve public bodies such as the National Health Service (NHS), or police authorities, quangos, appointed local agencies, voluntary groups, community groups and other councils such as parish, neighbourhood and community councils, as well as the private sector. The new arrangements have been criticised for undermining the public service ethos and creating a confusing duplication of services.

This enabling role has been taken a step further in recent years by Barnet Council which, with its strategy of 'One Barnet' in 2010, pioneered the idea of the 'easy council' modelled on the no-frills budget airline Easy Jet. Barnet proposed outsourcing £600 million of services over a 10-year period to private sector companies. These included building control, planning, highways, transport, cemeteries and crematoria, trading standards, licensing and environmental health. It resulted in the handing over of 70 per cent of council services and a loss of 200 staff.

In 2010, Suffolk County Council took a step further by proposing to outsource most services and create a 'virtual council' or, as some councillors called it, 'council lite'. Suffolk would now simply commission services from the private sector and cut its budget by 30 per cent, leaving the council with just a few hundred staff. Services such as libraries, youth clubs, highways, individual living centres, careers advice, children's centres, registrars, parks and record offices would be outsourced. Interestingly, in Barnet and Suffolk there has been a public backlash, with splits in the Conservative ruling groups that have put these policies on hold.

Local government finance

New Labour governments accepted the Conservatives' council tax, which had replaced the poll tax that created riots and led to the downfall of the Thatcher government. The tax amounts to about 20 per cent of local government revenue, most funding coming from central government grants and centrally collected and distributed business rate. It brings in about £30 billion, but the current Coalition government has frozen increases in council tax for many authorities. The government is also implementing the idea that if councils want to raise council tax by more than 2 per cent, then local people have the right to keep tax bills down by holding a local referendum vote.

Alternatives have been put forward, such as a local income tax (supported by the Liberal Democrats). However, critics argue this would increase local taxation and provide more autonomy for local councils. Some argue local government should be completely funded by central government although this would take away its fiscal independence completely. Others argue that large expenditures on education and social services should be taken out of local government control and funded directly by central government. In 2013, local government spent about £178 billion (24 per cent of total public spending), and about 80 per cent of this money came through grants from central government. Austerity measures following the debt crisis have profoundly affected local government finances. Since 2011 local government spending has been cut by 28 per cent and there will be further cuts of 10 per cent in the next two years. This has particularly hit non-statutory services (services that councils do not have to provide by law) such as road maintenance and cultural activities, and inevitably it will mean the greater involvement of voluntary and private sectors.

New ethical procedures

Labour announced a new 'ethical framework' for English councils in March 1999 in the wake of a much-publicised fraud in Doncaster Council, where councillors had been imprisoned for expenses fraud and planning corruption, so highlighting the financial rewards allocated to committee chairpersons. In response to the Nolan report on local government standards of conduct, a new independent standards board was set up to investigate all allegations that a council's code of conduct may have been breached. Each council was required to keep a register of members' interests and to have a standards committee to oversee it. Regional standards boards and an appeals system to the national standards board were set up.

The 2011 Localism Act abolished previous ethical frameworks and introduced a new code of conduct. It covers general standards of behaviour and declaration of interests. Councillors with a financial interest in a council matter must declare an interest and withdraw from the meeting considering the matter. In an era when there is much more overlap between public bodies and the private sector, such standards are even more important.

Reinvigorating local democracy

Recent local elections have seen turnouts of about 36 per cent on average. Only 34 per cent voted in the referendum about changing the shape of London government, and in referendums in other parts of the country turnout was as low as 11 per cent (Southwark) and 16 per cent (Bedford), with highest turnout at about 30 per cent (Cheltenham). The government also wants to encourage experiments in new forms of voting to increase turnout, including the introduction of electronic voting, the use of the internet, mobile polling stations, entire elections elected by postal ballot and polling stations located in supermarkets and shopping centres. The government is also looking at rolling registration to include people who have recently moved into a new local authority area. In 2004, there were experiments using all postal votes in local and European parliamentary elections. There was a slight increase in voting in these pilot areas. However, there were a number of allegations of fraud. The Electoral Commission now opposes all-postal voting for the UK (www.electoralcommission.org.uk). In 2013, Labour became committed to reducing the voting age to 16, following the Scottish Parliament's decision to allow 16-year-olds to vote in the 2014 vote on Scottish independence. In the future, the government wants to consider the introduction of proportional representation across all local elections.

Devolution in Scotland, Wales and Northern Ireland

By far the most important and potentially most radical changes in sub-national government have been the devolution of powers to a Scottish Parliament and a

Welsh Assembly, which now operate alongside a unitary structure of local authorities (see Figure 13.3). In the second devolution elections in May 2003, a four-party system emerged with no party in control. However, in 2007 the Scottish National Party (SNP) became the largest party and in 2011 it achieved an overall majority with 69 Members of the Scottish Parliament (MSPs). The Scottish Parliament holds devolved powers over economic development, agriculture, education, the environment, health, housing, local government and planning, social work and transport. It has the right to change income tax by up to 3 per cent. A contentious issue between governments in Scotland and Westminster remains the 'West Lothian Question'. Basically, Scottish MPs in the Westminster Parliament can vote on domestic legislation that applies to England, Wales and Northern Island, whilst MPs are unable to vote on the domestic legislation of the Scottish Parliament.

After its victory in the 2011 elections, the SNP indicated that it would hold a referendum on Scottish independence in September 2014 on the question 'Should Scotland be an independent country?' The SNP is actively campaigning for a 'Yes' vote, although representatives from Labour, Conservatives and Liberal Democrats have come together in the 'Better Together' campaign calling for a 'No' vote. Several issues remain controversial, including whether Scotland would retain the monarchy, pound currency and nuclear weapons. There are also arguments about the proceeds from North Sea oil, and the level of national debt Scotland would inherit if independence came about. The Scottish Parliament has reduced the voting age from 18 to 16, and the referendum will be the first time when younger people will have the chance to vote (Runciman 2010). Parliamentary seats gained in the four elections since 1999 are shown in Table 13.1.

In the 2011 vote for the Welsh Assembly, Labour gained 30 seats, Conservatives 14, Plaid Cymru 11 and Liberal Democrats 5. Elected members are termed Assembly Members (AMs). The Welsh Assembly can implement laws that affect

TABLE 13.1 Scottish Parliamentary Elections 1999–2011

Party	1999	2003	2007	2011
SNP	35	27	47	69
Labour	56	50	46	37
Conservative	18	18	17	15
Liberal Democrat	17	17	16	5
Green	1	7	2	2
Independent	1	4	1	1
Scottish Socialist	1	6	0	0
Turnout (%)	59	49	52	50

economic development, agriculture, schools and colleges, the environment, food and health, housing, local government, sports and leisure, and some transport policy. Unlike Scotland, the Assembly cannot make laws and has no tax-raising powers. Final authority over British policy affecting Wales lies with Westminster, although the Secretary of State for Wales has a duty to consult with the Assembly and invite representations concerning Welsh matters. Scotland and Wales now have first ministers supported by appointed executives (cabinets), including ministers of finance, agriculture, health and so on. These executives have responsibility for day-to-day policy related to devolved matters.

Following the April 1998 Good Friday Agreement in Northern Ireland, direct rule from Westminster was replaced by a new Northern Ireland Assembly and a ten-member power-sharing executive made up of all political parties nominated by the Assembly. A new British–Irish agreement has also established a cross-border council composed of ministers from the Irish Republic and the Northern Ireland Assembly. At the demand of the Unionists, a British–Irish Council was established consisting of representatives of the British and Irish governments, the devolved institutions in Northern Ireland, Scotland and Wales, and Jersey, Guernsey and the Isle of Man. Areas for cooperation include the environment, tourism, transport and organised crime.

New forms of political structure

In the 1980s the polarisation and politicisation of relationships between central and local government led to the abolition of many key authorities that were Labour-controlled and seen as a direct threat to the Thatcher government's policies. The year 1985 saw the abolition of the Greater London Council and the six metropolitan authorities in Tyne and Wear, South Yorkshire, West Yorkshire, Merseyside, Greater Manchester and the West Midlands. The Blair government continued to reorganise local government. The emphasis was on larger unitary authorities, and in 2009 ten new single authorities were established. Blair also wanted to change how authorities made decisions and policies. In 1998 he wrote a paper calling for stronger leader-ship and a clearer separation between executive and non-executive roles in local government (Blair 1998).

Highly influenced by American municipal government, the 2000 Local Government Act made local authorities change their traditional committee-based system of decision-making to an executive model. Three models were open to councils to adopt:

- a directly elected mayor
- a council leader and cabinet system
- a mayor and council manager (dropped as an option in 2007).

Blair hoped that the mayoral system would attract personalities from outside con-ventional politics, such as actors, leading business people and media personalities.

There were criticisms that the mayoral system would attract mavericks and populist personalities. In Middlesbrough, a former senior police officer, Ray Mallon, was elected mayor on a populist zero-tolerance law-and-order policy. In Hartlepool in 2002, 'H'Angus the Monkey' (Stuart Drummond dressed in a monkey suit) was elected as independent mayor and served three terms before local people voted in a referendum to abolish the post. In both cases, the traditional party of power in local government was voted out. However, turnout in referendums for a change in the system has been low, around 29 per cent, and in 2012 referendums in major English cities saw the rejection of the mayoral system everywhere except Bristol and Liverpool.

In 2013, there were 16 authorities with directly elected mayors, including Lewisham, Tower Hamlets, Newham and Hackney borough councils in London; city councils in Liverpool and Bristol; borough councils in Watford and Middlesbrough and North Tyneside council. Most councils have opted for a council leader and cabinet executive system.

London government

The first experiment with this new form of local government was the establishment of the Greater London Authority (GLA) with a 25-member assembly and a directly elected London mayor. It was approved by 72 per cent (34 per cent turnout) of Londoners in a referendum in 1998. The GLA at City Hall near Tower Bridge has strategic (but no operational) responsibility for transport, police, fire and emergency planning, development and planning.

Blair's New Labour had wanted to distance itself from the 'old Labour' legacy of Ken Livingstone at the then Greater London Council (GLC), and in the first elections tried to block him as a candidate. Instead, he ran as an independent against the official Labour candidate and defeated Steve Norris (Conservative) and Labour's Frank Dobson, who was eliminated in third place. Livingstone won again as the Labour candidate in 2004, but was defeated by the Conservative Boris Johnson in 2008 and 2012. The GLA election results are shown in Tables 13.2 and 13.3.

The shape of local government

Today, because there are so many variations in the shape of local government, local journalists cannot assume anything about the way services are organised and delivered to their local communities. Does the council have a directly elected mayor or party leader and cabinet system? Is the authority unitary or two-tier? In short, you have to get to know your own local authority area, remembering that many authorities often combine delivery of services to a much wider area. A reporter needs to research their local area, get to know councillors and understand the priorities and needs of their local community.

TABLE 13.2 London Mayor Elections 2000–12

Year	Party	Percentage of vote
2000	Livingstone (Independent)	58
	Norris (Conservative)	42
2004	Livingstone (Labour)	55
	Norris (Conservative)	45
2008	Johnson (Conservative)	53
	Livingstone (Labour)	47
2012	Johnson	52
	Livingstone (Labour)	48

TABLE 13.3 Elections to London Assembly 2000–12

Party	2000	2004	2008	2012
Labour	9	7	9	12
Conservative	9	9	10	9
Liberal Democrat	4	5	3	2
Green	3	2	2	2
UKIP	0	2	0	0

As shown in Figures 13.2 and 13.3, local government operates under a one-tier, unitary authority or a two-tier system of county and district councils. In Scotland there is a devolved Parliament and a single tier of unitary authorities. Wales has a devolved Assembly and unitary authorities. Northern Ireland has an elected Assembly and borough, city and district councils.

Local government services

The main functions of the different tiers of local government are shown in Table 13.4. In general, the most important and expensive services are run by upper-tier and unitary authorities, although this is not true for London. Here, the 32 London boroughs still have effective control over service delivery.

Services are also provided by local agencies such as housing associations and trading and enterprise boards. Police authorities have become increasingly autonomous, often involving joint boards where single police forces provide services for several local authority areas. For example, Thames Valley Police covers Berkshire, Buckinghamshire and Oxfordshire local authority areas, and also has close ties

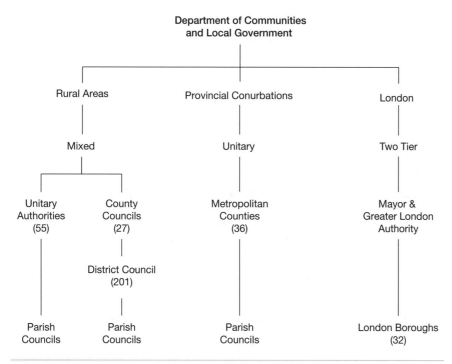

FIGURE 13.2
Structure of local government in England

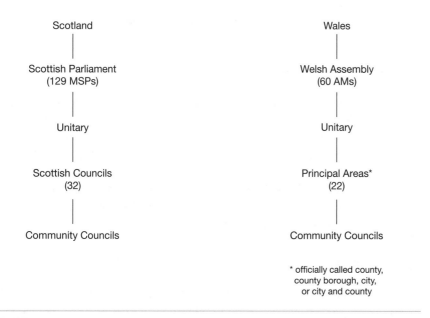

FIGURE 13.3
Structure of local government in Scotland and Wales

TABLE 13.4 Distribution of Local Government Services

Location	Upper-tier authority	Lower-tier authority	Parish or community council
Shire counties	Education (most budgets now delegated to schools); social services; waste management; transport; libraries; strategic planning; consumer protection; police; fire	Housing; waste collection; local planning; licensing; cemeteries and crematoria; council tax collection	Public toilets; parks; ponds; war memorials; local halls; community centres; allotments
Unitary authorities	Education; social services; housing; transport, planning; waste management and collection; libraries; consumer protection; licensing; cemeteries and crematoria; police; fire; council tax collection		Public toilets; parks; ponds; war memorials; local halls; community centres; allotments
Metropolitan counties	Education; social services; housing; transport; planning; waste management and collection; libraries; consumer protection; licensing; cemeteries and crematoria; police; fire; council tax collection		Public toilets; parks; ponds; war memorials; local halls; community centres; allotments
London	Strategic planning; regional development; transport; police; fire	Education; social services; housing; local planning; waste management and collection; transport; libraries; consumer protection; licensing; cemeteries and crematoria; council tax collection	Public toilets; parks; ponds; war memorials; local halls; community centres; allotments

with Hampshire County Council. It provides policing for 180,000 people and has 18 different local authorities in its area. All these are usually coordinated by joint committees representing each local authority in the region. In 2012, the Coalition government abolished Police Authorities and brought in directly elected Police and Crime Commissioners with the objective of cutting crime, making the police more transparently accountable and improving community responsiveness. Some 41 were elected in England and Wales, but turnout was very low, at between 10 and 20 per cent, questioning whether commissioners had a real mandate.

Councillors

There are about 22,000 councillors in 410 local authorities in the UK, and in 2008 a councillor's average age had risen to 59 years. Councillors under the age of 45 had fallen to just 13 per cent. Figures also showed that 32 per cent were women, 13 per cent people with disabilities and 4 per cent from the ethnic minorities.

Women are also less represented in the higher echelons of local authority positions. In 2008, just 12 per cent of council leaders were women and 13 per cent elected mayors. Evidence from a census of councillors in 2010 indicated that about 32 per cent said they would not stand again after one term in office, this figure rising to 51 per cent in London, with a larger proportion of women dropping out. The picture is one where younger councillors from more diverse backgrounds are standing down, with older, traditional councillors staying on and getting older. Most councillors stand down because they cannot meet the demands of two jobs and have a family life at the same time. On average, they work about 25 hours a week, with an average payment of £6,000 or (£10,000 in London).

A district, borough or city councillor represents a ward, and a county councillor a county district. Electoral wards may have more than one councillor. Reporters need to ground local political stories in terms of human interest, so getting a quote from a local councillor or cabinet member about a school closure or new day centre is crucial. Sometimes local councillors will have opposing views from those of their party. For example, it was reported that local Liberal Democrats opposed the Coalition's 2011 Localism Act making it easier for councils to approve the building of house extensions. Elections take place every four years, although in some urban county districts there are elections in three years out of four, when a third of councillors are elected each time.

The council system

Figure 13.4 is a simplified diagramme showing a top-tier authority with a leader and cabinet or directly elected mayor and advisory committee system. The full council of all councillors elects the council leader, deputy leader and councillors given responsibility for particular policy portfolios. The cabinet has a more specialist role in formulating and promoting council policies.

Party group meeting

Most councillors see their role as representing the party they stood for at the local election, and Widdicombe (1986) confirmed this, giving evidence that the party group was the most dominant factor in local government. In Labour-controlled councils, 99 per cent of groups voted together, and 92 per cent in Conservative councils; 87 per cent of councillors in Labour councils and 61 per cent in Conservative councils said their main task was to implement their party manifesto. Party group meetings are outside the formal local government system and are often held in local party headquarters rather than council buildings. It is important for a journalist to get to know leading local party politicians in their area and to build up contacts that may give them some indication of future council policy.

Executive

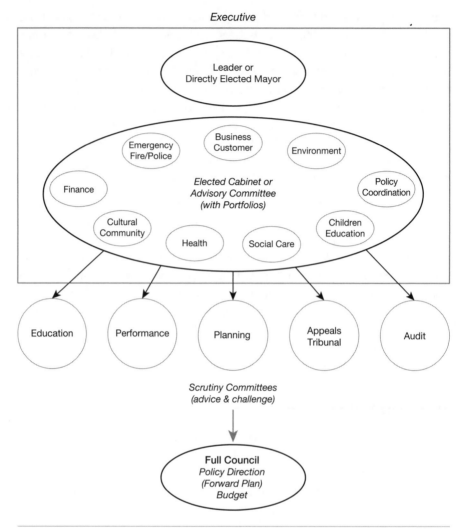

FIGURE 13.4
Cabinet system of local government

The executive

The executive is made up of the leader and nine portfolio holders who cover key policy areas including social care, education, environmental and community services. There are also portfolio holders for finance, public health (coordinating policy with the local health service) and policy coordination. One member of the cabinet will be appointed deputy leader. The leader usually takes responsibility for overall council strategy, communications and external partnerships and liaison with lower-tier authorities. The leader and cabinet, acting as the council executive, create a policy framework for the implementation of future policies.

Scrutiny committees

The executive is monitored by scrutiny committees which are also elected by the full council and are given delegated powers. Non-cabinet councillors as well as cabinet members sit on these committees. They have the task of advising and challenging the policy decisions made by the executive. A typical upper-tier authority might have scrutiny committees covering education, planning and performance, along with appeals and audit.

Full council meetings

The full council meets on average six times a year and is mainly responsible for deciding the budget and policy framework. It is usually the least interesting meeting to attend because most policies have already been decided by the executive and approved by scrutiny committees. It is these bodies that were given delegated powers to make decisions for the full council. The public can attend these meetings and ask questions, and can also submit petitions. Journalists can attend most meetings, and each council publishes a 'forward work plan' showing when meetings will take place. Meeting papers are usually published a week in advance, and minutes of meetings are published summarising the decisions that were taken. The meeting is usually taken up with the approval of policy positions and reports. Minutes of other meetings are received and approved.

Officers

Officers are officially the servants of the council and, like civil servants in Westminster, try to resist attempts to politicise their role. The streamlining of local government using a leader and cabinet system means lines of authority are clearer. The work of officers is circumscribed by legal constraints and they are greatly influenced by their professional training. Many still think of themselves foremost as engineers, architects, planners, social administrators or accountants. A journalist usually has to go through the public relations or press department of the council, which has its own agenda, and the journalist must be careful to clarify the difference between publicity and news.

Local councillors and their press officers have been identified as primary definers of the news agenda, controlling the flow of information and defining situations and issues. Local news reporting is particularly dependent on local sources and the council's new management. Local journalists therefore often reproduce the interpretations, or spin, put on stories by these primary definers. Local councils, like other organisations, attempt to protect their image and promote particular ideologies consistent with their political composition. In general, local reporting has been criticised as too descriptive and non-analytical; too dependent on council sources; and having editorials that tend to be consensual and non-critical and approaches to stories that are too conservative and conformist (see Cox and Morgan 1973; Curran 1987).

Press officers have found it increasingly difficult to be an intermediary between committed politicians and a more hostile national press, and this has changed their role significantly. They are much more interested in negotiating a compromise between both sides. The press office is likely to direct the reporter to the head of a service department, and it will have a corporate view as laid down by the policy framework. The continuous adverse reporting about issues related to social care, education and the environment makes officers more sensitive about what they can say in public.

NATIONAL POLITICS

At the national level, the main local contact is the constituency MP. There may be three or four in the local area. It is even better if a local MP is also a government minister or an outspoken critic on the backbenches. Speeches, general interviews, votes in the Commons, local party contacts and other public duties can provide material for stories. Background on an MP's personal and business life provides information for the local reporter.

A local paper will obtain a report of their local MP's speeches in the House from a stringer or news agency. Many regional and local papers have correspondents based at Westminster, some of whom are members of the lobby. The local newsroom will use Hansard Parliamentary Reports, and local MPs will be more than forthcoming in sending journalists copies of speeches. This may also include speeches at party conferences in October, when a local paper may wish to send a reporter or will again use a stringer.

Labour Party

The Labour Party has a federal structure controlled by a National Executive Committee (NEC), which is elected by the party conference. The NEC is made up of representatives from the trade unions, constituency parties, socialist groups, co-ops and a women's section. The leadership has moved power in the party away from the constituency parties and activists, and has given ordinary members voting rights, one member one vote (OMOV) in the election of the party leader, replacing the old block-vote system which gave votes to the trade unions, MPs and constituency parties. The party conference is no longer a policy-making body, more a venue for keynote addresses from the leadership. Since 2008, conference can no longer submit motions for policy debate. The Blair leadership also distanced the party from the trade unions, although most of its income still derives from the trade union political levy. Labour has received about £60 million in donations since the election. About half comes from trade unions, the most, about £12 million since 2010 (20 per cent), from Unite. In 2013, Ed Miliband, the new leader of the Labour Party, suggested abolishing trade union affiliation fees and moving to membership fees only. In the same year, Labour had about 180,000 members (Rawnsley 2010).

Conservative Party

The Conservative Party has a more top-down structure, with considerable power residing with the leadership. The party leader chooses the party chairman, who runs Central Office, the party's organisation. Central Office is like the personal machine of the leader, raising funds, organising campaigns, selecting candidates and carrying out policy research. At the regional level there are twice-a-year meetings of the Conservative Union, which has delegates from the constituency associations and which elects an executive committee. At the local level there are associations made up of ward organisations, which appoint a committee. The Conservatives have around 170,000 members and have had funding of £45 million since 2010; £28 million is from individual donors, mainly from business owners in the financial sector.

The party conference is always a stage-managed affair. Speeches by the leadership tend to be orchestrated, and representatives are mainly out to display their loyalty. It is not a policy-making body, although it is a good barometer of party feeling. In 1998, William Hague, then Tory leader, changed the method for electing the party's leader. After his general election defeat in 2001, this new method was used, involving the party's rank-and-file for the first time. After the Tories' third election defeat in a row in 2005, and the resignation of a third opposition leader who had failed to improve the party's electoral prospects, the party accepted the need for a new approach that would attract more than just their core vote. In 2005 David Cameron defeated David Davis for the leadership and proposed modernisation of the party, calling it 'compassionate Conservatism'. He has increased the number of women and ethnic minority candidates, and the expenses scandal allowed him to remove some of the older members of the parliamentary party. Cameron talked of a 'big society' rather than big government, relying more on voluntary work and charity than on state intervention to solve social problems (Bale 2010). In 2010 he won the election but could not achieve a majority and was forced into a Coalition government with the Liberal Democrats.

Liberal Democrats

The Liberal Democrats also have a federal structure, with different organisations in England, Scotland and Wales. There are 12 regional parties who appoint representatives to the regional council. In 2012 they had about 42,000 members, a loss of 30,000 in the past ten years. They received funding of about £1 million, mainly from individual donations. The conference is the most powerful body, electing a coordination committee to oversee the day-to-day running of the party. At the constituency level there is the local party. The party leader is elected by the party membership on the basis of one person one vote.

United Kingdom Independence Party (UKIP)

Founded in 1993, UKIP is a Eurosceptic, right-wing party that campaigns mainly on the issues of EU membership and immigration into the country. In 2013 it had about 30,000 members. It put up 572 candidates at the 2010 general election and won just 3.1 per cent of the vote. However, the party does have nine MEPs, and in 2013 took 23 per cent of the vote in county council elections, gaining 147 councillors, with particular successes in Kent, Essex and Lincolnshire. In September 2013, polls indicated it was polling support at around 20 per cent – enough to take away votes from the Conservatives at the 2015 general election.

Scottish National Party (SNP)

The Scottish National Party was founded in 1934 and gained ground at the Hamilton by-election in 1967, boosting its membership and party organisation. In the 1980s many in Scotland were alienated by Thatcher's policies and there was resentment that the poll tax was first tested north of the border. Real change came in 1999 with devolution and the Scottish Parliament. In 2007, the SNP won most seats in the Parliament and formed a minority government under leader Alex Salmond (Runciman 2010). In 2011 the SNP achieved a landslide victory, taking 69 of the 129 seats on 45 per cent of the vote. It holds six of the 59 Scottish seats at Westminster and is the largest party in local government in Scotland, holding 12 out of 32 authorities. In 2014 there will be a referendum in Scotland on independence, with the SNP actively campaigning for a 'Yes' vote.

Welsh Nationalist Party (Plaid Cymru)

Founded in 1925, the Welsh Nationalist Party made a breakthrough at Carmarthen in 1966 and strongly contests seats against Labour in the valleys, West Rhondda and Caerphilly. Again, the party was given a boost by devolution and the setting up of the National Assembly of Wales, where it holds 11 of the 60 seats. It has three MPs at Westminster and one MEP, and holds about 16 per cent of council seats. It is currently led by Leanne Wood.

Ulster Unionist Party

The Ulster Unionist Party dominated Ulster politics from 1922, when Northern Ireland was established, until 1972. With the 'Troubles', unionism was fractured in the 1970s when direct rule was imposed from Westminster in the wake of increasing sectarian violence. Since 1999 it has lost ground to the Democratic Unionists and formed an alliance with the Conservatives in 2009, forming the Ulster Conservative and Unionists – New Force (UCUNF).

Democratic Unionist Party (DUP)

Founded by Iain Paisley in 1971, this is the largest party in Northern Ireland, holding 38 of the 80 Assembly seats. Its leader, Peter Robinson, is First Minister of Northern Ireland. The DUP also has eight MPs at Westminster and one MEP, and holds about 30 per cent of local council seats.

Social Democratic and Labour Party (SDLP)

The Social Democratic and Labour Party replaced the old Nationalist Party in 1971 and has been prepared to negotiate within the existing political framework, despite its ultimate goal of a united Ireland.

Sinn Fein

Founded in 1905, Sinn Fein is often referred to as the political wing of the illegal Provisional Irish Republican Army (IRA), which has been engaged in an armed struggle against the British presence in Ireland since the 1960s. Sinn Fein received semi-illegal status when Thatcher imposed a ban on Sinn Fein politicians talking directly to radio and television. This ban was lifted when the Major government sought to involve Sinn Fein in all-party talks on the future of Northern Ireland. In April 1998, the Belfast Agreement (Good Friday Agreement) was reached between the British and Irish governments and interested parties in Northern Ireland. A new devolved Northern Ireland Assembly was established, Sinn Fein now has 29 of its 80 seats, and Martin McGuinness is deputy first minister.

Green Party

Founded in 1973, the Green Party was called the Ecology Party in 1975. It became the Green Party in 1985, emphasising its links with the more successful European green movement. Currently, the Greens have two members in the London Assembly, two MEPs and one MP for Brighton, Caroline Lucas. In the 2011 general election the Greens polled 285,616 votes and currently have 136 councillors in England and Wales.

ELECTIONS

People are most aware of politics and political parties at election times, and national elections especially provide journalists with a good source of stories. By-elections can be used as a barometer of government popularity and will always attract leading MPs from all parties, including ministers and frontbench opposition speakers. They are often used to register a protest vote against the government of the day, so can provide an angle on current policies. The local agent for the candidates is the most important contact for the reporter, pointing them towards the appropriate meetings and photo opportunities. An agent may distribute a copy of a proposed speech in advance, highlighting the key passages which the party wants reported. Otherwise most reports will be centred on candidates' comments on each other's party programme and the personal stance taken by specific politicians. Journalists should be prepared to challenge candidates about issues and party commitments.

PARLIAMENT

House of Commons

The House of Commons is the central focus for reporting of national politics. Most political stories emanate from parliamentary reporting, and many local papers have their parliamentary specialists, often located at Westminster. Otherwise, local papers will employ London-based stringers and the task of the local reporter will be to follow up such stories with a local angle and local interview.

In 2009 a committee on the reform of the House of Commons was established under the chairmanship of Tony Wright, who produced a report on reform, 'Rebuilding the House'. It proposed reducing the number of departmental select committees, chairs and members of committees to be elected by MPs rather than appointed; backbench business to be decided by MPs and not government; and one backbench motion to be debated at least once a month. However, these good intentions were soon overtaken by the worst scandal to hit the Commons in years. In 2009, information obtained as a result of the Freedom of Information Act regarding MPs' expenses was leaked to the *Daily Telegraph*, which published details by instalment (see Chapter 10). At first the government tried to exempt MPs' expenses from the Freedom of Information Act, but as details of fraudulent claims emerged, public anger and disillusionment increased. Parliament was put on the defensive as items claimed as expenses emerged, such as cleaning a moat, buying a duck house, paying for a full-time housekeeper, buying a tin of dog food and tuning a piano. Resignations, including those of several government ministers, sackings, deselections and retirements followed, and several MPs were prosecuted and received prison sentences.

The power of government, and especially that of the prime minister, has increased in recent years. The government controls the business and procedures of the Commons, the leader of the House outlining the timetable of business after Prime Minister's Questions. The guillotine and closure motions are increasingly used to push legislation through, curtailing debate by putting a time limit on the discussion of amendments to bills. The Commons acts with the permission of government. Most of its time is devoted to the passage of public (government) bills through Commons procedures, with the government's control of its majority ensuring legislation is passed.

The work of government has grown in complexity. In one session there are about 150 government bills to be considered, most receiving the royal assent, and about 2,000 statutory orders and regulations. Backbenchers and the opposition parties can use the following limited devices for influencing government. Their interventions can provide copy for reporters.

- *Prime Minister's Questions*: once a week for 30 minutes on Wednesday afternoons, Prime Minister's Questions provides a set piece between government and opposition. There is little scrutiny here, with rhetoric crowding out information. A planted question from a government backbencher allows the prime minister to take up a subject that can be used to attack the opposition.

- *Private Members' Bills*: a good source of news. MPs ballot for the opportunity to introduce them, and are then inundated with suggestions from pressure groups on suitable topics. There is very limited parliamentary time for such bills and few get through, the more controversial usually being talked out by the use of the filibuster.

- *Ten-Minute Rule Bill*, *Adjournment Debate and Early Day Motions*: ways for backbenchers to draw public attention to specific issues.

- *Supply Days and Emergency Debates*: used by the opposition parties to debate and vote on issues of importance. The government ensures it has a majority to ward off such attacks, the main intention of the opposition being to embarrass ministers and the government.

House of Lords

From 1997, New Labour was committed to the reform of the House of Lords. In 1999, all but 92 hereditary peers were removed and a royal commission under Conservative peer Lord Wakeham was established. He recommended a mainly appointed house, with only 100 of 500 members directly elected. In 2001, Labour continued with Lords reform, Blair suggesting that just 20 per cent of peers should be elected by the public. Both the Tories and Liberal Democrats argued that there should be at least 80 per cent of members elected directly, but in 2003 Blair backed a wholly appointed Lords, suggesting that elections would create a 'rival rather than a revising chamber'. The Commons rejected all options for reform, and since 204 the issue has dropped off the political agenda. It remains a strange assembly, with 23 spiritual peers, 92 hereditary peers and 667 life peers, mainly appointed by the prime minister. Around 77 per cent of Lords are men.

Select committees

In recent years, the most notable attempt to increase the Commons' influence over government has been the introduction of new select committees. With the televising of Parliament these now have a much higher profile. They are made up of about 12 MPs, and can call ministers, civil servants, union leaders and business chiefs to give evidence on particular topics. Select committees oversee the work of the main government departments, including agriculture, defence, education, employment, environment, foreign affairs, home affairs, social services, trade and industry, transport, the military and the civil service.

They produce reports, sometimes critical of government policy, but are weakened by the evasiveness of ministers and civil servants, hiding behind collective cabinet responsibility. Select committees hold sessions which journalists can attend. Usually, officials and ministers are questioned by MPs about aspects of a contemporary issue. Sometimes discussions can be a little heated, and notes from the meeting can be used in conjunction with follow-up interviews with interested parties. Civil servants have a set of instructions, the Osmotherly Rules, drawn up in 1977, which govern their evidence before select committees. They are instructed to be helpful but guarded, to ensure good government and national security. As a result, many important issues relating to government are kept from select committees, including advice to ministers, how decisions are made in departments, the level of consultation, the work of cabinet committees and how policy is reviewed.

Standing committees

Standing committees of between 20 and 50 MPs are appointed to examine the details of bills as they progress through Parliament. The committee can be of the whole House, as with the Maastricht Bill or the Finance Bill, and amendments to a bill can be tabled. A local MP may be on a standing committee or may have a particular interest in the legislation. There is a *First Reading*, when a bill is formally introduced without a vote; a *Second Reading*, when the general principles of the bill are discussed; a *Committee Stage*; a *Report Stage*, when committee amendments are considered by the House; and a *Third Reading*, when the bill is reviewed and further amendments added. The bill then goes to the Lords, the Committee Stage usually being of the whole House, and the bill returns to the Commons with *Lords' Amendments.* These then need to be resolved before the bill receives the *Royal Assent* and becomes an *Act*.

Government and the civil service

The decline in the power of Parliament is matched by a growth in the power of the executive, and in particular the power of the prime minister's office. Much of this power emanates from party control and the growth of the cabinet office since the First World War. The anonymity of civil service procedures reinforces this power at the centre (Ponting 1986). The prime minister appoints the government, dismisses ministers, chooses appropriate ministers for cabinet committees, controls cabinet agendas and chairs discussions with the cabinet secretary writing the minutes on behalf of the prime minister. The prime minister also controls the system of patronage, approving ministerial appointments to the chairmanship of quangos.

Cabinet government remains secretive and divisions between ministers are usually concealed by the notion of *collective cabinet responsibility*. Under this convention, decisions of the cabinet are collective and ministers are not allowed to contest the view emanating from the cabinet office. This makes it difficult for journalists to record the true flavour of the political debates and discussions taking place at the heart of government. The work of the civil service is also kept secret by means of *ministerial responsibility*. This convention states that the buck stops with departmental ministers, ensuring that, when questioned in select committees, senior civil servants can dodge answering by referring to their minister.

Cabinet committees

Issues concerning the resignation of Nigel Lawson and Geoffrey Howe from Thatcher's government raised questions about the relevance of the notion of collective cabinet government. In the 1980s the cabinet met less often, some 45 times a year compared with nearly 100 times in every year since 1945, and the number of cabinet committees and papers also fell (Hennessy 1986).

Under Thatcher, a large proportion of cabinet work was determined by cabinet committees. Many major items of public policy were dealt with by committees, including the abolition of the GLC and six metropolitan authorities, the introduction of the poll tax, the banning of trade unions at GCHQ, the privatisation of British Telecom and reforms of the NHS.

The three principal committees deal with economics, overseas and defence, and home affairs. With more decisions made in committee, the whole cabinet system has become fragmented, with policy being decided by relatively isolated groups of ministers and civil servants.

Prime minister's office

Another recent trend has been the bypassing of the cabinet system altogether. Increasingly, policy has been determined by informal groupings centred around the prime minister. Government information flows as much through the prime minister's office as it does through the cabinet secretariat. As a consequence, policy reaches the cabinet and departments in a fairly developed form, providing ministers with a *fait accompli* and little time to organise opposition to it. The Broadcasting White Paper of 1989 was developed in a series of breakfast meetings between Thatcher and like-minded newspaper editors.

Under New Labour there was a burgeoning of political advisers and spin doctors, with a threefold increase in advisers, over 100 being taken on since 1997 with a spiralling salary bill. Lord Waldegrave, giving evidence to Lord Neill's public standards inquiry, pointed to a 'new political apparatchik system equivalent to an alternative civil service'. Tony Blair was one of the most active prime ministers in appointing life peers between 1997 and 2007. Patronage still remains an insidious part of British government and culture, and with the wider culture of secrecy, places a question mark over democratic practice and accountability.

CHAPTER 14

On or off the job – or both?

Training and careers

The best way to learn how to be a journalist is to go out and do some journalism. There is simply no substitute for talking to real people about real issues that affect their lives. You may have great ideas about the nature of reporting, you may know all about ideology and the history of the press in eighteenth-century England. But if you cannot bash out a quick story on a local murder you are useless.

That was the dominant view in the industry at the beginning of the twentieth century. It remains largely the same at the start of the twenty-first. There have been slight changes. Training courses have developed with the support of newspaper managements and trade unions. They have even spread into the learned corridors of universities. But mutual suspicion persists between the press and academia.

On one hand, there is a prevalent belief that journalists are born, not made. You've either got the nose for news or, sadly, you haven't. As Sir David English, former editor of the *Daily Mail*, said: 'Journalism is a skill that can only be acquired on the job and at the end of the day it depends on whether someone has a burning individual talent.' On the other hand, there is the belief that journalism is a profession with its own ethical and work-related standards which can be both taught and assessed. Thus certain educational qualifications are laid down for entrants, while the development of training courses becomes an essential part of the formation of the journalist's professional identity. Caught between these two views are students and trainers. A further twist emerges when attempts are made by educators to promote reflective, critical approaches to dominant professional attitudes (as, for instance, reflected in this text). Scepticism about the value of theoretical studies for aspiring reporters remains widespread.

THE CONTRASTING US/UK TRADITIONS OF TRAINING

The training of journalists in Britain is a relatively new phenomenon. In the United States, university training started in the late nineteenth century with the first journalism school founded in 1908 at the University of Missouri. Ten years later there were 86 schools offering at least some journalism coursework, while by 1940 this figure had jumped to 542.

In Britain, in contrast, it was not until the mid 1960s that any major programme of journalism training was launched. A diploma course had run at King's College London between 1922 and 1939, but this was not restarted after the war. After the 1949 Royal Commission on the Press drew attention to the need for better training, the National Advisory Council for the Training and Education of Junior Journalists was set up in 1952 (Stephenson and Mory 1990). Three years later this body changed its title to the National Council for the Training of Journalists (NCTJ) and brought together representatives from the NUJ and the Institute of Journalists (the two trade unions), the Newspaper Society (owners of provincial newspapers in England and Wales and suburban London weeklies) and the Guild of British Newspaper Editors. Later they were joined by the Newspaper Publishers' Association (linking owners of national newspapers) and by the two bodies formed by the owners and managers of newspapers in Scotland.

Since the 1960s, many colleges and universities have developed courses in journalism. Initially, the media were considered largely within their sociological or broader theoretical contexts in courses usually titled 'mass communications'. But over recent decades the focus has shifted, largely in response to student demand, to the development of practical skills. Many mass communication courses have integrated a practical element, while both postgraduate and (since the early 1990s) undergraduate journalism degrees have emerged. By 2013, the Universities and Colleges Admissions Service (UCAS) website listed more than 400 undergraduate courses with 'journalism' in their title. In addition, more than 450 postgraduate master's courses were available. The vast majority of these, however, are not designed to qualify their students for a career in the industry; only a small percentage have the professional accreditation that editors seek.

THE IMPORTANCE OF THE NCTJ

The NCTJ was formed in 1951 as a result of the Royal Commission on the Press. Its role in maintaining and enforcing the standards of professional journalism training is arguably more important now than it has ever been. Under the dynamic leadership of chief executive Joanne Butcher, the NCTJ has boosted its profile in the industry with the appointment of high-profile journalists to its board and the inclusion of senior editorial figures from the worlds of television and radio.

Major changes to NCTJ qualifications have been made in recent years. Alongside its Diploma in Journalism, introduced in 2007, and the National Qualification in Journalism, introduced in 2013, it has also announced plans for new apprenticeship and foundation certificate qualifications. Qualifications cover news, magazines, production journalism, sports, business and finance, online journalism, video, radio and television journalism.

EDUCATIONAL QUALIFICATIONS

In 1965, the trade unions and the Newspaper Society agreed that the minimum qualifications for entry to the profession was three GCEs, one being in English. Since 1970 the required minimum has been five passes at O level or GCSE at grades A, B or C, with English language still being among them. Some other examinations have been approved by the NCTJ as being educationally equivalent, and in exceptional cases (when the editor has their eye on an individual) the qualifications are waived.

The trend over recent decades has been towards the formation of an increasingly graduate profession. In 1965 only 6 per cent entering local newspapers had a university degree while a further 33 per cent had one or more A levels. In 1990 53 per cent of entrants to provincial papers boasted degrees while most of the others had two or more A levels. By 2012, the Journalists at Work survey found that 73 per cent of working journalists had degrees while 34 per cent had a postgraduate qualification too (NCTJ 2012a).

Even so, academic qualifications in themselves have never been sufficient to guarantee a chance to become a trainee journalist. As Sarah Niblock (1996) comments: 'Some editors may feel journalists who are well read in media criticism may lead them to question editorial policy, so do not think having such a qualification will automatically give you a head start.' In addition to showing academic abilities, the successful applicant must be able to demonstrate a special commitment to working in the field. Many school pupils go to newspapers on work attachments, others manage to persuade editors to let them observe the newspaper operations during their holidays. Some students help with hospital radios; others send in letters and articles to their local newspapers. All this counts well for any applicant, whether to a newspaper or a college.

PRE-ENTRY TRAINING: POST-A LEVEL

One year pre-entry courses are provided at further education centres dotted about the UK, such as City College Brighton and Hove; Crawley College; Darlington College; East Surrey College, Redhill; Harlow College; Sutton Coldfield College; Warwickshire College; West Kent College; and Wolverhampton College.

THE DEGREE ROUTE

In the early 1990s, for the first time the US-style undergraduate route to journalism emerged with the launch of degrees at five centres in the UK. They were to be joined later by a host of others. Journalism can now be studied alongside an extraordinary range of subjects: Staffordshire University offers journalism and citizenship; Sheffield University offers journalism and Russian; Sunderland University offers journalism with comparative literature.

For most newspaper editors, however, the degree is significantly less important than the NCTJ diploma – the qualification that tells them a prospective reporter is capable of taking accurate shorthand notes, has a good grounding in media law, understands how national and local government structures work, and can formulate a decent news story (among many other skills). Of the 82 universities offering some sort of undergraduate degree programme in 2013, just 14 had programmes that were accredited by the NCTJ. They are listed alphabetically below:

Bournemouth University

Brunel University

De Montford University

Glasgow Caledonian University

Nottingham Trent University

Staffordshire University

Teesside University

University of Brighton

University of Central Lancashire

University of Kent

University of Lincoln

University of Portsmouth

University of Sheffield

University of Sunderland

PRE-ENTRY TRAINING: THE MASTER'S OR POSTGRADUATE DIPLOMA ROUTE

In 1970, the first university journalism course was launched at University College, Cardiff. Largely the inspiration of Tom Hopkinson, former editor of *Picture Post*, and modelled on a programme at Columbia University, New York, it initially attracted between 15 and 20 postgraduate students. A similar one-year postgraduate diploma course was begun at City University, London, in 1976, initially with 13 students.

By the late 1980s, postgraduate courses had grown in numbers enormously, spanning a wide range of diplomas and MAs: newspaper, periodical, broadcast, European (linking Cardiff and City with colleges in Utrecht, the Netherlands and Aarhus, Denmark) and international.

As with the degree programmes, the value for many newspaper editors lies with the ability of these courses to deliver students who have passed the NCTJ's diploma in journalism. But suspicions of universities by the press persisted. As Professor Hugh Stephenson of City University commented: 'The academic community in this country has always been distrustful of courses in journalism and media employers have been distrustful of people with education.'

GRADUATE TRAINING SCHEMES

In-house training schemes set up by individual newspaper groups come and go depending on the economic climate at any given time. In 2013, the *Daily Mail,* the *Daily Telegraph,* the *Sun,* the *Financial Times* and *The Times* were running graduate schemes, as were Reuters and Press Association Sport. These are highly competitive schemes that aim to take on the cream of the country's aspiring journalists, sending them to learn the ropes at various corners of their empires in the hope that they will emerge as the star journalists of the future.

ON-THE-JOB TRAINING

The days have long since passed when the majority of local newspapers took on school-leavers and trained them to be reporters from scratch. The vast majority of first jobs now go to applicants who have already achieved a basic journalism qualification such as the NCTJ diploma. However, training does still continue whilst on the job – which is why your first job title is likely to be 'trainee reporter'. During their first 18 months on the job, trainee journalists can then work their way through NCTJ's National Qualification in Journalism (NQJ, formerly known as the NCE) to be fully qualified as a senior reporter. The NQJ builds upon the diploma.

THE NEW APPRENTICESHIPS

As journalism increasingly has become a profession whose newest recruits have at the very least a degree-level qualification, many in the industry began to feel uneasy that potentially great journalists from less academic backgrounds no longer had any way of forcing their way into a newspaper's newsroom. As a result, the diversity of their organisations was continuing to be diminished. In response to this, the NCTJ set up a pilot scheme for the Advanced Level Apprenticeship in Journalism, which began in September 2013 with apprentices from Archant London; BBC radio; the *Independent*; *i*; the Kent Messenger Group; and the *London Evening Standard* studying one day a week at Lambeth College.

OTHER ROUTES

In addition to these entry routes there are many others. For instance, there are two-year HNDs, BTECs and many evening class centres now running courses in freelancing, feature writing and press photography. There are privately run journalism training centres (most claiming extraordinary success for their graduates in gaining jobs in the industry), and you can even learn journalism via a correspondence course on the internet. The range of courses is bewildering.

Many universities provide media studies courses. During the 1990s, media-related courses became the most fashionable to study and inevitably attracted the suspicions of Fleet Street (once reserved for sociology and peace studies). Many editors argue that they require applicants with broad interests and knowledge rather than bookish experts in the narrow academic discipline of communications. Yet, increasingly, theoretical media courses are incorporating practical vocational elements. It is to be hoped that journalists' traditional reluctance to encourage the reflective, critical approach will dwindle as more media graduates enter the industry.

There are conflicting research findings over the job success rate of media graduates.

A FOOT IN THE DOOR: GETTING THE FIRST JOB

Journalism has always been a notoriously difficult world to enter. With staff cuts in virtually all newspapers since the late 1980s, the job hunt has become still more difficult. Admittedly, the internet is beginning to provide large numbers of new jobs for journalists, but not only are colleges producing more trained young aspirants, but also the newspaper jobs market is becoming jammed full with experienced journalists made redundant and on the hunt for employment.

Contacts are crucial. Spend time while training concentrating on building up sources and links in the industry. Also try to get freelance work published. After completing work attachments on newspapers, ask your supervisor to write you a reference. Compile an attractive portfolio of your cuttings and references and attach an up-to-date CV: that will provide an invaluable aid to you during job interviews. You may even want to post your CV on the internet, including links to other works you have completed. As Damian Barr (1999) advises: 'Provide the URL (the name of your website) in your prospective letter or email so that an employer can click to it easily without having to bother with attachments.'

INTERNSHIPS

The application

Because newspapers are inundated with job applications, there is often little need to advertise many of the jobs that fall vacant. But a number are still advertised in a number of places, including the websites of *Press Gazette* (www.pressgazette. co.uk), the *Guardian* (www.jobs.guardian.co.uk), Hold the Front Page (www.holdthe frontpage.co.uk), www.journalism.co.uk and Gorkana (www.gorkanajobs.co.uk).

Your letter of application should be brief and to the point. The accompanying CV should summarise your achievements to date. It should list your name, address, date of birth, education (school, college, university, evening classes etc.) with dates and qualifications (briefly), professional qualifications, work on student/university publications, any job/s you have held (perhaps on a local hospital radio), desktop publishing skills, publications, special interests, languages and references (with addresses and contact details). Remember that presentation is a key element of journalism – a poorly designed CV is not going to do you any favours.

Remember that if your CV does not show a professionally accredited qualification – the NCTJ diploma being the most obvious – it is increasingly likely to go in the bin.

The interview

It is vital to prepare for any job or college interview. Find out everything you can about the newspaper. Get hold of some recent copies and look at them critically. If it is out of your area – trainee journalists should be prepared to travel anywhere in the country in search of a job, rather than expecting one to crop up on their doorstep – make sure you have researched the key individuals on that patch. Who is the local MP? The police chief? The council leader? You should also arrive at the interview armed with ideas for stories for the next edition of the paper. Nothing impresses an editor more than an applicant who is clearly able to be an instantly productive member of the newsroom.

Your portfolio is vital here too. Editors will want to see evidence of the work you have produced at university or college, as a freelance or on work placements. Keep this cuttings file well presented and up to date. The interviewer will also expect you to be able to speak confidently about the national media – both print and broadcast – and the internet.

Dress tidily and be prepared to go out and find a story – some interview days now include a task like this as part of their recruitment process. And always go prepared to ask questions. Good luck.

Useful information and contacts

INDUSTRY ORGANISATIONS

Audit Bureau of Circulation

Provides audited measurement of newspaper and magazine circulation and distribution across print and digital channels.
www.abc.org.uk

Journalists' Charity

Originally known as the Newspaper Press Fund, the charity provides help and support for journalists who have fallen on hard times.
www.journalistscharity.org.uk

National Council for the Training of Journalists (NCTJ)

A charity set up following the first Royal Commission on the Press to oversee the training of professional journalists. Most newspaper journalists hold a qualification accredited by the NCTJ. The organisation has modernised significantly over the past decade. Chief executive: Joanne Butcher (see Chapters 3, 4, 5 and 13).
www.nctj.com

National Readership Survey

A continuous survey of 36,000 people to establish their news reading habits across print and online newspaper publishing.
www.nrs.co.uk

The Newspaper Publishers Association

Represents the UK's national newspapers on matters of press freedom and commercial interest.
www.n-p-a.org.uk

The Newspaper Society

Established in 1836, the NS is the voice of Britain's regional and local media. It exists to promote newspapers' interests in all political, legal and regulatory matters and to promote their strengths as news and marketing media. Director: David Newell.

www.newspapersoc.org.uk

Press Association

National news agency providing words, pictures and video to its subscribers. It is ultimately owned by 27 shareholders, most of which are national and regional publishing companies.

www.pressassociation.com

Scottish Newspaper Society

Represents Scotland's newspapers on matters of press freedom and commercial interest.

www.newspapersoc.org.uk/tags/scottish-newspaper-society

Society of Editors

A network of senior journalists from print, broadcast and online journalism that lobbies on behalf of its members on matters of press freedom and promotes standards, media independence and self-regulation for the industry. Executive editor: Bob Satchwell.

www.societyofeditors.co.uk

UK Press Card Authority

Voluntary scheme for issuing credentials to professional newsgatherers who may need to identify themselves as such to the public or officials. The press cards are issued by 16 'gatekeeper' organisations, which include the NUJ, the CIoJ, the BBC and Sky.

www.presscard.uk.com

UNIONS

British Association of Journalists

Aims to be a non-political union, representing its members on employment matters and promoting ethical journalism. Considerably smaller than the NUJ in terms of membership numbers.

www.bajunion.org.uk

Chartered Institute of Journalists

Granted a Royal Charter by Queen Victoria to protect the interests of journalists. Combines the role of a professional society with that of a union, the Institute of Journalists (IoJ).

www.cioj.co.uk

National Union of Journalists
Represents its members' interests on employment matters, and promotes ethical journalism. Controversially backed statutory press regulation without consulting its members in 2012 – which led to a number of high-profile journalists leaving the union. General secretary: Michelle Stanistreet.
www.nuj.org.uk

ASSOCIATIONS

Association of British Science Writers
Looks after the interests of scientific journalists.
www.absw.org.uk

Association for Journalism Education
The AJE represents journalism educators at higher education institutions in the United Kingdom and Ireland.
www.ajeuk.org

Commonwealth Journalists Association
Looks after the interests of journalists operating in Commonwealth countries.
www.commonwealthjournalists.org

Foreign Press Association
Long-established club for foreign correspondents. Organises regular political briefings.
www.fpalondon.org

Sports Journalists Association
Looks after the interests of sports journalists.
www.sportsjournalists.co.uk

World Association of Newspapers and News Publishers
Global organisation of the world's press, representing more than 18,000 publications, 15,000 online sites and over 3,000 companies in more than 120 countries.
www.wan-ifra.org

Women in Journalism
Networking, campaigning, training and social organisation for women journalists who work across all the written media, from newspapers and magazines to digital media.
http://womeninjournalism.co.uk

PUBLICATIONS

The Drum
Magazine covering all aspects of media in Scotland, including newspapers.
www.thedrum.com

Ethical Space: The International Journal of Communication Ethics
Peer-reviewed journal of the Institute of Communication Ethics.
www.communicationethics.net/espace/

Hold the Front Page
Jointly owned by several regional newspaper publishers, this website offers news about the regional press.
www.holdthefrontpage.co.uk

Index on Censorship
Committed to freedom of speech and expression. Highlights cases of censorship, harassment, jailing or intimidation of journalists, writers, intellectuals and campaigners globally.
www.indexoncensorship.org

InPublishing
Bi-monthly magazine covering the production side of newspaper publishing.
www.inpublishing.co.uk

Journalism.co.uk
Independent website with news and views from the digital journalism sphere.
www.journalism.co.uk

Journalism Practice
Peer-reviewed academic journal published by Taylor & Francis.
www.tandfonline.com

Journalism Studies
Peer-reviewed academic journal published by Taylor & Francis.
www.tandfonline.com

Journalism: Theory, Practice and Criticism
Peer-reviewed academic journal published by Sage.
http://jou.sagepub.com

The *Guardian* Media
The media section of the *Guardian* website provides news and features from around the media village.
www.guardian.co.uk/media

Niemann Journalism Lab
Online publication of the Niemann Foundation for Journalism at Harvard University.
www.niemanlab.org

Poynter Institute
US website hosting news and academic study from the world of journalism.
www.poynter.org

Press Gazette
Formerly a weekly newspaper for the journalism industry. Now an online-only publication covering newspapers, magazines, broadcast and online journalism.
www.pressgazette.co.uk

AWARDS AND PRIZES

The British Journalism Awards
Launched in 2012, this annual event recognises journalism from any platform in several categories, but with an emphasis on public interest. Run by *Press Gazette*.
www.pressgazette.co.uk/subject/British Journalism Awards

EDF Energy Regional Media Awards
Organised in conjunction with Hold the Front Page (see above), these awards are for regional newspaper journalists in three regions: East of England; South West England; and London and the South.
www.edfenergy.com/media-centre/media-awards

FPA Media Awards
Run by the Foreign Press Association to highlight the best in international journalism in print, broadcast and online.
www.fpalondon.org

George Viner Scholarship fund
Set up by the National Union of Journalists to address the shortfall of journalists from minority backgrounds in newsrooms and to broaden the diversity of journalists working in the British and Irish media.
www.nuj.org.uk/rights/george-viner-memorial-fund/

The *Guardian* Student Media Awards
Many winners of these prestigious awards have gone on to great careers in journalism. Individual categories include student writers, designers, broadcasters, editors and photographers. There are team awards for publications too.
www.theguardian.com/student-media-awards-2013

National Union of Students Awards
Includes a Student Journalist of the Year category and a Best Student Media category.
www.nusawards.co.uk

NCTJ Awards for Excellence

Recognise and reward the best journalism students completing NCTJ-accredited courses and journalists/photographers with less than two years' experience on the job.

www.nctj.com/Awardsforexcellence

Paul Foot Award

Run by *Private Eye* in memory of one of the country's finest investigative and campaigning journalists.

www.private-eye.co.uk/paul_foot.php

The Press Awards

Formerly the British Press Awards. Now run by the Society of Editors, this annual awards event recognises great journalism in national newspapers.

www.pressawards.org.uk

The Regional Press Awards

Also run by the Society of Editors, this annual awards event recognises great journalism in regional newspapers.

www.theregionalpressawards.org.uk

Sports Journalism Awards

Run by the Sports Journalists Association to highlight the best in sports journalism in newspapers.

www.sportsjournalists.co.uk/sja-journalism-awards/

ETHICAL AND CAMPAIGNING WEBSITES

Amnesty International

www.amnesty.org.uk

Campaign for Freedom of Information

www.cfoi.org.uk

Campaign for Press and Broadcasting Freedom

www.cpbf.org.uk

Human Rights Watch

www.hrw.org

Institute for Global Ethics

www.globalethics.org.uk

Institute for War and Peace Reporting

www.iwpr.net

Bibliography

Adams, Sally (1999) 'Writing features.' In Wynford Hicks with Sally Adams and Harriet Gilbert, *Writing for Journalists*, London: Routledge, pp. 47–98.

Adams, Sally with Hicks, Wynford (2001) *Interviewing for Journalists*, London: Routledge.

Aitchison, Jean (1988) *Writing for the Press*, London: Hutchinson.

Alexander, Anne (2013) 'Where are Britain's black journalists?' *Guardian*, Comment Is Free (accessed on 20 July 2013 at www.guardian.co.uk/commentisfree/2013/jan/10/where-are-britains-black-journalists).

Alia, Valerie (2004) *Media Ethics and Social Change*, Edinburgh: Edinburgh University Press.

Allan, Stuart (1999) *News Culture*, 1st edition, Buckingham: Open University Press.

Allan, Stuart (2004) *News Culture*, 2nd edition, Maidenhead: Open University Press.

Allan, Stuart and Thorsen, Einar (2010) 'Journalism, public service and BBC News Online.' In G. Meikle and G. Redden (eds) *News Online: Transformations and Continuities*, Basingstoke: Palgrave Macmillan, pp. 20–37.

Almond, Gabriel and Verba, Sidney (1963) *The Civic Culture*, Princeton, NJ: Princeton University Press.

Anderson, Kevin (2010) 'Journalists: Belittling digital staff is not acceptable', Strange Attractor blog, 18 January (accessed on 23 July 2013 at http://charman-anderson.com/2010/01/18/journalists-belittling-digital-staff-is-not-acceptable/).

Andersen, Michael (2009) 'Four crowdsourcing lessons from the *Guardian*'s (spectacular) expenses-scandal experiment', Nieman Journalism Lab, 23 June (accessed on 13 September 2012 at www.niemanlab.org/2009/06/four-crowdsourcing-lessons-from-the-guardians-spectacular-expenses-scandal-experiment/).

Anderson, Patricia (1991) *The Printed Image and the Transformation of Popular Culture, 1790–1860*, Oxford: Clarendon Press.

Anderson, Peter J. and Ward, Geoff (eds) (2006) *The Future of Journalism in the Advanced Democracies*, London: Ashgate Publishing.

Andrews, Robert (2012) 'Two years after the tipping point, papers' web readership is booming', Paid Content, 8 August (accessed on 20 July 2013 at http://paidcontent. org/2012/08/08/two-years-after-the-tipping-point-papers-web-readership-is-booming/).

Arthur, Charles (2009) 'They've got your number', *Guardian*, 13 April (accessed on 11 September 2012 at www.guardian.co.uk/media/2009/apr/13/investigative-journalism-protecting-sources).

Arthur, Charles (2010) 'Analysing data is the future for journalists, says Tim Berners-Lee', *Guardian*, 22 November 2010 (accessed on 11 December 2013 at www.theguardian. com/media/2010/nov/22/data-analysis-tim-berners-lee).

Article 19 (2003) *What's the Story? Results from Research into Media Coverage of Refugees and Asylum Seekers in the UK*, London: Article 19 (www.article19.org).

Aubrey, Crispin (ed.) (1982) *Nukespeak: The Media and the Bomb*, London: Comedia.

Bagnall, Nicholas (1993) *Newspaper Language*, Oxford: Focal Press.

Bainbridge, Cyril and Stockdill, Ray (1993) *The News of the World Story*, London: HarperCollins.

Bale, Tim (2010) *The Conservative Party from Thatcher to Cameron*, Cambridge: Polity Press.

Ball, James, Schneier, Bruce and Greenwald, Glenn (2013) 'NSA and GCHQ target Tor Network that protects anonymity of web users', *Guardian*, 4 October (accessed on 1 November 2013 at www.theguardian.com/world/2013/oct/04/nsa-gchq-attack-tor-network-encryption).

Balmer, John (1998) 'Corporate identity and the advent of corporate marketing', *Journal of Marketing Management* Vol. 14, No. 8, pp. 963–96.

Barber, Lynn (1991) *Mostly Men*, London: Viking.

Barber, Lynn (1999) 'The Art of the Interview.' In Stephen Glover (ed.) *Secrets of the Press: Journalists on Journalism*, London: Allen Lane/Penguin Press, pp. 196–205.

Baresch, Brian, Knight, Lewis, Harp, Dustin and Yaschur, Carolyn (2011) *Friends who Choose your News: An Analysis of Content Links on Facebook*, International Symposium on Online Journalism (accessed on 23 June 2012 at https://online. journalism.utexas.edu/2011/papers/Baresch2011.pdf).

Barker, Dennis (1998) 'The question posers', *Press Gazette*, 11 September.

Barr, Damian (1999) 'Let them read all about you', *The Times*, 8 November.

Barsamian, David (2002) 'John Pilger', *Progressive*, November (accessed on 8 October 2004 at www.progressive.org/nov02/intv1102.html).

Bartlett, Rachel (2013) 'FT to focus on "smart aggregation of content"', journalism.co.uk, 9 October (accessed on 11 December 2013 at www.journalism.co.uk/news/lionel-barber-on-future-of-ft-print-product-will-derive-from-the-web-offering-/s2/a554389/).

Bates, Daniel (2012) 'Rupert Murdoch's iPad-only newspaper The Daily closes after less than two years', *Daily Mail*, 3 December (accessed on 4 December 2012 at www.dailymail.co.uk/news/article-2242283/Rupert-Murdochs-iPad-newspaper-The-Daily-closes-years.html).

Battle, John (2003) 'Silenced in court', *Guardian* Media section, 24 February (accessed on 5 December 2013 at http://media.guardian.co.uk/mediaguardian/story/0,901391, 00.html).

BBC News (2009) 'Man behind expenses leak revealed', 23 May (accessed on 13 September 2012 at http://news.bbc.co.uk/1/hi/uk_politics/8064731.stm).

BBC News online (2011) 'BBC's Andrew Marr "embarrassed" by super-injunction', 26 April (accessed on 24 August 2013 at www.bbc.co.uk/news/uk-13190424).

BBC (2011) 'Court results put on Twitter by West Midlands police', 19 April (accessed on 13 December 2013 at www.bbc.co.uk/news/uk-england-birmingham-13127533).

Beal, Joan C. (2004) *English in Modern Times*, London: Arnold.

Beech, Matt and Lee, Simon (2008) *Ten Years of New Labour*, Basingstoke: Palgrave Macmillan.

Bell, Martin (1998) 'The Journalism of Attachment.' In Matthew Kieran (ed.) *Media Ethics*, London: Routledge, pp. 15–22.

Berrey, R. Power (1933) *The Romance of a Great Newspaper*, London: *The News of the World*.

Berry, Stephen J. (2009) *Watchdog Journalism: The Art of Investigative Reporting*, New York: Oxford University Press.

Black, Tim (2011) 'A demeaning epidemic of injunctionitis', Spiked online, 23 May (accessed on 24 August 2013 at www.spiked-online.com/newsite/article/10538#. UhjM7rxhyK8).

Blackhurst, Chris (2013) 'Editor's Letter', *Independent*, 21 June.

Blair, Tony (1998) *Leading the Way: A New Vision of Local Government*, London: Institute for Public Policy Research.

Blair, Tony (2010) *A Journey*, London: Hutchinson.

Blake, Matt (2011) 'John Yates's confession prompts calls for him to step down', *Independent*, 11 July (accessed on 17 September 2012 at www.independent.co.uk/ news/uk/crime/john-yatess-confession-prompts-calls-for-him-to-step-down- 2311634.html).

Bloch, Jonathan and Fitzgerald, Patrick (1983) *British Intelligence and Covert Action*, London: Junction.

Bowater, Donna (2011) 'Leveson Inquiry: David Beckham's former PA Rebecca Loos "received six-figure sum"', *Telegraph*, 12 December (accessed on 12 September 2012 at www.telegraph.co.uk/news/uknews/leveson-inquiry/8951138/Leveson- Inquiry-David-Beckhams-former-PA-Rebecca-Loos-received-six-figure-sum.html).

Bowcott, Owen (2013) 'Press Intrusion: Don't name suspects in the media until charged, urges MP', *Guardian*, 21 April (accessed on 22 April 2013 at www.theguardian. com/media/2013/apr/21/press-intrusion-name-suspects).

Bower, Tom (1988) *Maxwell: The Outsider*, London: Mandarin.

Bower, Tom (1992) 'Maxwell: A very British experience', Sixth James Cameron Memorial Lecture, City University London.

Bradshaw, Paul and Rohumaa, Liisa (2011) *The Online Journalism Handbook*, London: Pearson.

Brockway, Fenner (1986) *98 Not Out*, London: Quartet Books.

Brook, Stephen (2006) 'Galloway guns for "fake sheik"', *Guardian*, 30 March (accessed on 22 April 2013 at www.theguardian.com/media/2006/mar/30/pressandpublishing.politicsandthemedia).

Brook, Stephen and Gillan, Audrey (2009) 'The truth about the cabinet's expenses', *Guardian*, 18 May (accessed on 18 September 2012 at www.guardian.co.uk/media/2009/may/18/mps-expenses-how-scoop-came-light).

Brooke, Heather (2011) *The Revolution Will Be Digitised: Dispatches from the Information War*, London: Random House.

Brown, Gerry (1995a) 'Fines are just fine by me', *Guardian*, 24 July.

Brown, Gerry (1995b) *Exposed! Sensational True Story of Fleet Street Reporter*, London: Viking.

Browne, Christopher (1996) *The Prying Game: The Sex, Sleaze and Scandals of Fleet Street and the Media Mafia*, London: Robson.

Browne, Christopher (1999) *The Journalist's Handbook*, London: A. & C. Black.

Buchanan, Matt (2012) 'The biggest sites in social publishing', Buzzfeed.com, 23 October (accessed on 24 October 2012 at www.buzzfeed.com/mattbuchanan/the-biggest-sites-in-social-publishing).

Burden, Peter (2009) *News of the World? Fake Sheikhs and Royal Trappings*, London: Eye Books.

de Burgh, Hugo (ed.) (2000) *Investigative Journalism: Context and Practice*, London: Routledge.

Burkeman, Oliver (2002) 'Voice of America', *Guardian*, 1 March.

Burrell, Ian (2004) 'The wit and wisdom of Dan Rather', *Independent*, 29 November.

Burrell, Ian (2012) 'Grant sees "war" over Leveson Report on press', *i*, 17 September 2012.

Campbell, Duncan (2013) 'The decline of the British trial', *New Statesman*, 12 November (accessed on 13 December 2013 at www.newstatesman.com/lifestyle/2013/11/decline-british-trial).

Campbell, Duncan and Connor, Steve (1986) *On the Record: Surveillance, Computers and Privacy*, London: Michael Joseph.

Campbell, Lisa (2013) London Live to offer 'Urban' TV, *Broadcast*, 11 July (accessed on 12 July 2013 at www.broadcastnow.co.uk/london-live-to-offer-urban-tv/5058183.article).

Cathcart, Brian (2013) 'Hacked Off and the midnight pizza deal: Another silly myth', Hacked Off website, 18 July (accessed on 19 November 2013 at http://hackinginquiry.org/news/hacked-off-and-the-midnight-pizza-deal-another-silly-myth/).

Caulfield, Brian (2012) 'Facebook IPO: Time for a drink', Forbes.com, 17 May (accessed on 23 June 2012 at www.forbes.com/sites/briancaulfield/2012/05/17/facebook-goes-public-time-for-a-drink/).

Cellan-Jones, Rory (2013) 'Twitter plans stock market listing', BBC News online, 13 September (accessed on 14 September 2013 at www.bbc.co.uk/news/business-24075010).

CFOI (2008) 'A thousand freedom of information stories demonstrate Act's value', Campaign for Freedom of Information press release, 30 September (accessed on 23 May 2013 at www.cfoi.org.uk/pdf/FOIStories2006–07.pdf).

CFOI (2012) 'Government's FoI reforms would block difficult FoI requests', Campaign for Freedom of Information report, 18 December (accessed on 23 June 2013 at www.cfoi.org.uk/pdf/foipostlegscrutiny_cfoicommentgovtresp.pdf).

Chalaby, Jean (1998) *The Invention of Journalism*, London: Macmillan.

Chapman, Jane L. and Nuttall, Nick (2011) *Journalism Today: A Themed History*, Oxford: Wiley-Blackwell.

Chilton, Paul (ed.) (1985) *Language and the Nuclear Arms Debate: Nukespeak Today*, London: Frances Pinter.

Chippendale, Peter and Horrie, Chris (1999) *Stick It Up your Punter: The Uncut Story of* The Sun *Newspaper*, London: Simon & Schuster.

Chittum, Ryan (2013) 'The *NYT*'s $150m-a-year paywall', Columbia Journalism Review website, 1 August (accessed on 2 August 2013 at www.cjr.org/the_audit/the_nyts_150_million-a-year_pa.php).

Chomsky, Noam (1999) *The New Military Humanism: Lessons from Kosovo*, London: Pluto.

Chossudovsky, Michel (1998) 'Global poverty in the late 20th century', *Journal of International Affairs* Vol. 52, No. 1 (accessed on 29 May 2014 at www.mtholyoke.edu/acad/intrel/chossu.htm).

Clarke, Bob (2010) *From Grub Street to Fleet Street: An Illustrated History of Newspapers to 1899*, London: Revel Barker.

Clarkson, Wensley (1990) *Confessions of a Tabloid Journalist*, London: Fourth Estate.

Cockerell, Michael, Hennessy, Peter and Walker, David (1984) *Sources Close to the Prime Minister: Inside the Hidden World of the News Manipulators*, London: Macmillan.

Cohen, Stanley (1980) *Folk Devils and Moral Panics*, London: Robertson.

Cole, Peter and Harcup, Tony (2010) *Newspaper Journalism*, London: Sage.

Coleman, Terry (1993) 'Best chat lines of our time', *Guardian*, 6 November.

Colman, Clive (2008) 'Will the internet kill off our creaking contempt laws?', *The Times*, 11 March.

CRE (2005) *Why Ethnic Minorities Leave London's Print Journalism Sector*, Commission for Racial Equality (accessed on 11 December 2013 at http://workinglives.org/fms/MRSite/Research/wlri/Photo%20gallery/Why%20ethnic%20minorities%20leave%20London's%20print%20industries.pdf).

Conboy, Martin (2002) *The Press and Popular Culture*, London: Sage.

Conboy, Martin (2003) 'Parochializing the Global: Language and the British Tabloid Press.' In Jean Aitchison and Diana M. Lewis (eds) *New Media Language*, London: Routledge, pp. 45–54.

Conley, David (2002) *The Daily Miracle: An Introduction to Journalism*, 2nd edition, Melbourne, Australia: Oxford University Press.

Cooke, Lynn (2005) 'A visual convergence of print, television, and the internet: Charting 40 years of design change in news presentation', *New Media & Society* February Vol. 7, No. 1, pp. 22–46.

Cookson, Robert (2013) 'Johnston Press writes down £250m in assets', *Financial Times*, 28 August (accessed on 29 August 2013 at www.ft.com/cms/s/0/947b6480–0fc1–11e3-a258–00144feabdc0.html).

Cottle, Simon (1999) 'Ethnic minorities and the British news media.' In Jane Stokes and Anna Reading (eds) *The Media in Britain*, London/New York: Macmillan Press/St Martin's Press, pp. 191–200.

Council of Europe (1950) *European Convention on Human Rights* (accessed on 18 September 2012 at www.hri.org/docs/ECHR50.html#Convention).

Cox, Harvey G. and Morgan, David (1973) *City Politics and the Press*, Cambridge: Cambridge University Press.

Cudlipp, Hugh (2009) *Publish and Be Damned*, Malta: Revel Barker.

Culbertson, Hugh and Somerick, Nancy (1976) 'Quotation marks and bylines: What do they mean to readers?', *Journalism & Mass Communication Quarterly* September Vol. 53, No. 3, pp. 463–508.

Curran, James (1987) *Interim Report: Goldsmith Media Research Group*, London: Goldsmiths College.

Curran, James and Seaton, Jean (2003) *Power without Responsibility: The Press, Broadcasting and New Media in Britain*, 6th edition, London: Routledge.

Curtis, Liz (1984) *Ireland and the Propaganda War*, London: Pluto.

Cusick, James (2013) 'Leveson: Newspapers and magazines reveal "Independent Press Standards Organisation"', *Independent*, 8 July (accessed on 23 July at www.independent.co.uk/news/media/press/leveson-newspapers-and-magazines-reveal-independent-press-standards-organisation-8695559.html).

Dacre, Paul (2011) Speech to the Leveson Inquiry seminar, 12 October (accessed on 13 December 2013 at www.theguardian.com/media/2011/oct/12/paul-dacre-leveson-speech/print).

Dale, John (2011) *24 Hours in Journalism: 1 Day, 1 Million Stories*, London: CreateSpace Independent Publishing.

Daly, Jimmy (2012) 'Crowdsourcing criminals: How a local newspaper uses Pinterest to catch bad guys', StateTech.com, 10 December (accessed on 11 December 2012 at www.statetechmagazine.com/article/2012/12/crowdsourcing-criminals-how-local-newspaper-uses-pinterest-catch-bad-guys).

Davies, Andrew (2009) 'Crowdsourcing news: *The Guardian* and MP expenses', Idio, 24 June (accessed on 14 September 2012 at http://idioplatform.com/2009/06/crowdsourcing-news-the-guardian-and-mp-expenses/).

Davies, Nick (2000) 'Keeping a foot in the door', *Guardian*, 10 January.

Davies, Nick (2008a) *Flat Earth News*, London: Vintage.

Davies, Nick (2008b) 'PA can deliver an accurate report of what was said – but is it always the truth?', 9 February (accessed on 13 December 2013 at www.pressgazette.co.uk/story.asp?storycode=40201).

Davies, Nick (2009a) 'Murdoch papers paid £1m to gag phone-hacking victims', *Guardian*, 8 July (accessed on 11 December at www.theguardian.com/media/2009/jul/08/murdoch-papers-phone-hacking).

Davies, Nick (2009b) 'Trail of hacking and deceit under nose of Tory PR chief', *Guardian*, 8 July (accessed on 18 September 2012 at www.guardian.co.uk/media/2009/jul/08/murdoch-newspapers-phone-hacking).

Davies, Nick and Hill, Amelia (2011) 'Missing Milly Dowler's phone was hacked by *News of the World*', *Guardian*, 5 July (accessed on 15 August 2013 at www.theguardian.com/uk/2011/jul/04/milly-dowler-voicemail-hacked-news-of-world).

Davies, Russell (1995) *Foreign Body: The Secret Life of Robert Maxwell*, London: Bloomsbury.

Delano, Anthony and Henningham, John (1995) *The News Breed: British Journalism in the 1990s*, London: London College of Printing.

Dent, Susie (2004) *Larpers and Shroomers: The Language Report*, Oxford: Oxford University Press.

Department of National Heritage (1995) *Privacy and Media Intrusion*, London: HMSO.

Deuze, Mark (2001) 'Online journalism: Modelling the first generation of news media on the world wide web', First Monday, Vol. 6, No. 10 (accessed on 15 August 2012 at http://firstmonday.org/ojs/index.php/fm/article/view/893/802).

Dickenson Quinn, Sara (2012) 'New Poynter Eyetrack research reveals how people read news on tablets', Poynter.org, 17 October (accessed on 15 August 2012 at www.poynter.org/how-tos/newsgathering-storytelling/visual-voice/191875/new-poynter-eyetrack-research-reveals-how-people-read-news-on-tablets/).

van Dijk, Teu (1988) *News as Discourse*, Hillsdale, NJ: Lawrence Erlbaum.

van Dijk, Teu (1991) *Racism and the Press*, London: Routledge.

Dorril, Stephen and Ramsay, Robin (1991) *Smear*, London: Fourth Estate.

Dougary, Ginny (1994) *Executive Tarts and Other Myths*, London: Virago.

Douglas, Torin (2006) 'How 7/7 democratised the news', BBC News online, 4 July (accessed on 15 August 2012 at http://news.bbc.co.uk/2/hi/uk_news/5142702.stm).

Doyle, Jack (2012) 'Investigative journalists who breach data protection rules could face two years' jail', *Daily Mail*, 29 November (accessed on 15 August 2013 at www.dailymail.co.uk/news/article-2240715/Leveson-Report-Investigative-journalists-breach-data-protection-rules-face-2-years-jail.html).

Doyle, Margaret (1995) *The A–Z of Non-Sexist Language*, London: The Women's Press.

Dyson, Steve (2010) 'Dyson at Large: How not to grab readers' attention', Hold the Front Page, 21 September (accessed on 23 June 2012 at www.holdthefrontpage.co.uk/2010/news/dyson-at-large-how-not-to-grab-readers-attention/).

Economist (2010) 'The year of the paywall', 5 January (accessed online at www.economist.com/node/15207305 on 29 July 2013).

Economist (2013) 'Out of dead trees', 6 April (accessed on 23 July 2013 at www.economist.com/news/britain/21575824-successbut-unfortunately-not-model-others-out-dead-trees).

Evans, Harold (1974) *The Freedom of the Press: The Half-free Press*, London: Hart-Davis MacGibbon.

Evans, Harold (1983) *Good Times, Bad Times*, London: Weidenfeld and Nicolson.

Evans, Harold (1997) *Pictures on a Page*, London: Pimlico Press.

Evans, Harold (2000) *Essential English for Journalists, Editors and Writers*, London: Pimlico Press.

Fedler, Fred (1989) *Reporting for the Print Media*, 4th edition, San Diego, CA: Harcourt, Brace, Jovanovich.

Filloux, Frederic (2012) 'Blog strategies', Monday Note, 29 February (accessed on 23 June 2012 at www.mondaynote.com/2012/02/19/blog-strategies/).

Fishman, Rob (2013) 'The social media editor is dead', Buzzfeed, 29 May (accessed on 24 July 2013 at www.buzzfeed.com/robf4/the-rise-and-fall-of-the-social-media-editor).

Fiske, John (1989) *Understanding Popular Culture*, London: Unwin Hyman.

Fitzwalter, Raymond, and Taylor, David (1981) *Web of Corruption: Full Story of John Poulson and T. Dan Smith*, London: Granada.

Fowler, Roger (1991) *Language in the News: Discourse and Ideology in the Press*, London: Routledge.

Franklin, Bob (1994) *Packaging Politics: Political Communication in Britain's Media Democracy*, London: Edward Arnold.

Franklin, Bob (2005) 'McJournalism: The local press and the McDonaldization thesis.' In Stuart Allan (ed.) *Journalism: Critical Issues*, Maidenhead: Open University Press, pp. 137–50.

Franklin, Bob and Murphy, David (1991) *What News?*, London: Routledge.

Friedlander, Edward Jay and Lee, John (2004) *Feature Writing for Newspapers and Magazines*, Boston, New York, San Francisco: Pearson Education.

Friend, Tad (1998) 'Stars in their eyes', *Guardian*, 20 April.

Frost, Chris (2000) *Media Ethics and Self-Regulation*, London: Longman.

Gans, Herbert J. (1979) *Deciding What's News*, New York: Random House.

Garcia, Mario (2012) *iPad Design Lab*, New York: F+W Media.

Garrahan, Matthew (2011) 'Murdoch's MySpace dream turns to dust', *Financial Times*, 30 June (accessed on 13 August 2013 at www.ft.com/cms/s/0/9262f82c-a289–11e0–9760–00144feabdc0.html#axzz2bqfQkqIQ).

Geere, Alan (2013) 'Destination journalism: What happened next to the brightest and best.' In John Mair, Richard Lance Keeble and Neil Fowler (eds) *What Do We Mean by Local*? 2nd edition, Bury St Edmunds: Abramis, pp. 202–14.

Gilligan, Andrew (2013) 'Royal Charter: The men who want to kill off our free press', *Daily Telegraph*, 24 March (accessed on 23 July 2013 at www.telegraph.co.uk/comment/9949855/Royal-charter-The-men-who-want-to-kill-our-free-press.html).

Gilmor, Dan (2004) *We the Media: Grassroots Journalism for the People, by the People*, Sebastopol, CA: O'Reilly Media.

Glover, Stephen (1999) 'What columnists are good for.' In Stephen Glover (ed.) *Secrets of the Press: Journalists on Journalism*, London: Allen Lane/Penguin Press, pp. 289–98.

Golding, Peter and Murdock, Graham (2000) 'Culture, communications and political economy.' In James Curran and Michael Gurevitch (eds) *Mass Media and Society*, 3rd edition, London: Arnold, pp. 70–92.

Gompertz, Will (2012) 'Robert Redford: Documentaries have replaced journalism', BBC News, 29 March (accessed on 11 September 2012 at www.bbc.co.uk/news/entertainment-arts-17534932?print=true).

Gordon, Paul and Rosenberg, David (1989) *Daily Racism: The Press and Black People in Britain*, London: Runnymede Trust.

Graham, Christopher (2012) 'Justice Select Committee post-legislative scrutiny of the Freedom of Information Act', ICO blog, 26 July (accessed on 23 July 2012 at www.ico.org.uk/news/blog/2012/foia-post-legislative-scrutiny).

Greenslade, Roy (1992) *Maxwell's Fall*, London: Simon & Schuster.

Greenslade, Roy (1995) 'Breaking the silence', *Guardian*, 6 February.

Greenslade, Roy (2004) 'Have the regional takeovers run out of steam?', *Guardian*, 29 November.

Greenslade, Roy (2010) 'The death knock: How a journalist coped with journalists on the doorstep', the *Guardian* media blog, 21 July (accessed on 14 December 2013 at www.theguardian.com/media/greenslade/2010/jul/21/local-newspapers-press-association).

Greenslade, Roy (2012) 'The *Evening Standard* goes into profit', *Guardian* online, 16 October (accessed on 23 July 2013 at www.theguardian.com/media/greenslade/2012/oct/16/london-evening-standard-evgeny-lebedev).

Greer, Chris and Reiner, Robert (2012) 'Mediated mayhem: Media, crime and criminal justice.' In Mike Maguire, Rod Morgan and Robert Reiner (eds) *Oxford Handbook of Criminology*, Oxford: Oxford University Press, pp. 245–97.

Gripsrud, Jostein (1992) 'The Aesthetics and Politics of Melodrama.' In Peter Dahlgren and Colin Sparks (eds) *Journalism and Popular Culture*, London: Sage, pp. 84–95.

Gun, Katharine (2004) 'The truth must out', *Observer*, 19 September.

Hague, Rod and Harrop, Martin (2010) *Comparative Government and Politics*, Basingstoke: Palgrave Macmillan.

Halliday, Josh (2013) 'Lord McAlpine Row: George Monbiot reaches "unprecedented" settlement', *Guardian*, 12 March (accessed on 23 July 2013 at www.theguardian.com/media/2013/mar/12/george-monbiot-libel-lord-mcalpine).

Halliday, Josh and O'Caroll, Lisa (2013) 'New press regulator with "real teeth" could be set up within months', *Guardian*, 8 July (accessed on 23 July 2013 at www.theguardian.com/media/2013/jul/08/new-press-regulator-months).

Hanstock, Terry (1999) 'The thirteenth pillar: The death of Di reconsidered', *Lobster* 38, pp. 2–8.

Harcup, Tony (2004) *Journalism: Principles and Practice*, London, Thousand Oaks, New Delhi: Sage.

Hargrave, Sean (2004) 'The blog busters', *Guardian*, 9 August.

Harker, Joseph (2013) 'Amol Rajan will have his work cut out to change the face of *The Independent*', *Guardian*, Comment Is Free, 17 June (accessed on 27 July 2013 at www.guardian.co.uk/commentisfree/2013/jun/17/amol-rajan-change-face-independent).

Harman, Harriet (2000) 'A house of men', *Guardian*, 27 March.

Harris, Nigel (1992) 'Codes of conduct for journalists.' In Andrew Belsey and Ruth Chadwick (eds) *Ethical Issues in Journalism and the Media*, London: Routledge, pp. 62–76.

Harris, Robert (1990) *Good and Faithful Servant*, London: Faber & Faber.

Hastings, Max (2012) 'A rotten day for freedom', *Daily Mail*, 30 November (accessed on 23 July 2013 at www.dailymail.co.uk/news/article-2240677/Leveson-inquiry-Yes-got-things-right-tragic-blow-liberty-publics-right-know.html).

Hennessy, Brendan (1993) *Writing Feature Articles*, Oxford: Focal Press.

Hennessy, Peter (1986) *Cabinet*, Oxford: Blackwell.

Herbert, John (2004) *Journalism in the Digital Age*, Oxford: Focal Press.

Herman, Edward S. and Chomsky, Noam (1994) *Manufacturing Consent: The Political Economy of the Mass Media*, 4th edition, London: Vintage.

Hermida, Alfred (2007) 'Social media poses digital dilemmas for journalists', Centre for Journalism Ethics website, 8 June (accessed on 23 July 2013 at www.journalism ethics.info/feature_articles/social_media_poses_digital_dilemmas.htm).

Hermida, Alfred (2010) 'From TV to Twitter: How ambient news became ambient journalism', *Media/Culture Journal*, Vol. 13, No. 2, May 2010.

Hermida, Alfred and Thurman, Neil (2008) 'A clash of cultures: The integration of user generated content within professional journalistic frameworks at British newspaper websites', *Journalism Practice*, Vol. 2, No. 3, pp. 343–56.

Hicks, Wynford (1998) *English for Journalists*, 2nd edition, London: Routledge.

Hold the Front Page (2010) '"We need more court reporters," say judges', 4 October, Hold the Front Page (accessed on 13 December 2013 at www.holdthefrontpage. co.uk/2010/news/we-need-more-court-reporters-say-judges/).

Hollander, Gavriel (2013) 'Local World's David Montgomery: "We will harvest content and publish it without human interface"', *Press Gazette*, 21 May (accessed on 23 July 2013 at www.pressgazette.co.uk/david-montgomery-we-will-harvest-content-and-publish-it-without-human-interface).

Holmes, David (2010) 'Court reporting in decline.' Powerpoint presentation to the Association for Journalism Education annual conference, Strathclyde University, Glasgow, 10 September.

Holmwood, Leigh (2009) 'Decline of local news may allow corruption in public institutions to grow, *Guardian* editor warns', 22 July (accessed on 13 December 2013 at www.theguardian.com/media/2009/jul/22/local-news-scrutiny-future-journalism/print).

Holovaty, Adrian (2006) 'J-Schools, computer programming and the bigger picture', www.holovaty.com, 2 October (accessed on 14 December 2013 at www.holovaty. com/writing/343/).

House of Lords (2012) *The Future of Investigative Journalism*, London: Stationery Office.

Howard, Philip (1984) *State of the Language*, London: Hamish Hamilton.

Howe, Jeff (2006) 'The Rise of Crowdsourcing', *Wired*, June (accessed on 23 July 2013 at www.wired.com/wired/archive/14.06/crowds.html).

Hughes, Lotte and McCrum, Sarah (1998) *Interviewing Children*, London: Save the Children.

Humphrys, John (2004a) *Lost for Words: The Mangling and Manipulating of the English Language*, London: Hodder & Stoughton.

Humphrys, John (2004b) 'Lost for Words', *Independent*, 8 November.

IDC (2012) 'Consumers increasingly using mobile devices as their default gateway to the internet, IDC says', IDC press release, 29 October 2012 (accessed on 25 April 2014 at www.idc.com/getdoc.jsp?containerId=prUS23756512).

Inglis, Fred (2002) *People's Witness: The Journalist in Modern Politics*, New Haven, CT/ London: Yale University Press.

Ingram, Mathew (2010) 'Video killed the radio star, but might save newspapers', Gigaom, 22 December (accessed on 23 July 2013 at www.reuters.com/article/2012/01/23/us-google-youtube-idUSTRE80M0TS20120123).

Ingram, Matthew (2013) 'No: The job of social media editor isn't dead – but it sure as heck better be evolving', Paid Content (accessed on 25 July 2013 at http://paid content.org/2013/05/30/no-the-job-of-social-media-editor-isnt-dead-but-it-sure-as-heck-better-be-evolving/).

Jaconelli, Joseph (2002) *Open Justice: A Critique of the Public Trial*, Oxford: Oxford University Press.

Jarvis, Jeff (2007) 'New rule: Cover what you do best, and link to the rest', buzzmachine. com, 22 February (accessed on 23 July 2013 at http://buzzmachine.com/2007/02/22/new-rule-cover-what-you-do-best-link-to-the-rest/).

Johnson, Wesley (2012) 'Leveson Report: Forcing journalists to sign contracts with sources would be "unworkable"', *Daily Telegraph*, 29 November (accessed on 23 July 2013 at www.telegraph.co.uk/news/uknews/leveson-inquiry/9715100/Leveson-Report-Forcing-journalists-to-sign-contracts-with-sources-would-be-unworkable.html).

Ju, Alice, Jeong, Sun Ho and Chyi, Hsiang Iris (2014) 'Will social media save newspapers?' *Journalism Practice*, Vol. 8, No. 1, pp. 10–27.

Judge, Lord (2009) Speech to Society of Editors' annual conference, 16 November (accessed on 13 December 2013 at www.societyofeditors.co.uk/userfiles/file/Lord JudgeKeynoteAddress.doc).

Kalb, Marvin (2010) 'Rupert Murdoch: The making of a modern media mogul', Kalb Report, 6 April (accessed on 23 July 2013 at www.gwu.edu/~kalb/2010/Rupert_Murdoch/337-THE%20KALB%20REPORT-RUPERT%20MURDOCH.pdf).

Karp, Scott (2008) 'Re-inventing journalism on the web: Links as news, links as reporting', Publishing 2.0, 20 February (accessed on 23 July 2013 at http://publishing2.com/2008/02/20/reinventing-journalism-on-the-web-links-as-news-links-as-reporting/).

Kavanagh, Dennis (1983) *Political Science and Political Behaviour*, London: Allen and Unwin.

Kavanagh, Dennis and Cowley, Philip (2010) *The British General Election 2010*, Basingstoke: Palgrave Macmillan.

Keeble, Richard (1997) *Secret State, Silent Press: New Militarism the Gulf and the Modern Image of Warfare*, Luton: John Libbey.

Keeble, Richard (1999) 'The three secret wars in the Balkans 1999.' In Peter Goff (ed.) *The Kosovo News and Propaganda War*, Vienna: International Press Institute.

Keeble, Richard (2000) 'George Orwell – the journalist', *Press Gazette*, 21 January.

Keeble, Richard (2001) *Ethics for Journalists*, London: Routledge.

Keeble, Richard (2004) 'Agents of the Press', *Press Gazette*, 27 July.

Keith, Susan M. (2009) 'Sinking subs and collapsing copy desks? The evolution of editing at newspapers and their web sites'. Paper presented at the Second Biennial Conference on the Future of Journalism, Cardiff, Wales, September.

Kelion, Leo (2013) 'Amazon boss Jeff Bezos buys *Washington Post* for $250m', BBC News online, 6 August (accessed on 8 August 2013 at www.bbc.co.uk/news/business-235810850).

Kelso, Paul (2004) 'Beckham assistant ready to take affair claim to court', *Guardian*, 15 April (accessed on 10 September 2012 at www.guardian.co.uk/media/2004/apr/15/ pressandpublishing.football).

King, Graham (2000) *Punctuation*, Glasgow: HarperCollins.

Knightley, Phillip (1998) *A Hack's Progress*, London: Vintage.

Knightley, Phillip and Kennedy, Caroline (1987) *An Affair of State: The Profumo Case and the Framing of Stephen Ward*, London: Jonathan Cape.

Kovach, Bill and Rosenstiel, Tom (2003) *The Elements of Journalism*, London: Guardian Books.

Lambourne, Helen (2012) 'Editor's role scrapped for five Johnston Press weeklies', Hold the Front Page, 20 August (accessed on 23 July 2013 at www.holdthefrontpage.co.uk/2012/news/editors-role-scrapped-for-five-johnston-press-weeklies/).

Lambourne, Helen (2013a) 'Highfield reveals local TV plans for Johnston Press', Hold the Front Page, 22 January (accessed on 25 July 2013 at www.holdthefrontpage.co.uk/2013/news/highfield-reveals-local-tv-plans-for-johnston-press/).

Lambourne, Helen (2013b) 'Waters out, Pickover in at EDP as editor role axed', Hold the Front Page, 30 August (accessed on 1 September 2013 at www.holdthefrontpage.co.uk/2012/news/waters-out-pickover-in-at-edp-as-editor-roles-axed/).

Lashmar, Paul (2000) 'Is a Good Story worth a prison sentence?', *Independent*, 28 March.

Lazaris, Louis (2010) 'The case against vertical navigation', *Smashing Magazine*, 11 January (accessed on 23 July 2013 at www.smashingmagazine.com/2010/01/11/the-case-against-vertical-navigation/).

Leahul, Dan (2009) '*New York Times* hires its first social media editor', Brand Republic, 27 May (accessed on 24 July 2013 at www.brandrepublic.com/bulletin/digitalam bulletin/article/908527/New-York-Times-hires-its-first-social-media-editor/?DCMP= EMC-Digital-AM-Bulletin).

Leapman, Michael (1983) *Barefaced Cheek*, London: Hodder & Stoughton.

Lehmann, Janette, Castillo, Carlos, Lalmas, Mounia and Zuckerman, Ethan (2013) *Finding News Curators in Twitter*. Proceedings of the 22nd international conference on World Wide Web companion, Rio de Janiero, Brazil, pp. 863–70.

Leigh, David (1989) *The Wilson Plot*, 2nd edition, London: Heinemann.

Leigh, David and Harding, Nick (2011) *Inside Julian Assange's War on Secrecy*, London: Guardian Books.

Leigh, David and Vulliamy, Ed (1997) *Sleaze: The Corruption of Parliament*, London: Arnold.

Leonard, Andrew (1999) 'Open source journalism', salon.com, 8 October (accessed on 23 July 2012 at www.salon.com/1999/10/08/geek_journalism/).

Leslie, Ann (1999) 'Female firemen.' In Stephen Glover (ed.) *Secrets of the Press: Journalists on Journalism*, London: Allen Lane/Penguin Press.

Leston, Jean (2004) 'Debunking those myths of the freelance working life', *Press Gazette*, 26 November.

Leveson, Brian (2012) *An Inquiry into the Culture, Practices and Ethics of the Press: Leveson Inquiry*, London: Stationery Office.

Lewis, Justin, Williams, Andrew and Franklin, Bob (2008) 'Four rumours and an explanation: A political economic account of journalists' changing newsgathering and reporting practices', *Journalism Practice*, Vol. 2, No. 1, pp. 27–45.

Leyland, Adam (1998) 'The pen mightier than the sword but not the tape', *Press Gazette*, 17 July.

Liddle, Dallas (1999) 'Who invented the "leading article"?: Reconstructing the history and prehistory of a Victorian newspaper genre', *Media History*, Vol. 5, No. 1, pp. 5–18.

Linford, Paul (2012a) 'Reporter sacked after naming sex abuse suspect on Twitter', Hold the Front Page, 6 December (accessed on 23 July 2013 at www.holdthe frontpage.co.uk/2012/news/reporter-sacked-after-naming-sex-abuse-suspect-on-twitter).

Linford, Paul (2012b) 'Scottish daily nails Titanic myth as it goes tabloid', Hold the Front Page, 16 January (accessed on 23 July 2012 at www.holdthefrontpage.co.uk/2012/news/scottish-daily-nails-titanic-myth-as-it-goes-tabloid/).

Linford, Paul (2013) 'Editor roles to be axed in Archant Lond shakeup', Hold the Front Page, 23 May (accessed on 23 July 2013 at www.holdthefrontpage.co.uk/2013/news/editor-roles-to-be-axed-in-archant-london-shake-up/).

Linklater, Magnus (2006) 'Treating the law with an open contempt', *The Times*, 20 December.

Lloyd, John (2004) *What the Media Are Doing to our Politics*, London: Constable and Robinson.

Lohr, Steve (2013) 'Sizing up big data, broadening beyond the internet', *New York Times* blogs, 19 June (accessed on 20 November 2013 at http://bits.blogs.nytimes.com/2013/06/19/sizing-up-big-data-broadening-beyond-the-internet).

Loweth, Jenny (2013) 'Shipley robber tries to flee court as judge jails him', *Telegraph and Argus*, 24 September (accessed on 15 December 2013 at www.thetelegraphand argus.co.uk/news/10692974.Shipley_robber_tries_to_flee_court_as_judge_jails_him/).

Lyon, Reesh (2008) 'Robert Fisk: Truth compromised in Middle East reporting', Newswire.co.nz online (accessed on 23 July 2012 at www.newswire.co.nz/2008/09/fisk/).

Mackey, Robert (2009) 'Can a Tweet be a scoop?', *New York Times*, 16 January (accessed on 23 July 2013 at http://thelede.blogs.nytimes.com/2009/01/16/can-a-tweet-be-a-scoop/?_r=0).

MacKinnon, Kenneth (2003) *Representing Men: Maleness and Maculinity in the Media*, London: Arnold.

Madar, Chase (2012) *The Passion of Bradley Manning*, London: Verso.

Mahmood, Mazher (2008) *Confessions of a Fake Sheik*, London: HarperCollins.

Mair, John and Keeble, Richard Lance (2014) *Data Journalism: Mapping the Future*, Bury St Edmunds: Abramis.

Manning, Paul (2001) *News and News Sources: A Critical Introduction*, London: Sage.

Marr, Andrew (2004) *My Trade: A Short History of British Journalism*, Basingstoke, Oxford: Macmillan.

Martinson, Jane (2012) 'Why does this shocking dearth of women in the media persist?', *Guardian*, 15 October (accessed on 25 July 2013 at www.guardian.co.uk/lifeand style/the-womens-blog-with-jane-martinson/2012/oct/15/shocking-dearth-of-women-in-journalism).

McAndless, David (2009) *Information Is Beautiful*, London: HarperCollins.

McCann, Paul (2000) 'Make way for TV briefings', *The Times*, 17 March.

McGregor, Phil (2013) 'Siren songs or path to salvation: Interpreting the visions of web technology at a UK regional newspaper in crisis, 2006–2011', *Convergence*, 14 February (accessed on 11 December 2013 at http://con.sagepub.com/content/early/2013/02/14/1354856512472605.abstract).

McNair, Brian (2000) *Journalism and Democracy: An Evaluation of the Political Public Sphere*, London: Routledge.

McNair, Brian (2003) *News and Journalism in the UK*, 4th edition, London: Routledge.

McQuail, Denis (1992) *Media Performance: Mass Communication and the Public Interest*, London: Sage.

Media Lawyer (2012a) 'Judge slams press over attitude to errors' and 'Report "should have included judge's intervention"', *Media Lawyer*, 5 October.

Media Lawyer (2012b) 'Attorney General investigates journalist', *Media Lawyer*, 3 February.

Media Lawyer (2013a) '*Mail on Sunday* pays libel damages to banker', *Media Lawyer*, 31 January.

Media Lawyer (2013b) 'Newspaper fined for identifying sex case victim', *Media Lawyer*, 8 October.

Melin-Higgins, Margareta (1997) 'The social construction of journalist ideals: Gender in journalism education'. Paper presented at conference 'Journalists for a New Century', London College of Printing, 24 April.

Mendick, Robert (2011) 'John Yates: I failed victims of *News of the World* phone hacking', *Daily Telegraph*, 9 July (accessed on 23 July 2013 at www.telegraph.co.uk/news/uknews/phone-hacking/8628052/John-Yates-I-failed-victims-of-News-of-the-World-phone-hacking.html).

Merritt, Stephanie (2003) 'Speaking for myself, I'm as guilty of using tired old cliché as the next man', *Observer*, 13 April.

Meyer, Philip (2004) *The Vanishing Newspaper*, Columbia, MO: University of Missouri Press.

Meyer, Philip (2008) 'The elite newspaper of the future', *American Journalism Review*, October/November (accessed on 23 July 2013 at http://ajr.org/Article.asp?id=4605).

Mills, Jane (1991) *Womanwords*, London: Virago.

Milne, Seamus (1995) *The Enemy Within: The Secret War against the Miners*, London: Pan.

Ministry of Justice (2012) *Judicial and Court Statistics 2011*, London: Ministry of Justice (accessed on 13 December 2013 at www.gov.uk/government/publications/judicial-and-court-statistics-annual).

Moore, Suzanne (1996) *Head over Heels*, London: Viking.

Morgan, Piers (2005) *The Insider*, London: Ebury Press.

Morton, Andrew (1992) *Diana: Her True Story*, London: Michael O'Mara.

NCTJ (2012a) 'Journalists at work: Their views on training, recruitment and conditions', National Council for the Training of Journalists (accessed on 16 December 2013 at www.nctj.com/downloadlibrary/jaw_final_higher_2.pdf).

NCTJ (2012b) 'NCTJ announces compulsory ethics module for diploma students', National Council for the Training of Journalists, 30 November (accessed on 23 July 2013 at www.nctj.com/latestnews/NCTJ-announces-compulsory-ethics-module-for-diploma-students).

Newman, Nic (2009) *The Rise of Social Media and Its Impact on Mainstream Journalism*. Working paper, Reuters Institute for the Study of Journalism (accessed on 23 July 2013 at https://reutersinstitute.politics.ox.ac.uk/fileadmin/documents/Publications/The_rise_of_social_media_and_its_impact_on_mainstream_journalism.pdf).

Newspaper Society (2013) 'Editors' Survey', 13 May (accessed on 13 December 2013 at www.newspapersoc.org.uk/local-newspaper-week-2013-editors-survey).

Newton, Jackie and Duncan, Sallyanne (2012) 'Hacking into tragedy: Exploring the ethics of death reporting'. In John Mair and Richard Lance Keeble (eds) *The Phone Hacking Scandal: Journalism on Trial*, Bury St Edmunds: Abramis, pp. 312–19.

Newton, Kenneth (1986) 'Mass media'. In Henry Drucker *et al.*, *Developments in British Politics*, London: Macmillan.

Niblock, Sarah (1996) *Inside Journalism*, London: Blueprint.

Nielsen (2012) 'Buzz in the blogosphere: Millions more bloggers and blog readers', Nielsen.com, 3 August (accessed on 23 July 2013 at www.nielsen.com/us/en/newswire/2012/buzz-in-the-blogosphere-millions-more-bloggers-and-blog-readers.html).

Norris, Bill (2000) 'Media ethics at the sharp end'. In David Berry (ed.) *Ethics and Media Culture: Practices and Representations*, Oxford: Focal Press, pp. 325–38.

Northmore, David (1996) *Lifting the Lid: A Guide to Investigative Research*, London: Cassell.

Norton, Philip (2005) *Parliament in British Politics*, London: Palgrave Macmillan.

Nussbaum, Emily (2009) 'The new journalism: Goosing the gray lady', *New York Magazine*, 11 January (accessed on 23 July 2013 at: http://nymag.com/news/features/all-new/53344/).

O'Carroll, Lisa (2012) 'Press Complaints Commission to close in wake of phone-hacking scandal', *Guardian*, 8 March (accessed on 23 July 2013 at www.theguardian.com/media/2012/mar/08/press-complaints-commission-close-phone-hacking).

ONS (2013) 'Statistical bulletin: Crime in England and Wales, year ending March 2013', Office for National Statistics, 18 July (accessed on 13 December 2013 at www.ons. gov.uk/ons/rel/crime-stats/crime-statistics/period-ending-march-2013/stb-crime–period-ending-march-2013.html).

O'Neill, Brendan (2013) 'This Defamation Bill is a disaster for free speech', *Daily Telegraph* online, 13 June (accessed on 23 July 2013 at http://blogs.telegraph.co.uk/news/brendanoneill2/100164840/this-defamation-bill-is-a-disaster-for-free-speech/).

O'Neill, Deirdre and O'Connor, Catherine (2008) 'The passive journalist: How sources dominate local news', *Journalism Practice*, Vol. 2, No. 3, pp. 487–500.

O'Shea, Gary (2011) 'Footie star's affair with Big Brother's Imogen Thomas', *Sun*, 14 April (accessed on 12 September 2012 at www.thesun.co.uk/sol/homepage/news/3526696/Footie-stars-affair-with-Big-Brothers-Imogen-Thomas.html).

Oakley, Chris (2012) 'The men who killed the regional newspaper industry'. In John Mair, Neil Fowler and Ian Reeves (eds) *What Do We Mean by Local?* Bury St Edmunds: Abramis, pp. 51–65.

Ochoa, Xavier and Duval, Erik (2008) *Quantitative Analysis of User Generated Content on the Web*. Proceedings of the First International Workshop on Understanding Web Evolution, Beijing, China, pp. 19–26 (accessed on 11 December 2013 at http://journal.webscience.org/34/).

Ooyala (2013) 'Tablet and mobile breaks record in latest global video index', Press Release, 19 June (accessed on 23 July 2013 at http://financeyahoo.com/news/tablet-mobile-video-break-records-040100616.html).

Oreskovic, Alexei (2012) 'YouTube hits 4 billion daily video views', Reuters, 23 January (accessed on 23 July 2013 at www.reuters.com/article/2012/01/23/us-google-youtube-idUSTRE80M0TS20120123).

Orlowski, Andrew (2013) 'UK.Gov passes Instagram Act: All your pictures belong to everyone now', *The Register*, 29 April (accessed on 24 April 2014 at www.theregister.co.uk/2013/04/29/err_act_landgrab/).

Orwell, George (1984 [1957]) 'Politics and the English Language.' In *Inside the Whale and Other Essays*, Harmondsworth: Penguin, pp. 143–57.

Owen, Paul (2012) 'When was the first live blog? 1923, it seems', *Guardian* shortcuts blog, 28 October (accessed on 23 July 2013 at www.theguardian.com/media/shortcuts/2012/oct/28/when-first-live-blog-1923).

Oxford, Esther (1992) 'Pay your money and pick your man', *Independent*, 18 November.

Page, Bruce (2003) *The Murdoch Archipelago*, London: Simon & Schuster.

Pai, Hsiao-Hung (2013) 'Brothel worker: I regret not working in sex trade as soon as I got here', *Guardian*, 15 April (access on 23 July 2013 at www.theguardian.com/society/2013/apr/15/brothel-regret-not-working-sex-trade).

Panel on Fair Access to the Professions (2009) *Unleashing Aspiration,* Cabinet Office (accessed on 24 April 2014 at http://webarchive.nationalarchives.gov.uk/+/http:/www.cabinetoffice.gov.uk/media/227102/fair-access.pdf).

Parker, R. (2007) 'Focus: 360-degree commissioning', *Broadcast*, 13 September.

PCC (2011) 'Press Complaints Commission v *Daily Mail*', adjudication issued 9 December (accessed on 11 December 2013 at www.pcc.org.uk).

Perez-Pena, Richard (2007) '*Times* to stop charging for parts of its website', *New York Times*, 18 September (accessed on 23 July 2013 at www.nytimes.com/2007/09/18/business/media/18times.html?_r=1&).

Pierce, Andrew (2000) 'Whispers in the corridors of power', *The Times*, 7 July.

Pilger, John (1996) 'The hidden power of the media', *Socialist Review*, September.

Pilger, John (1998) *Hidden Agendas*, London: Vintage.

Pilger, John (2004a) *Tell Me No Lies*: *Investigative Journalism and Its Triumphs*, London: Jonathan Cape.

Pilger, John (2004b) 'Iraq: The unthinkable becomes normal', *New Statesman*, 15 November.

Pilger, John (2004c) 'The secret files that reveal how a nation was deported', *Daily Express*, 18 October (accessed on 12 September at www.pilger.carlton.com/print/133386).

Platell, Amanda (1999) 'Institutionalised sexism.' In Stephen Glover (ed.) *Secrets of the Press: Journalists on Journalism*, London: Allen Lane/Penguin Press, pp. 140–47.

Ponsford, Dominic (2004) 'Editors toughen up code to outlaw phone text grabs', *Press Gazette*, 14 May.

Ponsford, Dominic (2006) 'Phone-hacking was "extremely prevalent among Sunday tabloids, it went on all the time"', *Press Gazette*, 11 August (accessed on 11 December 2013 at www.pressgazette.co.uk/node/35256).

Ponsford, Dominic (2009) 'Tony Watson: "Legislators must wake up to public service journalism threat"', *Press Gazette* (accessed on 13 December 2013 at www.pressgazette.co.uk/node/44643).

Ponsford, Dominic (2012) '*Sun* investigations chief: Bribery Act has forced us to turn away whistleblowers', *Press Gazette,* 13 November (accessed on 24 April 2014 at www.pressgazette.co.uk/sun-investigations-chief-bribery-act-has-forced-us-turn-away-genuine-whistleblowers).

Ponsford, Dominic (2013a) 'Monty's Local World vision: Editors "pretty redundant", 20-fold increase in content', *Press Gazette*, 25 January (accessed on 23 July 2013 at www.pressgazette.co.uk/montys-local-world-vision-editors-pretty-redundant-publishers-exploit-20-fold-increase-content).

Ponsford, Dominic (2013b) 'Defamation Bill passed: "It will change the landscape of free speech in Britain"', *Press Gazette*, 25 April (accessed on 23 July 2013 at www.pressgazette.co.uk/defamation-bill-passed-it-will-change-landscape-free-speech-britain).

Ponsford, Dominic (2013c) '*Telegraph* figures show "No Downside" to metered paywall', *Press Gazette*, 27 May (accessed on 23 July 2013 at www.pressgazette.co.uk/telegraph-figures-show-%E2%80%98no-downside%E2%80%99-metered-paywall).

Ponting, Clive (1986) *Whitehall: Tragedy and Farce*, London: Sphere Books.

Porter, Bernard (1992) *Plots and Paranoia: A History of Political Espionage in Britain 1790–1988*, London: Routledge.

Pöttker, Horst (2003) 'News and its communicative quality: The inverted pyramid – when and why did it appear?' *Journalism Studies*, Vol. 4, No. 4, pp. 501–11.

Poynter Institute (2007) 'Eyetrackng the news: A study of print and online reading', www.poynter.org (accessed online on 14 December 2013 at www.poynter.org/extra/Eyetrack/).

Price, Lance (2006) 'Rupert Murdoch is effectively a member of Blair's cabinet', *Guardian*, Comment Is Free, 1 July (accessed on 14 December 2013 at www.theguardian.com/commentisfree/2006/jul/01/comment.rupertmurdoch).

Preston, Peter (2004a) 'Are newspapers burnt out?', *Observer*, 21 November.

Preston, Peter (2004b) 'When race is a numbers game', *Observer*, 24 October.

Preston, Peter (2008) 'Damaged limitations', *Guardian*, 9 February.

Preston, Peter (2011) 'WikiLeaks is just the beginning', *Guardian*, 16 September.

Press Gazette (2012) 'Tweeting from court: "It's multi-skilling gone mad"', *Press Gazette*, 6 March (accessed on 13 December 2013 at www.pressgazette.co.uk/node/48890).

Pugh, Andrew (2011) 'Could accepting freebies land journalists in jail?' *Press Gazette*, 26 August (accessed online on 14 December 2013 at www.pressgazette.co.uk/node/47771).

Pugh, Andrew (2012a) '*Express & Star* scraps online paywall after 9 months', *Press Gazette*, 18 January (accessed on 23 July 2013 at www.pressgazette.co.uk/node/48585).

Pugh, Andrew (2012b) '*Times* becomes sixth newspaper to change editors in 16 months', *Press Gazette*, 12 December (accessed on 23 July 2013 at www.pressgazette.co.uk/content/times-become-sixth-national-newspaper-change-editor-past-16-months).

Rawnsley, Andrew (2010) *The End of the Party*, London: Penguin.

Reeves, Ian (1999) 'Reaping the whirlwind', *Press Gazette*, 18 May.

Reeves, Ian (2002) 'Is the demon just a pussycat?' *Press Gazette*, 10 May.

Reeves, Ian (2005a) 'I have been, I hope, an agent of change . . .', *Press Gazette*, 25 November (www.pressgazette.co.uk/node/32634).

Reeves, Ian (2005b) 'I have seen the future. And we're not in it', *Press Gazette*, 8 June (accessed on 14 August 2013 at www.pressgazette.co.uk/node/30750).

Reeves, Ian (2010) 'How I learned to stop worrying and love the code.' In John Mair and Richard Lance Keeble (eds) *Face the Future*, Bury St Edmunds: Abramis, pp. 275–89.

Reich, Zvi (2010) 'Constrained authors: Bylines and authorship in news reporting', *Journalism*, December, Vol. 11, No. 6, pp. 707–25.

Reid, Alasdair (2000) 'Newspapers bask in glow of dotcom boom', *Campaign*, Friday, 3 November.

Richards, Ian (2004) *Quagmires and Quandaries: Exploring Journalism Ethics*, Sydney: University of New South Wales Press.

Richmond, Shane (2008) 'How SEO is changing journalism', *British Journalism Review*, Vol. 19, No. 4, pp. 51–5.

Richmond, Shane (2009) 'Telegraph.co.uk: 15 years of online news', *Daily Telegraph*, 11 November (accessed on 13 August 2013 at www.telegraph.co.uk/technology/6545788/Telegraph.co.uk-15-years-of-online-news.html).

Richter, Felix (2013) 'Facebook is the No. 1 social traffic source for news websites', Statista.com, 26 July (accessed on 27 July 2013 at www.statista.com/topics/1164/social-networks/chart/1324/social-media-traffic-of-news-websites/).

Riley, Sue (2012) 'Life after the editor's chair', InPublishing, September/October (accessed on 11 December 2013 at www.inpublishing.co.uk/kb/articles/life_out_of_the_editors_chair.aspx).

Robertson, Geoffrey (1983) *People against the Press: An Enquiry into the Press Council*, London: Quartet.

Robertson, Geoffrey, QC (2011) 'Foolishness that threatens freedom', *Guardian*, 17 September.

Rogers, Simon (2009) 'Welcome to the data blog', *Guardian* (accessed on 26 July 2013 at www.guardian.co.uk/news/datablog/2009/mar/10/blogpost1).

Rose, Richard (1965) *Politics in England*, London: Faber & Faber.

Rowlands, Barbara (1993) 'Don't call me, please, and I won't call you', *Independent*, 24 August.

Rozenburg, Joshua (2009) 'Why newspapers lack interest in court reporting', *Law Gazette*, 26 November (accessed on 13 December 2013 at www.lawgazette.co.uk/53266.article).

Runciman, David (2010) 'Is this the end of the UK?', *London Review of Books*, Vol. 32, No. 27 May.

Rusbridger, Alan (2009) 'Trafigura: Anatomy of a super-injunction', *Guardian*, 20 October (accessed on 24 August 2013 at www.theguardian.com/media/2009/oct/20/trafigura-anatomy-super-injunction).

Rushton, Katharine (2012) '*Guardian* "seriously discussing" end to print edition', *Daily Telegraph*, 17 October (accessed on 23 July 2013 at www.telegraph.co.uk/finance/newsbysector/mediatechnologyandtelecoms/media/9614953/Guardian-seriously-discussing-end-to-print-edition.html).

Sabbagh, Dan (2011) '*Guardian* and *Observer* to adopt digital first strategy', *Guardian*, 16 June (accessed on 23 July 2013 at www.theguardian.com/media/2011/jun/16/guardian-observer-digital-first-strategy).

Sands, Peter (2009) 'The sub is dead. Long live the sub?' InPublishing, May/June (accessed on 23 July 2013 at www.inpublishing.co.uk/kb/articles/the_sub_is_dead_long_live_the_sub.aspx).

Sarikakis, Katherine (2004) *British Media in a Global Era*, London: Arnold.

Schudson, Michael (1978) *Discovering the News*, New York: Basic Books.

Searle, Chris (1989) *Your Daily Dose of Racism*, London: Campaign for Press and Broadcasting Freedom.

Sebba, Anne (1994) *Battling for News: The Rise of the Woman Reporter*, London: Hodder & Stoughton.

Segel, Edward and Heer, Jeffrey (2010) 'Narrative visualisations: Telling stories with data', *IEEE Transactions on Visualisation and Computer Graphics* November/December, Vol. 16, No. 6.

Sentencing Council (2013) 'Sentencing myths', Sentencing Council (accessed on 13 December 2013 at http://sentencingcouncil.judiciary.gov.uk/sentencing/sentencing-myths.htm).

Seymour-Ure, Colin (1974) *Political Impact of the Mass Media*, London: Constable.

Shafer, Jack (2012) 'So Warren Buffet likes newspapers again?', Reuters blog, 18 May (accessed on 23 July 2013 at http://blogs.reuters.com/jackshafer/2012/05/18/so-warren-buffett-likes-newspapers-again/).

Shaw, Adrian (2011) 'Rio Ferdinand loses kiss-and-tell privacy action against the *Sunday Mirror*', *Mirror*, 29 September (accessed on 23 July 2013 at www.mirrorfootball.co.uk/news/Manchester-United-defender-Rio-Ferdinand-loses-kiss-and-tell-privacy-action-against-the-Sunday-Mirror-article805964.html 24 August 2013).

Shawcross, William (1992) *Murdoch*, London: Pan Books.

Shirky, Clay (2009) 'How social media can make history', TEDEd (accessed on 23 July 2013 at http://ed.ted.com/lessons/clay-shirky-how-social-media-can-make-history).

Silverstreak (2013) 'How Pistorius' journalists have massively boosted their social media influence', 2Oceansvibe, 21 February (accessed on 13 December 2013 at www.2oceansvibe.com/2013/02/21/live-tweeting-the-oscarpistorius-case-just-how-journalists-have-massively-boosted-their-social-influence-analysis/).

Silvester, Christopher (ed.) (1994) *Interviews: An Anthology from 1859 to the Present Day*, Harmondsworth: Penguin.

Slattery, Jon (2009) '*FT* spells out £1.5bn fall in Johnston Press value', Jon Slattery blog, 31 March (accessed on 23 July 2013 at http://jonslattery.blogspot.co.uk/2009/03/ft-spells-out-fall-in-johnston-press.html).

Smith, Anthony (1978) *The Politics of Information*, London: Macmillan.

Snoddy, Raymond (1993) *The Good, the Bad and the Unacceptable*, 2nd edition, London: Faber & Faber.

Spark, David (1999) *Investigative Reporting: A Study in Technique*, Oxford: Focal Press.

Sparks, Colin (1992) 'Popular journalism: Theories and practice.' In Peter Dahlgren and Colin Sparks (eds) *Journalism and Popular Culture*, London: Sage, pp. 24–44.

Sparks, Colin (1999) 'The press.' In Jane Stokes and Anna Reading (eds) *The Media in Britain: Current Debates and Developments*, London: Macmillan, pp. 41–60.

Sparks, Colin (2003) 'Inside the media', *International Socialism*, No. 98, pp. 31–55.

Spender, Dale (1980) *Man Made Language*; London: Routledge & Kegan Paul.

Stanistreet, Michelle (2013) 'David Montgomery's "robot" journalism will terminate both jobs and local news', *Guardian*, Comment Is Free, 23 May (accessed on 23 July 2013 at www.theguardian.com/media/media-blog/2013/may/23/david-montgomery-robot-journalism).

Steel, Emily and Edgecliffe-Johnson, Andrew (2013) '*Mail* Online to expand as it hits top spot', *Financial Times*, 10 March.

Stelter, Brian (2008a) 'Finding political news online, the young pass it on', *New York Times*, 27 March (accessed on 23 July 2013 at www.nytimes.com/2008/03/27/us/politics/27voters.html).

Stelter, Brian (2008b) 'Mainstream news outlets start linking to other sites', *New York Times*, 12 October (accessed on 23 July 2013 at www.nytimes.com/2008/10/13/business/media/13reach.html?_r=3&adxnnl=1&oref=slogin&ref=media&adxnnlx=1378470430-goU+q3NFPdcM6jpvRyHgKg).

Stephenson, Hugh and Mory, Pierre (1990) *Journalism Training in Europe*, Brussels: European Community.

Stevens, Mary (2001) 'The new doorstep challenge', *Press Gazette*, 15 June.

Stevenson, Alex (2011) 'Phone-hacking inquiry triggers "long grass" fears', politics.co.uk, 14 July (accessed on 23 July 2013 at www.politics.co.uk/news/2011/07/14/inquiry-triggers-long-grass-fears on 16 August 2013).

Stewart, Graham (2005) *A History of* The Times, London: HarperCollins.

Stray, Jonathan (2010a) 'Designing journalism to be used', jonathanstray.com, 26 September (accessed on 23 July 2013 at http://jonathanstray.com/designing-journalism-to-be-used).

Stray, Jonathan (2010b) 'Why link out? Four journalistic purposes of the noble hyperlink', Nieman Journalism Lab, 8 June (accessed on 23 July 2013 at www.niemanlab.org/2010/06/why-link-out-four-journalistic-purposes-of-the-noble-hyperlink).

Subscraft blog (2013) 'Another sad week at *The Times*', Subscrsaft blog, 13 June (accessed on 14 January 2014 at http://subscraft.blogspot.co.uk/2013/06/another-sad-week-at-times.html).

Sweney, Mark (2013) '*Mail* Online powers into global expansion with onslaught on US', *Guardian*, 31 March (accessed on 23 July 2013 at www.theguardian.com/media/media-blog/2013/mar/31/mail-online-global-expansion).

Swinford, Steven (2013) 'Leveson could have "chilling effect" on press freedom, Information Commissioner warns', *Daily Telegraph*, 7 January (accessed on 23 July 2013 at www.telegraph.co.uk/news/uknews/leveson-inquiry/9786404/Leveson-could-have-chilling-effect-on-journalism-Information-Commissioner-warns.html).

Tait, Nigel (2011) 'Carter-Ruck's take on the Trafigura story: Who guards the *Guardian*', Legal Week, 17 October (accessed on 18 October 2011 at www.legalweek.com/legal-week/blog-post/2117745/carter-rucks-trafigura-story-guards-guardian).

Taylor, Matthew (2013) 'Ian Tomlinson: Family's four-year quest for justice finally ends', *Guardian*, 5 August (accessed on 6 August 2013 at www.theguardian.com/uk-news/2013/aug/05/ian-tomlinson-family-quest-justice).

Taylor, Matthew and Lewis, Paul (2013) 'Jimmy Mubenga case: From death on BA flight 77 to inquest verdict', *Guardian*, 9 July (accessed on 23 July 2013 at www.theguardian.com/uk-news/2013/jul/09/jimmy-mubenga-death-inquest-verdict).

Tench, Dan (2004) 'The law of secrets', *Guardian*, 8 March.

Tiffen, Rodney (1989) *News and Power*, London: Unwin Hyman.

Tindle, Sir Ray (2012) 'The future is local'. In John Mair, Neil Fowler and Ian Reeves (eds) *What Do We Mean by Local?* Bury St Edmunds: Abramis, pp. 1–2.

Tomkinson, Martin (1973) Private Eye *Extra: Guide to the Poulson Case*, London: Pressdram.

Trelford, Donald (2000) 'The freedom to be irresponsible', *Press Gazette*, 24 March.

Truss, Lynne (2003) *Eats, Shoots & Leaves*, London and New York: Penguin.

Tryhorn, Chris (2009) '*Telegraph* paid £110,000 for MPs' expenses data', *Guardian*, 25 September (accessed on 13 September 2012 at www.guardian.co.uk/media/2009/sep/25/telegraph -paid-11000-mps-expenses).

Tuchman, Gaye (1972) 'Objectivity as a strategic ritual: An examination of newsmen's notions of objectivity', *American Journal of Sociology*, Vol. 77, No. 4. Reprinted in Howard Tumber (ed.) (1999) *News: A Reader*, Oxford: Oxford University Press, pp. 297–307.

Tumber, Howard (ed.) (1999) *News: A Reader*, Oxford: Oxford University Press.

Tunstall, Jeremy (1983) *The Media in Britain*, London: Constable.

Turvill, William (2012a) 'Debt triples to £15k in ten years for new journalists', *Press Gazette*, 25 March (accessed on 23 July 2013 at www.pressgazette.co.uk/survey-debt-triples-%C2%A315k-ten-years-new-journalists-broadcasting-pays-double-newspapers).

Turvill, William (2012b) 'Weekly did not breach editors' code over story featuring Facebook injuries pic', *Press Gazette*, 27 November (accessed on 24 July 2013 at www.pressgazette.co.uk/weekly-did-not-breach-editors-code-over-story-featuring-facebook-injuries-pic).

Turvill, William (2013) 'Surge in number of privacy cases heard in UK courts', *Press Gazette*, 23 July (accessed on 24 July 2013 at www.pressgazette.co.uk/surge-number-privacy-cases-heard-uk-courts).

Tynan, Kenneth (1990) *Profiles: Selected and Edited by Kathleen Tynan and Ernie Eban*, London: Nick Hern Books.

UK Asian (2013) 'Amol Rajan: "Fleet Street needs to be more inclusive"', 19 June (accessed on 24 April 2014 at www.ukasiaonline.com/profiles/amol-rajan-fleet-street-needs-to-be-more-inclusive).

Vehkoo, Johanna (2013) *Crowdsourcing in Investigative Journalism*, Reuters Institute for the Study of Journalism Report, August (accessed on 11 december 2013 at https://reutersinstitute.politics.ox.ac.uk/fileadmin/documents/Publications/fellows__papers/2009–2010/Crowdsourcing_in_Investigative_Journalism.pdf).

Wade, Stephen (1997) *Freelance Writing*, London: Straightforward.

Wahl-Jorgensen, Karin (2008) 'Op-ed pages.' In Bob Franklin (ed.) *Pulling Newspapers Apart*, London: Routledge, pp. 67–74.

Wardle, Claire and Williams, Andrew (2009) 'Ugc@thebbc: Understanding its impact on contributors, non-contributors and BBC News', Cardiff University Report for the BBC (accessed on 14 December 2013 online at http://cardiff.ac.uk/jomec/resources/UserGeneratedContent_ClaireWardle.pdf).

Waterhouse, Keith (1981a) *Waterhouse on Newspaper Style*, London: Mirror Books.

Waterhouse, Keith (1981b) *The* Mirror's *Way with Words*, London: Mirror Books.

Waterhouse, Keith (1991) *English our English (and How to Sing It)*, London: Viking.

Waterhouse, Keith (1995) 'Talking of which . . .', *Guardian*, 25 September.

Weinberger, David (2009) 'Transparency is the new objectivity', Joho the blog, 19 July (accessed on 23 July 2012 at www.hyperorg.com/blogger/2009/07/19/transparency-is-the-new-objectivity/).

Wilson, David and Game, Chris (2006) *Local Government in the United Kingdom*, 4th edition, London: Palgrave Macmillan.

Wheen, Francis (2000) 'The *Sun*'s gypsy curse', *Guardian*, 22 March.

Widdicombe, David (1986) *Report of Committee Inquiring into the Conduct of Local Authority Business*, London: HMSO.

Williams, Granville (1994) *Britain's Media: How They Are Related: Media Ownership and Democracy*, London: Campaign for Press and Broadcasting Freedom.

Williams, Kevin (1998) *Get Me a Murder a Day! A History of Mass Communication in Britain*, London: Hodder Headline.

Winer, Dave (2005) 'Monday, December 12, 2005', Scripting News, 12 December (accessed on 23 July 2012 at http://scripting.com/2005/12/12.html).

Wingfield, John (1984) *Bugging: A Complete Survey of Electronic Surveillance Today*, London: Robert Hale.

Winnett, Robert (2009) 'MPs' expenses: *Telegraph* investigation exposes allowances', *Daily Telegraph*, 8 May 2009 (accessed on 13 September 2012 at www.telegraph.co.uk/news/politics/5293147/MPs-expenses-Telegraph-investigation-exposes-allowances.html#).

Wintour, Charles (1990) *The Rise and Fall of Fleet Street*, London: Hutchinson.

Women in Journalism (1999) *Real Women – The Hidden Sex: How National Newspapers Use Photographic Images of Women in Editorial*, report by Meg Carter, Mimi Turner and Maureen Paton, November (http://womeninjournalism.co.uk/real-women-the-hidden-sex/).

Yelland, David (2010) 'Former *Sun* editor David Yelland: "I was drunk every night for 24 years but I was saved by the love of my son"', *Daily Mail*, 27 March (accessed on 11 December 2013 at www.dailymail.co.uk/femail/article-1261200/Former-Sun-editor-David-Yelland-I-drunk-night-nearly-24-years-I-saved-love-son.html).

Zobel, Gibby (2000) 'Rights mess', *Guardian*, 3 May.

Index